David J. Beale

Through the Johnstown Flood

David J. Beale

Through the Johnstown Flood

ISBN/EAN: 9783744758246

Printed in Europe, USA, Canada, Australia, Japan

Cover: Foto ©ninafisch / pixelio.de

More available books at **www.hansebooks.com**

REV. D. J. BEALE, D. D.

THROUGH

THE JOHNSTOWN FLOOD.

BY A SURVIVOR.

A THRILLING, TRUTHFUL, AND OFFICIAL HISTORY

OF THE

MOST APPALLING CALAMITY OF MODERN TIMES.

PREPARED IN RESPONSE TO A REQUEST OF
THE LEADING CITIZENS OF JOHNSTOWN AND MANY OF THE FOREMOST MEN OF THE NATION,

By REV. DAVID J. BEALE, D. D.

ELEGANTLY AND APPROPRIATELY ILLUSTRATED.

EDGEWOOD PUBLISHING COMPANY.
1890.

NOTE.

THIS volume has been prepared by Dr. Beale in response to an urgent request from many leading citizens of Johnstown and eminent men of the nation, among them the following:

His EXCELLENCY, GOVERNOR BEAVER, of Pennsylvania.

HON. JOHN WANAMAKER, Postmaster General.

CHAUNCEY M. DEPEW, New York City.

His HONOR, HUGH J. GRANT, Mayor of New York.

HON. F. C. LATROBE, Ex-Mayor of Baltimore.

GENERAL D. H. HASTINGS, Harrisburg, Pa.

JAMES B. SCOTT, Pittsburgh, Pa.

REV. H. L. CHAPMAN, D.D., Pastor M. E. Church, Johnstown.

REV. R. A. FINK, D.D., Pastor Lutheran Church, Johnstown.

REV. JAS. P. TAHANEY, Pastor St. John's R. C. Church, Johnstown.

. JOSEPH COOK, Boston.

LT. COL. J. L. SPANGLER, Bellefonte, Pa.

REV. HOWARD CROSBY, D.D., LL.D., New York City.

REV. THEODORE L. CUYLER, D.D., Brooklyn, N. Y.

REV. JOHN HALL, D.D., New York City.

HON. THOMAS V. COOPER, Media, Pa.

W. HORACE ROSE, ESQ., Johnstown.

COLONEL JOHN P. LINTON, Johnstown.

C. SHERIDAN, M.D., Johnstown.

REV. SAMUEL J. NICCOLLS, D.D., St. Louis, Mo.

REV. B. M. PALMER, D.D., New Orleans, La.

REV. WAYLAND HOYT, D.D., Minneapolis, Minn.

REV. M. CARO, Rabbi Jewish Synagogue, Johnstown.

HERMAN BAUMER, Postmaster, Johnstown.

F. D. JOLLY, ESQ., Johnstown.

REV. F. L. PATTON, D.D., LL.D., President Princeton College.

ELLIOT F. SHEPARD, Proprietor *Mail and Express*, N. Y.

REV. H. L. WAYLAND, D.D., Editor *National Baptist.*

REV. J. C. GREER, Pastor U. P. Church, Johnstown.

T. A. BENFORD, Proprietor Hulbert House, Johnstown.

B. K. JAMISON, Banker, Philadelphia.

GEORGE H. THOMAS, of Drexel & Co., Bankers, Philadelphia.

REV. D. M. MILLER, Pastor Conemaugh Presbyterian Church.

TO MY

REVERED AND VENERABLE MOTHER,

IN HER EIGHTY-NINTH YEAR, WHOSE GODLY FAITH SUSTAINED HER THROUGH SIX DAYS OF
MATERNAL ANXIETY CONCERNING OUR FATE, OF WHICH SHE COULD GET NO TIDINGS; TO
MY BELOVED WIFE, ALWAYS THE INSPIRATION AND STRENGTH OF MY LIFE, BUT NEVER
SO MUCH SO AS WHEN WE WERE STRUGGLING TOGETHER WITH OUR CHILDREN
AMID THE RAGING WATERS; TO MY DEAR CHILDREN, MADE DEARER TO US
FOR THE PERIL THROUGH WHICH, BY THE HELP OF GOD, WE CARRIED
THEM; TO MY FELLOW-CITIZENS AND FELLOW-SUFFERERS OF JOHNS-
TOWN, WITH WHOM THE TIES OF FRIEND AND PASTOR HAVE
BEEN RIVETED BY THE BLOWS OF THIS TERRIFIC CALAMITY
—THIS BOOK IS DEDICATED BY THE AUTHOR.

(7)

PREFACE.

As the sun sank behind the western foothills of the Alleheny Mountains, Wednesday evening, May the 29th, 1889, he gilded with glory the spires of a score of churches, shed his parting beams upon more than five thousand dwellings, and lighted to their happy homes over thirty thousand people in the peaceful, picturesque and industrious Valley of the Conemaugh. When, on Saturday, the 1st day of June, the sun again, for the first time, looked out from behind the thick clouds, peeping over the eastern crest of the Alleghenies, he saw, indeed, the same deep valley and the same mountain peaks, but oh! how changed was Johnstown! The scene of destruction presented was unparalleled in the annals of American history, and for suddenness, destructiveness and awful horrors, perhaps, unsurpassed since the Noachian deluge. Within a few minutes nearly four thousand human beings had been launched into eternity, twenty-five hundred houses had been utterly demolished, and property destroyed the worth of which has been estimated by millions. The business man, the physician, the lawyer, the clergyman, the school-teacher, the clerk, the mechanic, the laborer, the rich and the poor, the stranger and the citizen, the old and the young, parents and children, the good and the bad—all, all had gone down together into a common watery grave.

So many persons have expressed their desire to have written a correct description and trustworthy record of this great calamity that I have been induced, upon the solicitation of a number of our citizens and others, to undertake the work. They represented to me that my personal and pastoral relations to Johnstown, my own experience, my official connection with the work of rescue and reconstruction, imposed it upon me as a duty. I could not possibly describe all that occurred during, and subsequently to, the flood; but as a participant in the terrible tragedy, as an eye-witness of the frightful scenes, and as superintendent of the morgues, brought into contact with most of the dead and living who were overwhelmed in the flood, I trust that my account will prove an acceptable, as it certainly is a reliable, one in all it contains.

I acknowledge my indebtedness to many of my fellow-citizens and fellow-sufferers of Johnstown for statements of their own experiences and for other favors furnished me; also to the many gentlemen and ladies who labored for our relief, and whose official reports add so much to the value of these pages; also to those whose artistic and editorial skill and care have done so much for the appearance of the volume.

DAVID J. BEALE.

CONTENTS.

I.

THE OVERWHELMING FLOOD.

(11)

II.

CARE OF THE SURVIVORS.

V.

REBUILDING.—RESTORATION.—RECONSTRUCTION.

VI.

MISCELLANEOUS.

VII.

HISTORICAL SKETCH OF JOHNSTOWN.

By W. Horace Rose, Esq.

ILLUSTRATIONS.

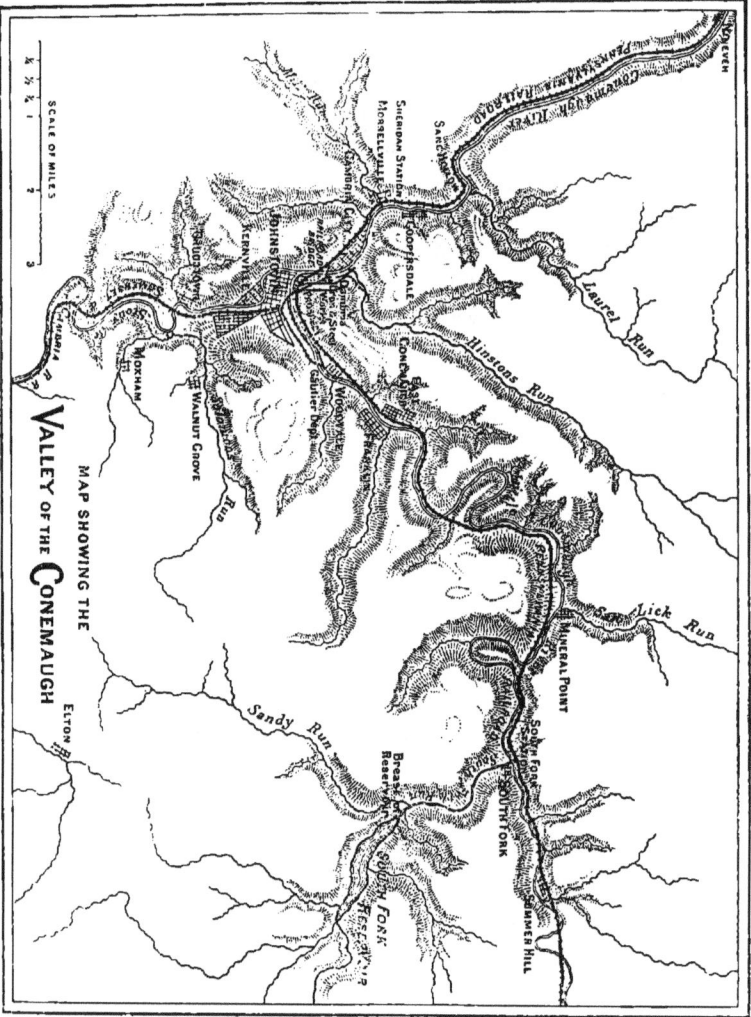

MAP SHOWING THE
VALLEY OF THE CONEMAUGH

SCALE OF MILES

I.

THE OVERWHELMING FLOOD.

" When thou passest through the waters, I will be with thee."—ISAIAH 43 : 2.

1.—THE AUTHOR'S EXPERIENCE.

THE day preceding the flood was "Decoration Day." Although the sky was overcast and there was a slight rainfall occasionally, this Thursday, upon the whole, was rather pleasant. The citizens of Johnstown were out in their strength, and a large number of strangers were present from Altoona, Hollidaysburg, Wilmore, Ebensburg, Somerset, Latrobe and other neighboring towns. The great concourse of people on the sidewalks, the long procession of soldiers and of various secret orders, the numerous bands of music, the display of flags and bunting along the principal streets, the strewing of flowers on the graves of deceased patriots, and Colonel W. D. Moore's eloquent oration in the Opera House, all contributed to make this a red-letter day for Johnstown.

After nightfall the clouds grew heavier, hanging nearer the earth, and at 9 o'clock a gentle drizzling rain set in, which, after 11 o'clock, was followed by an unprecedented outpour. In fact, there seemed to be a series of waterspouts during much of the night. Before 8 o'clock in the morning the banks of both the Conemaugh and the Stony Creek were full, and the lower parts of the city were slightly covered with water. By 10 o'clock the flood had reached half way up the First and Second Wards, and by 11 o'clock it had attained a depth of five feet at the corner of Main and Market Streets and at the Cambria Iron Company's store.

It was now frequently remarked that our periodic flood was upon us, and that it was already at a greater altitude than the highest point attained by the flood of June 7th, 1887. But as then, and on other occasions, no lives had been lost by the freshet, so now no one apprehended a different result. In the lower districts of the city, carpets were taken up, as was usual at such seasons of high water, and in some cases pianos and organs were lifted on chairs, that they might go unharmed. Gradually the streams rose higher, until in the very centre of the town the waters of the Stony Creek mingled with the waters of the Conemaugh. An aged citizen standing on the corner of Main and Market Streets remarked to me that he had seen the Conemaugh as high before, and that he had witnessed as much water in the Stony Creek, but that he had never before noticed both streams so high at one and the same time. Not one word, however, was uttered by him or by any one else concerning the Conemaugh Lake; and I am persuaded that few, if any, imagined there would be disaster arising from that source. I remarked that I thought our officers should have called out men to make rafts to remove people from the lower parts of the town, not for a moment supposing that we in the central parts should need them ourselves within a few hours.

Soon we and all others on the pavements sought refuge in our houses, for soon the water filled all the streets, so that by 2 o'clock there were from two to ten feet of water all over Johnstown proper. Although the water continued to rise, we had no news of any apprehended danger of the bursting of the dam. Nor do I suppose that many of our citizens believed that in the event of the breaking of the reservoir it would greatly increase the volume of the water at our distance from its location. When one of our leading citizens was asked at this time how much higher he thought the flood would reach, if the Conemaugh Lake or reservoir would give way, his reply was, " About two feet."

From 2 o'clock until 4 o'clock the water seemed to rise slowly; in fact, it was slightly falling, when, at 10 minutes after 4, the great avalanche rushed upon us. I had been in my study, on the first floor, preparing for the Sabbath services, when, contrary to my own judgment of the necessity of the case, I was induced to go into my parlor to assist in taking up the carpet. In a moment after I heard a sound as of an approaching railroad train, when all at once the mighty torrent struck our residence. I cried " Upstairs! up-stairs!" and when I saw all my family and Mr. Lloyd and his sister—neighbors who were present at the time—safely in advance of me, I followed, with the family Bible in my hand, pushed upward by the incoming water. Mrs. Beale, with great presence of mind, had turned off the natural gas, which we employed for heating purposes, and one of my daughters had seized the canary cage and carried it above stairs. The water was on the second story sooner than I was, and carried the hat-rack with such force as to strike me on the back, just as I reached the head of the stairs, up to my waist in water. In a moment the family had rushed on to the attic, when a man was washed through a window beside me as if shot out of a catapult. I said, in one breath, "Who are you? Where are you from?" He did not give his name (although I recognized him as one whom I had frequently seen near the woolen mill), but struggling for breath, he merely replied, "Woodvale." He had been carried on a roof a mile and a quarter, and was dashed through the window into my second story as the roof on which he had been borne, with a great shock, struck the parsonage.

Soon we were all together on the third floor, and I had found the Forty-sixth Psalm, a part of which I read to our company, con-

sisting of ten persons.   Several of them wished to see and read
the passage for themselves, which they did, as the Bible was passed
around.   The entire company engaged in ejaculatory prayer, and I,
also, led them in prayer, renewedly dedicating ourselves to God
and our Saviour, expecting in a moment "to be present with the
Lord."

One of my little sons, a lad of twelve summers, shouted out:
"Surely, papa, God will take care of us, for we are His children,"
and then he prayed aloud in a most touching manner, closing in
the language of the Twenty-third Psalm, "Yea, though I walk
through the valley of the shadow of death, I will fear no evil: for
thou art with me; thy rod and thy staff they comfort me. Amen."

During all this time, and for several minutes after, scores, aye,
hundreds of houses and parts of houses, wrecked and ruined
structures, were dashing, rocking, grinding, tipping and tumbling
past our shattered, broken and twisted parsonage on the right of
us, and on the left of us; for, superadded to the water already on
our streets, from 16 to 40 feet more, dependent on the width of
the valley, rushed down upon us, bearing on its bosom houses,
barns, freight cars, city passenger cars, locomotives, tenders, iron
bridges, the Gautier plant, trees, lumber, animals and human
beings, dead and alive, and all kinds of wreckage, pitching, tossing, banging and smashing to pieces in one indiscriminate mass.
We were in the midst of an angry, raging sea.

I recognized J. Q. A. Benshoff, our leading bookseller; Mrs.
John Fulton and daughter, Charles Barnes, Mrs. Young, of Park
Place, and scores of others as they were dashed past our residence.
I saw two little children alone, and almost nude, clinging to the
comb of one roof as it floated by, and three or four young ladies,
on another roof, clinging to each other in agonized embrace
amidst the swirl and swash of the sweeping waves.   I observed
that for several squares west and north and south of us nearly every

house had been torn from its foundations, and we all were in momentary expectation of a similar disaster. But it now appeared that the waters flowed less rapidly and in a different direction, for the immense stone bridge on the Pennsylvania Railroad had become the breast of a turbulent sea, which submerged our fair city, and hurled the waters back again.

The houses which first passed our residence were now completely crushed together, with trucks of cars, tons of steel and piles of lumber at the railroad bridge; but those which came last were returned near my locality by the back water. At this moment, seeing Captain A. N. Hart, his wife, sister and two children struggling among wreckage which had drifted near the parsonage, I descended into the water in the second story and succeeded in getting them into my house through a window. Now our company numbered fifteen in the parsonage garret.

Soon the wreckage to the west of us began to move off, and, our house, which is a large, new frame building, began to shake and rock and sag in the middle. Captain Hart and Mr. Lloyd insisted that we were in immediate peril, as, in their judgment, the house was giving way. Finally, after some hurried conference and an unsuccessful attempt to get upon our own roof, we gained egress from the highest window upon a floating roof below. This was indeed a hazardous alternative. Seizing a rope at hand, I let Captain Hart out first. He assured me that the roof was worthy; and then, in quick succession, all the occupants of the attic were passed out of the window, when I followed them. Just as I was about to pass David and Wilson, our youngest boys, out of the window, they expressed the desire that their dog, which stood by, mutely pleading for his life, should be saved, and accordingly "Guess" was let down upon the roof. No sooner had he reached it than, true to doggish nature, he and a neighbor's cur engaged in an earnest and free fight for the supremacy.

We had hoped at first to have reached the church, but we soon ascertained that an intervening space of fifty feet or more was entirely uncovered with wreckage, over which we had hoped to have walked; and so we abandoned that attempt, and began a perilous journey to Alma Hall, the largest, strongest building in the city, of four very high stories, half a square distant, walking and jumping from one moving house or roof, or box-car to another; and sometimes we were on opposite sides of roofs, and therefore out of sight of each other: then, again, we were compelled to bridge over deep watery spaces with loose boards or planks. One of the young ladies, when walking on a piece of scantling, fell into the watery chasm, so that we could see nothing but her hair floating on the surface. She was rescued by being pulled upon some floating timbers, and just before dark we succeeded in reaching the Hall. We found that very many from different parts of the city had sought refuge there before our arrival. Some of our number now went out on the wreckage, taking the rope brought from the parsonage, and succeeded in extricating a number who were either fastened in amongst the timbers, or were too much exhausted to help themselves.

A meeting of the men in the Hall was held on the second staircase, and James M. Walters, Esq., was elected Director of the building, and Dr. W. E. Matthews, Captain A. N. Hart and myself, respectively, were appointed controllers of the three stories now peopled with two hundred and sixty-four rescued ones. On motion, being requested, I offered, in each room, prayer. We also gave thanks to Almighty God for His gracious deliverance of those present, and sought sustaining grace for the bereaved ones. Mr. Walters, who accompanied me, suggested that all should reverently bow their heads during the prayer, which request was complied with. That was, indeed, a solemn and impressive occasion. In this service, Jews and Gentiles, Catholics and Protestants, Africans and Chinamen united.

Orders were given that there should be no lights in the Hall during the night, lest the escaping natural gas explode; and all persons having spirituous liquors were required to give them to the Directors of each hall of the building. These orders were cheerfully obeyed, and those having pocket flasks willingly surrendered them.

It is doubtful if any one in that entire building on that awful night, the last of May, 1889, refused to pray to his Maker. One can scarcely conceive of an assembly convened under circumstances more affecting than those which massed us together on the floors of Alma Hall. The suppressed moans of the bruised, the agony and dread suspense of separated friends and relatives; the cries of little children for food and water, which could not be supplied; the howlings of terror-stricken brutes; the darkness and confusion throughout the building; the sickening and stifling odors; the dying scenes on the wreckage about us, and in the conflagration at the railroad bridge; and the expressed opinions of contractors present, that the great building would yield to the fearful strain, combined to make that night one of indescribable horror.

At break of day, the waters had somewhat subsided, having forced a way through the wreckage under the arches of the great bridge, and formed a partial outlet by washing away the roadbed between the station and the stone railroad bridge; and yet the wreckage on many of the streets was almost as high as the few remaining buildings.

Except those who had broken bones, or were otherwise disabled, nearly all sought an early opportunity to leave Alma Hall. We departed from the building through a window on Main Street, the whole length of which to Adam—nearly five blocks away—was filled with rubbish, such as cars, houses, bridges, trees and furniture, together with dead bodies, the mass piled up fifteen or twenty feet, over which we walked and crawled the entire distance. We of

Alma Hall, with a large company of others, rescued elsewhere, made our way over this rubbish with great difficulty, until we reached the hill at the foot of Frankstown Road, beyond the line reached by the waters of the flood.

There were here gathered at least three thousand persons of all ages, and of every condition, many of them stripped of nearly all their clothing, and all chilled, haggard and quite distracted with the dreadful experience of the night. Our first thought was to find some refuge for our wives and children and those who were too feeble to care for themselves. With my family I climbed Singer hill to the house of Mr. Cover, and, leaving them there, hastened back to the multitude, with the purpose of aiding others and effecting something like order out of the confusion.

It is wholly impossible to give any conception of the scene presented at that spot. Every one of the vast crowd was either injured in some form, or had been bereft of their kin and loved ones. Their agony was so intense as to be oppressive, and held expression as with the grasp of a vise, so that no one was seen to shed a tear. As fast as possible, the women and children were distributed in the homes and shelters on the hills, which were kindly offered by the occupants. These being few, and for the most part small, were taxed to the utmost. In one, thirteen families were located; on a floor in another, nineteen persons had to sleep, without change of clothing.

For ten days, such was our need, and I was so occupied with the dead and living, that I wore without change the clothes with which I came out of the flood, and went without food for twenty-four or thirty hours, having turned over that which was sent to me to children and ladies who, I knew, could not endure the fast as well as I. Perhaps the constant labor and anxiety which were upon me enabled me the better to endure it.

As from this point we gazed back upon our city, or where our city was, our hearts sank within us. To the right stood the blackened walls of St. John's Roman Catholic Church, which had burned during the horrid night, its rafters still smoking. Here and there above or beyond the massed piles of bricks in the city there were a few houses standing, some of them out of plumb. The spires of churches once our pride were gone; the most of our homes destroyed, and their fragments scattered over the wide vale below.. It were vain to undertake to tell the world how or what we felt, when, shoeless, hatless, and many of us almost naked, some bruised and broken, we stood there and looked upon that scene of death and desolation. This was not the time for yielding to emotion ; and with the recollection of the fact that Paris was overrun with thieves the day of its capitulation to the German army, I ran to a little boy who was passing on horseback, and, giving him some money which I had in my pocket, ordered him to telegraph immediately to Governor Beaver, to send the military to us at once. The boy did as bidden, and the practical response soon came.

Everything about us was in inextricable confusion, showing the effects of the terrific convulsion through which nature and humanity had passed. Here were uprooted trees, houses upturned or demolished, furniture of every description—hardware, woodenware, parlor ornaments and kitchen utensils, mattresses, bodies of horses, cattle and swine, corpses of men, women and children, railroad cars and locomotives—overturned or on end, and pressing down upon the half-buried bodies of the drowned.

As I was climbing over the debris a young man, whom I did not know, recognizing me, handed me a handsome gold-headed cane, saying, " Dr. Beale, here is a valuable cane which I picked up amid the wreckage." After several weeks I found the owner, Mr. C. W. Lewis, to whom I returned it. Another person, whom also I did not know, handed me a watch and several gold chains. These

I committed to my wife's care, after we had reached our place of refuge, Mr. Cover's. Two months afterward the owner was found, a Mrs. Randolph, to whom they were delivered. These acts are but samples of many occurring in those days of misery.

2.—EXPERIENCE OF W. HORACE ROSE, ESQ., ATTORNEY AT LAW.[*]

"Truth is stranger than fiction."

I AWOKE on the morning of May 31st, 1889, to find the waters of the Stony Creek and Little Conemaugh, within seventeen hundred feet of whose confluence I reside, so swollen that the gutter in front of my dwelling was full. This was higher than the water had ever attained, except in June, 1887, when my cellar was flooded. I had resided in Johnstown all my life, had seen the floods of 1847, 1862, 1867; was at home a few hours after the sweep of 1887, and although I now saw that the water had attained a higher level (except the flood line of June, 1887) than I ever witnessed, I took no special alarm. The flood of 1887 was exceptional, and I did not believe there would be any greater damage done, or that the waters could possibly attain a much greater elevation than did the flood of that year.

In all the great floods that had swept the valley, the periods when the highest flood had occurred in the Stony Creek and the Little Conemaugh were not simultaneous, and the one or the other of the streams had discharged the volume of its flood before its confluent had reached its climax. The Stony Creek drains a much larger area of territory, and its rise is much slower than the precipitous Little Conemaugh. The Stony Creek flows from the South, while the Conemaugh drops from the East down the mountain side of the Allegheny. I had expected the same state or condition that had marked all other floods I had witnessed.

---

[*] Dictated by himself.

After breakfast I found the waters rapidly rising and discovered that both streams were rising simultaneously. I aided my boys in hitching my team of horses in an open wagon, prudently refusing to use my best harness or attach the horses to my fine carriage, because I did not desire to have them wet or injured by the heavily falling rain. By the time we were harnessed up, the water was on my stable floor, and I caused my cow to be driven to the hillside, expecting to have her returned in an hour or two, when the flood subsided.

I personally drove the wagon along the Main Street, intending to remove any from their houses on the lower part of Main Street who desired to go, but I found that by 9 o'clock the water was so deep in the lower part of the town that it was unsafe for me to return below my own residence. I then drove toward the upper end of the town, and found the water flowing across the town on Main Street at its intersection with Clinton and Bedford Streets. A man led his cow in the direction of the hill at the upper end of the town, where she stopped and drank water on Main Street at its intersection with Clinton and Bedford.

I stood on the corner of Main and Clinton Streets conversing with Charles Zimmerman and D. W. Harshberger ; I remarked to Mr. Zimmerman: "Charley, you and I have scored fifty years, and this is the first time we ever saw a cow drink Stony Creek River water on Main Street." He remarked: "That's so, but the water two years ago was higher." This was between 9 and 10 o'clock in the forenoon. The rain began to fall heavily, and I went and purchased rubber coats for my two youngest sons, who were in the wagon, and with them I went to my office, located on Franklin Street, within one hundred feet of the Stony Creek River.

The flood of 1887 had reached the altitude of about one foot in my office. I found on arriving at the office that the Stony Creek was still rapidly rising. I immediately set about placing my papers above the flood line of 1887, and then started for my dwelling. On my way home, I met my neighbor, John Dibert; we discussed the situation and mutually agreed that the filling up of the margins of the streams was the cause of the town being overflowed for the want of sufficient outlet for the water; and that if the two streams continued to rise simultaneously, the Cambria Iron Company having reduced the width of the channel below the confluence of the Little Conemaugh and Stony Creek to such an extent that there was insufficient room for the escape of the water, it would be backed up and our cellars overflowed, which was the full extent of the damage we anticipated.

The width of the Stony Creek had been fixed by ordinances of the borough and an agreement with the Cambria Iron Company at one hundred and seventy-five feet; its actual width before the adoption of this ordinance, as was marked by the spans of the bridge at the end of Franklin Street, was two hundred and forty feet. The width of the Little Conemaugh, as fixed by the ordinances of the boroughs of Johnstown and Millville, and an agreement between the two boroughs and the Cambria Iron Company, was one hundred and ten feet, making a total water-way of the two streams, as fixed by the ordinance, of two hundred and eighty-five feet; whereas the Conemaugh proper being the stream below the confluence of the Stony Creek and Little Conemaugh was reduced by the Cambria Iron Company, filling on either side, so that the water was less than two hundred feet in width.

This was the point discussed by Mr. Dibert and myself, and he proposed that after the flood was over, a meeting of the citizens should be called to take steps toward compelling the Cambria Iron Company to remove its deposits from the bed of the river and restore the stream to its original width and give an outlet for the waters, so that the property-holders in the lower end of Johnstown should not, every spring and fall, be inconvenienced by the flooding of their cellars by the back waters. We separated, and I never saw him again. I made my way to my home, arriving there about 11 o'clock. I could not reach the house by the front door, the water then being nearly four feet deep, but improvised a raft in an adjoining lot and floated into my back porch. Finding the water was still rapidly rising, we immediately commenced removing the furniture and carpets from the lower story, being overtaken in the kitchen before we had the carpet raised there. Slowly but surely, the water continued to rise, and I marked with sadness that it reached above the wash-board, and with its muddy freight stained the beautiful paper I had recently put upon the walls of my dwelling. My family were now all in the house except Forest, the next to my youngest son, who, after taking the team to the hillside in the Sixth Ward, had only been able to make his way back as far as the residence of my neighbor, Mr. Fisher, on the opposite side of the street and two doors above me, from whence he made known to us his presence and safety. My eldest son, Horace, who is married and resides on the hillside, in the Sixth Ward, had early in the day made his way to my house to assist us in removing any articles likely to be reached by the rise of water, which he anticipated would not be higher than that of 1887. At any time after 11 o'clock it would have been impossible for him to have left the house.

So unsuspecting of danger was I that, from the time we removed the furniture to the second floor, until within fifteen minutes of the final catastrophe, I amused myself by shooting rats from an upper window, or joking with my neighbors, Squire Fisher and Mr. Hamilton, across the street. I shot a rat as it struggled along the wall of a stable in an adjoining lot; a moment after I cast my eye to the right and noticed that the water was rapidly rushing from the Little Conemaugh toward Main Street, and that there were four courses of brick between the water and the bottom of the window-sill of my neighbor, Mr. Dibert's, house. I drew my watch from my pocket and, noting the time, said to my youngest son, a lad of 14 years, who stood by my side at the attic window: "Percy, it is just a quarter to 4 ; I have shot a rat, and there are just four courses of brick between the water and Dibert's window-sill ; after a while we will look and see whether the water is rising or not." I then went down to the second floor, where the women folks had broken up a box, started a fire in the grate and made some coffee. I walked to a window, raised it, and called to Bessie Fronheiser, a neighbor's child, who stood at an opposite window, and asking her to come over, she laughingly said : "I can't." I then told her to come to a window in the front part of the house and I would give her some candy ; a minute after, she and her mother appeared at a window directly opposite one in our house, where the distance between the houses was about five or six feet. I took a broom; some member of my family poured a lot of mixed candy on it, and I passed the same across the open space to Bessie and her mother ; as she took the candy from the broom, Mrs. Rose said to Mrs. Fronheiser, "You are not looking well—wait till we hand you some coffee ; we have made some on the grate." She then handed me a tin-cup of coffee, which was placed on the broom and passed over to Mrs Fronheiser, who took it and raised it to her lips. She never tasted it. There came a crash; she lowered the cup and exclaimed : "My God! what is that?" My daughter said : "Our fence is breaking down !" I rushed to the back part of the house, saw the side of my carriage house fall out into the lot, and the carriage being driven through the opening. I heard loud screams, the sound of breaking timbers, the alarm of a bell, and the loud scream of a steam whistle. I said : "Something awful has happened !" and rushed to the third floor of the building, followed by all who were in the house. I ran directly to the northeast window, which overlooked the valley of the Little Conemaugh, when a sight was presented which absolutely appalled me, and I at once made up my mind that the days of myself and family were numbered. My view extended for nearly a mile up the valley. I saw stretching from hill to hill a great mass of timber, trees, roofs and debris of every sort, rapidly advancing toward me, wrecking and carrying everything before it. It was then about the midst of what was known as the Gautier Works, a department of the Cambria Iron Works, which covered perhaps ten or twelve acres of ground. A dense cloud hung over the line of the rolling debris, which I then supposed was the steam and soot which had arisen from the hundreds of fires in the Gautier Works as the waves rolled over them. I stood and looked as the resistless tide moved on and saw brick buildings crushed and in an instant pass out of sight, while frame tenements were quickly crushed to atoms.

Members of my family asked me if there was no escape. I answered, "No; this means death to us all." My wife with blanched face said, "Won't our big strong house stand?" I replied deliberately: "No, Maggie, no building can stand this awful jam, and we are all lost."

The press of the heaving, surging mass rolled steadily on, and in less than three minutes, as nearly as I can estimate time from the moment I saw the front of the angry torrent, it was upon us. The great municipal building above me fell with a crash. The stately dwelling of my neighbor, John Dibert, was broken to atoms. I walked rapidly to the southeast window and saw the front of the brick dwelling above and adjoining mine, crushed to rubbish. Several persons were floating directly down Main Street, in front of me; a large frame building, directly opposite me, careened, at the attic windows of which I saw a number of ladies, one of whom held an infant in her arms; there was a crash, a sensation of falling, a consciousness that I was in the water, and all was dark. A moment later, I felt the press of a heavy shock, a sense of excruciating pain, involving my right breast, shoulder and arm. The thought came upon me that I was being crushed to death, that I could not long endure the agony I then suffered, and that death would soon come. I watched for the change, expecting in a moment to know the reality of eternity. I heard the moan of my eldest son, who was at my side when the crash came.

I felt myself struggling with my left hand, clutching at something, I know not what. I heard the voice of my youngest son, as I thought, imploring me to aid him. I told him I was powerless to succor him. A moment later and I realized that he was endeavoring to have me reach a higher elevation, when I told him my whole right side was crushed; he came to my relief and aided me in getting upon a fragment of a slate roof. A moment after, a little boy, whom I had sheltered, appeared and informed me that my wife was drowned; he had barely made this announcement, when I saw my only daughter, June, rise up out of the water among the debris to perhaps her waist and immediately sink out of sight. As she sank, I saw my wife rise out of the water to about her waist and almost immediately sink out of sight; a moment after they rose together, and I saw my son Winter, a lad of 20 years, a strong, robust person, and heard him say: "Ma, hold on to me, and I can save you." I was lying on my left side, perhaps twenty to twenty-five feet distant from where my wife, daughter and son were struggling, the skin torn from the right side of my face, the blood flowing profusely from the wound, the skin torn from the back of my left hand, my right collar-bone broken, my shoulder-blade fractured, the ribs crushed in upon my lung, my right arm from shoulder to wrist lying limp on my side, powerless to give aid or assistance to my loved ones. At this moment, a young man seemed to shoot up out of the debris at my side; I realized that he was an acquaintance, but could not name him. I at once, however, addressed him, saying: "Young man, won't you go and help Winter save

ALMA HALL. DISCIPLES' CHURCH. PRESBYTERIAN PARSONAGE. PRESBYTERIAN CHURCH.

DR. BEALE AND HIS AIDS ON THEIR FIELD OF LABOR.

my wife and daughter? I am helpless, my whole right side and arm are crushed." He made no reply, but at once hastened across the debris and aided in relieving my wife from the timbers in which she was pinioned. Then he immediately disappeared from my sight; but I afterward learned he was Harry Phillips, who was reared in Johnstown, was then practicing his profession of dentistry in Pittsburgh; was home on a visit and in the house of Dr. L. T. Beam, and was the only person who escaped with his life, while his mother, niece, nephew and brother-in-law were lost in the flood. My eldest son had disappeared. I believed I had heard his dying moan. All the other inmates of my house at the time it was struck were now floating on different fragments of houses, and being rushed with fearful velocity in a westerly course to and across the Stony Creek River.

Here I saw a stout roof floating on the outer edge of the mass of debris; I told my family that if that roof could be reached, there was a chance to escape, as the roof might drift to the hillside, where escape was possible; we were then slowly drifting down the stream toward the stone bridge; we all reached the roof in safety, my boys assisting me to gain it. After we had reached it, an elderly lady was observed floating near us upon a shutter or door, on her bended knees, her hands clutching each side of her frail support. Winter made his way across the debris, took her in his arms and brought her to the roof; and there were now upon it, this elderly lady, with my wife, daughter, two sons, the strange boy, a domestic and myself. Scarcely was the complement of passengers complete, when the current turned, and our ship was driven with terrific velocity directly up the channel of the Stony Creek, following, as near as I can tell, its southwestern bank, distant, perhaps, twenty feet from the margin. In this manner we were carried a distance of half a mile, following the sinuosity of the stream, coming to rest above Morris Street, in the

3

Fifth Ward ; here we lay for a considerable length of time, while buildings and fragments of building and all sorts of material passed on up the stream. At length there was dead water about us, when some unknown and to me inexplicable force drove us across the river into the mouth of Franklin Street, where we rested for a considerable period of time. The current having changed, the buildings and debris were now being driven rapidly down the stream, some of them being jammed and crushed to atoms, while persons who had taken refuge on them, with wild shrieks, sank to watery graves. A cold and pitiless rain poured down upon us, causing me to have frequent and severe chills. At this time the spire of St. John's Catholic Church was on fire, and as we floated about we were in plain view of the flames as they leaped up the magnificent spire and consumed the emblem of Christianity which graced its lofty top. As we lay at the mercy of the waves, within, perhaps, a hundred feet of my office, which stood hard by the Lutheran Church, on whose spire was affixed the town clock, with its ponderous bell, far above the flood tide, the mechanism of the clock moved on, the hands reached the hour, the spring was raised, and five times the ponderous hammer struck the massive bell, tolling the dreadful knell of the thousands who had perished in that awful hour. No one except him who has passed the same ordeal can imagine the horrible sensation the slowly beating strokes of that clock sent thrilling through the floating survivors of that terrible hour, the climax of the catastrophe.

By a sudden freak of the flood, we were driven again into the stream and floated down a distance of a hundred yards, where we were struck by a heavier building and driven over the bank and lodged among a lot of debris and brought to rest. Finding ourselves at rest, and seeing that the house of Dr. S. M. Swan, a three-story brick building, stood intact, we made our way over roofs, timber, logs and the like, and just as the clock tolled the hour of six, having had two hours of terrible floating, we entered the haven.

I shall not attempt to describe the terrors of the following night, with its thousand and one alarms, as the crash of buildings was heard as they settled in the water or were crushed by the weight from above ; suffice it to say, it was a night of awful terror, and over all was the ghastly and lurid light that came from the burning debris at the stone bridge below. At length morning came, and with it the first sense of relief, for then we learned with certainty that the waters were subsiding, that an outlet had been made by the giving away of the embankment of the Pennsylvania Railroad, and there was no further danger to be apprehended, as the flood had reached and passed its climax, leaving a torn and devastated town, upon whose wreck the stoutest heart on that Saturday never dared to dream would be rebuilt a town. By 4 o'clock on Saturday, my two sons, who had been separated from us in the flood, rejoined us, and we found all had safely escaped with life and limb, I alone being injured. From my injuries I have not yet recovered, and am only able to dictate this narrative, which fact must be my excuse for any want of directness and polish.

3.—STATEMENTS REGARDING OTHER SUFFERERS.

. . . " The ties that strengthen
Our hearts in hours of grief."

ONE of the most prominent citizens of the Conemaugh Valley, a brave soldier in the civil war, lately remarked, in substance, as follows : " I have seen two contending armies meet each other on the field of battle ; I have seen cannon belching forth smoke and iron hail into the ranks of the enemy, and have felt the yielding earth tremble beneath my feet at each discharge ; I have heard the terrible roar of musketry and all the noise of battle, and have witnessed comrades falling all around me ; and after the battle was over I have followed the long and bloody lines of carnage and destruction, beholding the results of the awful conflict, until, with an aching heart, I turned away from the scenes of bloodshed and distress ; but I declare to you that the sights and sufferings attending our appalling flood were the most sickening and terrible I ever witnessed." In fact, Colonel Jacob Higgins and Major Robert Litzenger, two of our most thoughtful citizens, who have been through two wars, assure me that nothing occurred in their army life to be compared with the horrors of the evening and night of the 31st of May, 1889. The presence, in the indescribable calamity, not only of men, as is usual on the battle-field, but also of mothers, wives, sisters and daughters, and of the whimpering little ones pleading for protection and food ; the falling of brick buildings, crushing both men and women beneath them ; the floating of frame houses, carrying off and destroying their occupants ; the agonies of maternity ; the burning of many of our citizens alive at the fatal bridge ; together with an awful sense of helplessness that oppressed us all—these circumstances presented a state of things unparalleled in its appalling character.

Of the breaking of the artificial lake, which was the largest human factor in this awful calamity, the Rev. G. W. Brown, pastor of the South Fork United Brethren Church, writes me : " The lake was a little over two miles south of our village, and, by the water course, fifteen miles from Johnstown. It covered 750 acres of ground, and had an average depth of over 30 feet. Having heard the rumor that the reservoir was leaking, I went up to see for myself. It then wanted 10 minutes of 3 o'clock in the afternoon of Friday, May 31st. When I approached, the water was running over the breast of the dam to the depth of about a foot. The first break in the earthen surface made a few minutes later was large enough to admit the passage of a train of cars. When

I witnessed that, I exclaimed, 'God have mercy on the people below,' but I did not then suppose that the destruction of the lake would be attended by so great loss of human life.

"The dam melted away, oh, how quickly! Only a few moments were required to make an opening more than 300 feet wide and down to the bottom. I watched it until the wall that held back the waters was torn away, and the entire lake began to move, and until, finally, with a tremendous rush that made the hills quake, the vast body of water was poured out into the valley below. Only about 45 minutes were required to precipitate those millions of tons of water upon the unsuspecting inhabitants of the Conemaugh Valley; and right here it began its work of destruction. A mill, house and stable, owned by George Fisher, were demolished in an instant. Fortunate it was for him that, a few minutes before, he and his family had moved to higher ground. He had conveyed a milk wagon, a plow and other implements to a more elevated spot, supposing they would be safe there; but the mighty rush of water leaped over the hills and carried off his and other people's property, to be seen no more.

"It was but an instant apparently before the mighty torrent tossed into the air the iron bridge that spanned the South Fork, and crushed, beyond recognition, the house and two barns belonging to George Lamb. Onward dashed the destructive flood, roaring like a mighty battle, tree-top high, toward South Fork village, rolling over and over again rocks that weighed tons and tons, carrying them a mile or more from the spot where they had lain for ages."

The Chicago and New York limited train, upon which the Rev. James W. Putnam, of Philadelphia, and Frank Hatton, Esq., of the *Washington Post*, were passengers, had been detained at South Fork village from early in the morning, on account of a washout some miles beyond. Learning of the impending danger the engineer pulled out just in time to escape the destruction. A freight train was less fortunate; for the officers were able only to uncouple the engine from the cars, and in great haste pull across the Conemaugh bridge just a moment before it was swept away. The abandoned train was entirely wrecked, and two of the brakemen, Thomas Henderson, of Derry, and Thomas Kehoe, of Altoona, went down with the flood. Two citizens of South Fork village, Michael Mann and Howard Schaffer, also perished, and considerable property was there destroyed.

Let us follow the line of devastation down to what is known as the viaduct, the only bridge of the old Portage Road, utilized by the Pennsylvania Railroad Company. The railroad at this point, a mile and a quarter west of South Fork Station, was completely wrecked. In fact, for most of that distance, the roadbed was entirely washed away.

In passing from South Fork, before reaching the viaduct, the Conemaugh River makes a sudden bend to the left. The following cut will give the reader some idea of the locality :

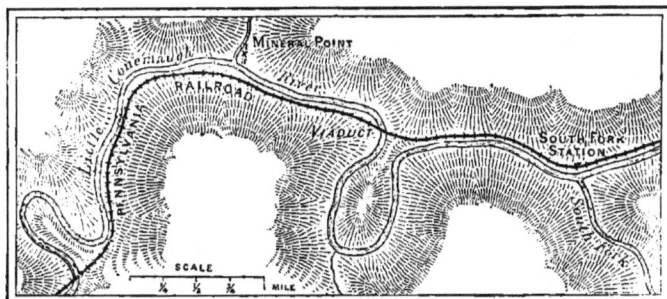

The dotted line represents the railroad, and the continuous line the course of the creek, or Little Conemaugh River.

At the point where the river bends suddenly to the left, the roadbed is cut through the narrow rocky ledge, a distance of about seventy-five feet to the point where it strikes the river again. Where it leaves the river at the eastern bend, the altitude is about twenty feet above the bed of the stream, and at the viaduct the roadbed was over seventy feet above the bed of the river, but now measuring over eighty feet, more than ten feet having been washed out by the flood. Whilst the distance around the bend is two miles, the cut straight across is less than one hundred feet. Here occurred one of the wonders of the deluge, a sight which, if any human eye was permitted to witness it, must have thrilled the soul of the beholder: when the rushing torrent reached the bend of the river, it divided, one part passing through the cut in the mountain and plunging down over the viaduct, and the other following the proper channel. A volume of water twenty feet deep poured through the railroad cut and over the viaduct, carrying with it debris of every description—trees, buildings, rocks, etc.,—depositing them to a greater height than was wreckage afterward hurled at the stone bridge. The tell-tale marks that the flood left behind it go to show that the debris was piled up 125 feet above the bed of the stream. But all this accumulated rubbish was carried away when the rush of water that followed the regular course of the stream reached that point, and then with gathered force, exceeding that with which it had issued from the reservoir itself, it swept on down to the next village called Mineral Point, where forty houses were carried away in a shorter time than it requires to read this page, and where the following named sixteen persons found a watery grave: Samuel Kohler, James Wilson, Samuel Page, wife and two children, Mrs. Christopher Gormley and six children, Mrs. Abram Byer and mother, and Mrs. Burkhardt.

The pastor of the M. E. Church of that place informs me that when his church building was moved from its foundation, the bell began to toll and continued to strike a singular dirge until the edifice went to pieces.

Sweeping around the great bend above East Conemaugh, the grand and terrific scenes of the viaduct were repeated. Regarding the first view of the great wall of water as it approached East Conemaugh and Franklin, two of the upper villages of our cluster of towns (included in what is commonly called the city of Johnstown) situated on opposite sides of the river, the Rev. J. A. Smith, pastor of the United Brethren Church, sends me the following statement : "Whilst looking from the up-stairs window of our residence, on the Franklin side, having an elevated view of the river and town, watching the piles of drift borne upon the surging current, marking the gradual rise of the water on the river banks, the roar of the mighty torrent fell upon my startled ears, and, at once, the appalling situation of the people in the valley was apparent. At that moment, the shriek of a locomotive, that came rushing full speed into the yard, sounded forth the tocsin of alarm. This was engine Number 1124, class R., J. C. Hess, engineer, and J. B. Plumer, fireman. They had been up the railroad about a third of a mile, their engine looking west, with a number of freight cars ahead of them, when they suddenly heard the roar of the waters up the valley, and looking in that direction beheld the immense avalanche rushing toward them. Mr. Hess immediately opened up the throttle of the engine, and pushing ahead of him the intruding cars, made his way in advance of the swift deluge in the chase until he reached the Pennsylvania Railroad yard, just opposite the house of Master Mechanic Syane. Here he abandoned his faithful engine, still sounding out the alarm whilst he ran to his home near by and carried his family to the hills just in the nick of time.

"The Pennsylvania Railroad property was all swept away, and much of their track was torn up and washed off. The Round

House succumbed to the force of the current like a toy in the hands of a giant, and more than thirty huge engines rolled down the stream like so many pebbles."

The sections of the day express and also the mail train had been detained at this point here in consequence of the washout already referred to.

In answer to my request for his experience in our disaster, the Rev. Dr. T. H. Robinson, Professor in the Western Theological Seminary, at Allegheny, Pa., a passenger on the day express, writes that his train was put on a siding upon reaching Conemaugh. He continues: "Another passenger train was there before us, and soon after section 2 of our train joined us. After a little, it was seen that the river was working in on our track, when we were moved back, soon after which the track fell into the river. We were moved again, and the second track fell into the river. While these things were going on, I and other passengers were walking about in the rain, up and down the tracks, watching the rise of the river, the destruction of tracks, the descent of floodwood and the encroachment on two bridges near by; or we sat in our trains reading, writing, conversing, etc., unconscious of danger. There we were from a little after 10 A.M. until 4 P.M. I was busy part of the time making up a diary of events for my wife. Soon a crash told us that one of the bridges had gone; still we felt safe. Rumors were about of a reservoir up the road somewhere that might give way, but we knew nothing of the real peril. All at once, as I had taken up my book to read again, a shrill, long whistle sounded from an engine near by. The people in my car rose to their feet and began asking what it meant. No one knew. I said to a lady near by me, 'I presume there is no danger;' but looking out of my car window, I saw a huge mass of trees and flood-wood and water, about two or three hundred feet away, moving toward the train. I at once cried, 'We must get out as soon as possible.'

Our passenger trains and a freight were lying side by side, the freight nearest the river, our train next, the other train between us and the town and safety. As I got out of my car, I saw three ways before me: climb over section No. 2 or crawl under it, or run down the track with the flood four-car lengths and around the train. I instantly chose the latter. No one else followed me so far as I saw, but all attempted the other courses. I got safely around the trains. Between me and the first street of the town ran a ditch quite deep. Happily for me, just below where I struck it, there was a plank across, and in a moment I was over it. This ditch was a fatal place to some. A man, his wife and sister, who sat by me in the car, attempted to get over or under section 2. The man and his wife's sister were not seen again, but the wife, climbing back into the car, was saved. My flight down stream had taken me away from the rest of the people, and I found myself almost wholly alone, pressing up an alley toward the hillside back of the town. I ran to the second street, and, hoping I might be safe, I turned and looked. The houses were floating away behind me, and the flood was getting round above me. I ran on to the third street and turned again; the water was close behind me, houses were toppling over, and the torrent again pushing round as if to head me off. I ran now up rising ground at the foot of the mountain and soon found I was beyond the flood. What an awful sight presented itself as I turned and looked: houses falling and sweeping down stream; some six or eight rods away, two men were dragging a woman with all their might; one car broken loose and going down stream in plunging water, two men on top, others inside. It was awful to see the men as the car rolled from side to side trying to keep on top. Then all the trains started down the river, a number (I know not how many) inside. I cried out in anguish, 'They are gone!' They went about five hundred feet, and were stopped very strangely, our engine being lifted up and flung upon the head of the other train. Engines from the Round House were rolled down against it, a mass of trees was lodged here and a breakwater formed. The rear cars also, one or more, were thrown from the track against the freight train, and the whole four trains, save two or three cars, were held in the midst of the flood."

George M. Graham, M.D., of Port Royal, Juniata County, Pa., who was also a passenger on one of these trains, writes : " I stepped on the platform of one of the gondola cars, and looking east of the river, I saw what appeared like a bank of water coming with fearful velocity. Rolling at great height in its passage it showed trees, roots and bodies of trees, with debris of all kinds. I quickly reported the danger to those in the car. The passengers tumbled out in all haste, some passing under the train on the north track, as that was the direction of escape and safety. An old minister of Kalamazoo, Michigan, got out of the rear car with his wife, and, seeing the waters so close, called to her to come back, which she did, both re-entering the car. There was a gully or ditch a few rods north of the train, running parallel with the track. It was about ten feet wide and five and one-half deep. After passing around the rear car of the second section, I jumped across the ditch to the farther bank. I then had open space to see the approach of the torrent, and I felt safe, as by running fifty or sixty yards over level ground would allow me to enter the street where the grade ascended. Feeling secure myself, I determined to help others. Just to my left, into the ditch, arm-pit deep, I saw nine women and girls tumble. I instantly grabbed the hand of the first and quickly pulled her out ; the meanwhile all the others reached for me at once. I succeeded in saving them all except one old lady. I said to her, ' Give me your hand quick ! quick ! quick ! Give me your hand !' She evidently was bewildered, for she replied, ' I will go this way,' and, walking toward the maddened waters, she was lost.

"The water was within ten feet of me when I reached the street corner. I ran about fifty yards up the street, took a long breath, and, upon turning around, saw a building half way across the street at the point I had passed not thirty seconds before. The next instant it dashed against the corner and was surrounded by five or six feet of water. The force of the water lifted up and dashed the buildings one against another. The roaring of the rushing, fearful water, the tumbling and crashing of the buildings, and the wailing and cries of the women and children, no pen can describe. One poor woman came to me in agonizing distress, with her gaze so intent as if to pierce the water, crying out, 'Oh my baby! My dear baby is in the water!'"

During all this time of terror the scene among the citizens, both in the village of East Conemaugh on the railroad side of the stream, and in Franklin or the south side, was awful beyond all description. Frank Traut, on his way to work, was caught by the fatal waters near the ticket gate of the fair grounds. He scrambled upon the roof of the ticket office and afterward on a telephone pole, which soon was broken off. Then he seized a passing log, on which he dashed ahead, all the way to the stone bridge, a distance of over two miles, where he took hold of some wreckage which, by the back water, landed him near the Presbyterian church on Main Street, whence he worked his way to Alma Hall and was saved.

John Keiper, fireman on the Pennsylvania Railroad, also caught hold of a drifting log which carried him across Johnstown proper over to the upper end of Kernville, a distance of more than three miles.

Two daughters of Gustavus McHugh, of East Conemaugh, were saved at the Woodvale Woolen Mill, by some men, who threw a rope to them as they approached on some drift, and pulled them in through a window.

J. W. Burkhardt and family were carried in their house, which kept intact until it struck the side of the steep hill below the Chemical Works, where it was delayed long enough for them all to make good their escape from the roof.

Among the victims of the flood from this place, none have been more widely lamented than John C. Wilson, M.D., and his estimable family. The Doctor had been over among the passengers at the trains, where, thinking of no danger, he had held pleasant and protracted conversation with a brother physician, Dr. Graham, of Juniata County. Some time before the torrent came, he had returned to his beautiful residence, which, with its occupants, went down in the deluge. Being a ruling Elder and Sabbath School Superintendent in the Presbyterian Church of the place (the Rev. D. M. Miller, pastor), he had in his charge the Church records, all of which were destroyed.

Not only were the Doctor's dwelling and the dwellings of other citizens destroyed, but even the lots upon which these dwellings stood were washed away, and the place covered with water and rocks so as to be beyond reclaim.

These are the names of the resident victims from East Conemaugh and Franklin :

Dr. J. C. Wilson and his wife, Carrie Wilson.
Essie Kiefer and child.
Sarah Leech and daughter Allie.
W. W. Mills.
Miss Devlin.
Peter Rubritz, wife and daughter Maggie.
Mrs. Robine and two children.
Ida Loudensteine.
G. Constable.
Solomon Boyer.
Sarah Soy and son Newton.
John Atkinson.
Mrs. McHugh, daughter and son.
Mrs. Burk.
Mrs. McKinn.
Mrs. Sample.

The following are the names of those known to have been lost off the trains at East Conemaugh:

Miss Long, of Curwinsville, Clear-field County, and three children in her charge.

Miss J. B. Rainey, of Kalamazoo, Mich.

Miss Paulson, of Pittsburgh.

Mr. Ross (a cripple), Pittsburgh.

Miss Elizabeth M. Bryan, of Phila-delphia, Pa.

Mr. Ewing, of Ligonier, Pa.

Christ. Meisel, of Newark, N. J.

W. Shelley, Newark, N. J.

E. Lyon, of New York.

J. R. Day and daughter, Prospect, Harford Co., Md.

F. Phillips, the colored porter, of Phila-delphia.

Mrs. J. F. King, unknown residence.

Miss Annie Bates, of Racine, Wis-consin.

Mrs. E. Swineford, of New Berlin, Ohio, and her daughter-in-law of St. Louis, Mo.

Mrs. McCoy and two sons, residence unknown.

Mrs. H. R. Smith and 3-year-old child, residence unknown.

Miss A. C. Christman, New Orleans, La.

Woodvale, the next town below, the upper part of which is about a quarter of a mile distant, and containing, as Judge Mas-ters informs me, nearly eight hundred buildings, like another Chamouni, was swept off the face of the earth. Although most of the buildings were wooden, yet such solid brick structures as the residence of John Hannan, the school-houses, and the Rosen-steel tannery were swept away. The only walls left in that village were parts of the large woolen and flouring mills. More than one-third of the population were drowned, among whom were such prominent citizens as the Alexanders, the Allisons, the Rosensteels, the Nixons, the Joneses, and others, for particulars regarding whom, see chapter on Morgues.

Mr. Charles B. Clark, the compiler of the valuable directory of Johnstown, speaking in regard to the destruction in the Wood-vale part of our city, writes, "Here was the greatest comparative loss of life, excepting, perhaps, Washington Street in Johnstown proper, for the people were mostly in their houses and went down with them. Some of them, hearing the noise, attempted to run to the hills, forty to sixty rods distant, but not many succeeded in reaching a place of safety, as the water was already too deep for rapid running; and what added to the horror of the situation, a train of freight cars was standing between them and the hill. These cars started to move with the flood, and thus many perished just at the portal of safety."

On swept the mighty torrent with its increased freight and Conemaugh Borough was reached. Here also there was an almost total destruction of the lower half of the town, including the section about and below the Gautier Mills. When it struck those works, with their numerous fires and immense machinery, the explosions that took place were simply terrific, destroying human life, and scarcely leaving a trace of those great industries. As the Rev. Dr. Fink expressed it, who was watching the approaching flood from an upper window of his house in Johnstown proper, "It seemed as if the whole works arose and moved forward on the water slide, as the whole came down the valley."

Among those who had the most awful experience in this part of the city was Mrs. Jacob Molzie, who was floated across the Seventh Ward, and, helpless in the wreckage, lay all night in the water, fast among timbers, with only a part of her face above the flood, and within easy reach of seven dead persons. She says that the luxuriant hair of a dead woman frequently during that black Friday night swept across her face. Mrs. Molzie was rescued on Saturday.

Mrs. John Ludwig, a wealthy German lady, well educated in her own language and a leading member of the German Lutheran Church, said to me in her broken English, " My son Henry and his wife, my son Charles and my son-in-law, August Young, all got drowned. My pastor and his wife and four nice little children were lost, and there is not one brick of our good, big church left on top of another; and here is the key of our church, and that is all that we got of our church. Mr. Beale, I think my heart must break with my much trouble." This excellent woman, like many others, sank under her grief and died a few days after.

Before sweeping Johnstown proper, between which and Conemaugh Borough there is no break of buildings, the great volume of water divided into three parts, the first following the natural channel of the river, the second crossing above and through Conemaugh Borough and the upper wards of Johnstown, destroying hundreds of stone buildings, including the German Lutheran Church and the Hulbert House, and the third crossing the central part of the city, demolishing the Municipal Buildings, the Y. M. C. A. Hall, and scores of the most elegant private residences in the city. I shall now give the experience and observation of a number of citizens of the First, Second, Third and Fourth Wards, or what is known as Johnstown proper.

More persons perished in the Hulbert House, one of our best hotels, situated on Clinton Street, near Main, than in any other single building in the whole city. Most of the guests were in the office, on the second floor, when an unusual whistling of engines was heard. Thinking that a fire had broken out, everybody except F. A. Benford, proprietor, Walter Benford, clerk, and Mr. H. W. Galager went up stairs to ascertain where it was. About three minutes afterward Walter Benford walked to the front window, and looking toward the Conemaugh saw the cloud of dust, and thinking Prospect Hill had caved in, called out, "My God, the hill is falling;" then F. A. Benford ran to the door, and looking up street realized what had happened, and told Walter and Galager to go up stairs, remarking that he would go back to the kitchen and tell the girls of the danger. When he had done so he looked out of the side door, and saw the first wave of the flood coming. He remembers that Mr. Butler and Misses Carrie and Mollie Richards were in the parlor on the second floor, and that Mrs. DeFrance

SITE OF HULBERT HOUSE AND WRECKED BUSINESS BLOCK ON MAIN STREET.

and Miss Jennie Wells had already reached the third floor. Just as he started to reach the fourth floor, Miss Carrie Deihl ran down, exclaiming, " Oh, this is terrible." He had just reached the fourth floor when the building fell. Walter and Galager went to the third floor and started to go to the back part of the building, and when at about two-thirds of the distance the brick work was washed out from under them, leaving the upper or mansard story a floating wreck. They got upon this without even wetting their feet, and by it were saved. All stories told in regard to traveling men pinning cards on their coats, bidding each other good-by, etc., are mere fabrications. The crash came too suddenly for such premeditated farewells. Mr. J. L. Smith, one of the saved, says that the flood broke instantly on the house, and that the walls fell before the people realized what had happened; and that they all rushed for the stairway leading to the fourth floor; but none of them got farther than the landing before the rest of the building fell.

The saved were :

F. A. Benford, proprietor.
Walter Benford.
William Marshall, colored.
Mary Early.

Laura Rodgers.
Elmira Prosser.
Maggie Jones.

The following is a list of the lost :

Mrs. E. E. Benford, widowed mother of the proprietor.
Miss Maria M. Benford.
" May Benford.
Mr. G. L. Benford.
Mrs. Jacob Katzenstein and son.
" J. L. Smith and three children.
" H. T. DeFrance.
Miss Carrie Richards.
" Mollie Richards.

Miss Jennie Smouse.
" Ellen Johnson, colored.
Mr. James G. Cox, of Philadelphia.
" W. L. Spitz.
" J. A. Little, of Pittsburgh.
" Jonathan Carlin, of Philadelphia.
" James Murray.
" N. F. Dow.
" Charles Dewatt.
" George Randolph.

4

Miss Jennie Wells, of Shippensburg, Pa.
Miss Carrie Deihl, of Shippensburg, Pa.
Miss Laura Hamilton.
" —— Horner.
" Nellie Clark.
" Ella Byrne.
" Minnie Huston.
" Maggie Irwin.
" Jane Maloy.
" Mary Ridgers.
" Ellen Harrigan.
" Bertha Stoppel.
" Lottie Yost.

Mr. John Byrne.
" J. W. Weakland.
" Charles F. Butler.
" Charles Marshall.
" Elmer Brinkey.
Dr. J. C. Brinkey.
Mr. J. C. Clark.
Dr. St. John.
Albert Wherry.
Mr. —— Herron.
" Charles Wilson.
" William Henry, colored.
" Samuel Etcheson.
Unknown young lady, monogram J. H. G.

Mrs. Agnes C. Chapman, wife of the Rev. Dr. Chapman, pastor of the M. E. Church of Johnstown proper, gives me this statement:

"About 4 o'clock, Mr. Chapman, who had gone to the front door, returned pale and affrighted, exclaiming that doubtless the reservoir had broken. I looked out of the study window and saw the waves coming; it seemed to me half as high as our house. I ran for our little grand-daughter Nellie, and started up stairs. There were present myself and Nellie, Mrs. Brinker, a neighbor, who had come into our house for safety; our servant girl, and a young Mr. Parker. Mr. Chapman ran into the study to turn out the natural gas in the parlor fireplace. Upon reaching the second floor I looked down to see if Mr. Chapman was coming, when I saw the front door burst open and the water rushing in. It seemed to me to be half way up the front stairs in a moment. I called to Mr. Chapman to come quick, but he was nearly up the back stairs by that time, and we were all in the attic in a few moments. We all stood there in the middle of the floor, waiting our turn to be swept away, and expecting every minute to be drowned. When our porches were torn loose, and the two book-cases fell over, the noise led us to think the house was going to pieces. But fortunately it stood, because the church stood between us and the swift current. When the noise of houses scraping against ours and the great rush of water had somewhat diminished, Mrs. Brinker asked Mr. Chapman to look out and see if their house was still standing. But, said she, "If it is not, don't tell me." He looked out, then turned back, but said nothing. Our little Nellie, only 7 years old, then peeped out and said: "Yes, Mrs. Brinker, your house is gone—your house is gone." We knew we had to stay there all night, every moment of which was one of anguish and suspense, as there were eighteen feet of water around us and under us. There were nine saved in the attic with us, four of whom got into our second story windows and ran up to where we were; some were as wet as they could be. We gave them clothing and blankets to wrap around them. When daylight came, we all walked and crawled out over the roofs of houses or anything that would hold us until we reached the hillside."

The Rev. James A. Lane, the well-known local preacher in the M. E. Church, an official of the Cambria Iron Works, lived in an elegant brick house on Locust Street, about midway between the high hill back of the town and the Point, or stone bridge. Mr. Lane's family consisted of his wife and her mother, Mrs. Teeter; their daughter Jessie and her husband, Mr. Harry G. Rose, Esq., District Attorney of Cambria County. On this fatal day they were all at home on account of the high water. The first indication of the coming of the awful catastrophe was seen by Mr. Lane himself as he stood in the stairway looking down, and saw large logs dashing in at the window. He hastened to get his family up into the third story.　He had hardly succeeded in this when the two lower stories fell away, leaving the third floor, covered with a mansard roof of tin, floating deep in the swelling waves.　He found himself in darkness, up to the neck in water, and wedged in between floating logs.　The whole family were in the same condition, and Mr. H. G. Rose was killed by the force of the crushing timbers.　Mother Teeter's arm was cut off at the wrist, it is supposed by glass from the mirror of a dressing bureau which fell over and struck her.　She was so seriously injured that she afterward died. Three times Mr. Lane struggled to get out from among the logs, and finding his pantaloons held him, he took out his knife and cut the suspenders.　He then was free, and with his fists knocked off the boxing around the trap-door, and got out on the roof.　In his anxiety to get his family out he was heard loudly calling for some one to bring him an axe.　In pulling Mrs. Rose from among the wreck, she received considerable injury.　He was himself much bruised, and came out of the struggle almost naked.

On the top of the roof, they were drifted within reach of another house, and got upon the comb of its roof.　Within the attic of this house were several persons, among them Mr. Thomas Watt, ticket agent of the Pennsylvania Railroad.　Mr. Walters from the inside and Mr. Lane on the outside effected an opening in the roof, through which Mr. Lane's party succeeded in escaping from the storm, and remained in the attic all night.　The house had careened, and kept cracking and threatening to go to pieces ; while fire from the stone bridge seemed to be approaching, and filled them with dread lest it should reach their tottering shelter. About 10 o'clock next day Mrs. Lane and Mrs. Rose escaped into the Morrell Institute.　But owing to the condition of Mother Teeter, Mr. Lane remained in the attic with her until 4 o'clock in the afternoon, when they joined the others in the safer building, and thus escaped.

Among the varied experiences of many in escaping from what appeared to be certain death, perhaps few, if any, were more thrilling than that of Rev. D. M. Miller and family.

Mr. Miller is pastor of the Conemaugh Presbyterian Church in that part of the city commonly called East Conemaugh, and his residence was at No. 94 Vine Street, in Johnstown proper. The family assure me that they had no warning of the bursting of the reservoir, until they heard a fearful noise and saw buildings suddenly rising from their foundations a half square away and floating toward them, crushing fences, shade and fruit trees, and telephone and electric light poles. Mr. and Mrs. Miller were in the second story of their residence. Instantly the room was waist deep with water. Mrs. Miller jumped upon a bed, which suddenly rose to the ceiling, where she was scarcely able to breathe. In the meantime the rest of the family sprung through a window upon floating boards and timbers, urging her to follow. But the water having risen above the open part of the window, the lower sash being raised, she could not escape until by great effort she tore the strip from one side of the window, and Mr. Miller, having recovered himself from his first plunge into the seething mass, with one hand caught hold of the spouting under the eaves of the house, and with the other broke the glass of both sashes, cutting his hand severely. Then with his foot he broke the sash near where she was hemmed in, so that diving out under the cap of the window, she sprung out where a small porch roof had attached to the house ; but unfortunately it had just been torn away, and she sank out of sight. Just then the water seemed to rise several feet, and she was thrown to the surface, surrounded with rubbish of every kind, and seized hold of the spouting. The building at this moment was rapidly floating toward the Stony Creek, immediately beyond which was an almost perpendicular mountain four hundred and fifty feet high. When the tide crossed the river and struck the mountain, there was a fearful rebound, which upset many buildings that had been before floating upright. Now this part of the flood, with its scores of buildings and people, divided into three currents. One turned to the right and went down the already overflowing stream to the terrible gorge at the large stone bridge of the Pennsylvania Railroad; and one turned to the left and flowed rapidly up the channel of the Stony Creek, carrying buildings and people nearly a mile up that stream; the other between these two currents was thrown back in the direction in which it came, but in such a way as to cause all floating material to describe a circle, embracing perhaps fifteen or twenty acres, or about four squares of the city. This return tide caught Mr. Miller's dwelling, and after describing about two-thirds of a complete circle, it landed on the junction of two streets not more than a hundred yards from its starting point, very much the worse for its unfortunate journey. Mr. and Mrs. Miller in the meantime were still clinging to the water-spout, and were being dragged through the debris, with only their heads above the water, until they discovered on their housetop two of their neighbors, Price Davis and John Hennecamp, who, having been separated from their families, had been thrown upon this roof, in some way, they knew not how. These men, upon discovering the heads of the unfortunate husband and wife, at once crept down to the edge of the wet, slippery roof—for it was raining hard—and undertook the difficult task of dragging them out of the water over the wide cornice, and up to the comb of the roof. This feat only strong, steady and cool-headed men could have accomplished, risking their own lives as they did to save others; but they were successful, and the clergyman and his wife were saved, yet not without cuts and bruises, which for a time threatened fatal results. Soon after a lady and boy were also drawn out of the flood upon the same roof, and all sat together in the rain and wind on the comb of the roof until about nightfall. The house being full of water, their only refuge was the unfinished attic, where they sat upon a narrow board, without room to stand or floor on which to lay the sick and faint. With no clothing except the remnants of wet and filthy garments which still clung to their persons, they spent the long, dark, cold and dreary night, as well as the next day, until the middle of the afternoon, before they were reached by rescuers, when, after climbing over many crushed buildings, they gained the river and were taken in a rude boat across to the steep mountain on the other side. They then walked in mud and water nearly half a mile, where they found friends and refuge, having been without food, drink or sleep for twenty-eight hours. The scenes they witnessed, the sounds they heard, and the experiences through which they passed can never be described.

On this same roof were the wife and only child of John Hennecamp, both of whom perished at this time.

My friend, Mrs. Masterton, who lived on Vine Street, near Market, writes me:

"We had been watching the rivers rise and overflow the town all day. I had rather enjoyed it, as it was my first experience of the kind. Mr. Masterton came home from his business before noon, having heard that the water was in our part of the town. Fortunately the water rose so rapidly that he could not leave the house again, or God alone knows what would have been his fate, for you know his portion of the store was completely demolished. We could see quite a distance up the Conemaugh River from the windows of our second story and were standing there talking to our neighbors, the Whites, when the great rush of water came upon us. Mr. Masterton called to Mr. Delaney, Mr. White's son-in-law, that there must have been a terrible explosion up the river, for the water coming looked like a cloud of the blackest smoke I ever saw. Almost before Mr. Delaney could answer, his house was lifted and turned upside down. There were twelve members of their family in the house at the time, and you know the fate of six of them. Mr. Masterton took our little girl in his arms, and we ran to the attic, the water following us up the stairs. I cannot tell you when our house was carried away, for I was not conscious that it had moved until I saw that we were just back of the Market Street School-house. Our house must have turned several times, for we were bound very securely with telegraph and electric light wires, which I think helped to keep it from overturning as all about us had done. When we had recovered ourselves a little, we began to look around us to see what we could do. We succeeded in getting twenty-seven people into our attic, but the names of all of them I cannot tell you, as they were entire strangers to me.

"The first person we rescued was Joseph Hipp, our mail carrier; he had floated from Conemaugh Borough and was very badly bruised. Mr. and Mrs. Kirwin, with Mr. and Mrs. Williams, their three children and a young Welsh girl, whom I did not know, were the next. Mrs. Williams, during the night, gave birth to a child, which you afterward baptized 'Moses.' Mr. and Mrs. William Moore, with their two children; Miss Alice Kinney and her brothers Wills and Samuel; two young men by the name of Stattler (members of our church, I think); Mr. John Jones and David Davis, carpenters; two women with two children, none of whom I knew, and a very old woman, I think they called her Auntie Whannell, and her son.

"Our attic was perfectly dry, and as I had all our winter clothing packed there, I had something to give the poor drenched creatures who came to us. We were taken from the house about 10 o'clock on Saturday morning. Of the twenty or thirty houses around us, I think ours was the only one that was not crushed or overturned. It was burned, however, in the fire of June 24th."

Mr. William T. Colliver, a machinist, who lived in a low part of the Second Ward, on Friday afternoon sat with his wife and daughter Mary in the second story of their house, which was already flooded. Mrs. Colliver is an invalid, who for seven years had not walked without assistance. Mr. Colliver was quite cheerful, and, having watched for some time the waters in the street, was assuring his neighbors that the worst was over and that the water was already receding; but he shortly changed his mind, for he saw the rush of the great flood from the Conemaugh Lake, and the houses coming toward them. He said to his family: "Something awful has occurred, and we probably must all die. But let us be calm, and give ourselves wholly to the Lord." At the same time he hurried them up into the attic, but before this could be accomplished they were already knee-deep in the water. The house was lifted from its foundation and borne swiftly away, but by the favor of Providence did not turn over. His daughter Mary said,

"Papa, I do not like to die this way."

"No, daughter, I don't like to die this way either, but we must submit to God's will."

"But, papa, I have not been as good as I might have been. But, father, you have always tried to be good."

"So have you always tried to be good, Mary; but let us give ourselves wholly to the Lord, and He may yet save us."

"But you won't leave us, papa, will you?"

"No, my dear, whatever happens we will stick together; if we must die, we will die in each other's arms."

By this time they had drifted out of the swift current toward Union Street School-house. There they struck upon something which anchored the house and held it fast. They began to feel secure, but presently they saw a large livery stable coming swiftly toward them, and they expected that their house would be knocked to pieces; but before it reached them it was caught in a counter-current, and whirled around and passed by without touching them. When it began to get dark they found that so many houses had gathered between them and the school-house that it was possible, by climbing over roofs, logs and other drift, to reach that more comfortable place. Several had already done so. Mr. Colliver shouted to Mr. Williams, whom he saw in the window of the school-house, to come and help him get his invalid wife over. He and Mr. Owens came, and, with the assistance of Colonel J. P. Linton, succeeded in getting them all into that place of refuge, where they found nearly two hundred who had been rescued in various ways. A number of these were suffering from injuries, and were groaning from pain, while others, having been exposed in the waters, were shivering with cold. Not one could sleep, and it was a long night of misery and terror. When daylight appeared, such was the joy that Mr. Colliver climbed upon the roof and shouted, "It is morning! It is morning!" After they got safely away the next day he had a curiosity to know what had anchored the house in such good time. He found that five open railroad cars had drifted into the neighborhood, and one of them having fallen with one end into a cellar, the shaft of the brake-wheel had run through the bottom of the house and held it there.

Mr. J. C. McNeice, agent of the Adams Express Company, allows me to use the following concerning his experience :

" My wife, two children and myself were all in the second story of our residence on Lincoln Street, where we had been driven by the water coming into the first floor about 8.30 A.M. The water had been rising very slowly for almost two hours, and upon going to the rear of the building which was of brick, about 4 P.M., I noticed that the current had increased, also that some drift which had been held for some time by the fence-post had moved away.

" Being unable to account for this, I started toward the front of the building, when I heard a commotion and people crying out,

'The reservoir has broken!' Hastening to the window, I saw a frame building cross Lincoln Street at Market Street with a huge wave of water following. I turned round to inform my family, but at that moment water came pouring into the second story. My wife seizing one child and I the other, we got up to a window-sill, over which the water was pouring into the room, and, getting on the outside, we held the children and ourselves by clinging to the window-sash.

"While standing there, with the water in front and in the rear of us, and rising rapidly, and buildings being removed from one lot to another on the opposite side of the street, a large double frame dwelling was thrown against our building, causing the bricks to fall all around us. At this time the water had reached to our waists, when suddenly a pair of large box steps came shooting up out of the water and settled, broadside up, directly in front of us. Seizing the steps, I got my family on them and transferred them, together with Mrs. Linton, to the Armory building roof, which had swung around and anchored against the lower corner of our building.

"As the rafters under the tin roof of the Armory building began to give way, we scrambled to the roof of the house occupied by Mr. T. H. Watt, the Pennsylvania Railroad agent, and Mr. Anderson H. Walters, where we remained, with some thirty others, for about two hours in a heavy rain. Those who were on the roof were Mr. and Mrs. Watt, Mrs. Ramsey, grandmother of Mrs. Watt; Mrs. Linton, Mr. I. E. Roberts, Frank and Ed. Buchanan, Mr. Stackhouse, Mr. and Mrs. Breniser and son, who came down with their dwelling from Locust Street; Mr. and Mrs. Mertz and family, Mr. and Mrs. Owens, from Locust Street; Mrs. Harris and family, Mrs. Carroll and Mr. Oswald, Mr. and Mrs. Lane, Mrs. Harry Rose and Mrs. Teeter, the latter being badly injured when rescued from the ruins."

By crawling over debris, part of those mentioned reached Morrell Institute and were saved.

Alfred Easterbrook states:

"Our home was on Union Street, which is about the lowest part of the town, and as early as 7 o'clock in the morning of that fatal day, the water was rising rapidly. We began moving the furniture and other things up to the second story of our house, and at 8 o'clock we were all chased up stairs on account of the water coming into the dwelling. We remained there, thinking all the time that the water would go down, and at 3 o'clock we thought it had gone down about an inch. At this time it was five feet in our house. At about 4 o'clock we were all frightened by the cries of the people on the neighboring hills, and before we could realize what had happened, we saw our neighbors' houses floating toward us. I rushed for the attic, and then dragged my wife and children up after me; we did not all reach the attic before our house was afloat, but at last I succeeded in getting my children up, when all at once the flue of my house fell out. I then rushed to get out, and I succeeded. Then my eldest son got out of the attic window, on to the side of the house. The house turned over again, and parted in the centre, and my daughter shot out of the house, but just as she was half way out, the house was forced together again, holding her fast. By a great effort we released her from this position. All this time my wife and youngest son were under the water. I then saw my youngest son coming toward us. I reached out, caught him, and by dragging him out, and my wife having a hold of him under the water, I happened to see her hair floating on the water, and I caught it and dragged her out. Once more we were all together. We then began to consider which way we could reach the hill. At last the ruins gorged together, and we climbed from one thing to another over the debris and were then near enough the hill to be drawn up with ropes."

Abram Mangus lived at 27 Main Street. Mrs. Mangus, his wife, says that first, the long porch went. Then some heavy object struck the building and knocked out the under part and left the attic afloat. Several persons got into the attic as they floated within reach, among them an entirely naked babe. None of them knew where this child came from, but they supposed some one had thrown it in while being carried by, in order to save it. Mrs. Mangus seeing the babe was cold wrapped it in a skirt. Three times their wrecked building floated down near to the bridge and the burning debris, and each time was carried back by the reacting current. Finally they found it possible to get into Union Street School-house, by climbing over the masses of wreck. In order that she might have the use of her hands in climbing into the window of the school-house, Mrs. Mangus took in her teeth the muslin which wrapped the babe, and thus carried it into the place of safety. Much curiosity was excited among the people gathered there about the babe. One woman came and looked at it and exclaimed, " That is my baby." And so it actually was. The babe after its perilous ride was restored to its mother.

Miss Annie Fisher lived in a cottage. It had no attic, but the family had gone into the second story for safety from the flood, which was high in the first story. Her family consisted of her brother Pierson, Milton and his wife, Aunt Susan (Mrs. Pershing), Bertie Jones, her nephew, and a servant girl. Milton had just returned from Philadelphia, where he had been in a hospital on account of serious ill-health. He was still helpless and in bed. Miss Fisher was at the front window looking out, when she saw neighbors across the way on the roof of their house looking excitedly at something. She called across to know what was wrong. "My God," was the answer, " the reservoir is broken, and we are all lost." In a few moments she saw the awful mass of spray, looking like smoke, and the black wreck coming, and could not imagine what it was.   It looked like the smoke of a fire, and she thought it was the end of the world.   She turned back to where the family were so frightened that they asked what was the matter.   "Oh," she replied, "something awful has happened; I fear that the end of the world has come.   But let us be calm, and we will all die together."   It was but a moment until the house seemed wrenched from the foundation with such a cracking and grinding as filled them all with inexpressible horror.   Miss Fisher compares it to the sensation of wrenching out a tooth.   It produced an awful sense of helplessness, as if every earthly dependence was gone.   "Aunt Susan" went down under the wave, and some one said she was drowning.   Miss Fisher caught her and held her head out of water.   A large log crushed into the window, and following came a big dog which leaped upon the bed and lay down upon the sick brother.   The bed being lifted up came apart, and they had to place him upon the wardrobe and hold him on while it was borne up nearly to the ceiling.   As soon as the house had been lifted up from its foundation it began moving swiftly, borne along by the current.   It passed the brick residence of her sister, Mrs. Byron, which was still standing, but carried them on until it reached South Street, in the Kernville part of the city.   Here it was arrested in its course near a higher building, which had an attic.   With a plank they punched the window in, and after considerable effort got the invalid brother and all the family into the attic.   Here they remained until the waters had receded.

Rev. Dr. Chapman gives me the following incident:

" David Valiance was an aged man who was converted at our protracted meeting last winter.   Of all our 165 converts no one was more faithful than he.   With his aged wife he was to be seen at every prayer-meeting and at his class regularly.   He joined the Young People's Society, and was a regular attendant.   Religion seemed to be the source of his highest enjoyment every day.   He

lived with his wife and one daughter in a brick house, one of a row of six, on the brink of the Conemaugh River. Of the six families occupying this row, only two persons escaped. The last that was seen of this good old man was on his roof by some one going by.
· He was on his knees shouting, 'Glory to God.' The rest of his story must be learned in Heaven."

Mr. John Fenn lived opposite the M. E. Church, on Locust Street. No man in the city loved his family more, and none had a more interesting group of little darlings to love. The cut given on page 75 presents all the children except the youngest.

> " They grew in beauty side by side,
> They filled one home with glee.
>
> " The same fond mother bent at night
> O'er each fair sleeping brow ;
> She had each folded flower in sight—
> Where are those dreamers now ?"

Ah, their present home is not uncertain. They and their godly father entered the blissful world together. In life they were lovely ; in death they are not parted.

Miss Bertha T. Caldwell, who has been a mission teacher among the Mormons in Idaho for several years, had, just a few days before the flood, returned to her father's house in this city. The abstract that follows is from an interesting letter written by her : "Our house is high from the foundation, and we were not very much afraid that the water would reach the lower story, and yet we took up our carpets and first floor furniture, that we might be on the safe side. My sister and I went above stairs to write, while our parents remained below reading. All at once we heard a shrill whistle. I called to papa to know what it meant, when he replied that there was probably fire up town, in the direction of

Woodvale. In a few moments I heard another whistle, and then came an awful roar and crash. It flashed through my mind in a minute that the South Fork Dam had broken. I screamed the alarm to my parents, when papa, rushing up-stairs, cried out, 'We're lost! We're lost!'

"We all ran to the third story and saw, a block away, a great perpendicular wall of water, seemingly a mountain in height, with smoke, dust and vapor flying in every direction, and on its surface houses, engines, people, cars, logs, everything, coming right toward us. We saw brick buildings, three stories high, knocked down like toy houses. I heard something splash, splash, in our lower hall, and I called, 'Is any one drowning? Oh, come up here.' We expected every second the house would be struck and broken to pieces, as were many we saw around us. The house of our next door neighbor went down, and the poor souls drowned before our eyes. The children screamed and stretched out their arms to us, saying, 'Oh, help us; for God's sake, help us.' Papa called back, 'God help you; we, too, will go in a minute.'

"The crash we expected did not come. We rushed to the rear of the house, up to our waists in water. My father put his arms around us and said we would all die together. The water was running into our second-story windows, sending a spray many feet high. I leaned far out and saw a roof-top below, and believing that we would be lost if our house would fall, I caught hold of mother when we jumped on the roof below, calling upon the others to follow. We walked and crawled over house-tops and other timbers until we reached Main Street, about a block from our home. Here, in a big three-story building, we found many other rescued ones; and the town clock struck five. We still heard the shrieks of drowning people and their cries for help. Now, for the first time, I realized that I had no dress on. It must have been torn off me. I stood shivering in a skirt, wet to the

DAISY.   JOHN F.   GEORGE
       VIRGINIA.   GENEVIEVE   BISMARCK.

THE FENN CHILDREN—ALL LOST IN THE FLOOD.
(Father and Baby also lost.)

waist. Some of our number had scarcely any clothing, and some had limbs broken. There were one hundred and twenty persons in the building; the only little child present was my brother's babe. There we sat all night through, each hour seeming as long as a day. It rained incessantly, and the cries for help never ceased. Our family clung together shivering and half dead from fright and exposure. I wondered whether my work in Idaho was finished, regretting that I had not done more when I had the opportunity. I wondered if my body would be recognized when found, and where I would be buried. The suspense was horrible. I could hear men pray who heretofore had spoken God's name only in an oath. The women bore up better than the men. Morning came at last, and, oh, what a scene presented itself to our view! My grandmother, two aunts and three cousins were drowned. Ours is a sad home. We are so thankful that our lives have been spared and that we have been supplied with necessary clothing from the Presbyterian headquarters. I realize that the Blessed Master is not through with me yet, and that there remains much for me to do."

The Rev. R. A. Fink, D.D., pastor of the Lutheran Church, gives me this account :—

" My house is on Somerset Street, on the south side of Stony Creek, opposite Clinton Street. During the flood I was standing at the front second-story window. I saw the wire-mill rise and the wreck come sweeping down toward us, prostrating everything in its course. When it crossed Stony Creek and struck my house, I saw a boy, twelve or thirteen years of age, on the front of the wreck, bareheaded, and his face bleeding. When he observed me inside the window, he recognized me and exclaimed : ' Mr. Fink, can I come in ?' I opened the window and took him in. He was a son of Mr. Updegraff from Woodvale, and had floated two miles, his brother being drowned on the way. We immediately had to

5

flee to the third story of my house, where we remained all the night and were saved. On the opposite side of the street stands the large brick Church of the Brethren. Into an upper window of the church an old gentleman made his way from the wreck. During the whole night he wept and screamed and prayed, calling over to me to pray for him, exclaiming that all his family were drowned. In the morning he was rescued by some young men who went to his aid.

"Sitting by the window in the third story, by the light of the burning steeple of the Catholic Church, and the light of the wreckage at the stone bridge, listening to the cries and screams of the old man in the church, I spent a long and memorable night."

Irwin Rutlege, Esq., who resides on the south side of the Stony Creek, sends me the following account of his experience:—
"On the afternoon of May 31st, 1889, I was alone in my house on Water Street, Fifth Ward, the family having sought different points for safety from the water, which was backed up on our city, at the dark hour of 4.10 P.M. Mrs. Parker, who lived opposite me, was screaming at the top of her voice. I went to the door to ascertain the cause of her alarm, when she said, 'Rutlege, for God's sake get out of your house; the reservoir has broken, and we will all be drowned.' I jumped out in some six feet of water and caught hold of the iron fence of my neighbor, which was under water some two feet, and was making my way toward the Franklin Street bridge—one hand down in the water, holding by that fence—when the tidal wave caught me, and I was riding or swimming on some fifteen feet of water. At this stage, a team of mules belonging to P. A. Cobaugh, hitched to a wagon, made for me for protection, as the poor brutes were frightened and fighting with the surging waves. A bay horse, without a rider, came also and crossed the tongue of the wagon in front of the mules. I was tangled up with them and passed away from them between the wagon and the

drowning animals, for they all drowned there and then at my feet. At this point the waves and debris from the stone bridge and Levergood Street met and lifted the bridge, and it floated up Stony Creek a few feet, after which it came back again and passed out of sight down the river.

"My son was in the upper story of Torney & Co.'s drug store, and, seeing me, jumped out of the upper window and pulled me to safety just as floating houses closed in upon where I had been. My son then went to the rescue of an old lady from one of the wrecked trains. She was a Grecian. He assisted and carried her to where we were then lodged—on the top of Joseph E. Morgan's house, where for nineteen hours about twenty of us remained, all that dreary, cold night and the next day until 3 o'clock, P.M., when the lamented Mr. Coffin came to our rescue with a skiff. From Friday morning at 6 o'clock until Saturday afternoon at 4½ o'clock, I ate one cracker. The old lady referred to above had her thigh broken or dislocated and her spine injured. She prayed nearly all those nineteen long, sad hours. My limbs were peeled from my knees to my ankles, and for five weeks I was under the physician's care."

George Moses lived in a beautiful frame house on the South Side, or Kernville. He had left his store in Johnstown proper to take care of itself, and was at home looking after the safety of his family. When the big torrent came they all hurried into the garret. There it was quite dark. When the house began to move, George felt an irresistible desire to look out, that he might know where they were going. He broke a hole through the roof so that he could get his head out. He found that his house was moving toward the river. Mrs. Moses was one of the sweetest singers in the city. She now commenced to sing for her children and for her own comfort, "Jesus, lover of my soul." While she sang the house received a sudden violent shock, and then stopped moving. The top end of a large tree had run in through the side of the house, and, by means of the weight of its roots and heavy end, had anchored the house right on the brink of the river. Here they remained until the waters had subsided.

Mr. William E. White, who dictated the following, lives in the Sixth Ward, near the Stony Creek :

" We would not leave our house in the morning, and after dinner could not get away. The water rushed in so swiftly at 4 o'clock that by the time we got the gas turned off and looked around it was almost to my waist. I found we would have to run up-stairs or be swept out, as the water had burst open the doors and was rushing through the hall carrying everything with it. I cannot describe the agony we suffered when we saw everything running up stream and expecting every moment to be taken along. Our house rose up, but fortunately the current turned in time to keep us back. The Unique Rink was a terrible sight, sailing past like a steamboat, which upon coming back was only prevented from floating down Somerset Street by striking a large log on the river bank when within fifty feet of our house, and almost opposite us. My thoughts all night were, Where are all the people we have seen clinging to the roofs or standing on boards, both going up stream and coming back ? When we got over our fright a little and looked out of the back attic window, we found we were completely surrounded by broken buildings and rubbish of all kinds. On the top of a house not twenty feet away, which had come from the lower end of Morris Street, stood a young man with a light shawl around his shoulders and his hair standing straight up with fright ; we called out who was he and where had he come from. He said his name was Harry Phillips, and he had come from Dr. L. T. Beam's, on Market Street. We wanted him to try to get out of the rain into our house, but he thought he was safer where he was until things had settled. Finally, he concluded to try and get to us, which he did with hard work. Next the families above us thought our house was safer than theirs, and they climbed over the debris and got into our windows, so that we would be company for each other. Harry Phillips told us how Market Street and the lower end of town had fared, and from our house-top we could see that Grandma Levergood's house was gone, and also that papa's house was standing, so we concluded they were safe. Harry Phillips said he never expected to see his mother or Dr. Beam alive. He also said that there were people in the house on which he was standing. He called over, and a young man said he was there with his old father and mother, that his father was dying, having taken a chill. We asked if they could not come over, and how they were fixed. He said the tops of the beds were dry, and they would stay there. About 6 o'clock he called to us that his father was dead. And there they remained all night alone. Climbing out the next morning they were compelled to leave the dead body of the father alone. That was a long night of agony and suspense. I cannot say it was dark, for the glare from the fire at the stone bridge made it light enough to see each other's faces. Our house is a mile from the bridge, but happily we did not know what was burning, and supposed it was the natural gas. The burning of the Catholic Church steeple was a beautiful yet awful sight—a blazing fire in the midst of water. At 4 o'clock on the next morning we could see people moving over the debris trying to release those who were in danger. About 8 o'clock we concluded to try to get to the hill, and were more than one hour climbing over the debris to go two squares."

Rev. E. W. Trautwein, pastor of the Roman Catholic Church in Cambria Borough, writes me: "Rose Carroll, of Conemaugh Borough, was half submerged in the water a short distance above the stone bridge, and her limbs were tightly held by a number of heavy timbers that were jammed around her body. I was told that directly beneath her was the body of her uncle, or some other relative, whose hand, the muscles of which were set in death, held her heel in a vise-like grip. I have not, however, been able to verify this by asking the young lady herself.

"She was the coolest person I saw that night at the bridge, though in the greatest danger, as the fire was gradually creeping up to where she was held. I several times thought we would be compelled to get an axe and cut off the one foot that was still held rather than let her be burnt alive; but, fortunately, this was not necessary, as she was taken out after several hours' hard work before the fire had reached her."

The following letter was written to Mrs. Beale by our next-door neighbor, Mrs. Dr. S. C. Poland. One of her children had been in the parsonage until the water had become two and a half feet deep on Lincoln Street, and until within a short time of the approach of the great torrent, when, having expressed a wish to return home, his uncle carried him there on his shoulders: "I have thought of you every day since the flood. I have had a very serious time in trying to recover from the dreadful bruises which I received whilst in the water. And now I am so thankful that I can write you that I am almost myself again. I was taken to Philadelphia for the treatment of my eyes, which were so badly injured that all, myself included, supposed I must spend the remainder of my days in darkness. Indeed, I suffered such intense pain in my brain that it was thought my reason would be dethroned. Oh! that fearful shock! I thought I could not survive it, and I sincerely desired to die; but it was not the will of God to take me then. My dear friend and kind neighbor, how awful was that moment when the dreadful crash. came; when, as we stood at the second-story window, looking toward the parsonage, some heavy timbers wrecked our dwelling, tearing open the lime and plaster, which fell into our eyes! The Doctor had both the little children in his arms when the house collapsed. We knew nothing until we had been floated a square away. When we came to our senses we were in more than thirty feet of water, and the Doctor and I were both fast in the wreckage. Our darling boys were both in the Doctor's arms, but the immortal spark had fled. The Doctor said he felt them struggling in his arms when he was under the water, but he could do nothing for them. Oh! if only dear Walter could have stayed at the parsonage, he might have been spared. The Doctor had two ribs broken, and I was so crippled up and black and blue with bruises, that my sister and brother did not know me when they first saw me. We have not secured one thing from our ruined house to remind us of home. Oh! if I only had some toy or book that belonged to my dear drowned children. I miss my darling babies more and more, and although I know they are better off and saved from sin, still that does not fill up the vacancy in my heart. Oh! it is dreadful to be robbed at once of home and of children; but I am trying to submit, as a Christian woman ought. It was a miracle from God that the Doctor and myself and your dear family were spared; and I do thank our Heavenly Father that my eyesight has been restored, and that my mind has become more composed. We expect to locate in Philadelphia, where we shall make a new start in the world."

Charles Boyle and wife, with their seven children, lived in an exposed part of Cambria Borough, or city, as it is sometimes called. Mr. Boyle, like everybody else, was surprised by the avalanche of water. With his family he rushed above stairs. When the water became waist-deep, he held two of the smallest children on his shoulders, until finally, the water rising still higher, they and he were drowned. The house was suddenly torn to pieces, destroying the other members of the family, save Mrs. Boyle and one son. Mrs. Boyle clung to a piece of timber, upon which she was rushed down the river nine miles to Nineveh, where her hair becoming entangled in the branches of a floating tree, which moved toward the shore, she was rescued.

> " Oft doomed to death,
> Though fated not to die."

She told Dr. C. Sheridan, her physician, that again and again in her awful ride she was under water, and that she once resolved to let go her hold, permitting herself to be drowned ; but just then thoughts of her living boy Hugh, who was at college in preparation for the priesthood, stimulated her for further.struggle.

Many other experiences have been narrated to me by fellow-citizens, which are almost as thrilling as any already given, but which, for want of space, must be excluded, except such as it may be possible to insert in Part VI.

4.—THE DISASTER SCIENTIFICALLY VIEWED.

THROUGH the courtesy of the *Engineering News* of New York I am permitted to insert the following extracts from its columns. The proprietors sent a corps of reporters, consisting of expert constructing and topographical engineers, who made exhaustive examinations, took photographic views and prepared accurate maps. Its resultant articles in four of its issues were by far the most complete and satisfactory account of the nature and causes of the disaster, as viewed from the standpoint of engineering science.

The construction of the dam, which in its later reconstructed form has just failed, was first authorized in 1836, but it was not till 1839 that $70,000 was appropriated for it, and Wm. E. Morris, Principal Assistant Engineer, and an able and experienced man, was placed in charge of it, and also of the dam near Hollidaysburg, on the east side of the mountains. The west dam, which has now failed, raised the water 62 feet, was 850 feet long on top, covered 400 acres of ground, and stored up 480,000,000 cubic feet of water, the estimated cost being $188,000, one year being required for construction. The engineer, Mr. Morris, in his report, dated Johnstown, November 1st, 1839, said:

"The western division of the Pennsylvania Canal is supplied by water taken by feeders from the Little Conemaugh River and Stony Creek, which form a junction at this place. The valley of Stony Creek is not well suited for a reservoir, as it has a steep descent, and in time of floods the stream is far too large and unmanageable.

"The main branch of the Conemaugh has but one reservoir site on it, and that would flood the village of Jefferson and the railroad. Of the other branches, the *south* (the one adopted) is the only one that drains sufficient country to furnish a *certain* supply. This branch, when gauged in September, after one day's rain, discharged in 24 hours 60,000,000 cubic feet of water. At the same time there were flood marks two feet higher, and a *moderate* estimate of full discharge in 24 hours is 160,000,000 cubic feet. The best site for a dam is two and a quarter miles from the mouth. A dam 62 feet high and 850 feet long on the top is suggested.

"The valley is narrow at the dam and widens immediately above into an extensive basin. There is solid rock at both ends of the dam in which channels may be cut for flood water discharge. Drifts and shafts were sunk to insure in advance good foundations.

"Two plans for the dam were presented: (1) a crib dam of timber and stone with weir on top to pass over freshet water; and (2) a mound of stone and earth, made perfectly water tight, raised 10 feet above the surface of the pool, having a waste weir in *solid rock* at one or both ends of dam!"

Mr. Morris, however, pointed out that there were serious objections to the first plan, especially difficulty in uniting the body

of the dam with the embankment to prevent breakage under the
pressure; danger of undermining base; perishable nature of material; constant repairs, etc., and concluded that the second plan
promised a permanent and durable dam, maintainable at small
expense. He then presented estimates of quantities of material and labor needed, showing a total cost of $188,000.

In the annual report of the Canal Commissioners ending
November 30th, 1852, it is stated

" *The western reservoir* will be entirely finished in a very short
time. . . . It has been constructed in a most substantial manner, reflecting great credit on the contractors and engineers in
charge. The sluice gates were closed in June, 1852; by August
the water was 40 feet deep."

There had been some intermediate delay due to legal proceedings; but the dam appears, from the reports, to have been
executed precisely according to the original plans, which, from the
quantities and some incidental notes, appear to have been for a
structure closely resembling the accompanying sketch:

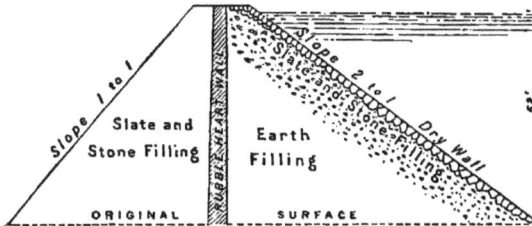

Approximate Sketch of the Section of the Original Dam on South Fork.—Constructed from the description and
quantities of material used, and believed to be substantially correct.

After the abandonment of the State canal, soon after its purchase by the Pennsylvania Railroad in 1857, a breach developed
in this dam that involved no serious disaster. The gap was about

15c feet across at the top and extended down nearly to the bottom of the dam, yet still leaving enough of the old dam intact to retain a small remnant of the original reservoir. This gap is stated to have been closed and the damage repaired in 1879–81, at a total cost of $17,000, a sum hardly adequate to properly repair even a much smaller gap, not to speak of raising the original level; which latter would not only have been a rash and dangerous procedure, without reconstructing the dam complete, but would have involved a heavy expenditure of money, however rashly done.

The engineer in charge of the reconstruction was General James N. Morehead. The primary cause of failure lay in no part of the work which he reconstructed, but in lack of sufficient spill-way. The considerable leakage reported from the dam, however, would indicate that the reconstruction was none too secure, as would also its low cost, and it may well be that its lack of the substantial solidity of the old structure aggravated the disaster by aiding the dam to go out all at once instead of gradually.

If anything can be said to be clear about this catastrophe, it is that the dam—poor structure as we must now believe that it was—failed just when and as it did merely for lack of *a little* more sectional area in the spill-way. For nearly half a century this spill-way has sufficed; it may have been at times severely tried, but it has never before caused water to actually run over the top of the dam, and it probably would not have done so on this occasion had there been slightly more provision for normal discharge; because the area of the impounded water was not very large, not over 450 acres at most, to judge by the old reports, and the water took many hours to rise to the crest level.

The original estimates were for half earth and half rock and slate spoil. We can readily understand how this could be, and yet the dam be made practically all of earth. A rotten, slaty shale rock lies close beneath the surface, which for a foot or two disintegrates into earth almost completely after excavation. It was probably contemplated to excavate half the material from this soft rock, and a good deal was so excavated, but the large borrow pits on each side at the bottom of the reservoir indicate that a good deal of material was taken from lower down on the valley slopes, where there was more earth and perhaps a rottener rock. Be this as it may, there was hardly a piece of rock as big as a man's fist in any of the central part now exposed to view. The lower edge of the northeast side of the gap showed an interior coating of spalls ; but while these may be the outer evidences of a similar lining extending along the old work, inside the heavy riprap, it is more likely that it is a mere exterior coating of a few stones,which chanced to lodge there in the washout or fall from above. There is no similar evidence of interior stone in the southwest end.

The excessive phenomenal rainfall, the second contributing cause of the disaster, began Thursday night, May 30th, after several days of moderate prior rains, and continued almost till the dam gave way. The lake, although discharging its best through the contracted spill-way, gradually rose at the rate of a foot an hour for several hours before the break, implying that the crest of the dam was 7 feet or so above the normal level, as the old records indicate, until, at 2.30 P.M., of Friday, May 31st, water began to run over the crest.

The dreaded catastrophy was then certain, and could not be long delayed, no earth dam being capable of sustaining such a discharge over it. It took half an hour for the increasing current to gradually cut away the earth support from the lower side of the rubble heart wall, and then, at 3 P.M., the dam gave way. The breach once made was instantly enlarged to nearly its final dimensions, 250 feet across. In fact, some of the eye-witnesses state that it "burst with a report like thunder," which it is quite possible would have been the effect, even if the real course of events was gradual but very rapid disintegration of the embankment in the torrent.

The foregoing account corresponds most correctly with that given by intelligent eye-witnesses of the break. A workman, who seems to have some grudge against the fishing company, absurdly declares that the dam had been leaking badly for weeks, and that on the morning before the disaster "jets squirted out for thirty feet from the face of it," and that these leaks rapidly increased until the whole gave way, without any running of water over the top. This is so far consistent with other facts that the dam is known to have been leaking for several years past, and has been the subject of considerable apprehension, especially since the spring floods of 1888.

The very remarkable fact that the dam is stoutly claimed by the company officers themselves to have been "inspected twice a month," by some engineers as yet unknown, tends to show that it was in a dubious condition, for a dam in good condition has no need of such frequent inspection ; and it is also specifically reported that the dam was inspected by Robert L. Halliday, Superintendent of the Lewiston and Sunbury Division of the Pennsylvania Railroad, "some years ago," and declared unsafe. But on the whole, the evidence is decided that it was the flow of water over the top of the dam, and not in any sense inability of the dam to sustain the static pressure of water, which caused the disaster.

The dam stands about 450 feet above the town of Johnstown, the valley connecting it being about twelve miles long, counting all the bends of the channel, or about ten miles long by the railway. In the valley were situated the following places, to which we add also the census populations of 1880 and the estimated populations of 1889.

TOWN OR VILLAGE.	DISTANCE FROM DAM BY VALLEY.	POPULATION. 1880.	Est'd 1889.
South Fork, ...	2 miles	893*	2,000
Mineral Point, ...	5 "	437*	800
Conemaugh, ...	10 "	1,372*	2,500
Woodvale, ...	11 "	637*	2,000
Conemaugh Borough, ...	12 "	3,498 ⎫	
Johnstown, ...	12½ "	8,380 ⎬	30,000
Cambria, ...	14 "	2,223 ⎭	
Intermediate country population .		957*	400
Total to Penn. Railroad bridge, .		18,397	37,700

It appears alogether probable that the population on the day of the disaster was fully 37,000, including Cambria City, which was below the fine stone bridge, which withstood the flood, and was speedily so choked by drift and human bodies as to form a second dam to drown out Johnstown.

The fates which have befallen the above towns may be thus briefly summarized, according to the best information now at hand :

South Fork—No very serious results ; a few drowned.

Mineral Point—"Entirely wiped out."

Conemaugh—"Almost depopulated," and every building swept away.

Woodvale—The same.

Conemaugh Borough—The same, with more escapes to the hill.

Johnstown, Cambria—The average opinion of a number of leading citizens is that 10 per cent. of the population is lost.

It is generally estimated that one-third of the bodies, at least, will never be recovered at all, being burned up, buried under sand and detritus, or carried down the river. We do not see how it can ever be expected to determine the loss much more accurately

---

* These are township populations.

than by the rude process we have just used, unless it may be by
a census of the remaining population combined with an estimate
based on the vote of the last Presidential election.

That the chances for life of any one in the way of the flood
after the dam had once given way were very small, is evident
when we remember that, as in all such cases, the flood advances,
not with a comparatively shallow advance guard, but with a solid
wall in front, which strikes a house or human being with terrible
velocity, and directly downward rather than from the side. All
accounts agree that the water did in fact advance "like a wall 30 or
40 feet high," and it is wholly in accordance with physical laws that
it should do so—in fact, it cannot well do otherwise. The water
which first flows out, being retarded by the rough surface, trees,
rocks, houses, animals and other obstacles, speedily loses its own
velocity, but furnishes an almost frictionless surface over which
other water can slide, like ice down a plank, with almost the full
theoretical velocity due to the fall. Thus the top of the flood is
continually moving much faster than the bottom, and falls over the
end of it when it reaches it, to be itself retarded and to surrender
a large part of the energy due to its velocity in tearing up the
ground and *beating down*, not driving forward, any unfortunate
creature or structure which stands in its path. The bottom of
the flood is relatively stationary, the top has its full theoretical
velocity due to the fall, and the average velocity of advance hence
becomes but slightly more than *half* the top velocity; the water,
in fact, rolling over itself at the front very much as a wheel rolls,
except that the lower part of the flood-wheel never rises again
when it once strikes the ground. The fall from the reservoir to
Johnstown having been about 450 feet, the actual time taken by
the flood to reach Johnstown corresponds very closely with that
which this theory requires. The top of the water would have nearly
the theoretical velocity due to a fall of 450 feet, which is about 100

miles per hour, that due to the 160 feet fall of Niagara Falls being about 70 miles per hour. Allowing for all the frictional losses, a man who sustained the *direct* impact of this torrent had about the same chance of resisting it and escaping alive as he would in sustaining the impact of Niagara Falls itself. The tendency which such a flood would have to bury many bodies is also evident.

The reservoir, at its normal water-level, held 480,000,000 cubic feet of water, but at the break it contained nearly 640,000,000 cubic feet, or say 20,000,000 net tons. How vast a body of water this is will be better appreciated by comparing it with Niagara Falls. The discharge over the falls is in the neighborhood of 18,000,000 cubic feet per minute. It would therefore take nearly thirty-six minutes for Niagara Falls to discharge an equal body of water. The reservoir was emptied, all but the last harmless drippings, in just about that time, so that during its continuance a body of water substantially equal to the vast flood of Niagara Falls was pouring through the 429 feet gap in the dam.

Had this body of water struck Johnstown, there would have been even less of the city left than there is, but this did not occur. The whole valley above it had likewise to be filled with water. This valley is somewhat irregular in width, varying from 300 to 2,500 feet; but independent and closely agreeing estimates place its average width at 750 feet for a depth of 20 feet, giving a cross section of 15,000 square feet. The distance from the dam to the Johnstown bridge is by the river channel 18 miles. The railway is about two miles shorter, owing to cutting across bends. It would therefore require a total volume of about 14×5,280×15,000 =1,108,800,000 cubic feet to fill the whole valley 20 feet deep, or about 60 per cent. more than the reservoir contained. As nearly as we can ascertain, it took the flood fifteen minutes to cover the 12 miles between South Fork Station and Johnstown, or say twenty minutes from the break until the jam at the Johnstown bridge

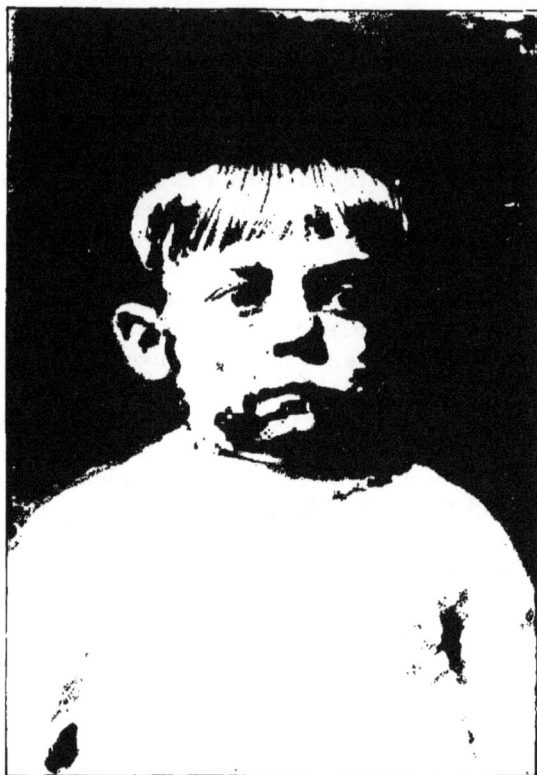

FREDDIE POLAND.
(Drowned, with his brother, in his father's arms.)

occurred. At the latter moment, therefore, the channel could not possibly have been 20 feet deep throughout, although it was probably deeper than that at the lower end.

The total energy communicated to the water, which had to expend itself in some way before the water could come to rest, and which was in fact nearly all expended between the dam and Johnstown bridge, was the inconceivably vast aggregate represented by 20,000,000 tons falling 400 feet.

The conclusion of the whole matter, as reached by the expert examination of the *Engineering News*, is thus summed up:

"The original dam was designed and built, as already stated, by the late Wm. E. Morris, Principal Assistant Engineer Pennsylvania State Canals, in charge of the Western Division. He was an able and experienced engineer, and the dam, under his supervision, was thoroughly well built by the late General James N. Morehead. It had no central core of masonry as the preliminary estimates indicated, but it was built in horizontal layers, thoroughly watered and rammed, riprapped on both slopes, and provided with an ample spill-way through rock, and an arch culvert underneath it, through which ran five two-feet cast-iron pipes for discharging the water during the dry season into the South Fork, from which the water ran down in the river channel to feed the State canal at Johnstown, 14 miles below by the river, which was the head of canal navigation. The canal, and the dam with it, were abandoned as public structures in 1857–1858.

"The first break in it, which occurred in July, 1862, was caused by a defect in the foundations of the culvert, through which the five two-feet discharge pipes were carried. This break did comparatively little damage, the reservoir having been only half full, and the discharge having been quite slow, wholly from the bottom, and choked from time to time by fall of material from above. So far as we can determine, it carried out only about

6

half as much material from the dam as the last break, or about
50,000 cubic yards.   There is great difficulty in determining
with exactness the quantity of material carried out in the first
break.   Most of those who ought to know say, '150 to 200 feet
wide on top,' but then most of the accounts of the last break
have called the gap only 200 feet, whereas it is actually more than
twice that.   No photographs taken after the first break are dis-
coverable, but it is probable that the gap was smaller than the
present one, especially on the upper side, where the remarkable
benches of old work, still remaining after two break-aways, testify
to the care and thoroughness with which the original embankment
was constructed, and rammed in regular layers.

"At the bottom of the old break, also, enough of the material
remained to make a little pond about 8 feet deep above the dam,
which remained in this condition, unused, until, in May, 1875, the
property, consisting of something over 500 acres, was sold to
Congressman John Reilly.   The lake itself was about 400 acres in
size, not 700, as has been reported.   After holding the property
unused till 1879, Mr. Reilly offered it for the sum of $2,000 to the
late Colonel B. F. Ruff, an old and successful railroad and tunnel
contractor, and the originator of the South Fork Fishing and
Hunting Club.   Colonel Ruff interested two other Pittsburgh
gentlemen in the project, and stated to them that the dam could
be reconstructed for a sum not to exceed $1,500, and that 'he
would take a contract to do it for $1,700.'

"On this basis the club was organized, and for some time
these three gentlemen were its only members.   Not one of them
is now connected with it.   Colonel Ruff's idea had been to recon-
struct the dam much lower, only 40 feet high; but it soon appeared
that to cut down the rock spill-way would cost more than to recon-
struct the dam to its original height, and by the time this had been
done the total expenditure, as shown by the pay rolls, had been

slightly over $10,000, or about twenty cents per cubic yard. There still remained to be done the riprapping of the slopes and other miscellaneous work, as to which our information is less precise, being only that it 'may' have cost $7,000, but not more, bringing the total cost up to the very small figures of $17,000, which have been given on other authority in newspaper dispatches. This work was all done in the summer of 1880. The original dam was estimated to cost $188,000, and actually cost nearly $240,000.

" Colonel Ruff engaged as foreman and superintendent for this work a Mr. Edward Pearson, of Pittsburgh. It is a general impression in the vicinity of Johnstown and Pittsburgh, among those who know anything about it, that Mr. Pearson was the 'engineer' of the repairs, but this is incorrect. He is not and never has been an engineer, but after 1880 was employed in the local freight department of the Pennsylvania Railroad at Pittsburgh, until he formed his present connection, which is with the firm of Haney & Co., general teamsters for the Pennsylvania Railroad freight department. We were also told that Colonel Ruff was 'the engineer,' but this statement also is incorrect. So far as we can ascertain by diligent inquiry, he not only was never an engineer, but he had never been engaged, before this time, even as a contractor on water-works or dam construction. If he was ever so employed at all, it would appear that it must have been to an unimportant extent. In fact, our information is positive, direct and unimpeachable that *at no time during the process of rebuilding the dam was* ANY ENGINEER WHATEVER, young or old, good or bad, known or unknown, engaged on or consulted as to the work. The precautions taken against failure were only such as an experienced railroad contractor's knowledge of hydraulic engineering indicated were admissible without further increasing a contemplated investment of $3,700, which had to be increased at best by over $10,000.

"Information gathered for us by Mr. T. S. Miller, M. E., of
the Lidgerwood Manufacturing Co., who assisted in our surveys,
corresponds with that gathered by us from other reliable sources,
that the work of reconstruction was done with the slight care
which the preceding facts make probable. The old material,
which had caved in, and so lost its compactness, was left un-
touched; the top of the dam was worked down on to it; the old
pipes and culvert, which still remained in somewhat injured condition, were covered over with earth and permanently closed, a
double row of hemlock plank sheet piling being driven across the
old channel. The water during reconstruction was carried across
the dam in a board flume, which was raised from time to time as
the work progressed. There was no careful ramming in watered
layers, as in the first dam, although some say there was some
ramming. There was much leaking during the process, and some
tons of hay and straw were filled in. The dam was finally made
fairly tight, but there has always been some leakage at the bottom,
and of late years this has been increasing. The truth as to the
exact amount of leakage is very difficult to ascertain. The original crest height of the dam was decreased from one to three feet,
and the spill-way was shortly after obstructed with gratings to
retain fish, and a trestle bridge was built across the opening.

"Negligence in the mere execution of the earthwork, however,
if it existed, is of minor importance, since there is no doubt that it
was not a primary cause of the disaster; at worst, it merely aggravated it. The primary causes of the disaster were the lowering
of the crest, the dishing, or central sag in the crest, the closing of
the bottom culvert, and the obstruction of the spill-way.

"Of the the final blow as it struck Johnstown, this may be said:

"The main body of the flood rushed directly westward, through
the very heart of Johnstown, sweeping it clean, and impinging
directly against the mountain-side. The bridge, whose 'resist-

ance of the torrent' has been the matter of so much talk, was a
noble four-track structure, just completed, fifty feet wide on top,
thirty-two feet high above the water line, consisting of seven skew
spans of fifty-eight feet each. It still remains wholly uninjured,
except that it is badly spalled on the upper side by blows from
the wreckage, but that it so remains is due solely to the accident
of its position, and not to its strength, although it was and is still
the embodiment of solidity. Had the torrent struck it squarely, it
would have swept it away as if it had been built of cardboard,
leaving no track behind; but fortunately (or unfortunately) its
axis was exactly parallel with the path of the flood, which hence
struck the face of the mountain full, and compressed the whole of
its spoils gathered in a fourteen-mile course into one inextricable
mass, with the force of tens of thousands of tons moving at nearly
sixty miles per hour. Its spoil consisted of (1) every tree the
flood had touched in its whole course, with trifling exceptions,
including hundreds of large trees, all of which were stripped of
their bark and small limbs almost at once ; (2) all the houses in
a thickly settled town three miles long and one-fourth to one-half
mile wide ; (3) half the human beings and all the horses, cows,
cats, dogs and rats that were in the houses ; (4) many hundreds of
miles of telegraph wire that was on strong poles in use, and many
times more than this that was in stock in the mills; (5) perhaps
fifty miles of track and track material, rails and all ; (6) locomotives, pig-iron, brick, stone, boilers, steam engines, heavy machinery and other spoil of a large manufacturing town. All this was
accumulated in one inextricable mass, which almost immediately
caught fire from some stove which the waters had not touched.
Hundreds of human beings, dead and alive, were caught in it,
many by the lower part of the body only. Eye-witnesses describe
the groans and cries which came from that vast holocaust for
nearly the whole night as something fearful beyond all power of
description."

CARE OF THE SURVIVORS.

I.—WHAT WE DID TO PROTECT OURSELVES.

Set all things in their own peculiar place,
And know that order is the greatest grace.—DRYDEN.

"WHAT have you there?" said I to a man, as hundreds of us were struggling over the debris toward the high ground on Saturday morning, June 1st. "Oh, nothing," was the reply. "But I know better; you are stealing; let those valuables lie where they are." He dropped them and sneaked away. Whilst good and true people acted nobly, and some of the most exalted traits of character shone out in our disaster, men who were weak in principle attempted to profit by this great calamity, and began stealing as soon as they could crawl safely over the wreckage, and thus illustrated some of the most mean and contemptible traits of our fallen humanity. Nor were the thieves all Hungarians, by any means. Some who, under ordinary circumstances, would have been horrified at the thought of robbery, had their sordid dispositions aroused by the sight of the ruin around them. From my own wrecked and ransacked house, and from many other partially destroyed dwellings, there were stolen clothes, silverware, money and many other things that escaped destruction from the water's overflow. Webs of muslin and linen, barrels of coal-oil and of ardent spirits, and other property were hidden by citizens and strangers. Residents who sat by their cellars guarding their valuables were overpowered by thieves, who stole silverware before their eyes. I was told, as an illustration of the audacity of thieves, that the valuable chair in which Madame Levergood was sitting, and had floated off bearing her dead form, still erect, about a mile and a half up the river into the Sandyvale Cemetery (having been carried there by the back-water), was stolen as soon as her body was removed therefrom. While such bold robbery was early suppressed somewhat by our own insufficient police, the thieves were not driven out until the detective corps of Mr. Mann, of Philadelphia, assisted us in recognizing the bad characters of both sexes.

There was another class of robbers, known as "relic-hunters," who carried away valuables of every kind as mementoes of this great disaster. Silver spoons, knives and forks, jewelry, harness —in short, anything not too heavy to be borne away—were "appropriated" and carried off. Invading the sanctuary of God, these "respectable thieves" stole hymn-books, copies of the sacred Scriptures and vessels used in the Holy Communion, which were shamelessly shown to fellow-passengers on the trains, and boasted of as trophies of the terrible flood. While many sought articles of little or no pecuniary worth, and others offered to purchase them from the owners, most relic-hunters, with a perverted taste, seemed to suppose that calling the articles they craved "relics," relieved them of dishonor in the act by which many such relics were obtained. A gentleman informed me that he saw two manuscript sermons in the possession of a person on the cars, who remarked that he had found them on Vine Street, nearly side by side. On the one he observed the name of Dr. Fink, of the Lutheran Church, and on the other that of the pastor of the Presbyterian Church. If, instead of carrying off this property and rejoicing over the souvenir, he had returned them to their rightful owners, the purloiner would have saved his credit and the bereaved preachers would have been made happy.

But the piracy of the relic-hunters was not our greatest afflic-tion. As the vulture afar off scents the carcass, and hastens to feast thereon, so the confusion and desolation, which called forth the pity of all the good and true, tended only to arouse the basest passions of thieves and profligates who from every quarter imme-diately flocked to our smitten city. The most wicked attempt at stealing that I witnessed was an effort on the part of a well-dressed stranger, with clandestine offer of presents of jewelry and money, to induce two beautiful, weeping, undefended girls to accompany him to a certain city, where he promised them delightful homes! Not knowing what was the precise nature of his remarks to the girls, I approached him and said, "Do you know these young girls?" He answered, "No, sir." I then said, "You then can leave here;" and not departing as speedily as I desired, I drove him from the place. Having afterward learned the nature of his proposal to the girls, I informed the police, but they were unable to find him. Besides, we were pestered with loafers—many mere sight-seers— who hindered others from work, who ate up part of our provisions, and who burdened us with the expense of return transportation. I mention these unpleasant facts to show the urgent necessity of the restoration of order in our midst. Had there not been a prompt organization of government which was a terror to evil-doers and the praise of those who did well, no man can conject-ure the evil consequences which might have ensued. Of course, we naturally looked to our Chief Magistrate to assume control in this herculean undertaking, but, by reason of the confusion of the hour and the urgency of the case, he could not at once be found. It will be impossible for me to represent to those not witnesses of the scene the almost hopeless distraction of the people and the gravity of the situation. I saw then, and I see now, that had the surviving city officers been able to convene in an executive session on the street, or anywhere—had they employed extra police to pro-

tect property; had they urged upon all good citizens in the adjacent towns and country places, upon the Sheriff of the County and
the Governor of the Commonwealth, the necessity of giving their
immediate assistance; had they sent out appeals to the whole
country for contributions in aid of our stricken city—order might
have been restored under the immediate direction of the proper
authorities, and all funds might have been transmitted to the Burgess and Council as the proper custodians and distributors of the
same.   But, when we consider that the community commonly
called Johnstown was made up of seven boroughs, each with its
own independent officers and government; that our Chief of
Police was overwhelmed by the loss of his family in the flood; that
no one seemed to know whether or not the Burgess of Johnstown
proper survived the disaster; and that the Burgess of Conemaugh
Borough was certainly among the drowned—when we consider
these circumstances it will not seem surprising that we who had
gathered together out of the flood, on Adam Street, felt compelled to organize a temporary government in the best and
speediest manner possible.   It was, perhaps, very imperfectly
accomplished, and accomplished, too, without any other authority
than that of supreme necessity.   The people were impressed with
the feeling that something must at once be done; that some recognized authority must be immediately established.

This sentiment sought expression more or less fully throughout the entire community.   On the Kernville, or south, side, then
cut off from us by the bridgeless Stony Creek, the survivors held
a meeting, which was presided over by Mr. Alexander Kennedy,
and which appointed Charles L. Dick, Esq., "generalissimo to direct all matters according to his own will."

Whilst the boroughs above the stone bridge were thus laboring to recover themselves, those below seemed so stunned or dazed
as to be unable to organize until Sabbath morning, when the Pitts-

burgh Citizens' Relief Committee reached Morrellville, Browns-
ville and Cambria City, whose representative citizens then assembled and appointed local committees, through whom supplies of
food and clothing were distributed.   The few policemen brought
by the Pittsburgh and Allegheny men, together with the efficient
work of Captains Hart and Gageby and Mr. Charles L. Dick, did
much to intimidate numerous thieves who came in upon us from
abroad, and especially upon that part of the city. Although there
was doubtless much pilfering of valuables found on the dead, it is
due to the truth to say that the reports of atrocities were exaggerated.   There were no fingers cut off by human ghouls, and no in-
furiated mob lynched such criminals.   There was little stealing
done by the Hungarians, and most accounts of outrages attributed to these people were apocryphal; and I am glad to say
that all statements of shooting and hanging them were without
foundation. I have this assurance from Mr. Dick himself, who was
reported to have killed several.

Chief of Police Hart and Captain Gageby, with their efficient
assistants, did good work in protecting property against the army
of marauders who, but for our local organization, were ready to
steal and destroy.   Within eighteen hours after the flood we had
three hundred duly qualified policemen protecting the First
National and Dibert's Banks, said to contain over $400,000 in
their vaults.   These officers recovered more than $6,000 cash
from trunks, valises and chests found in the wreckage.   They
did noble work, also, in the way of protecting us against fire until
the Pittsburgh Chamber of Commerce sent us aid.

The back-water had piled debris of every sort along all the
streets of the First and Fourth Wards of Johnstown proper and
much of Conemaugh Borough.   Dr. Wm. Caldwell, one of our
oldest and best-known merchants, did useful service by standing
at the corner of Adam and Bedford Streets and calling to farmers

and others, as they gathered in crowds, to go to work at once in the removal of wreckage. Charles Zimmerman, Chairman of Committee on Dead Animals, removed within a short time about two hundred carcasses. Thomas L. Johnson, one of the owners of the great plant at Moxham, brought all his well-known energy to bear upon the removal of debris from the streets. On Thursday, as soon as the waters in the rivers had fallen sufficiently for communication to be somewhat established between the different boroughs, the appointments we had made in Johnstown proper seemed by common consent to be recognized and respected throughout the entire community. It was at the meeting held near the corner of Main and Adam Streets that the officers were chosen to whom reference is here made. General Manager John Fulton, of the Cambria Iron and Steel Company, had been first named as one competent to be at the head of all the committees that might be created; but, upon learning that he was out of the city, Mr. A. J. Moxham, of the Johnstown Steel Street Railway Company, was unanimously chosen Director. In making this choice we had a practical consolidation of Johnstown proper, of Conemaugh Borough, of Woodvale and of the new town of Moxham, having representatives from each present. Manager Moxham accepted the position to which he had been so cordially chosen, and did honor to himself by his good work for the suffering city. Under him the following named committees were chosen and set to work :

(1) On Finances—W. C. Lewis, John D. Roberts, George T. Swank and Dwight Roberts.

(2) On Supplies or Commissary—Rev. James P. Tahaney John Thomas, Louis Von Lunen and C. B. Cover.

(3) On Morgues—Rev. David J. Beale, D.D., and Rev. H., L. Chapman, D.D.

(4) On the Removal of Dead Animals and Debris—Charles Zimmerman and Thomas L. Johnson.

(5) On Police—Captain A. N. Hart and Captain J. H. Gageby.

(6) On Hospitals—Drs. W. B. Lowman, J. C. Sheridan and W. E. Matthews.

These committees at once began their difficult and sorrowful duties, most of them asking and receiving no compensation therefor. The plans of these several departments were projected and their arduous labors entered upon before assistance from abroad came to hand. The same committees, with some additions to them (*e. g.*, Mr. James McMillen and Cyrus Elder, Esq., on the Finance Committee), were continued by Director James B. Scott, and afterward by General Hastings. They faithfully discharged their duties until the government of the various boroughs was restored.

2.—THE COUNTRY TO THE RESCUE.

Breathes there a man with soul so dead
Who never to himself hath said,
' This is my own, my native land ? ' —Sir Walter Scott.

(a) WHAT PITTSBURGH DID.

THE first statements regarding the terrible loss of life and the enormous destruction of property were received in Pittsburgh on the morning of June 1st, through the columns of the daily press. The fearful tidings passed through the city like the wind.

Through the agencies of the telegraph and the telephone, a call by the Mayor of Pittsburgh for a meeting at City Hall for 1 o'clock P.M. was rapidly spread, resulting in an overflowing assemblage. A committee was selected to take immediate action in the name of the community, which committee instantly began its work with energy and intelligence.

An organization was at once effected, including a committee to proceed to Johnstown in the name of the Pittsburgh Relief

Committee. The intense interest and devotion of the citizens toward the relief of their stricken brethren in the Conemaugh Valley were manifested by the fact that by 4 o'clock P.M. a train of nearly twenty cars, manned by as many volunteers as could be taken, was ready on the track of the Pennsylvania Railroad, headed for the desolated valley. Off it started, making its way, over and through the crowded tracks of the great roadway, on which were gathered the numberless trains halted all along its lines. At length Sang Hollow was reached about 10 o'clock at night. At this point the roadbed was entirely washed away, and the progress of the train completely arrested; but not so the advance of the men bound for Johnstown. Over the great gap of nearly three-quarters of a mile, created by the flood, willing hands and shoulders carried, trip after trip, their precious burdens of food for suffering brothers and sisters from the loaded cars; while beyond the gap, for the intervening space on toward the fated town, improvised means of transportation were rapidly secured, and by unflagging industry and untiring zeal the remaining four miles were covered, with the result that long before daybreak of the Sabbath morning the first installment of food was deposited at the now famous "stone bridge," beyond which it was impossible to proceed. Meanwhile, there was displayed one of the most remarkable instances of human energy ever witnessed. All around the great bend of Sang Hollow not a vestige of a railway had been left by the destroying waters, but so great were the facilities of the corporation of which every Pennsylvanian is proud that it was able, through its allies and connections, to collect men and material so promptly and thoroughly that by 7 o'clock on that Sunday morning the laden train passed over the newly laid tracks, and on it went, halting only at the stone bridge. A rapid examination of the situation showed that the immediate relief of all the various boroughs and villages had to be made from diverging

roads west of the bridge. Every available resource of men and
teams was pressed into the service, and from that moment until
railway communication was reasonably well resumed, the daily
rations of a large population were furnished from points within
two miles west of Johnstown. On Monday morning the well-
directed energy of the Baltimore and Ohio Railroad officials had
secured an entrance to the south side of Johnstown. By this time
the Pittsburgh committee at Johnstown had secured a telegraph
wire, and by it ordered all supplies from Pittsburgh for Johnstown
proper to be sent around by the Baltimore and Ohio Railroad, whose
entire facilities were made subject to the relief of the people.

The Pittsburgh Relief Committee continued the work as it
began it, never relaxing its activity until the change of affairs was
assumed by the natural and proper agency, viz., that of the Commonwealth. Not even then, as it continued to work in immediate
and constant association with the officials appointed by the Governor. All this time the Pittsburgh Relief Committee had the
direct control and supervision of the entire supply and labor furnished for the provisioning of the people, and the sanitary work
in clearing the towns of their horrible wreckage. The great proportion of the material in food and clothing forwarded by the
wonderful sympathy and generosity of a great nation naturally
came to and through Pittsburgh, whose organization was so well
prepared to forward and distribute these great supplies, which
came with a largeness that threatened even to overwhelm those
for whom they were intended.

When the country at large had learned of the organized
agency for relief at Pittsburgh, the generosity of the people
assumed the shape of money contribution.

All gifts in money sent to the Pittsburgh Relief Committee
were taken in charge for the benefit of the Conemaugh Valley.
Meanwhile, under the direction of that same committee, an army

of between 6,000 and 7,000 laborers had entered the field, and, under leadership of the most efficient character, pushed the work of clearing the highways and properties of their hideous encumbrances. With these at work, a population of nearly 30,000 souls had to be furnished with its daily food, and it was the duty of the Pittsburgh Relief Committee to act as its constant and untiring commissary. What that meant but few people know, and only those who have had an experience in provisioning an army of men.

In this case the demand was almost without warning, and could not have been met except by the resources of a large and well-equipped city like Pittsburgh, handled by a devoted body of men who dropped all other matters in the interest of their fellows. And so bravely the work went on, nor did the labor and attention cease so long as anything remained to be done through the agency of the Pittsburgh Relief Committee, whose office was never closed from the noon of the day following the great disaster until the time when the "Flood Commission of the State of Pennsylvania" assumed the task of distributing the immense fund of money contributed by the unparalleled generosity of a great people. Part of this "Flood Commission" consists of some of the members of the Pittsburgh Relief Committee, which thereby continues to be connected with the work in Johnstown and vicinity.

While the general conduct of affairs for the relief of the sufferers by the flood amongst us had been assumed by the men composing the Pittsburgh Relief Committee, a large and important work was also being conducted in Pittsburgh by an organization of ladies known as the Ladies' Committee.

It can be understood that a large number of the inhabitants of our fated valley, who, even with spared lives, found themselves homeless and destitute, eagerly turned their faces toward the city glowing with the light of the highest type of charity and Christian sympathy.

Streams of terror-stricken and homeless persons, widows and orphans, poured toward the city of refuge and its vicinity, where loving hearts and helping hands awaited their coming. Many of these people had their personal friends in the neighborhood of Pittsburgh ; but to most it was an unknown haven, except in their confidence as to its certain shelter and rest. The Ladies' Committee was early organized, and secured its first quarters in the spacious rooms connected with the Second Presbyterian Church, where they were ready for work on Tuesday, June 4th. Its rooms were open day and night, ready for the reception of refugees at any hour during the twenty-four. This was necessary, owing to the uncertainty of the arrival of the trains, incident to the crippled condition of the railways. Special committees took charge of the various departments of work. Committees met every train on both the Pennsylvania and Baltimore and Ohio Railways, one committee relieving another in constant succession, with means of conveyance from the depots to the general headquarters, where nourishing food was furnished to every weary refugee ; and in most cases entire changes of clothing were also provided. The greater part of such clothing was sent to the Ladies' Committee from various sections of the country for the use to which it was applied, and in many cases accompanied by tender and touching notes addressed to the unknown recipients of the garments.

Other sub-committees secured comfortable quarters in the sister-cities of Pittsburgh and Allegheny, whereby every sufferer was furnished with accommodation and shelter until able to determine his or her ultimate destination.

Many refugees took advantage of this opportunity to reach their personal friends and relatives at points beyond Pittsburgh, many of them very distant ; and through the generosity of the railway officials all such persons were furnished with free transportation when applied for by the Ladies' Committee.

REMAINS OF THE BROKEN DAM AT SOUTH FORK.

A Bureau of Information was also established by the Ladies' Committee, through which agency many found their friends and members of their families whom they had supposed to be drowned; while the whereabouts of others were successfully traced.

Situations were procured for many who wished to enter service in different forms, while in many cases families were assisted to permanent residence in the two cities, the Ladies' Committee continuing its watchful care so long as necessary, even to the anticipation of possible wants for the coming winter. This work will proceed through the winter, care being taken in the investigation of applicants as to their genuineness. A large amount of winter clothing and new flannel received by the Ladies' Committee was taken in charge and recently sent to our city for distribution by local ladies' committees.

Separate from and independent of the large sums of money sent to the Pittsburgh Relief Committee, the Ladies' Committee was put in possession of a considerable amount contributed directly by private generosity, which amount was expended in the relief of the Conemaugh sufferers.

Hundreds of applications from evidently reputable people were made to the Ladies' Committee for orphans for adoption. These applications were made for children wholly orphaned by the flood. It is a singular fact, however, as shown by the Ladies' records, and indicative of the disruption of the families of Johnstown and vicinity, that of the great number of children coming under the care of the Ladies' Committee, there were only two who were without both parents, and those two were in charge of relatives. All the others had lost one parent.

The work accomplished through this committee was the result not only of intelligent direction, but of hearty and continuous assistance by a great number of ladies of the two cities, and was in every respect as thorough and efficient within its depart-

7

ments as the work performed by their brothers of the Pittsburgh Relief Committee.

I regret beyond all expression that the good Pittsburgh and Allegheny gentlemen and ladies who furnished me the foregoing facts forbid me to mention their names, and render them the tribute in which all my fellow-sufferers would cordially concur. The inclination to disregard this unselfish request is very strong, believing that the names of those who did for us such excellent service in our time of need should be put on record for all time to come. It is at least due to our feelings to say that these noble, nameless brothers and sisters have the unaffected gratitude of our hearts and homes ; and that, without doubt, "the blessing of the Lord that maketh rich and addeth no sorrow" will be theirs.

I shall take the liberty of appending the report of Mr. H. E. Collins to Mr. James B. Scott, who was chosen by the Pittsburgh Relief Committee to direct the men and provisions sent to succor us :

The relief train left Union Station, Pittsburgh, June 1st, 1889, at about 4 o'clock P.M., with three members only of the transportation and distribution committee on board, together with some seventy volunteer aids, who, during the progress to Sang Hollow, were distributed into two companies about equal, which were placed under the personal direction of J. A. Logan and myself respectively. The relief train arrived at Sang Hollow at about 10.30 P.M., at which point the tracks of the Pennsylvania Railroad ended, and from which point the road was completely demolished for about three-quarters of a mile. By your instructions, myself and aids pushed on with such provisions as could be carried, and in this manner about one and one-half car loads were transported for about three-quarters of a mile across the break. From this point, for about one mile farther, these provisions were transported on a hand-car and push-car, as the track was not in condition to run a locomotive over it. In the meantime, four young men sent forward for the purpose, and who had first secured the hand-car and push-car, succeeded in getting the division superintendent of the Pennsylvania Railroad to bring the construction train, which, fortunately, remained intact on that part of the road, to a point where the provisions were transferred to it, and from thence to the Conemaugh bridge, at the head of Cambria City, where we arrived at about 2 to 2.30 A.M., with part of the provisions, the other part having being left at Morrellville, in charge of aids who were instructed to transport the same over the mountain, some five miles, to Kernville, as soon as daylight should enable them so to do. This was successfully done, the provisions arriving in Kernville about 7 o'clock Sunday morning. The provisions taken to Cambria City were stored in the only room which we could find in the town that was not occupied by the dead. When morning came, these were distributed in small rations to the people in Cambria City by those left in charge of same. To reach Johnstown Saturday night was impossible, for while the stone bridge across the Conemaugh at that point was intact, the railway embankment for about 100 feet beyond was washed out, and through this channel ran an almost impassable torrent of water. The debris which had lodged against the stone bridge, and covering ten to twelve acres in extent, was at this time thoroughly on fire, and lit up the valley of the Conemaugh for miles, disclosing a lake covering the sites of Johnstown, Woodvale, Conemaugh, etc., as far as the eye could reach. While we were not a stone's throw from Johnstown proper, it was impossible at this time to go there without making a detour of many miles, or to get supplies or provisions into Johnstown in adequate quantity via the Pennsylvania Railroad. The people of the flooded district seemed to be stunned or dazed, and the presence of the few policemen brought with our party to guard the relief stores suggested to their minds that they were to receive police protection for their homes and families, and this was demanded by them.   They were promptly informed that this was impracticable, and they were counseled to get their best and representative citizens together as promptly as possible in the various communities ; to first appoint local committees, through whom we could distribute supplies of food and clothing to the stricken people, with reasonable precaution, under the circumstances, against imposition ; also to form themselves into vigilance committees for the protection of their homes.   These suggestions were acted upon promptly and carried out by the people of Morrellville, Cambria City, Minersville, Kernville and Brownstown, and no place could be more orderly or safe than these communities immediately following such organization.   The local committees co-operated with us promptly and effectively, and by noon of Sunday the necessities of the above-named communities were quite generally relieved for the time being as to food, and partially as to clothing.

We had no sooner reached Cambria City than reports of atrocities, said to have been committed by Hungarians upon the persons of the dead, reached us, but investigation failed to disclose a single case of mutilation.   Rewards for cases of mutilation were offered to those making charges, but without disclosing a single case.   The reports, however, continued, and grew until they became so absurd as to defeat themselves, when a reaction of public feeling came about, and it was quite generally admitted that, while some pilfering of valuables found upon the dead had been perpetrated, the Hungarians were no more guilty than others. It is my conviction that these reports had no other foundation than race prejudice in the minds of the older population against the Hungarians.   The local committees were counseled to make no distinction between Hungarians and others in the distribution of food, as all were alike unfortunate and hungry; and this suggestion was promptly accepted and acted upon by the local committees, the result being that no more willing volunteers were found to handle the relief supplies from cars to store room than the Hungarians. This I submit in interest of the truth of history, and in justice to a much libeled race.

During Sunday morning the tracks of the Pennsylvania Railroad were sufficiently repaired to permit the relief train to proceed to Morrellville, and during Sunday provisions were issued freely to all of the above-named communities, and considerable quantities of provisions were transferred across the Conemaugh into Johnstown proper, by means of a rope and snatch block stretched across the chasm from the end of the Conemaugh viaduct, at which point General Hastings took charge of the provisions and issued them to the people of Johnstown. Small quantities of provisions were also ferried across the Conemaugh in skiffs from Kernville into Johnstown proper, which were distributed by Mr. Moxham's local committee. During Sunday a temporary bridge was thrown across the Conemaugh from the end of the viaduct, constructed of rope and boards by a number of the Pittsburgh aids. In this connection it is only just to say that the volunteer aids attending the Pittsburgh committee vied with each other in heroic work in the relief of the suffering people of the flooded districts; the youthful members seeming to feel it necessary to do themselves some bodily injury to emphasize their zeal and earnestness, and all did so admirably that it would be invidious to mention the names of any.

During Monday supplies of provisions and clothing came forward freely, in charge of various local committees from many points in Pennsylvania, Ohio and Indiana, and the distribution of provisions to all the points above named were ample to meet all wants for the time being. In this connection I would state that the survivors of the flood naturally over-ran and sought shelter in the non-flooded communities and parts of communities adjacent to the flooded district, that all houses were open to the refugees, and that provisions and clothing were generously shared with the sufferers by those that were not inundated, so that by Monday the people that were not flooded were as dependent upon the relief supplies as the victims of the flood ; indeed, during Sunday and the days following, vast numbers of interested parties, sightseers, photographers, tramps and thieves, over-ran the flooded district, and as they came without provisions, and as all houses were open to friend and stranger alike, this influx of population was as dependent upon the relief stores as the residents, and its members were as certainly fed from the relief stores as if provisions had been issued to them directly. This put so great a tax upon the relief stores as to be unbearable, and measures became necessary to reduce or eliminate this evil as much as possible.

On Monday, P.M., Captain Clark arrived at Cambria City with a car of skiffs, two of which proved very useful in transporting supplies to Minersville across the Conemaugh from Cambria City. During Tuesday, June 4th, relief supplies came forward freely by the Pennsylvania Road, and the work of relief proceeded effectively through the organized agencies in the communities named above, and some five car loads of provisions were transferred across the Conemaugh to the custody of General Hastings, in Johnstown proper. Adjutant-General Axline, of the State of Ohio, and his aids, had taken possession and control of the stone bridge and temporary foot bridge, which had been erected connecting with Johnstown proper, and the above-named supplies, together with many car loads of coffins, were transferred across this bridge, under the direction of General Axline, by sightseers, who were compelled to do this kind of duty as toll for use of the foot bridge, thus making themselves useful to this slight extent, at least. On this day direct telegraphic communications were opened with

General Hastings. The enormous quantities of construction material which the Pennsylvania Railroad required in repair of its tracks east of Morrellville, so crowded their limited track room that it became almost impossible to move relief supplies by rail east of Morrellville, and it was manifest that this point must be adopted as a base of supplies for Cambria City, Minersville, Brownstown and Kernville, and this was done on June 4th, and so continued as to Kernville until the pontoon bridges were completed across Stony Creek from Johnstown, and thereafter as to the other localities named and adjacent communities. It was also manifest that the Baltimore and Ohio Railroad must be relied upon to transport supplies for Johnstown proper, which must eventually become the base of the committee's operations. Therefore, during the afternoon of the fourth, three members of the Pittsburgh Transportation and Distribution Committee, including yourself, attended a meeting of the Johnstown Relief Committee and representative citizens of Johnstown, with the result that you were chosen " Director " of the entire flooded district, with plenary powers, so far as such representative body could confer same, and an organization was promptly effected for the further work of relief and treatment of the innumerable questions which the situation presented, involving the welfare of the entire flooded district.

At this time a large number of cars containing relief supplies had arrived in and near Johnstown, and many more were on the way to that point ; but there was not a single station or platform of any kind on the line of the Baltimore and Ohio Road within the limits of Johnstown, and the work of providing necessary terminal facilities, warehouses and depots for relief supplies of all kinds was intrusted to myself. Upon my leaving Morrellville for Johnstown, all of the Pittsburgh aids had been turned over to Mr. Logan, of the Transportation and Distribution Committee, who

was left in charge at that point. An examination of all the buildings available for storage purposes developed only a wagon shed
some 30 by 60 feet, near the Baltimore and Ohio tracks, the lumber yard of the Johnstown Lumber Company, with sheds 72 by
22 feet, corner Baltimore and Ohio Railroad and Bedford Avenue,
two store rooms in the Oddfellows' building on Main Street, and
various churches. With the exception, however, of the German
Catholic Church, the churches were not available for storage by
reason of their construction and dilapidated condition ; but all the
other properties named were taken possession of, and preparations
were made to put them into proper condition for use. The sheds
of the Lumber Company were cleaned out on Wednesday, June
5th, and an additional shed, 70 by 22 feet, was constructed with the
aid of a party of some twenty members of the Junior Order of
United American Mechanics of Greensburg, Pa., who volunteered
for this work. Ample platforms were also laid at this point, some
2,000 superficial feet in extent, and the work of unloading cars and
distributing to the various supply stations in Johnstown was at
once commenced. The wagon shed was also cleaned out, floored
and filled with supplies on June 5th. On the 6th and 7th, a general
commissary depot was built on the Lumber Yard property, consisting of a main building 60 by 20 feet, with surrounding additions
35 by 12 and 18 by 12 feet. On the 9th, the general commissary
depot and issue departments were transferred to these buildings,
and same were in the meantime completely filled with provisions
of all kinds. The general depot, corner of Bedford Avenue and
Baltimore and Ohio Railroad, that had been used up to this time,
was on this day filled with clothing. On June 10th, the floor of
the Catholic church was sufficiently advanced to commence the
storage of goods, and by the time the floor, 60 by 100 feet, was
completed, the next morning, the building was nearly filled with
relief supplies of every description. The store rooms on Main

Street were also in condition for use on the 10th, and a warehouse, 35 by 100 feet with platform 20 feet wide, was well under way alongside the main track of the Baltimore and Ohio, near the old passenger station.

On the morning of June 11th, the State authorities took possession of Johnstown, and relieved the citizen organization entirely, and all the above-named warehouses, with their contents, were turned over to the State on that day, excepting the store room on Main Street, which was important to private interests, and did not seem to be essential for storage purposes, the Baltimore and Ohio Railroad by this time being practically relieved, and were turned over to their owners. The cheerful acquiescence of all parties in the use of private property for the public welfare is worthy of note.

On Saturday, June 8th, the Government Engineers had completed the pontoon bridge across Stony Creek, and from this date the entire population in Kernville (some 6,000), as well as all of the sub-commissaries in Johnstown, were supplied from the Bedford Street commissary in Johnstown. Besides very considerable quantities of provisions were sent to General Hastings's commissary, across the Conemaugh River, at the Pennsylvania Railroad depot.

On June 9th, a committee composed of Mr. John Thomas, P. H. Chapin and another citizen of Johnstown, General Axline, of Ohio, and myself, visited Kernville to consider the situation there with reference to removing the flood debris which covered a large part of the town. It was suggested that fire would be the most economical agency for clearing up the wreck, and that this might be necessary as a sanitary measure to prevent epidemic, which was generally believed to be impending in case the weather should turn warm, and the work of cleaning up be considerably delayed, which appeared to be certain by reason of the very great magnitude of the work involved. This proposition was submitted to a number of citizens and property owners, privately, all of whom, save one, favored promptly burning the entire mass, without reference to the consequences to their own property ; but the problems involved in the execution of such a measure which presented themselves were so complex and serious, that none of the committee felt inclined to make a report involving any recommendation. The situation at Kernville strongly suggested the necessity for State intervention, with its power and lawful methods, which quickly ensued.

On Wednesday and Thursday all the laborers and others employed by the Pittsburgh Committee were paid off and dismissed, and at 3 o'clock, Thursday, the two remaining members of the Transportation and Distribution Committee left Johnstown on the return to Pittsburgh, where they arrived at 12.30 at night.

In connection with the work of the committee, the officers of the Pennsylvania Railroad and the Baltimore and Ohio Railroad co-operated most cheerfully and efficiently, and the committee is indebted to said railroads and their officers for very great courtesy, and for nearly all of the comforts and conveniences of living had while in Johnstown.

As a result of my personal observation and of reports received constantly and systematically during the following Sunday, June 2d, I am of the opinion that not one in or about Johnstown suffered seriously for food or clothing as a result of the great disaster, as the relief furnished was prompt and ample.

I cannot close without again referring to the efficient work done by the Pittsburgh volunteer aids, who were indefatigable and indispensable in the work of relief. A partial list of these is annexed hereto, and also the personal narratives of as many as could be gotten to give their experience in this form. In this connection the work of the undertakers, so indispensable and difficult under the circumstances, cannot be exaggerated or too greatly commended, especially with reference to the care exercised in the performance of their functions and the satisfactory condition in which their attentions left the victims of this awful calamity.

Respectfully submitted,

(Signed), H. E. COLLINS,

Of Transportation and Distribution Committee.

Aids attending Pittsburgh Relief Committee to Johnstown— "Co. A:"

E. H. Allen.	O. S. Richardson.
C. J. Weisser.	John A. Reed.
C. W. Winterhalter.	Theo. Sproull.
J. B. Boyce.	Rev. F. Rowoff.
A. C. Stevenson.	C. M. Johns.
Isaac Craig, Jr.	A. M. Gow.
E. G. Graff.	H. A. Johns.
J. L. Dawson Speer.	C. D. Sprung.
W. L. Mustin.	W. M. Smith.
H. G. Pfhal.	J. P. Brown.
H. W. McClain.	J. B. McNulty.
B. L. Elliott.	E. S. Carpenter.
W. S. Trumpore.	W. J. Gill.
Thos. Ullom.	W. P. Bennett.
B. F. Aaron.	Theo. F. Farrell.
E. G. Pearson.	Jas. Hartzell.
Wm. De Wolff.	C. A. Carpenter.
S. D. Hubley.	W. E. Matthew.

I have not the names of "Co. B" or I would include them in list. (Signed), H. E. COLLINS.

The labors of the people of the twin cities, Pittsburgh and Allegheny, were incessant and abundant. Not only did they furnish food, clothing, shelter and money, but they became the media through which such cities as Wheeling, Cincinnati,

Indianapolis, Chicago, St. Louis, Minneapolis, Milwaukee, Detroit, Cleveland, Toledo, Buffalo and other towns and rural districts poured in their generous contributions. Wilmington, Delaware, Braddock, Pa., and a hundred other towns and country places deserve special mention. In the appended account of the Pittsburgh Relief Committee it will be seen the amounts the above-named and other cities contributed through them for the benefit of the Conemaugh Valley:

Cash receipts from

Alabama,	$852 77
California, .	1,209 00
Colorado, .	2,232 95
Dakota,	687 45
Illinois, . .	32,756 63
Illinois, Chicago, ...	137,699 81
Illinois, Chicago, expended for houses, request of committee, . . .	13,891 00
Indiana, . . .	19,491 97
Iowa,	1,616 27
Kansas,	1,027 37
Kentucky,	5,084 92
Louisiana, .	592 45
Michigan, . .	15,603 56
Michigan, Detroit, . .	35,775 18
Minnesota, . .	1,466 09
Minnesota, Minneapolis,	8,583 75
Missouri, . .	687 90
Missouri, St. Louis,	16,597 28
Montana,	6,642 42
Nebraska, . .	475 75
New England States, . .	5,407 74
New Jersey, . .	6,291 35
New York State,	15,768 72

New York State, Albany, . .	$16,000 00
New York State, Buffalo,	20,188 47
Rochester, . .	2,111 51
Troy, ...	12,158 57
New York (city), . .	7,860 75
State of Ohio, . . .	26,906 26
Cincinnati, . . .	10,402 85
Cleveland, . .	3,010 00
Dayton, .	5,640 85
Toledo, ...	10,260 63
Youngstown, .	7,966 83
Oregon, ...	2,709 60
State of Pennsylvania, .	74,160 32
Philadelphia, ...	5,200 00
Pittsburgh and Allegheny,	250,770 72
South Carolina, . . .	1,455 38
North Carolina, ...	312 00
Tennessee, ...	3,056 25
Utah, ...	6,086 50
Washington Territory, .	1,000 00
State of West Virginia, .	3,246 60
Wheeling, . . .	8,545 06
Wisconsin, . .	297 45
Milwaukee, ...	18,297 05
Sundry places, under $300, in United States, London, Paris, Buenos Ayres, Canada, etc., ...	3,209 74
	$831,295 62

THE EXPENSE COLUMN.

Groceries, . . .	$49,092 29
Bread and flour, . . .	13,636 63
Dry goods, ...	16,446 57
Boots and shoes, . . .	9,262 07
Hardware, . . .	10,987 35

Coffins, .	$8,093 56
Drugs and medicines, .	1,710 27
Lumber, . .	7,185 94
Stoves and furniture,	1,335 97
Electric light, .	985 55
Miscellaneous items, . .	976 40
Labor (recovering bodies, etc.), . .	83,306 67
Cash sent local committee at Johnstown,	3,700 00
Railroad transportation, . .	300 37
Aid rendered needy cases, . . .	104 00
Cash sent relief committee at South Fork,	5,000 00
Drafts and checks returned,	764 95
Cash refunded, ...	50 00
Transferred to State Flood Relief Commission,	560,000 00
Chicago houses, ...	13,891 00
Cash balance on hand, .	44,466 03

$831,295 62

Mr. Wm. H. Thompson, the Pittsburgh banker, to whom were intrusted the care and custody of the above funds, and to all the excellent gentlemen who gave their time and money in this emergency, there is due, a debt of gratitude, which the people of Johnstown gratefully acknowledge but cannot adequately express.

(b) WHAT PHILADELPHIA DID.

The quickness with which Philadelphia has always responded to cries of human distress, and the records and memorials of her benevolence and charity, attest the fitness of her name. Nothing that pertains to man is foreign to her. This recognition of the brotherhood of man long ago inspired her citizens to organize a Permanent Relief Committee, to be always ready with men and means to furnish immediate relief in times of sudden calamity

—an example that ought to be imitated by every city and large community. Responsive to ordinary demands for help, it is not surprising that this extraordinary calamity to the people of her own Commonwealth struck the great heart of the city, and sent its pulsations through every vein and artery of her corporate existence. All classes of society, all trades and occupations, the poor as well as the rich, strong men and tender women, little children, sprung to the work of relief. "A fellow-feeling makes us wondrous kind." In the absence of definite information, they only knew that a mighty flood had overwhelmed a portion of their State, and there were sufferers there who needed rescue and aid. The first authentic official information was a telegram on Saturday morning, June 1st, from the Mayors of Pittsburgh and Allegheny to Mayor Fitler, announcing the awful disaster. He summoned the Citizens' Permanent Relief Committee to his residence. This committee met daily thereafter, after having appointed a special committee to proceed to Johnstown and other stricken localities in the State, to ascertain their condition and needs. Messrs. Huber, R. M. McWade, Bonbright, Vandeever, Blankenberg and McCreary composed that committee.

Mr. McWade is the city editor of the Philadelphia *Public Ledger*. The *Ledger* Building is a school of charity. The distinguished proprietor, George W. Childs, since the time he went to Philadelphia from Baltimore, a youth who had nothing but his own honesty and industry, and an unfaltering trust in his mother's God, whom she had taught him to revere, has manifested his inborn philanthropy. He began to exercise this when he himself needed the helping hand of others, and as he enlarged the schemes of his enterprise, he expanded his heart and hand until his great journal and its consequent wealth have become a benediction to the world. Mr. McWade displays the same noble spirit in making his important station serve the purposes of mercy. He flew to the help of Charleston, after the earthquake there, with $25,000, which he personally raised, and has done many other unrecorded noble acts. At a moment's notice, he sped from home, at Wayne, to be present at the first meeting of the Permanent Committee. He offered the resolution to appropriate at once $5,000 from the permanent fund, which is kept in hand for emergencies of this nature. As the proportions of the disaster were yet unknown, the opinion was expressed that this amount was extravagant. Mr. McWade insisted upon it, stating that "when the facts are ascertained, ten times that amount will be required."

Others besides the committee went to Johnstown, not waiting for organized efforts. Among these were Professor Forbes, of Jefferson Medical College, and Mr. McElway, who accompanied carloads of goods, consisting of ready-prepared food, bread, cheese, bacon, coffee, and one carload of shoes. They also carried surgical instruments and supplies.

On June 7th, Mayor Fitler informed the committee that he had received $50,000 from Boston, which was duly accredited and sent with the amount already collected to Governor Beaver.

The people were now beginning to realize the nature of the calamity, and exerted themselves accordingly. Subscriptions to the relief fund assumed large denominations. Thus, on the 8th of June, Mr. Walter A. Wood stimulated them by a donation of $1,000 through the house of Drexel & Co.

Then the ladies of Gloucester and other localities thoroughly organized their efforts and sent moneys collected to the Philadelphia committee. On the same day, June 8th, the committee sent to Johnstown 125 single cots and a carload of vinegar.

At the meeting June 10th, the Mayor stated that Governor Beaver said the money raised by the citizens was to be devoted to the charitable demands of the disasters, that he favored assembling the Legislature to adopt measures for repairing damages,

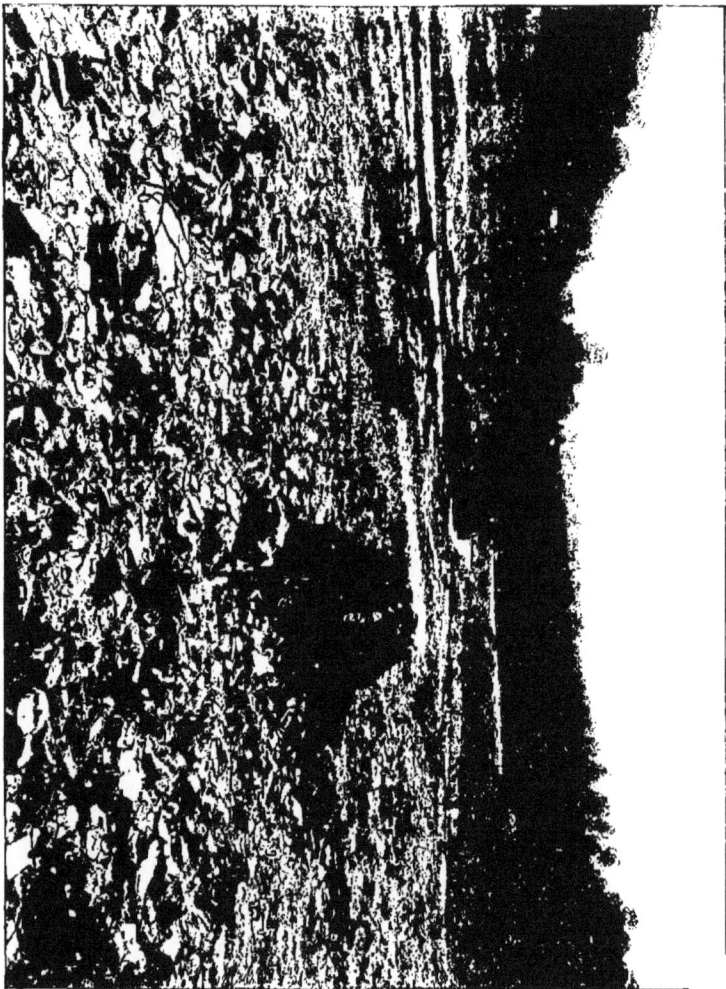
VIEW OF THE BROKEN DAM, LOOKING FROM THE LAKE BASIN.

and pledged himself to see to removing the debris and obstructions in the rivers. The proposed appropriation of a million of dollars was not made on the supposition that it was not legal.

On June 11th, Professor Forbes reported from Johnstown, calling the disaster "the Conemaugh hecatomb." He wrote in the highest terms of the conduct of citizens, and his words did much to dismiss the false impressions that heartless correspondents had created.

June 12th, Robert C. Ogden and Frank Reeves were added to the Permanent Committee.

June 14th, four steam fire-engines, with a complement of men, were sent to Johnstown at the request of General Hastings.

June 14th, the committee sent 1,200 market-baskets.

July 3rd, the Auditing Committee reported that Mayor Fitler had drawn checks from No. 1 to No. 18, amounting to $63,575.62. Part of this, however, was sent to other flooded districts than Conemaugh Valley.

July 11th was a golden day. On the motion of Thomas Dolan, the committee was authorized to place $500,000 in the hands of Drexel & Co., subject to the order of Governor Beaver; and Mr. McWade reported that a carload of fruit from California, which was donated to the relief fund, had been sold for $1,221.09, which was appropriated to the relief of Johnstown.

August 4th, Dr. Pancoast induced the committee to appropriate $10,000 to the Red Cross Hospital in Johnstown. The author is not able to state how this sum was expended, whether to the immediate wants of the sufferers or to the pay of employees.

On the same day, Robert C. Ogden, the new member of the committee, handed in $100,000 additional, which was placed with the Governor's fund.

This is but a partial and fragmentary account, and is really only the base line along which the charity and benevolence of

8

Philadelphia proceeded. It is impossible to give the total amount of money and supplies that were sent, because they passed through various mediums, to some of which access can not be obtained. The principal ones were Drexel & Co., the Fourth Street Bank, the Pennsylvania Railroad Company and the Cambria Iron Company.

One of the most reliable relief efforts in the city of Philadelphia was accomplished on this wise: The firm of Samuel M. Wanamaker & Co. decided, on the morning of June 3d, to wait upon Mayor Fitler, and ask permission to place upon the sidewalk in front of their store, on Chestnut Street, a large glass globe upon a pedestal, in which might be dropped the contributions of such persons as were disposed to aid the sufferers, by large or small sums, without the inconvenience of visiting the office of the Mayor, or any other designated depository of funds. Having received the desired authority a large glass globe, or aquarium, was placed in position at the curbstone, and was continually guarded by two stalwart policemen, specially detailed for that purpose. About 6.15 P.M., June 4th, the globe having been taken in for the day, a gentleman called at the door and requested to see Mr. Wanamaker. Having been accorded that opportunity he asked, "Do you receive contributions here for the Johnstown sufferers?" Being answered in the affirmative he said, "Here is my contribution," handing Mr. Wanamaker a roll containing twenty-five new crisp notes of the denomination of twenty dollars each. Mr. Wanamaker, after counting it, thanked the stranger and said, "I will give you a receipt for this amount, sir." The stranger, however, answered, "No; it is not necessary," whereupon Mr. Wanamaker said, "If you will kindly give me your name, sir, I will not make use of it, but it would be a great satisfaction for me to know who this generous benefactor is." The gentleman again said, "No, no," and turning toward the door, bade Mr. Wanamaker "good-night," and departed.

It may be well to state in connection with this interesting effort that many curious and interesting incidents occurred. One especially was an old lady who, after depositing her mite, stated that she had just deposited twenty cents, "all I have, and I wish I had more; for I would most willingly give it." It was not an uncommon occurrence to see newsboys and bootblacks step up and, after waiting with interest for a time, drop in their nickels. The same boys were noticed to return three and four times in one day and deposit similar amounts. Another incident was that of a gentleman who stood in deep thought for a few minutes and then, taking a cameo ring from his finger, dropped it in the globe, with a request to have it sold, the amount received from its sale to be contributed to the fund. The ring brought twenty-one dollars.

On June 6th a notice was placed on the globe to the effect that after its withdrawal it would be sold as a relic to the highest bidder. There were several bids offered of small amounts, but there was also a check dropped in for thirty dollars, with a statement that if it should prove the highest bid, the donor would be pleased to accept the globe, but if not the highest then the amount should be placed to the credit of the fund, which was done.

On the last day of displaying the globe, June 7th, we found a check from Mr. Wetherill for fifty-one dollars. He evidently presumed that some one would offer fifty dollars, and he, anxious to receive the souvenir, was willing to give one dollar extra. He received the globe and presented it to the Historical Society of Pennsylvania.

The result of the five days' work was as follows:

1st day, June 3d,	$659 11
2d " " 4th,	1,014 75
3d " " 5th, . .	623 24
The special gift of the stranger,	500 00

4th day, June 6th,		$400 72
5th " " 7th,		204 29
	Total,	$3,402 11
Sale of ring,	. .	21 00
Bid for globe,		30 00
Final sale of globe,		51 00
Grand total for five days,		$3,504 11

A similar globe collection was made by the *Philadelphia Inquirer* in front of its office, and at other prominent points.

We must remember in this connection that Philadelphia was at the same time generously extending aid to other stricken localities—Williamsport, Newport, Jersey Shore, Lock Haven, Harrisburg, Lewistown and Aaronsburg in Pennsylvania, and Harper's Ferry, Md.

(c) WHAT NEW YORK DID.

The city of New York awoke on a bright, beautiful morn, Sabbath, June 2d, 1889, in anticipation of a happy day of rest and worship. When, however, the morning papers were opened, a dark cloud of sorrow spread over it, a universal feeling of inexpressible grief weighed upon all hearts and homes. The news from Johnstown and other sections of Pennsylvania, though meagre and confused, was definite enough to satisfy the people that a fearful catastrophe had befallen them, involving great loss of life and suffering. When the congregations had assembled at the hour of morning service, the pastors announced in feeling and fitting words the great calamity, and some appealed to the sympathies of all hearts as Christians and citizens of a common country. Collections were immediately made for the sufferers. Probably the very first instance was that of Rev. Dr. John R.

Paxton, pastor of the West Presbyterian Church, 42d Street. My informant was present and made a note of the circumstance. Thus I am gratified to say that the first appeals in our behalf, and the first contribution in the greatest city of our country, which has ever distinguished itself for the help of other stricken and afflicted communities, were made in the house of God. Consecrated then by His service and spirit, no wonder the hearts and hands of its people were opened until nearly a million of dollars, besides other supplies, were freely contributed.

On Monday afternoon, June 3rd, Mayor Grant assembled a number of prominent business men in his office, by whom a relief committee was constituted. The celerity with which operations were begun was characteristic of New York men. Many contributions were immediately announced at their first meeting. Mr. Isidor Wormser reported $15,000 from members of the Produce Exchange; Mr. William R. Grace, that the Lackawanna Coal and Iron Company had authorized the Cambria Iron Company to draw upon it for $5,000. Mayor Grant stated that he had received during the forenoon by money and checks $15,000, to which he added his personal subscription of $500. Colonel Elliott F. Shepard reported that he had sent through the *Mail and Express*, $10,000 to Johnstown. Checks and subscriptions came in so rapidly that $27,000 were raised before the Committee on Organization had reported; and before the close of the day nearly $80,000 had been received at the Mayor's office. At the opening of the New York Stock Exchange, a subscription was inaugurated which on that day rose to $14,520, although comparatively few members were present. On the next day, Tuesday, June 4th, the work was resumed. A cablegram from the London Stock Exchange subscribed $5,000; Mr. John S. Kennedy cabled from London also $5,000; Mr. John Jacob Astor gave $2,500, and William B. Astor $1,000. With this generous beginning, the subscription list during the day was vastly increased.

The same course was pursued by the other exchanges, as the Produce, Cotton, Coffee, Metal, Real Estate, Lumber; the Hide and Leather Board of Trade; express companies, beginning with the Adams Express Company's subscription of $5,000; incorporated institutions, banks, insurance companies, associated societies. The most signal instances of the deep and all-pervading sympathy which our calamity aroused were the subscriptions by the children, especially those of the charitable and reformatory institutions, such as the House of Refuge on Randall's Island, the boys of which gave $258.22. The public school children likewise contributed. A beautiful example was furnished in Long Island City, opposite New York. The public schools there have a savings-bank, in which the pupils are encouraged to deposit their savings. Of the 4,000 enrolled pupils 2,272 donated out of their deposits in the bank $452.37 to the suffering children of Johnstown and the Conemaugh Valley.

At the close of the first week the subscriptions amounted to over $600,000. This was increased, by collection in the churches on Sabbath, June 9th, and benefit performances in places of amusement, to about $700,000.

It is impossible to ascertain the exact amount of money and supplies that were contributed from New York and vicinity, so much of them having passed through various channels. We know that nearly, if not quite, a million of dollars were raised.

From Mayor Grant's office the following statement is given as the last balance from the books:

Received by Hugh J. Grant, Mayor, .	$354,520 35
Received by J. Edward Simmons, .	162,417 34
	$516,937 69
Disbursements, . .	$500,737 84
Balance, . .	$16,199 85

This balance has been paid over to the Johnstown committee. Thus $516,937.69 went through the municipal authority of New York, and about $480,000 through the other channels of its commercial and social organization.

(d) WHAT BALTIMORE DID.

Of Baltimore, the scene of twelve years of my ministry, I employ not only words of appreciation, but affection. The alacrity and generosity with which its citizens hastened to our help recalled the many evidences of kindness I had personally enjoyed in the Monumental City.

On the 3rd of June, telegraphic communication having been reopened with Johnstown, the Baltimore and Ohio Railroad Company sent its first train from Pittsburgh, loaded with provisions. President Charles F. Mayer, of this company, with other officials, started on June 2d for Johnstown, to arrange for transportation and relief, in answer to a telegram from Mr. J. V. Patton, their Superintendent. Mr. Mayer left orders that contributions of supplies should be received at Camden Station and sent with dispatch, free of expense. This great corporation, with all its lines of railroad, is intimately interwoven with every interest in the city of Baltimore: whatever it does is due to the inspiration, and is propelled by the pulsations, of its heart. The train of ten loaded cars, to which the various towns on the line had contributed, arrived at 2 o'clock in the morning of June 3d.

Large portions of Maryland, near the seacoast and in the mountains, and of West Virginia, were overflowed, and demanded Baltimore's aid. The citizens, with the co-operation and direction of Mayor F. B. Latrobe, were already engaged in the work of relieving their own flooded districts when the Johnstown calamity was reported. The Baltimore *Sun* had sent a reporter along the

Potomac River into Western Maryland to ascertain the extent of damage and the needs of the people, and make arrangements for immediate transportation and relief. He was instructed to co-operate with the Merchants' and Manufacturers' Association of Baltimore, which had voted to use most of its funds for the sufferers in Western Maryland. He began to report from Point of Rocks, and as he proceeded found increasing destruction and distress, which taxed the charity and generosity of Baltimore and the other cities of the State very heavily. Thus the noble city, which stands in the front ranks of philanthropic enterprise, took upon itself the additional work of aiding stricken Pennsylvania.

Mayor Latrobe, who was then occupying the Mayoralty for the fifth time, instituted measures to meet this additional appeal to their sympathy and help. The newspaper offices opened subscription lists, the churches made Sabbath collections, the ladies organized committees, and during the first week about $35,000 were raised.

The peculiar value of Baltimore's aid was in its immediate supply of provisions and clothing, for which transportation was afforded by the Baltimore and Ohio Railroad. Among the first shipments were 600 pieces of clothing to my care, by the King's Daughters of the Twelfth Presbyterian Church. Other churches of different denominations followed with equally valuable gifts.

The Baltimore *Sun* telegraphed to me at once for information, with a view of helping with the liberality characteristic of the proprietors of that journal. The *American* telegraphed to Governor Beaver the following : " Draw on us at sight for $2,000 more, making altogether $4,000 subscribed at the counter of the Baltimore *American* for Johnstown sufferers. FELIX AGNUS, *Manager.*"

The aggregate amount given by Baltimore cannot be stated. The draft upon its citizens' sympathy was closer than upon other Eastern cities. Trains of twelve to fifteen coaches a day arrived

HOUSE OF JOHN SCHULTZ, NEAR THE STONE BRIDGE.

at Camden Station with people from all parts of the West, Maryland and Pennsylvania, impoverished and rendered homeless by the flood. Fifteen hundred arrived in one day. Thus somewhat of the dire results of the floods was brought to the door of Baltimore, and it generously responded to demands of humanity.

(e) WHAT BOSTON DID.

The response from Boston and New England was quick and large. Characteristic of the people of that little corner of our country, it was business-like, systematic and consequently complete. The world thinks mainly of New Englanders as a manufacturing, money-making people, and Boston as a literary centre. It attributes to them all those qualities that are essential to the acquisition of money and personal advancement in thrift, letters and science, and it has unreasonably concluded that this has made them the less warm-hearted and sympathetic. Their noblest and one of their most distinctive traits is their philanthropy. Boston is really the home of modern philanthropy, where originated the schemes and methods that embrace all forms of human suffering and human demands—methods that have become so common throughout the country that they cease to cause wonder. The sons of New England, not only at home, but wherever they have emigrated and become domesticated, have been prominent in deeds of humanity, and in advancing the intellectual, moral and religious condition of man. The merchant list of Boston is crowded with the names of philanthropists.

At the first intimation of Johnstown's disaster, Governor Long of Massachusetts and Mayor Hart of Boston organized a system for contribution, and worked together for an abundant and speedy relief. The House of Representatives, then in session, on June 3d, admitted a bill appropriating $10,000 to the sufferers, and on the next day, when further particulars were received, increased it to $30,000. Messrs. Kidder, Peabody & Co. were appointed treasurers for subscriptions of the people, and on June 5th these amounted to $35,400. Complete lists of the subscribers, published from day to day, showed that every class in the community contributed. The towns and country near Boston, and distant cities, nobly conspired in the work. Among the many munificent donations, there are hundreds of dollars in the aggregate given by single ladies, children, a number of orphans in asylums, bootblacks and newsboys, and many subscriptions with only initials attached. The funds in the hands of Messrs. Kidder, Peabody & Co. increased so rapidly that they telegraphed a number of times to Governor Beaver, desiring him to draw upon them or instruct them for its speedy appropriation.

The following items, selected from a multitude, are evidence of the sympathy which pervaded the heart of New England:

Lasell Seminary, Auburndale, has sent three large boxes filled with clothing for women and children; also $107 in money, directed to Williamsport.

A committee of Newton ladies has collected fourteen boxes of clothing, which will be shipped to Johnstown immediately. The Auburndale Congregational Church collected $151.75 on Sunday.

Next Sunday collections will be taken in all the Marblehead churches. The Dickens Dramatic Club has voted to reproduce "Bardwell vs. Pickwick," specially dramatized by Rev. J. Kay Applebee. Circulars will be sent out, and the schools will be asked to contribute their mite. The town clerk has also been empowered to receive subscriptions.

Rev. V. A. Cooper, superintendent of the New England Home for Little Wanderers, was in the West with a company of twenty-five children, for whom he was obtaining homes, when the Johnstown disaster occurred. He immediately telegraphed that the Home would take and care for twenty-five or more orphans or destitute children. He has gone to the scene.

The fund from Boston went through the hands of Governor Beaver, and amounted to over $500,000.

3.—THE COMMISSARY DEPARTMENT.

The quality of mercy is not strained ;
It droppeth as the gentle rain from heaven
Upon the place beneath. It is twice blessed :
It blesseth him that gives and him that takes.
—MERCHANT OF VENICE.

WHAT a spectacle for angels and men was visible in the valley of the Conemaugh as the day dawned on the first of June! There were several thousand people still clinging to the wreckage in parts that could not be reached, or imperiled by the fire at the bridge, or making their way over debris toward the hills, all hungry, and many of them injured, wet, cold and with insufficient raiment. Many had died, and several had been born, during the dismal night. Our first want was food, our second clothing, and our third shelter. Of the latter I shall write under the first chapter in Part V.

As for food, many had eaten none after Friday morning, because at dinner time they were so busily engaged in removing their carpets and furniture out of the reach of the water, that they neglected the noon meal ; and, of course, those who were washed out had no supper on Friday night, and not many had breakfast on Saturday morning. A few loaves and some crackers and bananas picked from the wreck were carried over the debris to Alma Hall and other places of rescue by some persons early on Saturday morning ; but what were these among so many? Most of the men and generally the women insisted that this food should be given to the feeble and to the children. It was very difficult to find food that was uninjured, for in scores of houses that had not been moved from their foundations the water had impaired the food in their kitchens and cellars. The provision and grocery stores were either carried off, or in the case of those on the outskirts of the place, the food in them was rendered unfit for use. Dependent entirely upon the outside world for something to eat, many persons traveled miles into the country before they broke the enforced abstinence. But most of us had some nourishment by noon on Saturday. The sympathy and generosity of the people on the hillsides and of the farmers for miles out in the country displayed an energy and promptitude that was beyond all praise. Realizing that it was more blessed to give than to receive, most of these country people showed marked kindness and a magnificent sympathy that was practical and hearty. Those who wished to sell their wares at exorbitant prices, or refused to take orphans to their homes because no one was authorized to foot the board bill, were few in number.

The rescued ones were gladdened by Reigart, Troll, Rogers, Graham and others issuing out milk by tinsfull to all comers, without money and without price. The people of our own County Cambria, of Somerset, of Bedford and of Legonier Valley in Westmoreland County, all contiguous to us, were the first to come to our relief. They brought prepared food and cooked provisions and flour, meat, potatoes, butter and eggs. But it was very apparent that our immense population must have more provisions than could be thus supplied. Some suggested that our citizens must at once scatter through the country for subsistence, abandoning the ruined city. Few persons were willing to believe that, cut off as we were, without railroad or telegraph facilities, our pressing wants could or would be supplied. Superintendent Pitcairn, of the Pennsylvania Railroad, seemed to have been one of the few who, at a distance, adequately took in the situation. At his instance the meeting was called of the citizens of Pittsburgh and Allegheny for 1 P.M., Saturday, the results of which are elsewhere fully given.

On the opening of the Baltimore and Ohio Road, on June the 2d, through the efficient action of General Superintendent J. V. Patton, large supplies of food and clothing were brought from

Somerset, Cumberland and Baltimore. At first the trains could not reach nearer the city than the distance of a mile or more, whence the donations were conveyed to the large, unfurnished building on the corner of Stony Creek and Bedford Streets, of which the Commissary Committee had taken possession.

Mr. James B. Scott, who had reached the north side of the stone bridge with provisions, finding it impossible to convey boxes and barrels over the swollen Conemaugh River into Johnstown proper, now telegraphed to Pittsburgh that all further supplies should be sent by the Baltimore and Ohio Railroad to Rockwood, and thence to Johnstown by the Cambria and Somerset Railroad. Superintendent Patton telegraphed to various points, asking for provisions and clothing. Transportation now fully opened, the railroad people said to the public: "We will place our cars on the track; you fill them, and we will pull them into Johnstown." Captain William Jones, of Braddock, as well as the Pittsburgh people, now sent large supplies over the Baltimore and Ohio Railroad by way of Rockwood. Too much credit cannot be given Captain Jones and Superintendents Pitcairn and Patton for their wonderful energy in pushing supplies through to the suffering city. Of course, the trains did not reach us on schedule time, and the goods were not manifested, but that was of little consequence. The people who desired it were enabled to leave the place by the outgoing trains, while those who remained to work were fed and clothed.

While the building on the corner of Stony Creek and Bedford Streets continued to be the chief depot, distributing commissaries were established in Kernville, at Cambria and other places. Young's livery stable, at Morrellville, was used as a commissary store, from which clothing was distributed.

Subsequently Captain H. H. Kuhn was put in charge of the receiving department of the commissaries, erecting several necessary buildings for the storage of supplies; Mr. John Thomas and his assistants had charge of the issuing department. A sub-department under Col. Thomas Stewart, Commander G. A. R. and staff officers, was established on Adam Street for the supply of Conemaugh Borough. Another depot was established on the south side, or Kernville, under charge of Major Singer and Peter Cobaugh, that they might supply the 5th and 6th Wards. There was also a small sub-department under the charge of Daniel Ott in the 7th Ward, or Hornerstown. Grubbtown and Upper Yoder were supplied by sending car loads of provisions to Osborn Station, in charge of responsible citizens.

A general department was also established at the Pennsylvania Railroad Station under charge of Col. J. L. Spangler, who organized sub-departments at Cambria Borough and Morrellville under charge of competent assistants, for the accommodation of those towns and Coopersdale. This efficient officer also supplied, from his general headquarters, Prospect, East Conemaugh, Franklin Borough, Mineral Point, South Fork and other points. These centres were sufficient to meet the wants of the entire district suffering from the flood; and to these noble men mentioned, together with Majors Irving and Austin Curtin, Mr. Bush and others, whose names may never be chronicled, belongs a meed of praise which no language can express. Captain Kuhn, one of our own honored citizens, finally consolidated and closed up the entire commissary department.

Through the courtesy of Gen. D. H. Hastings and Col. J. L. Spangler I am permitted to append the complete report of the latter to the former upon his withdrawal from our city, which report is a most important contribution to the story of Johnstown, furnishing as it does the official statement of what was done by the State authority, and by the final Director of the restoration at the desolated city.

JOHNSTOWN, PA., July 2d, 1889.

General D. H. Hastings, Adjutant General of Pennsylvania.

GENERAL:—I have the honor to report on the distribution of relief to the people of the Conemaugh Valley, made by this Department.

On arriving at Johnstown the day after the great disaster, June 1st, 1889, in company with yourself, intending simply to offer my services to you in the good work of relieving the sufferings of a great community, I found the place and its people in a most chaotic condition. There was no head, no organization, and the dazed inhabitants, under the effect of this frightful wreck, were in no condition to plan or organize. The people were entirely absorbed in the work of gathering their dead and searching for their missing relatives.

You gathered to your side, on the night of the 1st of June, a few citizens and strangers, and at that meeting you directed that immediate steps be taken to care for the dead and provide for the living. You assigned me to the duty of taking charge of the few supplies that were then coming in by wagons across the country, from Ebensburg and Altoona. The next morning additional supplies were received from Pittsburgh. These supplies were brought to the Pennsylvania Railroad Station, on the north side of the Conemaugh, and at this point a commissary was established for the relief of the people of this part of the valley. This commissary subsisted for a period of ten days over 10,000 people. Communication with Johnstown proper was cut off, and I had little connection with any relief distributed on the south side of the Conemaugh at this time, and communication was only established when temporary bridges were thrown across the streams. The people in this part of the valley were well taken care of by James B. Scott, Esq., and his valuable assistants.

I am indebted for many kindnesses shown me by Mr. Scott's able committee prior to June 12th, when the State assumed the control of relief.

In the practical management of the relief furnished to the people prior to the 12th of June I was compelled to employ many people to assist me in the work on hand. These obligations have all been met and discharged. Very many people, strangers in the valley, came forward and tendered their services in the great work of relief without any hope of reward, except that which arises from the discharge of duty to a suffering people.

Among the many noble men who rendered invaluable services to the people in the early part of June were General H. A. Axline, Adjutant General of the State of Ohio, and his assistants. His tents for sheltering the people, and his contributions from his friends in Ohio, did much to stay the sufferings of an afflicted people. I am deeply grateful to him and his friends for the enthusiastic and intelligent support they rendered in the distribution of relief at that time.

I wish to commend the services of the many traveling salesmen and practical merchants who acted as clerks in my commissary at this time. I wish I could mention them by name. In the excitement and confusion of the hour no record even could be kept, and I cannot, therefore, name them in this report. Wherever they may be now, I tender them my sincere acknowledgments for their generous aid furnished without compensation to the people subsisted through our joint efforts.

Provisions and clothing for the benefit of the sufferers began to pour in from every section of the country in vast quantities. This whole country was stirred with sympathy for the unfortunate. The great calamity of May 31st, without doubt the greatest and the saddest that has ever been witnessed on this continent, was only paralleled by the magnificent charity of the people of the United

VIEW FROM PROSPECT HILL, LOOKING SOUTH.

States. The great wave of ruin that struck the stone bridge was a central shock which sent its widening circles to the limits of the land, and on the returning vibrations the people placed their generous offerings, which poured into Johnstown like another flood. Relief came in every conceivable shape and condition. The two public highways, the Pennsylvania Railroad and the Baltimore and Ohio Railroad, abandoned their own business, and, with a magnanimity and generosity that will never be appreciated but by those who witnessed it, greeted the survivors of the flood with overloaded trains of provisions and clothing, which aroused the starving people of the valley, and gave them hope and cheer as they gathered about their ruined homes and coffined dead.

Let the country thoroughly understand and appreciate its absolute dependence upon the railroads in a disaster so widespread as that of Johnstown. Without compensation, and with a rapidity and promptness highly commendable, these roads saved the day at Johnstown. Their crippled equipment, their overworked people and their superintendents were in the field at the earliest moment, and their efforts never ceased by day or night until relief came in abundance.

On the 12th day of June, when you assumed control under the State, the relief cars from every section of the country reached here with no mark or address indicating from whence they came. They were simply consigned to the "Johnstown sufferers." Every effort has been made by this Department since you assumed the management to secure the names and addresses of the contributors with a view to making a special acknowledgment in each case. I have only been partially successful. Hundreds of acknowledgments have been made by the Department; and I would have other contributors who did not receive acknowledgments from me to appreciate the situation here, and feel assured that all contributions were duly received and appropriated by the Department and distributed for the benefit of the people.

9

After the 12th of June, system and organization were brought out of chaos. The whole district from South Fork to Coopersdale, a distance of thirteen miles, was divided into commissary districts. What is called Johnstown is made up of a number of boroughs and villages. These boroughs and towns are South Fork, Mineral Point, East Conemaugh, Franklin, Woodvale, Conemaugh Borough, Johnstown Borough, Grubtown, Walnut Grove, Moxham, Prospect Borough, Millville Borough, Cambria City, Morrellville, Rosedale, Brownstown and Coopersdale.

I established two post commissaries, one on each of the railroads, for the purpose of receiving relief goods and furnishing them in bulk daily to the fourteen district commissaries which I established at such points as would seem best for distribution of clothing and provisions directly to the people. These district commissaries were established at the following points, and were intended to supply the wants of the people, as shown by the population set opposite each station:

South Fork,	300	people.
Mineral Point,	200	"
East Conemaugh,	1,000	"
Franklin, .	600	"
Woodvale, .	600	"
Conemaugh Borough,	5,000	"
Kernville, . .	7,000	"
Morrellville,	3,500	"
Cambria City,	2,800	"
Prospect Hill,	4,000	"
Johnstown, .	2,500	"
Minersville,	1,425	"
Rosedale, . .	407	"
Coopersdale,	622	"
	29,954	"

This would appear to the casual observer a large population for the number of houses left in the region, but subsequent examination showed that nearly every house was crowded to its fullest capacity by refugees from the flooded districts. Day after day brought in friends and relatives searching for their missing ones, and these also drew their supplies from the commissaries and helped to swell the population. The entire population had to be subsisted from my commissaries for the reason that all business was paralyzed, rendering it impossible to purchase supplies. For some days subsistence was furnished, for the reason given above, to workmen of the Cambria Iron Company, to workmen of the contractors, and to the various organizations employed in the morgues, the Bedford Street Hospital, the grave diggers, the Odd Fellows' Society, the Masonic Relief, Children's Aid Society and others. Believing that the contractors were not entitled to subsistence from relief supplies, I have invariably charged them for the goods furnished upon their orders, and account to the relief fund for the same in this report.

You will observe at once that the subsistence of so large a population required the employment of competent men for the management of different departments, with a large corps of workmen. To each commissary were assigned a Quartermaster and a Sergeant, with orders to employ sufficient force to aid in the distribution, and make daily reports to me at 6 o'clock P.M.

The names of the various officers of the National Guard, officers of the regular army, and civilians assisting me in the management of this work are given in a separate statement hereto attached, and marked " Exhibit A."

The work of the officers was arduous in the extreme. It was their duty to make daily requisitions upon this Department for provisions, clothing and household furniture. They made a canvass of the sufferers in each district and ascertained their residences, their needs and their wants, with a list of such persons as were affording them shelter and a home under their own roof. Those who had no place to stay were furnished with tents by the Quartermaster General, who promptly honored all requests from this Department for any supplies required. Nearly every Quartermaster erected a temporary building of sufficient capacity to meet the wants and requirements of his station. These buildings contained a grocery department, a clothing department, a flour and bread department and a boot and shoe department. As soon as the canvass had been made, a ticket was furnished to the head of each family entitled to relief, with the days of the month printed thereon, and this ticket, in the hands of the holder, was good for one day's rations at the district commissary situated in the district in which he lived. A separate ticket was usually given for clothing and household furniture, on which was kept an account of what had been received and what was still needed. In the distribution of stoves, mattresses and other articles of furniture, the Quartermaster detailed a competent man to visit the houses of the people, and after being satisfied that the applicant had a room or place that he could call his own for a few months, these articles were furnished from the commissaries on his orders, and receipts taken in each case.

A meeting of the Quartermasters was held each evening in my Department at 8 o'clock. A report of stock on hand was submitted, and a requisition for supplies for the next day filed. The wants and needs of each district were taken up and discussed. This enabled me to submit a daily report to the Adjutant General's Office, for the purpose of determining what would have to be supplied by purchase to make a full assortment of supplies for the use of the people.

Besides the regular force employed at each district commissary, I required the detailing of a number of gentlemen, whose special duty it was to canvass the district, take orders for supplies and deliver them by wagon to the temporary homes of those persons who were averse to applying publicly at the commissaries for the assistance which they regarded in the nature of a charity. Within four days after I had commenced the work of relief under your direction I discovered that there were a large number of persons who, prior to the flood, had been in positions of affluence and wealth, but who were now as poor as the poorest, and were naturally diffident in asking for supplies at a commissary. Such persons, as well as all others who desired it, were daily supplied by giving their orders to gentlemen whose duty it was to solicit them.

I desire to mention in connection with this special work the names of Lieutenant George R. Burnett, an officer of the regular army; Mrs. Jerome, Frank A. Snyder, Esq., of Clearfield, Pa., a prominent lawyer of his county, with a corps of assistants, who remained with us during the entire month just passed.

Many strangers from all parts of the country temporarily sojourning here engaged in this kind of work, and many a home now comfortably furnished will attest the efficiency of their services. I would gladly mention them by name, but space and time forbid.

The popularity and success of the district commissaries are evidenced by the fact that many prominent people of this place assisted cheerfully in serving the people, and, in the course of time, came forward and received their supplies with their neighbors. When the day fixed by me to turn over the commissary department to the Citizens' Committee arrived, resolutions of regret at our withdrawal and complimentary to the officers in charge were passed by the citizens and forwarded to this Department—notably in the case of Lieutenant O. L. Nichols, at Cambria City, and Lieutenant Richardson, at Prospect Hill. Not a single serious complaint has reached this Department against any officer in charge of any of the district commissaries. I am naturally proud of the record made by the Quartermasters in my Department. No set of men, however experienced and prominent, could have performed this work with more fidelity, intelligence and efficiency. They knew no rich or poor, good or bad, and hence honestly endeavored to reach all and satisfy all. They regarded each sufferer entitled to the best that was on hand at the commissary at the time, and it was freely given. They early taught the people that this was their property, and not ours. It was here for them, and not for us, and it was distributed with kindness and politeness. Any subordinate who displayed a want of politeness in serving the people was promptly discharged and cashiered.

By reference to a former part of this report you will notice that this Department subsisted a population of 29,954 people. This was necessary, because for a number of days no supplies could be had here from any source but the commissaries. It simply meant the subsistence of all the people in the valley until proper arrangements could be made to bring in supplies. By June 23d there was a noticeable decrease in the goods received for relief by contributions, and about the same time a few stores began to resume business. Meat stands were started, several bakeries began to bake bread, and regular shipments were made to contractors. Wood, Morrell & Company reopened their store, and a pay day was had for all of their regular employees, and by reason of these circumstances I began to reduce the number subsisted: First, by refusing to sell to contractors; and, second, by withdrawing subsistence to the employees of the Cambria Iron Company and the employees of the Johnstown Company, by their own request, and all others who were in a position to purchase supplies abroad and get them here in regular shipments.

I gave directions to my Quartermasters at the meeting held

on the evening of June 22d, that an order for a reduction in the number subsisted would take effect on the following Wednesday, and that they should report to me the result.

At the meeting on Wednesday the consolidated report on subsistence, in view of the foregoing directions, showed as follows:

STATION.	CARDS LAST REPORT.	CARDS TO-DAY.	PEOPLE SUB. LAST REPORT.	PEOPLE SUB. TO-DAY.
Morrellville, ...	504	299	2,694	1,046
Cambria, ...	500	345	2,461	1,674
Prospect Hill, ...	432	427	3,068	1,484
Woodvale, ...	179	159	861	750
E. Conemaugh, ...	228	19	324	56
Franklin, ...	155	50	667	212
Minersville, ...	300	200	1,425	1,000
Rosedale, ...	90		407	50
Johnstown, ...	1,500	536	4,840	3,522
Kernville, ...	660	291	3,969	1,800
Conemaugh, ...	654	700	4,500	5,131
	5,202	3,026	25,216	16,725

At the last meeting of the Quartermasters, held July 1st, 1889, at 8 P.M., I was able to reduce the number of persons subsisted by this Department, as shown by the following statement:

STATION.	CARDS ISSUED TO DATE.	CARDS LIFTED TO DATE.	CARDS IN FORCE.	PEOPLE STILL SUBSISTED.
Franklin and Conemaugh, .	389	291	98	490
Conemaugh, ...	675	254	421	3,014
Johnstown, ...	1,180	454	726	3,630
Mineral Point, ...	30	20	10	45
Morrellville, ...	509	270	239	1,195
Cambria City, ...	500	259	241	1,600
Prospect Hill, ...	840	363	477	2,632
Woodvale, ...	171	147	24	120
Coopersdale, ...	50	20	30	150
	4,344	2,078	2,266	12,876

This leaves a number still to be subsisted—12,876 on 2,266 cards in force.

I had fully intended to make reductions so as to leave the number to be subsisted by my successor at 9,000 people, but upon close examination and inquiry I discovered that the average wages made here by the head of a family is from one dollar to one dollar and twenty-five cents a day. I know of but one payment made by the Cambria Iron Company to its employees, and I have concluded that though many of the sufferers are employed on regular pay, they have lost everything in the world in the form of property, and still have large families dependent upon them for support, and therefore it would be manifest injustice and cruelty to lift the cards of these people and deny them supplies at the commissaries at this time. Every consideration of humanity leads me to the belief that subsistence should be continued for a little while longer, until these people thus employed may get a little money ahead with which to make a new start in life. The responsibility of those in charge of commissaries, in this matter, is very great and serious. While it is the part of wisdom and good sense to encourage these people to stand alone as rapidly as possible by withdrawing their cards and denying them rations at the commissaries, it must not be done until the Department is satisfied beyond a question that the persons so denied are fully able to take care of themselves, and that no suffering will be entailed. The thought of somebody going hungry by mistakes in lifting cards should admonish those in charge to be certain and clear in the premises.

I have asked your permission to turn the commissary department over to the management of the Citizens' Committee, recently appointed. My reason for placing the distribution of supplies in the hands of the citizens is this : The citizens have expressed a willingness to assume control, and that is the time, in my judgment, when this work of relief should go to them. The

WRECK OF THE B. & O. STATION.

system is on a good basis; the supplies come regularly by the double method of relief contributed and of purchases regularly made; business is resuming; business men are once more hopeful; buildings are rapidly going up; work is plenty; money is paid out; and, therefore, the sooner the management of this relief is put under the control of persons residing here and knowing their own people, the better for all concerned. The great care and caution required from this time on to so manage relief as not to interfere with legitimate business, such as bakers, storekeepers, butchers, etc., constrained me to ask to be relieved from this work. I believe that the Citizens' Committee will be able rapidly to bring this relief down to those classes of persons who are incapacitated from earning a livelihood, either by age, youth, sickness, or inability to obtain work.

In view of the foregoing considerations and your acquiescence, I instructed my officers to make careful inventories of all stock on hand, and to-day, July 2d, at noon, I have conveyed all this vast property, consisting of commissary buildings, supplies on hand of every conceivable kind, at all the stations in the valley, to Captain H. H. Kuhn, a resident of Johnstown, highly capable of managing it, as was fully proved by the executive ability he displayed in organizing the relief and inspiriting the people in the early days following the disaster. The Citizens' Committee have selected him to receive this trust, and I am fully satisfied that he will not disappoint them in the performance of his duty. Captain Kuhn has been associated with me in this work from the beginning, and I have no doubt he will make many and valuable improvements in the work thus begun.

The stock on hand in the two post commissaries and the district commissaries on July 2d, 1889, at noon, and transferred to Captain H. H. Kuhn, was as follows:

Bread	104 crates.
Ham,	11 bbls.
Sugar, .	16½ "
Salt, . .	112 "
Oil, . .	5 "
Potatoes,	140 "
Vinegar, .	7½ "
Crackers, .	3 "
Rice, .	2 "
Flour, .	125 "
Flour, . .	200 sacks.
Canned Goods, .	250 cases.
Soap, ...	216 "
Mattresses, . . .	20
Coffee, .	830 lbs.
Crockery, .	2 crates.
Corn Meal,	381 sacks.
Cheese, .	14 boxes.
Butter,	85 packages.
Shoes,	425 pairs.
Blankets,	600.
Lard, .	5 packages.
Tobacco, . .	81 boxes.
Lamp Chimneys, .	10 "
Torches, .	2 "
Tinware, .	2 bbls.
Paper Bags,	5 bundles.
Pipes, . . .	40 boxes.
Oatmeal, ...	1 keg.
Beans, ...	10 bbls.
Yeast, ...	2 boxes.
Matches, ...	10 "
Cots, ...	25
Candles, ...	20 boxes.
Coffee Mills, . .	3 "
Tea, ...	2 "
Bedsteads, .	4

JOHNSTOWN, July 24th, 1889.

Colonel J. L. Spangler, Johnstown, Pa.

DEAR SIR:—We have on our sidings cars relief goods, etc., as follows :

C. St. L. & P. merchandise 9,313.
M. L. 2,370 sugar.
C. M. & St. P. 1,102 merchandise.
C. St. L. & P. 9,655 merchandise.
C. Co. 998 woodenware.
P.R.R. 41,109 meat & canned goods.
P. R. R. 49,034 merchandise.
A. V. 1,342 merchandise.
P. R. R. 41,046 canned goods, etc.
C. Co. 1,515 ear corn.
C. M. & St. Paul, 6,414.

P. R. R. 12,063 shelled corn.
C. St. L. & P. 9,405 lumber.
P. R. R. 70,425 furniture.
P. C. & St. L. 2,064 flour.
T. H. & I. U. L. 16,408 flour.
P. C. & St. L. 2,857 hams.
N. C. 7,147 stoves.
P. R. R. 1,050 furniture.
P. C. & St. L. 6,014 flue pipe.
P. C. & St. L. 6,835 disinfectant.
U. L. 3,886 merchandise.

20 small lots of goods.

Yours, etc.,

F. S. DECKERT,

Agent, P. R. R.

Also a large quantity of stoves, fixtures, cooking utensils and clothing.

Receipts were taken from Captain Kuhn for all these articles.

I made some attempt to secure a report of the value of the relief distributed in all the various forms in which it was sent here, from the 12th of June to the date of transfer of the commissary to the citizens. Of course, no accounts could have been kept by the Quartermasters, because the necessity of prompt action and the want of proper facilities prevented anything of the kind. From the meagre reports in my possession I would estimate the value of supplies distributed between the dates referred to at $600,000, and as much more from the 1st of June to the 12th, making a total of $1,200,000. This does not embrace the value of the great quantities of supplies distributed by the Red Cross, the Odd Fellows, the Masons, the veterans and private parties.

In the distribution of these supplies over an area of territory of fifteen miles to ten different district commissaries, many of which had to be reached by wagons, I was necessarily compelled to employ a large force of men. In the employment of this force I tried to prefer citizens of the valley, but owing to the fact that they were principally engaged in looking after their living friends, and searching for their lost ones, I could not rely upon their continuance in my service. The wages established were $1.50 per day for laborers, $2.00 per day for clerks and the commissaries, $3.00 per day for foreman, and the regular pay allowed officers of the National Guard according to their rank. I have made a few special contracts for extra compensation with gentlemen of experience and ability, without whose invaluable aid I could not have managed and controlled the business of my Department. Ordinarily, the wages paid might seem liberal, but when it is known that these employees in all the departments were required to seek shelter at night in freight stations, barns, damp tents and insecure buildings, I am of the opinion that the wages were reasonable in the extreme. The work was so arduous and continuous that few men who started in from the first remained with me to the last.

I have also to report that a number of people were employed at your suggestion to do relief work prior to June 12th. A special pay roll was prepared by this Department, and the amount thus paid is contained in a financial statement marked " Exhibit."

In the matter of furnishing relief, owing to the irregularity of contributions, I was compelled to purchase butter and fresh meat from time to time. I also arranged with the gentlemen composing the Pittsburgh Relief Committee to furnish me regular supplies of bread and other articles. All my requisitions upon the Pittsburgh Committee were promptly honored. Until this arrangement was perfected I experienced a great deal of trouble in meeting the wants of the people. Their prompt action and liberal supplies enabled me to fill all my requisitions and satisfy the people. I also received large consignments of boots and shoes, mattresses, bedding, stoves, sugar and other articles from the Commission. A statement of the quantities thus received is hereto attached and made a part of this report, and marked "Exhibit B."

This report does not include any expenditures on behalf .of the Commonwealth. Owing to the great proportions which the business of this Department assumed in the distribution of contributions, I was relieved from making purchases for these headquarters and the Fourteenth Regiment. I have assumed the payment of officers of the National Guard in my Department, because their services were required and rendered in the distribution of relief alone.

This Department has had nothing to do with commissary business proper, but was solely used as a branch of the service for the purpose of relief in this valley. Hence all members of the National Guard are entitled to be paid out of the relief fund. If a different view be taken of this matter hereafter it can be adjusted accordingly, and the State can make good the money thus expended.

In closing this report on the work of this Department, I cannot refrain from giving utterance to the following sentiments:

1st. That the prompt relief furnished the distressed people of the Conemaugh Valley by this Department was mainly due to the efficiency of the National Guard as an organization. Coming here as a citizen, simply to do my duty, with a slight prejudice against the propriety of intrusting so great a charity to military people, I am free to acknowledge now that the use of Quartermasters and Sergeants at the district commissaries was a great advantage, both to the Department and to the people. Every man trained to obey and anxious to make a good record was a power-ful incentive to do two men's work, and to show the best possible results. The people of the State, as well as the Guard, have reason to be proud of their record at Johnstown.

2d. Relief for Johnstown must continue for some time yet. The people are comfortably subsisted and clothed, but the question as to the furnishing of homes has not been met. This Department has made a beginning, but the end is far off yet. There is a crying need every hour of the day for all those articles which constitute the furnishing of simply a kitchen. Let the generous citizens understand that stoves, mattresses, bedding and furniture are required here in great abundance. I sincerely hope that the various municipalities will appreciate this intelligence, and not cease until the ruined homes shall be partially restored. Think of the widows made, the orphans left and the homeless many, and let your charity come.

3d. Better than all, I sincerely recommend that, instead of sending relief in the form of household furnishings, money be extended to the people in their distress, and let them purchase for themselves. The Commission of the State already appreciates the situation, and in the person of Honorable H. H. Cummin is here to afford temporary relief in this direction. But where are the holders of the various other funds raised for the benefit of the Johnstown sufferers? Are they still discussing plans and theories of equitable distribution, while the people of this valley are hourly refused those articles of necessity which afford shelter and com-fort? I am sure that if New York, Boston and other cities understood and appreciated the situation among the people here, the earliest train would bring their committees, and in twenty-four hours they would be satisfied as to the good they could accomplish with money. I will only be too glad to give data and information on application to any of the representatives of these funds with a view to afford the people the means of a plain existence. The necessity is great. Let the remedy be prompt.

4th. I am deeply grateful in the management of relief in my Department to his Excellency Governor James A. Beaver, for prompt compliance with my requisitions at a time when relief was most needed; to the gentlemen composing the Pittsburgh Committee ; to General Wiley for assistance and protection afforded this Department by the use of the troops, and to the different departments of the National Guard for invaluable assistance whenever called for.

I cannot close this report without thanking you, General Hastings, for your aid and advice during the entire management of this Department. I know full well how the fear of a famine among this people, by reason of the failure of sufficient food, occupied and distressed your mind in the first ten days of my management. Your interest and your worry never ceased until the nightly reports from this Department and the free expression of the people on all sides convinced you that there was enough and plenty for all. The people of the State may hold you in high esteem for valuable public services rendered in your capacity as citizen, soldier and statesman, but your clear head, generous nature and kindly response to the demands of the distressed at Johnstown will be the brightest record and the best achievement you can ever hope to attain in this world, however exalted and noble your future station may be.

Very respectfully,

Your obedient servant,

J. L. SPANGLER,
Lt. Col. and Asst. Com. Gen. of Pa.

Officers of the National Guard, Regular Army Officers and Civilians on Duty in the Commissary Department:

Lieutenant Colonel J. L. Spangler, Asst. Com. General.
Lieutenant J. P. Albro, R. Q. M., 13th Regiment.
Lieutenant C. E. Brown, R. Q. M., 18th Regiment.
Lieutenant W. H. Bean, 2d Cavalry, U. S. A.
Major Austin Curtin, Com. 2d Brigade.
Major W. H. Horn, Com. 3d Brigade.
Major J. S. Singer, Com. 1st Brigade.
Major H. P. Moyer, Quartermaster 3d Brigade.
Captain Gageby, U. S. A.
Captain Amos Mullen, 5th Regiment, N. G. P.
Captain J. A. Loar, 10th Regiment, N. G. P.
Lieutenant George R. Burnett, Cavalry, U. S. A.
Lieutenant F. P. Koons, R. Q. M., 1st Regiment, N. G. P.
Lieutenant Miller, U. S. A.
Lieutenant Herbert Cox, 3d Regiment, N. G. P.
Lieutenant William R. Klein, R. Q. M., 4th Regiment, N. G. P.
Lieutenant S. H. Williams, R. Q. M., 5th Regiment, N. G. P.
Lieutenant J. M. Baker, R. Q. M., 6th Regiment, N. G. P.
Lieutenant W. F. Richardson, R. Q. M., 8th Regiment, N. G. P.
Lieutenant F. L. Hutter, Ins. R. P., 8th Regiment, N. G. P.
Lieutenant G. G. Mercer, R. Q. M., 9th Regiment, N. G. P.
Lieutenant F. L. KeKee, 2d Lieutenant, 9th Regiment.
Lieutenant O. L. Nichols, R. Q. M., 12th Regiment, N. G. P.
Lieutenant A. P. Buckholdt, R. Q. M., 15th Regiment, N. G. P.
Lieutenant E. D. V. Selden, R. Q. M., 16th Regiment, N. G. P.
Lieutenant Frank Cooper, R. Adjutant, S. F
Lieutenant U. G. Condon, R. Q. M., S. F.

Non-Commissioned Officers:

W. T. Singer, Com. Sgt., 2d Brigade.
William Williams, Ord. Sgt., 1st Brigade.
F. A. Bingham, Q. M. Sgt., 1st Regiment.

DEVASTATED DISTRICT VIEWED FROM GREEN HILL.

W. W. Bell, Jr., Com. Sgt., 2d Regiment.
Charles Bowen, Q. M. Sgt., 2d Regiment.
George Ryan, Sgt., 3d Regiment.
A. J. Adrian, Com. Sgt., 4th Regiment.
Green, Sgt., 6th Regiment.
D. G. Brindle, Com. Sgt., 8th Regiment.
R. S. Magee, Q. M. Sgt., 8th Regiment.
A. E. Collamer, Q. M. Sgt., 9th Regiment.
I. A. Weill, Sgt., 9th Regiment.
J. L. Cogswell, 16th Regiment.
J. W. Packer, Q. M. Sgt., S. F.

Civilians :

S. M. Buck, Bellefonte, Pa.
J. R. Rose, Allegheny, Pa.
H. P. Harris, Bellefonte, Pa.
W. F. Reeder, Bellefonte, Pa.
H. C. Quigley, Bellefonte, Pa.
H. S. Walker, Norristown, Pa.
C. C. Berry.
Frank Snyder, Clearfield, Pa.
H. P. Bush, Bellefonte, Pa.
J. D. Hicks, Esq., Altoona, Pa.

Statement showing supplies furnished this Department for distribution by certain Relief Committees.

Supplies shipped by the Citizens' Permanent Relief Committee of Philadelphia and forwarded to General Hastings:

6,927 pairs of shoes, assorted sizes.	12 gross hair brushes.
1,025 cots.	12 " hair combs.
100 cots donated.	12 " tooth brushes.
1,125 pillows.	20 " medicated paper.
250 sheets.	1,949 feet stove-pipe, elbows and joints.
125 pillow cases.	517 stoves.

10

121 mattresses.	512 cook pots.
510 pairs of blankets.	537 fry pans.
604 doz. hosiery and underwear.	470 tea kettles.

3 large tents.

Supplies shipped to General Hastings from June 18th to 27th on requisition through Governor Beaver:

96 bushels beans.	45,615 pounds ham.
1,000 gallons oil.	2,860 " lard.
952 pounds tea.	1,000 cases canned goods, 2,000 doz.
3,000 " candles.	20 boxes yeast cakes.
99,757 " sugar.	6,338 pounds rice.
10,337 " butter.	551 gallons vinegar.
19,586 " cheese.	312 pounds pepper.

23,965 pounds coffee.

Supplies shipped by the Pittsburgh Committee:

26 barrels bacon.	25 boxes beans.
1,000 gallons sirup.	25 " corn.
100 boxes cheese.	84 " corn beef.
50 " tomatoes.	50 " coffee.

15,000 pounds of bread daily from S. S. Marvin & Co. from June 15th to June 27th.

Other supplies were furnished by the Pittsburgh Committee, of which I have no record.

J. L. Spangler, A. C. G.

Statement.

To cash per item, ...		$28,720 67
By amount paid on pay rolls for labor, . .	$15,088 53	
Cash paid Lieutenant Colonel Gray from sale of relief goods, ...	61 20	
Cash paid Colonel Gray by Q. M. from collections from contractors for sale of relief goods,	2,776 37	

Cash amount paid labor by vouchers,			$3,925 82	
"	"	for provisions, .	5,637 27	
"	"	freight and express,	1,012 13	
"	"	lumber and hardware, .	57 10	
"	"	soap, ...	135 00	
"	"	butchers' tools,	19 75	
"	"	kitchen tools,	7 50	
				$28,720 67

4.—HOSPITALS.

"*Sweet mercy is nobility's true badge.*"—SHAKESPEARE.

FROM the entrance of sin into the world, the care of the sick, the suffering and dying has been a duty that has demanded the attention of the living, and has required considerable time and labor even in ordinary times. When the Johnstown flood had spent itself, it left the city not only in need of food, raiment and shelter, but the hundreds of sick and shocked people needed immediate medical attention, which was clearly impossible without greater hospital facilities and a larger medical staff than Johnstown could supply. Some accommodations for the treatment of the sick and wounded were necessary. We had but one hospital in the city, which is a private institution belonging to the Cambria Iron Company, and located on Prospect Hill. It was soon filled to overflowing, and good work was done there under direction of physicians from Altoona and Philadelphia. It was soon apparent that another hospital must be established, and, accordingly, on Saturday afternoon, June 1st, the Bedford Street Hospital was created. Our telegraphic communication being destroyed, a messenger was sent on horseback to Stoyestown, by Dr. J. C. Sheridan, bearing messages to be sent from there to Pittsburgh for hospital equipments, consisting of cots, mattresses, pillows, medicines and other necessities.

The first patient taken into this hospital was recovered from the wreck at daylight on Sunday morning. Supposing him to be dead, the carriers took him to the Fourth Ward Morgue, where, discovering that life was not extinct, we summoned a physician who sent him to the hospital. By the united efforts of physicians and nurses he rallied and became conscious, but he died the next day of congestion of the lungs, the result of exposure. The hospital at this time was placed under the immediate charge of Dr. Foster, of Pittsburgh. He was early in the morning assisted by Dr. White, of Connellsville, and afterward by Dr. James, of Ebensburg. The latter physician came to the city early on Saturday morning, and had already done admirable work at the Club House and the Morrell Institute, where his services had been demanded. Later in the day other physicians arrived, all of whom rendered invaluable service.

By 2 o'clock, on Sabbath, less than twenty-four hours after the sending of Dr. Sheridan's order, the hospital equipment arrived from Pittsburgh. This I am glad to cite as one of the striking examples of the intelligence with which the Pittsburgh Committee, so early constituted, recognized the necessities of the hour, and supplied every hospital want with that celerity and liberality which are characteristic of the people of that noble city.

By the time the hospital equipment arrived, every bench and counter, and even the floor itself, was full of sick and wounded, who were brought from all parts of the city. They were soon made as comfortable as possible under the circumstances. There was such a constant demand upon the enduring powers of the physicians that not one of them could bear up under the strain for many days in succession, and consequently frequent changes of directors were necessary. Dr. Foster having occasion to leave the work, Dr. Oldshoe, of Pittsburgh, took his place. He was ably assisted by physicians from Pittsburgh, Connellsville, Altoona,

Phillipsburg, Philadelphia and other places. Dr. Oldshoe worked incessantly. Under his intelligent direction the hospital soon assumed that peaceful quiet which, with his watchful and tender care, did so much to soothe the dying and to inspirit those who were recovering. Although suffering from a fatal disease himself, Dr. Oldshoe neither ate nor slept until all intrusted to his vigilant care were properly tended and made comfortable. This self-sacrificing man remarked, when about to return to Pittsburgh, that his physical condition was such that he could not expect long life, and that if he had not done all that he might have done for our suffering people, he at least had the consciousness that he had done the best he knew.

During Dr. Oldshoe's management a competent corps of out-door physicians was organized, who responded promptly to calls from all parts of the city. Branch offices were also established at different points, and supplies furnished them from Bedford Street headquarters, to which Mr. William De-Wolfe had conveyed from Pittsburgh a liberal supply of drugs. About this time, Dr. Wm. B. Lowman, one of our most skillful resident physicians, was made Medical Director of all the Hospitals, and his extensive acquaintance with the city and its wants greatly facilitated the work.

Dr. Oldshoe was succeeded by Dr. T. McCann, of Pittsburgh, whose skillful management continued and extended the noble work of the Bedford Street Hospital. Dr. McCann, after a few days' efficient service, was relieved by Dr. Joseph Dixon, of Pittsburgh, who remained in charge until affairs had assumed such shape that the local physicians could give the necessary attention, when those from a distance withdrew. The great work done by these excellent men and their assistants deserves highest mention, and the Johnstown people will never forget their aid and kindness during the distressing experiences after the flood.

When the visiting physicians withdrew, Dr. J. C. Sheridan, of this city, "a worthy son of a worthy sire," assumed charge of the headquarters until the hospital closed.

As already intimated, those who preceded him rendered most difficult and self-sacrificing services that honored their noble profession while they relieved the suffering. Dr. Sheridan shone even among this number for his unwearied, unremunerated and skillful attention during the days and nights of the mournful months succeeding the flood. His name must adorn the annals of the medical profession among those who recognize this supreme law of mercy to the suffering, and who have generously employed their skill in their behalf.

Many estimable women gave their services as nurses, and aided very materially in the good work, and are entitled to the highest praise and gratitude of the survivors and their friends. Among these "elect ladies," Miss Rose Young, Miss Kizzie Vance, Miss Reed, Miss Vickroy and others, and the Sisters of St. Joseph's Convent, are deserving of honorable mention. Miss Sallie Stroup, since gone to her reward, was also of this number.

The Dispensary in the Hospital was intelligently conducted by Charles Griffith. His incessant attention to this, necessitating neglect of his own affairs, added materially to his great losses already sustained. When he withdrew, Charles Young took charge and continued in the good work until the hospital closed.

From June the 2d until July the 3d, when the hospital was discontinued, there were received and treated over 500 patients. When the hospital became crowded the convalescents were sent to various places. For some time, a car load of patients was daily sent to Pittsburgh, where they were distributed among the hospitals of that city. Others were sent to friends in the country and to neighboring towns. Some were conveyed to each of the following cities: Cumberland, Baltimore, Philadelphia and

Boston. There were over 300 surgical cases. If this seems to be a small number in such an unspeakable disaster, it must be remembered that the great majority of the victims did not survive the flood. There were during this time in the out-door department over 3,000 patients, and over 5,000 prescriptions were filled.

In conveying patients to Pittsburgh and elsewhere, the Baltimore and Ohio Railroad, through Mr. J. V. Patton, the efficient superintendent, kindly furnished each day a hospital car, which, of course, did much to alleviate the suffering incident to such a journey.

5.—THE WORK OF THE STATE BOARD OF HEALTH.

By BENJAMIN LEE, A.M., M.D., Ph.D., *Secretary and Executive Officer.*

"On the thirty-first day of May and the first day of June, one thousand eight hundred and eighty-nine, the State Board of Health of Pennsylvania was holding one of its Sanitary Conventions in the city of Pittsburgh.

"If the Board had stationed a brass band at the door of the hall and put up a placard announcing that the Brown-Sequard Elixir would be administered at a dollar a head, no doubt the sessions of the Convention would have been crowded to overflowing with aspirants for longevity and their curious friends; but as it had no higher aim than to teach the citizens of the two great cities whose beautiful bridges span the Allegheny, how they might prolong and bless their lives and those of their children by simple attention to certain rules of domestic and civic sanitation, the attendance was extremely meagre. It is fair to say, however, that what was wanting in numbers was made up in intelligence, and that through the kind assistance of the enterprising press of the city the audience was multiplied a thousandfold. Whatever may have been the extent and character of the labors of the Board during the four months which followed—and which it is proposed here briefly to sketch—in the Board's own estimation, so far as final results are concerned, this two days' educational work was the more important of the two. For the still diminishing attendance of the second day, however, an unusual reason existed. The river had risen suddenly to an unusual height. The bridges and banks were covered with thousands, watching the immense masses of wreckage that swept down its seething surface ; there were rumors that dead bodies had been taken out ; a sense of intense uneasiness pervaded the air ; railroad communication with the East was cut off ; members feared that they would be subjected to serious delay and inconvenience in reaching their homes. There were vague reports of loss of life, but nothing definite could be ascertained.

"The papers of the following morning, however, which was that of Sunday, contained authentic intelligence which left no room for doubt that a calamity of most appalling magnitude had visited the little mountain city of Johnstown, and that this calamity imposed a grave and urgent responsibility on the State Board of Health. An informal meeting of the Board was hastily called. A resolution of sympathy with the survivors was adopted. The entire quarter's appropriation to the Board, amounting to the paltry sum of $500, was voted for the prosecution of sanitary work in the flood-swept region, and a member of the Board, Professor George G. Groff, of the Bucknell University, was instructed to accompany the Secretary to the scene of the catastrophe, and co-operate with him in taking measures to prevent disastrous consequences to the public health from the exposure of such immense numbers of dead bodies of human beings and of animals as were reported to have been destroyed, as well as from the unnatural conditions surrounding those who had escaped with life alone. The Secretary desires to take this public opportunity of testifying

RUINS OF THE SISTERS' HOUSE.

to the faithfulness and zeal with which Dr. Groff discharged this onerous duty, and to the wisdom and sound judgment which characterized his suggestions in the numerous emergencies which hourly confronted us. It was evident that whatever suffering there might be at the scene of the disaster, the immediate obligation resting on the Board was to protect the water supply of the two great cities of Pittsburgh and Allegheny from the most horrible of all pollutions—that resulting from the fact that hundreds of corpses and of carcasses were decomposing in the streams whence it was drawn. Accordingly the first stop was made at Nineveh, about nine miles below Johnstown, where 162 dead bodies were found awaiting identification and transportation, and numbers more were being hourly brought in. Steps were here taken to secure by telegraph the immediate and full co-operation of the authorities of all the counties bordering on the streams implicated, in the work of reclaiming the dead and of burning carcasses and debris. Early the following morning the swollen Conemaugh was crossed in a skiff, and arrangements were made for facilitating the identification and early burial of the twenty-five or thirty bodies which had been recovered on that side of the river. We returned by the first train that passed up in the morning and were carried to Morrellville, whence we walked to Johnstown.

"Putting ourselves in communication with Adjutant-General D. H. Hastings, who had assumed command of the volunteer relief movement, and whom we had apprised of our coming, by wire, the night before, we obtained passes from Sheriff Steinman, were ferried over the Conemaugh, and proceeded at once to the headquarters of the local committee, of which Mr. Moxham was the efficient chairman. We notified him that the Board would assume entire control of all sanitary operations, and requested that five thousand pounds of copperas and two thousand five hundred pounds of chloride of lime should be at once ordered from Pittsburgh. The chemist of the Woodvale Chemical Works, which had fortunately escaped the flood, had already given the secretary *carte blanche* to procure all the copperas that might be needed, but the problem was to get it, there being no available teams and the road being in great measure washed away. The Secretary also announced the presence of the Board to Mr. Horrell, the Burgess of Johnstown, and to the Rev. David J. Beale, who was in charge of the Morgue in the Fourth Ward school-house and who was officially designated to the general supervision of that branch of the work. Chaotic as the condition still was, it was a matter of surprise that within twenty-four hours after locomotion had become possible, following the most crushing and paralyzing of modern catastrophes, so much of system had been introduced. A local police force was on duty, armed to some extent with shot-guns, but principally with base-ball clubs obtained from the wreck of a store. Detailed forces were working day and night reclaiming the dead; several commissaries were supplying provisions and clothing with generous hands—as was perfectly proper in such an emergency, not with scrutinizing eyes— to famishing and shivering crowds, principally of women and children. The local committee had its sub-committees to attend to each branch of the work. I doubt if in any other country in the world such a spectacle of prompt organization, in the face of overwhelming disaster, could have been witnessed.

"A survey of the situation showed that the Board was confronted by a task of gigantic dimensions. Johnstown proper was partly a lake, partly several small streams, partly a vast sandy plain, and partly clusters of more or less ruined houses. Around among, between, inside and on top of these houses, wherever the rushing torrent had been checked, were piled masses of wreckage; trunks of mighty trees, household furniture, houses whole and in fragments, bridges, locomotives and railroad cars, hundreds of tons of mud and gravel. Thickly strewn through it all were hundreds of corpses and carcasses. The only communication between this section and the Pennsylvania Railroad and the village of Peelorville on the north, and Kernville on the south, was across swollen torrents in skiffs, which required constant bailing to keep them above water. From the stone bridge of the Pennsylvania Road, for a distance of half a mile, no river could be seen, simply a dense mass of drift from twenty to fifty feet deep, apparently inextricable, bound together with miles of wire, here blazing and there smoldering, and enveloping the bridge in a cloud of nauseating vapor and smoke, giving unmistakable evidence of the presence of burning flesh. Not a thoroughfare was passable for a team, and very few for a horse. Not only was the work immense, but the difficulties in the way of its accomplishment were such as can scarcely be comprehended by those who did not see them. On the first day little could be done beyond a thorough survey of the town and study of the situation. Locomotion was difficult, the mud deep, the streets obstructed often to the roofs of houses, the rain incessant. On the second day, however, the secretary was fortunate in meeting his friend, Dr. Webster Lowman, of Johnstown, who introduced him to Dr. W. E. Matthews, Chairman of the Sanitary Committee, appointed at a meeting of the surviving physicians of the place. Notwithstanding Dr. Matthews was suffering from a fracture of the ribs, he expressed his willingness to devote himself entirely to the work of the Board. He was accordingly appointed chief deputy inspector, with instructions to enroll a sanitary corps, to consist of deputy inspectors and laborers, and to select at once a depot for disinfectants. The headquarters of the Board were temporarily established in the same room with the local committee, the dining-room of the only tavern not swept away by the flood, and known as the Fourth Ward Hotel. The advantage of this situation consisted in the opportunity for immediate and constant communication with the local committees, each of which had its table in the room, and use of telegraphic facilities and messenger service. The noise and confusion which reigned here, however, were by no means conducive to deliberate judgment and judicious arrangement of business, and as soon as possible a room was secured on the opposite side of the street (Adam Street), which continued to be the office of the Board until it was provided with a commodious building of its own in the centre of the town by the kind ness of the Finance Committee. The organization of the sanitary corps was at first almost entirely voluntary. A number of physicians who had hastened to the stricken town from all parts of Pennsylvania and neighboring States to proffer their services to the sick and injured, finding that they were not needed in that capacity, offered them to the Board. They did yeoman's service in the discovery of the dead, and in dragging out and burning dead animals. The exposing and exhausting character of this labor cannot be overstated any more than its importance can be overestimated. Among those who thus distinguished themselves and to whom Johnstown owes a debt of gratitude were Dr. Fussell, of Manayunk; Dr. Smith, of Philadelphia; Dr. Marvell, of Atlantic City; Dr. McGrew, Dr. Philips, and others.

"Each of these gentlemen was placed in charge of a gang of laborers, and accomplished much good. On the same day that this organization was effected the Secretary received the following telegram from Dr. John B. Hamilton, Supervising Surgeon General of the United States Marine Hospital Service:

"'Washington, D. C., June 4th, 1889.—Dr. Benjamin Lee, Secretary State Board of Health, Johnstown:—The Bureau is ready to render any aid in its power, if you desire it. I have ordered Dr. Carrington from Pittsburgh, and he will confer with you. You may retain him for a few days if you need his services; otherwise he will regain his station after reporting.

HAMILTON, *Surgeon General.'*

"Dr. Carrington reported the day following, and was at once put on duty in charge of a corps of disinfectors, proving himself a most efficient aid. In reply to Surgeon General Hamilton's offer of aid a request was made for disinfectants, and all that were available in Washington were at once forwarded, as well as a large consignment of copperas from Baltimore. In a subsequent communication Surgeon General Hamilton mentioned the deep interest taken by President Harrison in the work of the Board, and a suggestion by the latter that deportation of women and children, so far as practicable, would be expedient. This step was urged by the Board in one of its official bulletins, and with evident good results.

"In the latter part of the same week Dr. Hamilton visited Johnstown personally and made many valuable suggestions for the organization of the force and the prosecution of the work.

"Co-incidently with the establishment of the sanitary corps a communication was addressed to Governor Beaver, describing the condition, detailing the steps which had already been taken, and setting forth the greatness of the undertaking and the necessity for ample pecuniary provision. Owing to the fact that all lines of communication were interrupted, this information took some time to reach him.

"A most acceptable and efficient addition to our force arrived the day following, a large detail of sanitary police from Pittsburgh, under the charge of Superintendent of Public Health Baker, and of a similar smaller squad from Allegheny, sent with instructions from Health Officer Madley.

"These men were too valuable of course to be employed as common laborers. A few of them were set to work as disinfectors under Dr. Carrington. The majority were detailed to make a house-to-house inspection of inhabited houses, with instructions to report all foul accumulations and all cases of sickness, to inform the occupants how to dispose of offensive material, and where to apply for disinfectants. As soon as it could be obtained, a cart accompanied those forces with disinfectants for distribution. The Pittsburgh force was retained for this purpose in Johnstown, and the Allegheny force was sent over to Kernville, on the south side of Stony Creek River. The service rendered by these trained sanitary officers was most timely, and was subsequently recognized by the Board in an appropriate resolution of thanks. The following incident will indicate the difficulties under which work was accomplished during this early period of the operations. The first disinfectant available was copperas. To use this in many places it was necessary to dissolve it in water, and to have vessels of some kind from which to sprinkle it. But not a utensil of any kind could be found. Accordingly, the Secretary, accompanied by Dr. Carrington with his squad of Pittsburgh disinfectors, clambered over the wreckage on Main Street, often up to the third story windows, and made a descent on wrecked stores here and there until they succeeded in finding a dozen tin coffee pots, more or less buried in mud, half a dozen watering pots of different sizes and a wash boiler. Supplied with these, they returned in triumph, the names of the owners of the stores and of the articles taken from each having been carefully noted. The wash boiler was filled from one of the hydrants which were running freely all over the town, and placed upon a fire in which horses were burning. A solution was soon made and applied to their comrades, deeply buried in the debris, whose carcasses were an impediment to the progress of the work.

"The condition of the rivers as a source of water-supply still caused the Board so much anxiety that, on the afternoon of the 6th of June, the Secretary, after a careful inspection of the drift at the stone bridge, which satisfied him of the impossibility of removing it by the means and force then available, and also of the absolute necessity of such removal from sanitary considerations,

proceeded to Pittsburgh, and on the following day despatched a
gang of wreckers, consisting of two squads with a foreman over
each and a superintendent, to proceed to the mouth of the Kis-
kiminitas, and carefully patrol both banks of that stream and of
the Conemaugh up to Johnstown, removing and reclaiming all
dead bodies and burning all dead animals and all drift heaps which
could not be dragged apart. A similar expedition was organized
and sent down the Ohio as far as the State line on the steamer
'Tide.' On the same day a telegram was sent to Governor
Beaver, stating that 4,000 men were needed to work on the drift
on the stone bridge. A written communication was also addressed to him, accurately describing the condition at Johnstown
and along the rivers, declaring, in the name of the Board, such a
condition to be a nuisance prejudicial to the public health. It
represented the nuisances beyond the power of the local authorities to remove, and requested him at once, as Chief Executive of
the Commonwealth, to employ such force as might be necessary
for the work.

"When the surviving resident physicians were in a condition
to devote time and service to others than their own families they
were assigned places on the Sanitary Corps, and the volunteers
from a distance were reluctantly permitted to retire.

"Dr. Wagoner well says in one of his reports: 'These
gentlemen in leaving took with them the respect and gratitude of
all who were benefited by their labors.'

"Other gentlemen from a distance, who rendered very efficient
aid during the early period, were Dr. Spencer M. Free, Medical
Inspector to the Board for the Western Slope District, who was
temporarily placed in charge of the entire region below the stone
bridge, at that time almost cut off from communication with
Johnstown, and Dr. R. Lowry Tibbet, Medical Inspector for the
Cumberland, who did admirable work in inspecting the more in-

accessible districts and reporting their needs. The Board were also cheered by the presence of the Secretary of the State Board of Health of Ohio, Dr. C. O. Probst, who in company with Dr. Carrington undertook the somewhat difficult task of inspecting the three sources of the water-supply of Johnstown among the mountains.

"The entire region, including the outlying boroughs as far up the Conemaugh as South Fork, about nine miles to the eastward, up the Stony Creek to Moxham, two miles to the southward, and down the Conemaugh to Nineveh, nine miles to the westward, was now divided into twelve districts, to each one of which an inspector was assigned.

"Each inspector was required to make a daily round of his territory and see that the different gangs of men, each under its foreman, were working faithfully and judiciously; to direct the immediate removal of all decaying animal or vegetable matter, to indicate where disinfectants were especially needed, and to instruct the people how to use them in cellars, yards and outhouses. At the end of each day a written report was made by each, including any new cases of sickness which might have been discovered. On these reports the work of the day following was laid out and instructions given before the men started for work. An accurate knowledge of the health of the entire valley was therefore always possessed by the Board.

"Each of these districts had its office and depot for disinfectants. In regard to the use of the latter, Dr. Matthews says in his report to the Secretary: 'The distribution of disinfectants was conducted with proper system. At first, stations were established and placards placed throughout the valley, informing the people that they would be furnished with disinfectants free of cost. The man in charge of a disinfecting station carefully instructed the people in the use of whatever was given them.'

ROMAN CATHOLIC CHURCH OF ST. JOHN—BURNED DURING THE FLOOD.

"Sub-stations were also established in large districts, where disinfectants were easily obtained. Deputy Medical Inspector Wagoner, whose district was the large and crowded portion of the town known as Kernville, thus reports: 'Large quantities of disinfectants were taken away by the people and used, and still larger quantities were distributed by the office from house to house at regular intervals. During the entire time the office was open, one gang of laborers was employed in sprinkling disinfectants over the entire district. Fifteen supply stations were established and from these they worked so that they covered the entire district twice a week. A gang was also detailed to gather up and burn the bedding, garments and carpets which had been ruined by the water and were thickly scattered throughout the entire wreck. An immense quantity of this material was destroyed. Each day's work averaged twelve wagon.loads.' This statement is measurably true of all the other districts, although it is no disparagement to say that among many earnest workers Dr. Wagoner was conspicuous for the zeal, fidelity and sound judgment with which his work was conducted. While on the subject of disinfectants it may not be uninteresting to interrupt the thread of the narrative and state the amount of disinfectants received by the Board. Other consignments undoubtedly came to Johnstown, which never reached our office. These figures represent only what have been accounted for and acknowledged :

> 4,000 barrels quick-lime.
> 500 barrels chloride of lime.
> 1,700 bottles bromine.
> 110 barrels Bullen's Disinfectant.
> 100 tons copperas.
> 100 gallons carbolic acid.
> 3 carboys muriatic acid.
> 40 gallons nitric acid.

11

180 barrels rosin.
200 barrels pine tar.
73 barrels pitch.
5 barrels liquid Phenyle.
15 barrels Sanitas.
3 barrels Phenique.
100 kegs Utopia.
10 carboys embalming fluid.
720 bottles sod. hypochlorite.
700 bottles Platt's chlorides.
116 pounds corrosive sublimate.
100 Werther's Disinfectant.
50 bottles Pennsylvania R. R. Co.'s disinfectant.
100 bottles Purity.
100 bottles bromo-chloralum.

A cargo of Quibells Brothers' Disinfectant, valued at five hundred pounds sterling ($2,500).

"All of the above were donations, with the exception of 100 barrels Bullen's Disinfectant, the bromine and a portion of the copperas. The rosin and tar, gifts of citizens of Wilmington, N. C., were used in cremating dead animals, and proved a most acceptable contribution, not only greatly facilitating combustion, but also entirely neutralizing the foul odors, while the tar was a great assistance in burning obstinate stumps and roots. Bullen's Disinfectant was used principally in the morgues. The donation of ten barrels, which arrived the day after the flood, proved of great service, from the fact that it was all ready for use, which at a time when there were absolutely no utensils of any kind for mixing or dissolving chemicals was a matter of great importance.

"The proprietary disinfectants generally, being in comparatively small packages, easily handled and accompanied by printed directions, were given to the people for home use, with very good results. The great dependence of our disinfectors, where putrescent masses and intensely foul cellars and privies required heroic treatment, however, was bromine. It is difficult to see how the work could have proceeded without it at some points. Quibell's Disinfectant was used extensively in a street-sprinkler for laying the dust, which it at the same time deodorized, leaving a peculiar freshness in the air. "Sanitas" was used in the same way with similar results. The chloride of lime, quick-lime and copperas were strewn thickly over surfaces from which filth had been removed, in cellars and on the dumped filth. Carbolic acid was also used effectively over large surfaces and in closets. It may be safely said that disinfection was never so thoroughly put to the test before, and that it came out of the test triumphantly.

"Of the condition which confronted us Inspector Matthews says: 'The homes that were not swept away were left in the most insanitary condition imaginable. The flood water was heavily charged with every kind of filth, and whatever this water touched it contaminated. As a result, every house in the flooded district was filled, in most cases to the second floor, with most offensive matter. There was not a place which the flood touched where a man could lay his head with safety.'

"Inspector Wagoner, after describing the limits of his district, says: 'After the waters subsided, this extensive district was covered with a compact mass of debris, under which lay scores of dead in the slum and filth that fell from the burdened waters;' and yet the same gentleman is able, in the latter part of his report, to bear this gratifying testimony:

"'With the concentration of 2,500 people into 380 houses, all subjected to intense mental strain by reason of the calamity and the radical changes in their habits of life, it is very gratifying to know that during the continuance of the Board's operations not a case of infectious disease developed in the district which could be attributed to bad sanitary conditions.' During the first ten days following the flood, Johnstown was favored with low temperature clouded skies and frequent rains. These, while they produced much discomfort and gave rise to a certain amount of rheumatism and pneumonia, were of great advantage in delaying decomposition. As soon, however, as a hot sun developed the germs of putrefaction and the large force, employed by the Pittsburgh Relief Committee and subsequently by the State, began to uncover numerous houses, cellars and yards, reeking with filth and often containing dead bodies and carcasses even in parlors and bedrooms, the necessity for a rapid enlargement of the purely sanitary work became manifest, if pestilence was to be averted. New men were therefore daily enrolled until at one time the entire force numbered 285. This was the strength of the corps for about two weeks, when it became possible to begin to reduce the number of inspectors as well as of workmen, so that on the 9th of July the roster was as follows :

Five medical inspectors.
Seven clerks.
Eleven foremen.
Four cooks.
Six messengers.
One hundred and twenty laborers.
The teams at work were as follows :
Five two-horse teams.
Two one-horse teams.
Eighteen carts.
Three saddle horses.

"The Board built its own barracks and stable, and, as soon as communications were opened, furnished its own commissariat. At first it was of course compelled, like all other bodies, to depend upon the charity of the relief commissaries to feed its men. Other objects to which special details of men were assigned were :

"The collection and destruction of garbage. To such an extent did the accumulation of filth of this nature prevail around the laborers' camps that it was found necessary to appoint a special Inspector of Camps. This duty was conscientiously performed by Dr. C. Sheridan.

"The construction of public latrines and their daily disinfection. Seventy-five of these necessary adjuncts to a civilized community were provided and cared for.

"The cleaning of offensive cellars, more than two hundred of which were excavated by our men. Subsequently the State contractors performed this duty ; but in all cases the sanitary corps was called upon to disinfect, both during and after excavation. The entire number of cellars thus treated has probably been upwards of twelve hundred.

"In response to the declaration of nuisance and request for means to abate it, Governor Beaver, who was then officially visiting the Naval Academy at Annapolis, Md., returned to Harrisburg and conferred with the financial officers of the State. He came from there to Johnstown, and, after a careful survey of the situation, decided to place the entire work of removal of wreckage under the supervision of the Board. This was done with little delay, the Relief Committee withdrawing its forces on the tenth day of June. The day following Adjutant-General Hastings reported for instructions to the Secretary. At frequent intervals an inspection of the entire.territory was made by General Hastings, Colonel H. T. Douglass, the Chief Engineer in charge, and the Secretary, and the course of operations decided upon. The relations of these officers to the Board were of the most friendly nature, and it is a pleasure to the Secretary to have an opportunity of thus publicly acknowledging their unfailing courtesy, and their readiness to comply with his suggestions. With not less justice can the same recognition be made of the ready and efficient services of Captain

George C. Hamilton, who, on the withdrawal of General Hastings
and the reduction of the force, on the eighth day of July, assumed
the position of Chief Engineer in charge. Indeed, the State of
Pennsylvania may well be proud of a National Guard which, at a
moment's notice, could place in the field such officers and such
men as prosecuted the work and kept the peace at Johnstown,
under circumstances demanding so unusual a degree of prudence,
judgment, scientific attainment and Christian forbearance.

"Independently of their official connection with the Board as
inspectors, the physicians of Johnstown were ever ready to aid it
by their counsel both as individuals and through associate action
in the County Medical Society. It was owing to their advice that,
at as early a moment as possible, the deposits which were removed
from the streets and yards were carted to the point below the
town instead of being dumped over the river-bank. An idea of
the immense amount of this material thus removed may be gained
when it is said that the level of this entire area, covering many
acres, has been raised at least fifteen feet.

"The first necessity of the people of Johnstown, like ship-
wrecked sailors on a desert island, when they found themselves still
living after the bewildering catastrophe, was food. This the volunteer relief committees, and notably that of Altoona, among the first
in the field, generously supplied. The second was shelter. This
want was attempted to be met by the Pittsburgh Relief Commission,
who ordered ready-made houses from Chicago. The first speci-
mens of these which arrived proved to be simply little shelters
intended for the use of sportsmen during the summer, and, both
on account of their diminutive size and their insufficient protection against inclement weather, the Secretary felt compelled to
protest against their adoption as homes for families. A larger
and more substantial pattern soon followed, and, by placing
a large and a small one together, a tolerably comfortable tem-

porary dwelling was arranged. This, however, was evidently capable of accommodating only a very small family, and the Relief Commission therefore authorized the construction of a larger two-story house to accommodate households in which there were several children. Subsequently, Miss Clara Barton, the indefatigable head of the National Red Cross Association, proposed the erection of several large boarding-houses in which families and women might have privacy and protection. But the proposal to erect dwellings of any kind at once brought the Board face to face with the question: 'How far will it be safe for families to occupy houses placed upon this filth-saturated soil?' At first the Secretary felt it his duty to taboo the entire flooded district of Johnstown proper, including a large portion of Kernville. Little by little the restricted regions were narrowed, but it was not until the middle of August that it was felt to be wise to allow habitations to be placed indiscriminately on former foundations or house-lots. This fact has been alluded to in order to correct an impression which seems to have prevailed that the people of Johnstown were themselves unnecessarily tardy and unenterprising in the matter of rebuilding. Another cause, and an entirely reasonable one, for a certain amount of hesitancy in erecting houses on the plateau between the rivers, has been the well-founded apprehension that the elevation of the river-beds by flood-deposits would render this district liable to be overflowed by every slight rise in the streams. As a natural sequence to this came the suggestion that an official survey might lead to the establishment of a new grade for this entire portion of the city, which would place a building erected on the old level at a disadvantage. The importance of these grave engineering problems cannot be overestimated, and it is to be hoped that the General Government will recognize the duty of attempting their solution.

"With the double purpose of giving the people information as to the precautions to be observed in order to preserve their health amid the trying circumstances which surrounded them, and of allaying the apprehensions excited both in Johnstown and at a distance by the reckless misrepresentations of irresponsible news-mongers as to the prevalence of pestilential disease, bulletins were frequently issued and circulars distributed. It is estimated that from twenty-five to thirty thousand pages of printed matter were thus disseminated through the valley, in addition to the wide circulation given many of these documents by the daily press of the place. In order to be thoroughly acquainted with the exact state of the health of the people, and of the conditions under which they were living, a sanitary survey was made of all the boroughs from South Fork to Nineveh, according to a form proposed by Professor Groff, which recorded the number of rooms in each house, how many families and how many individuals were living in it, how many of these were sick, the character of the drainage, and many other points bearing on their hygienic needs. In addition to this, blank forms for a daily report were sent to each hospital and each physician, on which return was made every evening of the number of cases under treatment, of new cases, of the nature of the diseases under which they were suffering, and of deaths. The Board was, therefore, always in possession of accurate information as to the prevalence or absence of epidemic disease. The writer may perhaps be pardoned for closing this description of the work accomplished by the State in the interest of the public health at Johnstown with the introduction of two personal allusions, which have a certain value illustrative of the history of the flood.

"Wandering along Prospect Hill on the evening of the day of his arrival, weary wet, and hungry, and, like many others, without a place where to lay his head, he was hailed from the porch of one of the trim little cottages which line the front street with an invitation to enter. An appetizing odor of frying ham enforced

WRECKED ENGINES BELOW THE ROUND HOUSE AT EAST CONEMAUGH.

the hospitable invitation which, needless to say, was cheerfully
accepted. The house was filled with a strangely composed company. Two or three rescued women, pitiably pale, and with eyes
ghastly at the flood-horror, the kind hostess with babe in arms
and a little one clinging to her skirts, a divine, a physician, a lawyer, two or three merchants, all members of the noble Altoona
Relief Committee, with a brave woman, an attachee of the same
energetic and devoted body. The little dining-room was too
small to hold them all; so, having supped in squads, they assembled on the porch. And there, looking down on the scene of
total desolation at their feet, which three days before was a flour-
ishing city—a scene part flood, part desert-waste, part ruin and
wreck fitfully lighted up by the colossal funeral pyre at the stone
bridge, by the numerous piles of blazing drift in which horses
were consuming, by the distant watch-fires of the homeless refugees on the mountain-side, and by the flickering torches which
disclosed the dark waters of the Styx-like stream, across which
a flitting, shadowy Charon could be fancied ferrying the dead—
they listened to the story of the great flood that swept down the
valley of the Conemaugh. The narrator was their hostess and
the hero her husband. 'The day before the flood,' she began,
'he had borrowed my brother's horse and buggy. My brother
had a store down in the town there. It stood not far from
where you see those lights where they're bringing that body
across to the depot. The next morning when we got up we saw
the streets all under water and the river still rising, and he thought
my brother might need the horse at his home up the Conemaugh.
But, seeing that the buggy would be of no use, he just went on
horse-back. As he came down the side of the mountain to get to
the road up above where my brother lived, he saw, by the way the
flood was coming down and the stuff it was bringing, that the dam
must be washing over; so he started full speed down to my

brother's house. When he reached it, who should he see but my
sister-in-law, with her little child by the hand, standing in the door-
way. He called to her to hand him the baby and jump up behind,
for God's sake, for the dam was bursting. 'You don't mean it,'
says she; 'you're only fooling me.'—'No; it's true, I tell you.
Jump up! only be quick.'

"'She saw then that he was in deadly earnest, but, instead of
obeying him, she said, 'Wait; I must go and call my husband,' and
rushed into the house. That minute my husband heard an awful,
crashing noise, and, looking up the river, saw all the rocks and trees
coming down. He knew he'd be lost if he waited, and could do
them no good; so he dug his heels into the horse's sides and just
got up the hill in time. When he turned to look back, the house
was gone—not a sign of it left—and they all swept away in it.'

"It was growing chilly, and the company, shivering, and with
a common impulse, silently sought the lighted room.   .   .   .

"The difficulty of passing the numerous faithful but somewhat
indiscriminating guards, during the first day or two, was vexatious,
and often interfered with the discharge of important duties. Even
with a scribbled pass in every pocket, detentions sometimes occurred. This the writer succeeded in remedying in the following
way. In the Pennsylvania Railroad Station, which was morgue
within and commissary without, and the floor of which was covered
with nude bodies of victims of all ages and of both sexes, he found
a small can of black paint and a brush designed for marking freight.
Tearing a strip from a piece of muslin used for enfolding the dead,
he rudely printed on it 'Sanitary Corps,' and pinned it on the front
of his hat. This worked like a charm, and, until he succeeded in
obtaining appropriate badges from Pittsburgh, was password, coun-
tersign and *open sesame* to the most obdurate sentinel. It was
curious to observe how naturally the idea of the necessity for a
sanitary authority in the emergency seemed to be accepted by all.

"The object of this sketch, which has simply touched upon the salient features of the work of the State Board of Health of the Commonwealth of Pennsylvania in Johnstown, has been not to glorify the Board, but, by special request, to add the simple contribution of an eye-witness to the history of a tragedy in modern annals, and the story of which will not cease to be read with interest as long as human hearts beat in sympathy with the woes of their fellows.

"It is to be hoped, however, that the lesson taught by the prominent participation of the Board in the rescue and recovery of Johnstown will engrave itself deeply on the minds, not only of those over whom it, for a time, in the sacred interest of the preservation of human life, assumed a somewhat rigorous control, but of all under whose eyes these pages may come.

"That lesson is tersely conveyed in the motto of the Board,

SALUS POPULI, SUPREMA LEX."

III.

CARE OF THE DEAD.

I.—CONCERNING THE MORGUES.

These when death comes like a rushing lion.
  *   *   *   *   *   *   *
She vanished. We can scarcely say she died,
For but a now did heaven and earth divide ;
This moment perfect health, the next was death.—DRYDEN.

THE dawn of the day after the flood disclosed the wide scene of its terrific disasters. The survivors, after the night of infinite horrors, beheld that which, even in the retrospect, is so overpowering that they are amazed at the retention of their sanity. By the grace of God upholding the faith of those who knew Him, and by the necessity of immediately grappling with the problems that confronted us, we were saved from despair and dementia. One of those pressing problems was the recovery and identification of the bodies of the drowned. Bodies of men, women and children lay scattered over the streets, in the wreckage and along the water-courses, many of them bruised and mutilated, and some of them partially buried in the mud, half concealed amid the debris, or bruised beyond recognition. Thousands from different homes were thus by the remorseless flood washed together in the agonies of death, the victims of the common catastrophe. While our noble and gentle women addressed themselves to the care of the

(204)

children and other rescued sufferers, some of the men at once began to recover the bodies of the dead; not only to lessen the perils which would ensue from putrefaction, but for the purpose of identification, that friends might reclaim their dead and give them decent burial, and also to secure personal effects or valuables that might be found upon their bodies. In the prosecution of the morgue work, the Fourth Ward school-house, the Presbyterian church, the Millville school-building, the Catholic church in the borough of Cambria, a saloon in Morrellville, and a private residence on the corner of Napoleon and South Streets, were converted into houses for the dead. For a short time, the Pennsylvania Railroad Station, the Peelorville school-house, the Grand View cemetery chapel and the Dibert soap factory were employed for the same purpose. At Nineveh, the bodies were laid out upon the green sward for identification. Owing to the piled-up wreckage and the swollen streams, for nearly a fortnight the multiplication of morgues was a necessity; but as soon as practicable they were all consolidated at the central one—Millville school-house— the only building in that borough left on its foundation.

Unlike the authorized and regularly constituted morgues in our large cities, these extemporized ones were destitute of the commonest conveniences, and of means of protection against intrusion and morbid curiosity. We had no record-books, not even paper, on which to make our records, and had to use with great economy that which we gathered amid the debris or happened to have in our pockets. Upon this we wrote the names of those we identified and descriptions of the unrecognized.

We were obliged to employ all comers, even when we entertained fears of their efficiency or were suspicious of their honesty, to gather up the dead and carry them into the morgues. Delicate and responsible as this work was, it had to be done as speedily as possible before identification was rendered impossible, and before thieves could rob the bodies of what was upon them that was valuable. Besides, we had no means of satisfying ourselves concerning the helpers, for many were outsiders and strangers to everybody. We learned later, when Pinkerton's detectives arrived, that a number of these volunteers were noted crooks and criminals from other cities. We only then realized that, in this most awful and solemn work, we were unconsciously giving notorious thieves the opportunity of robbing our dead. It revealed to us the black depths of infamy to which the heart of man can sink. My experience here convinces me that the time has not yet come for us to revise or soften the declaration of the Bible and our orthodox creeds on the subject of human depravity. In some cases we were subjected to annoyance from intoxicated men, and I was compelled to eject many of them forcibly from the morgues.

Our anxiety may be imagined from the fact that we had no bank, no protected place, no safes where to deposit money, jewelry, watches and other valuables found on the bodies. These, of course, were a sacred trust, committed to us as superintendents of the morgues. Their preservation was far more than ordinarily important, for the friends to whom they would be delivered had lost everything, and these would not only be valuable as relics, but might enable them to purchase food or other necessaries. Professional thieves would continually pass through the morgues, ostensibly to identify alleged relations and friends, but really with a view of claiming the valuables. At times, the only protection we could give them was to keep them about our persons, and then we were in fear of personal violence. Night after night I have sat or reclined in the effort to sleep, with $2,000 and valuables about me, so that they could not be taken without my awaking. We were under the necessity of eating our sandwiches and drinking our coffee in the midst of the dead, some of whom were mutilated and otherwise offensive.

Among the helpers in the morgues who are deserving of special praise were Undertakers Russell of Braddock and Henderson of Johnstown ; Doctors Jessop of Kittanning, Webster and Smith of Pittsburgh ; Rev. Messrs. J. S. Woodburn, Davin and Mingle, and Messrs. A. M. Jolly, Thomas L. Porter, W. C. Coon and others.

The exact number of the dead is unknown. I believe 3,500 to be a low estimate. Two thousand bodies have been recovered, and fully 1,500 more are still missing.

Following are the lists of the dead as they were brought to the various morgues, embalmed and numbered by the undertakers :

MORGUE "A"—FOURTH WARD SCHOOL-HOUSE.

1. Hamilton, Miss Laura (Mary).
   Was to have been married on the next Tuesday. Body delivered to her brother.
2. Knorr, Mrs. Berta.
   Supposed to have money stolen from her person.
3. Brinkey, Elmer.
   Had valuables.
4. Little, John A.
   Was lost in the Hulbert House. A Pittsburgh man. Had valuables. Body delivered to G. C. Stucke, of Sewickley.
5. Wilson, Charles H.
   Deformed. Clerk at the Hulbert House. Had valuables.
6. Unknown.
   A female. Blonde hair. Supposed to be Mrs. Luckhart.
7. Unknown.
   A girl about four years of age.
8. Unknown.
   A female. Large ; about forty years old. Supposed to be Mrs. Christy, of Butler, Pa.
9. Unknown.
   A girl about twelve years of age. Supposed to be a Fitzharris.
10. Unknown.
    A female supposed to be or resembles Miss Ella Layton. Necktie. Plain gold ring. Age about twenty.
11. Unknown.
    A female. " F. L. F." on envelope.
12. Unknown.
    A young lady. Plain ring on finger of right hand.
13. Unknown.
    A lady about twenty-five years of age. Bracelet on left wrist. Two rings on right hand.
14. Wells, Miss Jennie.
    Removed by Wm. A. Ocker.
15. Andrews, John.
    Found on Stony Creek.
16. Unknown.
    A female. Fair complexion. Dark hair. Weight about seventy-five pounds. Height five feet. Blue waist, plaid dress.
17. Unknown.
    A man about fifty years of age. Short hair, smooth face.
18. Burns, John.
    Brakeman Cambria Iron Co. Left eye gone. Buried at " Prospect," June 9.

19. Unknown.
    A young lady about twenty. Plain ring
    on right hand. Bracelet and ring on
    left wrist and band. Ear-drops. Brace-
    lets and rings, duplicates of Miss Well's.

20. Unknown.
    Hulburt House porter. Supposed to be
    William Henry. Colored. Valuables.

21. Unknown.
    A male. Fair complexion. Black hair.
    Gray eyes. Dark blue suit. Flannel
    shirt.

22. Unknown.
    A female. About twenty years. Fair
    complexion, light hair.

23. Wild, Jacob.

24. Wild, Mrs. Jacob.

25. Unknown.
    Female. Light hair. About fifteen years.

26. Jones, Mrs. W. W.
    Pearl street. Two rings on left hand.
    Valuables.

27. Powell.
    Male child, two years old. Son of
    Howell Powell.

28. Powell.
    Male child, a few days old. Son of
    Howell Powell.

29. Baldwin, George H.

30. Layton, William.
    Found near B. & O. station. Valuables.

31. O'Connell. Mrs.
    Sister of Capt. O'Connell, of Washington
    street.

32. Unknown.
    Female. Middle-aged. Hair on chin.

33. McCoy, Mr.
    Railroad street.

34. Unknown.
    Female. Middle-aged. Dark hair
    mixed with gray.

35. Unknown.
    Female. From Hulbert House. A
    medal monogram, "J. H. G."

36. Richards, John.
    Supposed to have been employed by W.
    A. Moses. Hair gray. Height about
    five feet eight inches. Body taken by
    Mr. Thos. D. Rees, his nephew, June 4.

37. Unknown.
    Female. About forty-five years. Plain
    string and bag around her neck. Ear-
    rings. Dark complexion. Weight
    about 170.

38. Raab, Amelia.
    Washington street. Keys.

39. Penrod, William.
    Portage street.

40. Murphy, James I.
    115 Park Place.

41. Murphy, Miss Bessie.
    Daughter of James I.

42. Unknown.
    Female. Blue eyes. Black hair. Ear-
    rings. About eighteen. Valuables.
    Two rings on left hand. Initial on one
    ring, "W H."

43. Unknown.
    Female. About twelve years. Dark
    brown eyes. Bracelet on right wrist.
    Supposed to be a Fitzharris.

44. Holter, Miss.

45. Unknown.
    Female. Sandy hair. Age about twenty-
    two.

46. Unknown.
    Female child. About four years. Light
    hair. Supposed to be Katie Krieger.
    (Mr. Murphy.)

47. Unknown.
    Female. About twenty. Black hair.
    Ring on left hand. Ear-drops. Nap-
    kin ring.

48. Davis, Miss M. L.
    119 Market street. Afterwards thought
    to be Miss Masterson. Body left on lot
    of Thomas L. Davis. Ring at Fourth
    Ward Morgue.

49. Unknown.
    Female. About forty. Large. Hair
    turning gray.

50. Streum, John.

51. Davis, Miss Mary.
    119 Market street.

52. Unknown.
    Female. Age about thirty. Red hair.

53. Harris, Frank H.
    Son of Chief-of-Police John Harris.

INTERIOR OF ROMAN CATHOLIC CHURCH OF ST. MARY, CAMBRIA CITY.

54. Smith, Arthur.
    Son of J. L. Smith, marble cutter.
    Buried at " Prospect," June 9.

55. Unknown.
    Female. Age about twenty. Dark hair.
    Light complexion. Watch and chain.
    Ring on right hand. Ear-rings.

56. Unknown.
    Female child. Age about four. Dark
    hair. Ring on left hand.

57. Unknown.
    Female child. Age about three. Dark
    hair. Breast-pin.

58. Barbour, Carrie S.
    Age about sixteen. Buried at " Pros-
    pect," June 9th.

59. Randolph, George F., Jr.
    Valuables. Beaver Falls.

60. Diamond, Frank (or Dimond).

61. Unknown.
    Female. Age about thirty. Dark hair.
    Ring on left hand. $5 bill.

62. Faloon, Miss Annie.
    Buried " Prospect," June 9th.

63. Unknown.
    Female. Supposed to be Mrs. Geis.
    Valuables.

64. Cox, James G.
    Philadelphia. Valuables.

65. Fronheisser, Mrs. James J.

66. Unknown.
    Male. About twelve. Sandy hair.

67. Butler, Charles F.
    Assistant Treasurer of Cambria Iron
    Company.

68. Jones, Mrs. S. M.

69. Hamilton, Miss Jessie.

70. McAley, P.
    Male.

71. Harrigan.
    Mary Ellen, twenty-two years; daughter
    of Jerry Harrigan, 17 Ridge avenue,
    Minersville, servant in the Hulbert
    House.

72. Murtha, James.

73. Davis, William L.

74. Eldredge, Samuel B.
    Policeman.

75. Penrod, William.
    12

76. Unknown.
    Female. Thirty years. Dark, luxuri-
    ant hair.

77. Marshall, Charles A.

78. De France, Mrs. H. T.

79. Poland.
    Male. Young son of Dr. Poland.

80. Poland.
    Male. Little son of Dr. Poland.

81. Katzenstein, Mrs. Ella.

82. Katzenstein, Edwin.
    Child of Mr. Katzenstein.

83. Long, Samuel.
    Butcher.

84. Unknown.
    Male. Burned.

85. Strause, Moses.
    Body taken by son-in-law, Freidman, to
    Pittsburgh.

86. Wheat, Frank.

87. Gageby, Sadie.

88. Layton, Mrs. Ettie.

89. Layton, Miss May.

90. Hoopgard, Conrad.
    Baker. Clinton street.

91. Holmes, Julia.
    Wife of Charlie Holmes.

92. Hellriggle, Charles.
    Woodvale.

93. Jones, Mrs.

94. Dunn, Miss Mary.
    Dressmaker. Sixteen. Peelorville.

95. Roth, John.
    Buried " Prospect," June 6th.

96. Brown, Peter.
    Woodvale.

97. Unknown.
    Male. Sandy beard and moustache.
    Supposed to be Mr. Farrell, of Wood-
    vale. (Cambria Iron Co., Miller.)

98. Hoffman, Bertha.
    Age eighteen.

99. Hoffman, Marion.
    Age fourteen.

100. Hoffman, Florence.
     Age six.

101. Hoffman, Freida.
     Age four.

102. Hoffman, Joseph.
Age three.

103. Hornick, Mrs. John G.
Broad street.

104. Hoffman, Mrs. Mary.

105. Beam, Dr. W. C.

106. Beam, Mrs. Dr.

107. Neese, Conrad.

108. Derris, August.
Portage street.

109. Carlin, Jonathan.
Buried at No. 12, Grand View. Body
lifted by Thos. B. Bickerton, June 28th,
and taken to Philadelphia for interment.
In Commodore Perry's expedition in
Japan, that opened up the first treaty.
Fifty-seven years.

110. St. John, Dr. C. P.
Alex. Adair has charge of body. Trav-
elling optician.

111. Weakland, John.
Lawyer.

112. Clark, John B.
Boy. Age about seven. "Prospect."

113. (1.) Unknown.
Female. Large. Weight about 200.
Supposed to be Mrs. Shabler, or Mrs.
McClaren, or Mrs. Murphy, of Hotel
Brunswick.

113. (2.) Spaller, Lee.

114. Unverzagt, George.

115. Unverzagt, George.
Age seven.

116. Fitzharris, Mr.
Saloon-keeper, Clinton street. Taken
to German Catholic Cemetery.

117. Behuke, Charles.
Late Private 187 N. Y. Vols.

118. Riddle, John, Sr.

119. Valentine, George M.

120. Veiring, Lizzie.

121. Butter, Sarah.
Taken by her brother.

122. Anderson, John.
In charge of son.

123. Owings, Daisy.
By brother-in-law, Charles Conrad.

124. Unknown.
Female. About thirty-five years of age.
Two rings on right hand. Chain with
cross attached.

125. Unknown.
Male. Valuables. Watch. Two dollar bill and one dollar in silver. Sun
glass. Bunch of keys.

126.

Male. Two years old.

127.

Male. A few days old.

128. Unknown.
Female. Heavy build. Full face.
Dark hair. Supposed to belong to the
Salvation Army.

129. Strause, Moses. No. 85.
A Hebrew. Age seventy-eight. Had
been fifty-five years in America. Embalmed, and at the request of Mr. Fried-
man enclosed in rough box.

130. (1.) Knee, George D.
Claimed by his son Henry, and buried
in Sandy Vale.

130. (2.) Bogus, W.
Hulbert House.

131. Marburg, Dr.
Claimed and received by Sherman
Stroup.

132. Bending, Jessie.

133. Bending, Elizabeth.
Died after flood.

134. Pleegle, Anna.
Of Somerset county. Recognized by
her mother.

135. Deihl, Miss Carrie.
Shippensburg, Pa. Claimed by Wm.
H. Ocker, of Philadelphia, to whom she
was engaged to be married, and removed by him to be buried at Shippensburg, Pa.

136. Shumaker, John S.
Son of James. Walter, Jennie and
Edith also drowned.

137. Unknown.
Female. Age eight. Light hair. Blue
eyes. About three feet eight inches in
height.

138. Layton, David.
Valuables.

139. Tingle, Mrs. Mary.
Identified by Mrs. Bingle. Her husband is injured and in the hospital.

140. Haynes, Walter B.
Valuables. Taken by his brother, Charles W.

141. Unknown.
Female. Fair. Long hair. Height five feet four inches.

142. Greenwald, Rosa.
Age forty-three. Wife of Martin Greenwald.

143. Unknown.
Female. Dark hair. Blue eyes. Blue underdress with red stripes. , Gingham apron. Brown sacque. Removed.

144. (See No. 53.)

145. Unknown.
Female. Dark red hair. Gray eyes. Black alpaca clothing.

146. Unknown.
Said to have been Mary Hamilton or Miss Mollie Richards, but afterward found to be wrong.

147. (1.) (See No. 30.)

147. (2.) Unknown.
Female. Light complexion. Fair hair. Brown eyes. Height five feet six inches. Age about twenty-five. Blue polka dress. Plain gold ring on finger of left hand.

148. Unknown.
Female. Age fifteen. Dark brown hair. Blue or hazel eyes. Red sacque with blue trimming. Plaid dress.

149. Unknown.
Male. Fair complexion. Black hair. Gray eyes. Dark blue suit. Flannel shirt.

150. Unknown.
Female. Dark hair. Blue eyes. Dark dress with blue waist. Supposed to be Miss Zimmerman.

151. Hains, Walter B.
Son of J. B. Hains.

152. Fitzharris, John.
Age twelve. Gold watch, No. 1528. Empty pocketbook. Given to his aunt, Ella Mulhern.

153. Fitzharris, Chris.
A boy. Penknife. Valuables given to his aunt, Ella Mulhern.

154. Fitzharris, Mrs. Margaret.
Valuables taken by her sister, Mrs. Ella Mulhern.

155. Fitzharris, Miss Sallie.

156. Jones, Eliza.
Pearl street.

157. Unknown.
Male. Supposed to be James Barrett or James Lewis. (Package.)

158. Werry, Albert.
Bank notes and silver. Lady's watch.

159. Unknown.
Female. Penknife and buttonhook. Supposed to be Katie Fitzharris.

160. Unknown.
Female. Tickets to exhibition by the pupils of St. John's School, June 20th. Blank book bought of Irwin Rutledge, Jr. Small amount of money. Removed.

161. McGuire, Kate.
Valuables gotten by Laurence McGuire. Age about fifty-five. Unmarried. 15 Walnut street. St. John's Cemetery.

162. Unknown.
Male.

† 163. Benford, Mrs. E. E.
Of Hulbert House. To "Grand View."

164. Unknown.
Supposed by two to be John Schnable.

165. Hennekamp, Oscar.
Male. Baby.

166. Hennekamp, Mrs. Rebecca.
Wife of J. H. Identified by her husband. Valuables given to him. Buried in lot 143, "Grand View."

167. Unknown.
Male. Age about thirty.

168. Unknown.
Male. Age about forty. Supposed to be Meredith, above Caldwell's store. Eagle on arm. Bunch of keys. "Prospect," 6 | 10.

169. Unknown.
Female. Afterwards identified as Mrs. Samuel Lenhart.

170. Keifling, Mrs. Catharine.
Taken by husband.

171. Keifling, Mary.
Taken by her uncle.

172. Unknown.
Female. Supposed to be Mrs. Conrad Snable, bar-tender in Kost saloon on Washington street.

173. Unknown.
Female. Face mangled. Ring on forefinger of left hand.

174. Carroll, Thomas.
Railroad street, Conemaugh borough. Valuables. 65 and collar-button worked in.

175. Rabb, Norma.
Female. Identified by Mrs. Julia A. Hatzinger. Buried in lot of C. Rabb, Sandy Vale.

176. McCauliff, Laura.
Taken by her father, William.

177. Reidel, John C.
Kernville. Some valuables. Buried Prospect, June 9th.

178. Unknown.
Female. Middle-aged. Full head dark brown hair. Seersucker dress.

179. Unknown.
Male. Sandy beard and moustache, slightly gray. Oroide watch. Sun glass. $2 note. $1.10 in silver.

180. Unknown.
Male. Black hair and moustache. Oroide watch. Two pocket-knives. Forty cents in silver. Postal card and envelope addressed to M. J. Murphy, 1030 Callowhill street, Youngstown, Ohio. Valuables taken by M. J. McAndrew.

181. Fitzharris, Christopher.
Cash $167.65. Silver watch, knife, etc., taken by A. Craver, of Ebensburg.

182. Keifer, Mrs. John A.
Age twenty-four. Also child found. Taken by husband.

183. Lewis, James.
Main street. Silver watch. Knife. Cigar case. Pocketbook containing ring, key and five cents. Envelope marked James Lewis, Main street, Johnstown.

184. Ludwig, Mrs. Kate Gerhart.
Breast-pin. Collar-button.

185. Von Alt, Henry.
Collar-button and spoon.

186. Ludwig, Henry.

187. Nathan, Adolph.
Claimed by Sol. Reiman. Valuables given to brother Simon. ($1.68, keys, etc.)

188. Howe, Mrs. Thomas.
Sixty-five cents. Two keys.

189. Howe, Robert.
Son of Mrs. Thomas Howe. Age about eight. Identified by brother.

190. Wild, Bertha (or "Gertie").
Young lady. No valuables.

191. Wolf, Joanna.
Aged. No valuables. Removed to Catholic Cemetery.

192. Maltzi, Jacob.
City butcher.

193. Brown, Miss Emily.
Of Woodvale. Removed. Ring given to her sister, Mrs. Wm. McAuliff. Little girl baby in her arms when found.

194. Unknown.
Female. Small child. Found in arms of Miss Brown. Supposed to be child of J. M. Shumaker.

195. Quinn, Vincent D.
Valuables placed in hands of John J. Geis.

196. Benford, Lewis (Louis).
Fifty cents. Collar-button and cuffbutton.

197. Unknown.
Female. Age about four years.

198. Montgomery, Alex.
$29.54. Silver watch. Cuff-buttons. Spectacles. Eye-glasses. Bunch of keys. Letters, etc., etc. Valuables given to Alex. McKean. Body sent to Greensburgh.

199. Unknown.
Female. Aged. Black hair, slightly gray. Waist of narrow striped black and white goods. Purse with key.

200. Werberger, William.
Professor of music. Silver watch. Four keys. Match safe. Valuables given to his son-in-law.

201. Kirkbride, Mrs. Ida.
Age about thirty. Ring with setting on right hand. Two plain rings on third finger of left hand. Small ball drop earrings.

202. Fisher, W.
Knife and register receipt.

203. Kirkbride, Lyda (Lynda).
Handkerchief. Bracelet and ring.

204. Unknown.
Female. Age twenty-five. Dark hair. No valuables.

205. Raab, C. George.
Purse with $1.96. Keys with name on stencil. Purse delivered to brother.

206. Larimer, James.
Purse with one cent. Two keys. Two knives. Buried at Grand View.

207. Lichtenberger, Rev. James, pastor German Lutheran Church.
Claimed by James Blander, his brother-in-law.

208. Phillips, Mrs. E.
Woodvale. Purse with $1.23. Buried Prospect, June 9th.

209. McKeever, Mrs. Mary.
Purse with seventeen cents. Catholic prayer-book. Crucifix. Valuables given to Sallic McKeen. Buried in St. John's Cemetery.

210. Unknown.
Female. Aged. Nearly bald. Wore a "switch." Upper and lower false teeth. Open (silver) thimble. Twenty-five cents. Gold earrings.

211. Hornick, John P. (or D.).
Cash $351. Gold watch. Bunch of keys. Badge engraved St. G. R. O. Taken by Frank Hornick.

212. Mahew, Joseph.
Recognized by his father. Age sixteen. Light hair. No valuables. At his father's request sent to Irish Catholic Cemetery. Two sisters and three brothers lost.

213. Unknown.
Male. Age about three years. No marks. Buried at Prospect, June 9th.

214. Thomas, Edward.
Woodvale. Middle-aged. Red moustache and beard. Four gold collar-buttons. Given to O. J. Bishop. Buried in his own lot at Sandy Vale.

215. Unknown.
Male. Age eight years. Valuables placed on body.

216. Young, Aug.
Valuables given to George Millheizer. Buried in his lot at Grand View.

217. Thomas, Lydia.
Age fourteen. Woodvale. No valuables.

218. Unknown.
Child, a few days old. Badly burned.

219. Lenhart, Emma.
Age eighteen. Medium size. Earrings. Gold ring with white setting on second finger of right hand.

220. Unknown.
Male. Age about twenty-five. Reddish brown hair. Cash twenty-five cents. Package of Japanese headache cure.

221. Murray, James.
Gold watch. Cash $12.74. Two bunches keys. Identified by his partner, Mr. Jas. A. Hayes, of Hayes, Murray Co., 1103 Race street, Philadelphia. Body shipped by B. & O. R. R. by Mr. Hayes' order. Valuables given to him.

222. Unknown.
Female. Age about six months. Buried at Prospect, June 9th.

223. Marshall, William.
Of firm of George G. Marshall & Co. Silver watch (open face), chain. Pocket knife. Bunch of keys. Order book. Purse with $5.61. Valuables given to John Marshall, his brother. Body shipped to Indiana, Pa., via. P. R. R.

224. Lewellyn, Mrs. J. J.
Removed to Bangor, Pa., for burial.

225. Unknown.
Female. Age about fifty. Brown hair, turning gray. No valuables. Buried at Prospect, June 9th.

226. Unknown.
Female. Age about thirty-five. Heavy dark brown hair. Empty purse. Buried at Prospect, June 9th.

227. Unknown.
Female. Slender. Knit purse with $7.75. Aged.

228. Unknown.
Male. Age about thirteen. No valuables. Buried at Prospect, June 9th.

229. Unknown.
Male. Aged. One cuff-button and large key. Afterwards identified as James Dillon, of Somerset. Also had watch, wallet and papers received from Safety Deposit Company and given to brother-in-law, E. P. James, Somerset. Buried at Prospect, June 9th.

230. Unknown.
Male. A few weeks old. Greatly decomposed.

231. Unknown.
Female. Young lady.

232. McKinstry, Annie.
Age fifteen. No valuables. Buried at Grand View, June 9th.

233. McKinstry, Mrs. May.
Dressmaker. Hager Block. Plain band ring. Engraved hoop finger ring. Valuables given to James H. Greer, brother-in-law. Buried at Grand View.

234. Unknown.
Male. Aged about thirty Blind in right eye. Pocket knife. Buried at Prospect, June 9th.

235. Hiss, Miss Jessie.
Two rings on finger of left hand. Kid gloves in pocket. Small pearl-handled knife, collar-button and breastpin. Valuables given to her brother, James H. Hiss.

236. Unknown.
Female. Age about twenty-five. Medium height. Heavy set. Dark hair. No valuables. Buried at Prospect, June 9th.

237. Tittle, Cyrus P.
Male. Gold watch. Two bunches of keys. Penknife. Match box. Stencil plate marked with name. Pocket-book containing $75.94. Valuables given to his brother James. Buried at Sandy Vale in lot of John Tittle.

238. Unknown.
Female. Age about five years. Buried at Prospect, June 9th.

239. Linden (or Layden), Mary.
Age about twenty. Brown hair. Full round face. From Merchants' Hotel. Identified by A. Adair. Buried at Prospect, June 9th.

240. Unknown.
Female. Large. Full face, full lips, small nose, light hair, pregnant. Key and one cent. Buried at Prospect, June 9th.

241. Eldridge, Abraham.
Package of photographs. Large key. Empty pocket-book. Fountain pen. Gold watch. Tape measure. Match case. Two pocket-knives. $5.08 in pockets. Three keys and a bunch of keys. Valuables given to Mrs. A. Young. Buried in lot of A. Young, June 9th, Grand View.

242. Unknown.
Female. Age about twenty-five. Heavy set. Dark hair. Buried at Prospect, June 9th.

243. Unknown.
Female. Age about thirty-five. Short in stature. Very heavy. Very large breasts. Dark brown hair. Wart on left ear. Gold ring with rhinestone set, rubbed with sand. Breast-pin. Buried at Prospect, June 9th.

244. Kimpsel, Christian.
Furniture dealer. Pocket-knife. Bunch of keys with name on stencil plate. $2,500 in bills, $600 in gold, $4.23 in silver and coppers. Buried in lot of Henry Hesselbrie, Sandy Vale, June 9th.

245. Unknown.
Female. Aged. Slender. Dark brown hair. No valuables. Supposed to be Miss Gordon of Hager Building. Buried at Prospect, June 9th.

246. Campbell, Peter.
Colored. Pair of cuff-buttons. Buried at Prospect, June 9th.

247. Believed to be Elrigle, Mr.
Heavy sandy moustache. Black hair. Rather spare face. Buried at Prospect, June 9th.

248. Unknown.
    Female. Large. Pregnant. Brown hair. Delicate nose. Medium stature.

249. Zimmerman, Theodore F.
    Gold watch Elgin No. 932,645. Four collar-buttons. Set ring. Purse containing $7.18 in silver and copper, $20 in bills. Valuables given to G. A. Zimmerman. Buried at Sandy Vale.

250. McNally, Patrick.
    Proper number lost. Buried St. John's, June 9th.

251. Reicke, Alexander.
    Pittsburg. Sent from the hospital there.

252. Flagle, David C.
    Sent to Morgue by Alexander Hart. Identified by Homer. Buried at Prospect.

253. Nightly, John.
    Cash $2.16. Bunch of keys. Papers, etc. Valuables taken by T. J. Espey.

254. Unknown.
    Male. Age about twelve years. Reddish brown hair. Rather heavy build. No valuables. Sent to Prospect for burial.

255. Raab (or Robb), Mrs. George B.
    Age about forty-five. Large. Weighs about one hundred and eighty. Dark hair. Porous plaster on breast. To Sandy Vale for burial.

256. Ripple, Jackson.
    Brought from Presbyterian Church Morgue, No. 58.

257. Flinn, Mary.
    Identified by paper on her person. Cash $8.19. Valuables to D. P. Hensill.

258. Adams, H. Clay.
    Conemaugh street, Johnstown. Oroide watch. 10 cts. in cash. Bunch keys. Match safe. Papers, etc. By order of Mr. Scott buried at Prospect, June 10th.

259. Unknown.
    Male. Slender. Light hair and moustache. Age about thirty. Silver watch. Bunch of keys. Knife. Collar-button. $1.94 in cash. Supposed to be Cooney or Conrad Schnable.

260. Slick, Cyrus.
    Gold watch-chain. Two pairs of gold glasses. One pair silver scissors. Railroad tickets. Penknife. Brass cneck. Cash $6.21. Identified by letters in pocket.

261. Raab (or Robb), George.
    Saloonkeeper on Washington street. Cash $2.19. Two collar-buttons. Two cuff-buttons. Valuables placed in hand of Mr. Ossenburg, brother-in-law. Interred in Sandy Vale or Grand View.

262. Alexander, John G.
    Valuables in hands of John H. Scott. Body sent to Blairsville, Pa., by John Henderson, June 10th.

263. Elsaesser (son of C.).
    Identified by Riley Cramer.

264. Unknown.
    Female. Age about thirty. Medium height. Full form. Light brown hair. Three gold rings placed on body.

265. Unknown.
    Female. Age about fourteen. Medium height. Black hair. Buried at Prospect.

266. Neary, Mrs. Kate.
    Purse with $1.19. Valuables placed in hands of her son Patrick. Buried at St. John's Cemetery.

267. Nugent, Mary Jane.
    Cash $79.09. Rosary. Breast-pin. Two keys. Spectacle case. Green purse. Breast-pin engraved. St. John's.

268. McGinley, James.
    Ex-policeman. Valuables in hands of Mrs. Ella Gurley.

269. Smith, Mrs. J. L.
    From Kernville. Philadelphia.

270. Unknown.
    Female. Age about twenty-six. Gold watch and chain, with horn attached. Breast-pin. Hair-pin. Diamond ring on third finger left hand with garnet. Gold ring on second finger with pearl setting. Two diamond earrings.

271. Howe, W. F.
    Silver watch. P. R. R. baggage check, No. 48,196. R. R. ticket. Pen and pencil. $13 in bills. 87 cts. in coin. Bunch of keys. Match safe. Silver pencil. Knife. Collar and cuff buttons. Finger-rings and gold stud.

272. Unknown.
Young lady. Light hair. Gold leaf earring, diamond set in centre. Old number lost. Buried Prospect, June 10th.

273. Roth, Mrs. Emil C.
From Presbyterian Church Morgue, No. 63.

274. Unknown.
Male. Age about sixty-five years. Knife. Match-safe. Watch-chain with keys attached. Pencil. Boots with brass heels. Buried at Prospect, June 11th.

275. Stahr, Fred.
Died from injury in the flood. Coffin furnished his father from the Morgue. Buried in Sandy Vale, June 11th.

276. Unknown.
Male. Age thirty to thirty-five. Weight 145 pounds. Brown hair. Medium stature. Bunch of keys. Prospect June 11, 1889.

277. Unknown.
Female. Age seventeen to eighteen years. 5 ft. 4 in. height. Weight about 110 pounds. Check gingham waist. Blue and white striped ticking skirt. Very heavy brown hair tied with blue ribbon. Plain gold ring with raised square centre and diamond set, on second finger of left hand. Samples of dress and skirt on coffin. Prospect, June 11th.

278. Christman, Miss A. C.
New Orleans. Draft for $275. Cash $32.70. Gold pin. Gold chain. Papers, etc. Body and valuables shipped to Beauregard, Tenn., on telegraphic order of Mrs. D. H. McGavock, Nashville, Tenn., on June 11th.

279. Unknown.
Male. Age thirty-five to forty. Sandy hair. Height 5 ft. 5 in. Pair of steel knuckles. Key. Ticket of admission to Johnstown Opera House. Prospect, June 11th.

280. Raab, Miss Lizzie.
Buried as unknown 216, from Millville School Morgue, at Prospect. Disinterred and buried in lot of Conrad Raab, Sandy Vale, June 12th.

281. Unknown.
Female. Age seven or eight years. Ear-drops, square one-half of the face of the ear-drop checkered, the other half engraved with a vine. Taken from body and placed with valuables. Prospect, June 12th.

282. Alexander, Aralia Kline.
Age thirteen. Identified and removed by her mother. Buried on lot of A. J. Haws, Grand View, June 13th. Effects delivered to mother.

283. Unknown.
Male. Age about forty. Medium stature. Weight about 140. Dark brown hair. Rosary and scapula left on body. St. John's, June 13th.

284. Gard, Andrew.
Clerk Penna. R. R. station. Identified by papers, watch, etc. Grand View, June 14th.

285. Unknown.
Male. Age about fifty. Weight 150. Dark hair, turning gray. Medium height. Bunch of keys. Spectacles with case. Prospect, June 14th.

286. Young, Frank.
Identified by his mother, to whom valuables and body were delivered. Grand View, June 14.

287. Unknown.
Male. About 5 feet 6 inches height. Striped coat and pants. Open-faced silver watch. Heavy plated chain with black stone set. Bunch of keys. Package of Japanese headache cure. Rubber eraser. Pen-holder. Button-hook. Cash 54 cts. Prospect, June 14th.

288. Unknown.
Female. Very much decomposed. Afterwards identified as Mrs. Frawater, mother of Colonel Frawater. Identified by A. Kerflure. Prospect, June 14th. No goods.

289. Unknown.
Male. Age ten to twelve. Very much decomposed. Hair cut short, very dark color. Gray pants and coat. Blue shirt waist. Prospect, June 14th. No goods.

STORE OF MR. CLARK, ON MAIN ST.—PROPRIETOR 1851.

290. Unknown.
  Male. Manhood age. Face very much disfigured. Medium size. Jean pants and coat. Coarse laced shoes. Small piece of green ribbon. Pocket knife, black handle, one blade. Wooden pipe. Padlock, key and 15 cts. in pockets. Prospect, June 14th. Believed to be John Rausch.

291. Unknown.
  Female. Age not known. Heavy set. Height about 5 ft. 5 in. Hair light brown. Weight 160. Plain gold ring. Medium size breast pin above shaped Q with one brilliant set. Plain old-fashioned earring. Prospect, June 14th.

292. Rapp, George.
  Son of Phillip Rapp, of Hornerstown. Died after flood. Age two years. Sandy Vale, by friends, June 15th.

293. Dewald, Charles B.
  Presbyterian Church Morgue No. 81. One watch and chain. Pocket knife. One pin K. of P. Finger rings. One watch chain, one tooth brush, cash $1.20. June 15th. Received of J. A. Russell all above-named articles. A. Dewald, father, care of Jos. F. Miller, 4422 Leipert St., Frankford, Philadelphia, Pa., June 10th.

294. Diamond, Mrs. Anna.
  Silver ring. Purse. $10 bill. $1.29 silver. St. John's, on lot of James Diamond. Valuables recovered by James Diamond. June 15th.
  Witnesses { Charles Diamond, E. B. Gosline.

295. Viering, Mrs. Henry.
  Grand View, June 15th. Identified by her husband, Mr. Henry Viering, formerly reported from Nineveh, was incorrect.

296. Viering, Herman.
  Infant child of Mr. and Mrs. Henry Viering aged one year. Identified by the father. Grand View, June 15th.

297. Viering, Henry.
  Son of Henry Viering. Age fourteen years. Identified by the father. Grand View, June 15th.

298. Unknown.
  Young man. Medium weight. Height 5 ft. 7 in. Light brown hair. Silver open-faced watch. Double chain with square slide and square locket, charm black stone set on one side and blue stone set on the other. Emblem pin of A. O. K. of M. C. Pocket comb and maroon leather case. Prospect, June 15th.

299. Gardner, Rosa,
  Daughter of Mr. John Gardner. Age twenty to twenty-five. Height 5 ft. 7 in. Long, dark brown hair, calico dress. No valuables. Upper Prospect, June 17th.

300. Snyder, Mary.
  Age eleven. Sandy Vale.

301. Froenheiser, Catharine.
  Daughter of James J. Froenheiser. Age three months. Grand View.

MORGUE "B"—PRESBYTERIAN CHURCH.

Dibert, John.

Weaver, Mrs. Sue.

Dibert, Blanche.

Weaver, John Dibert.

NOTE:—The following thirty-four bodies were received at the Morgue in the Presbyterian Church, between 1 p. m., June 3d, and 3.30

p m., June 4th. Only the "Unknown" or those not positively identified were numbered. (Signed), H. A. Look, M. D.

Williams, Joseph.

Harris, Margaret T.
  Wife of John T. Harris.

Harris, Maggie.
  Daughter of John T. Harris.

Harris, Sarah.
  Daughter of John T. Harris.

Harris, William L.
  Son of John T. Harris.

Wenner, Karl.

Wenner, Jennie.
  Wife of Karl Wenner.

Wenner, Mary.
  Daughter of Karl and Jennie.

Marlbourgh, Dr.

Bending, Jennie (or Jessie).

Knee, George D.

Lambert, Miss.

Clark, John B.

Clark, Hamilton.
  Had initial J. C. on arm.

Gallagher, Mrs. Lizzie.
  nee Barnes.

Neary, Mary Ellen.

Fisher, Moses.

O'Connell, Mary.

Rosenstell, Mrs.

Hoffman, Charles B.

Unverzagt, Mrs.

Unverzagt, Miss.

McDowell, George.
  Age three years.

McDowell, Lilly.
  Age four years.

IV. Unknown.
  Female. Colored. Supposed to be Mrs.
  Brown or Mrs. Holmes.

V. Unknown.
  Supposed to be Annie Fitzner, but very
  doubtful. An autograph album near
  her hand belonged to Blanche S. Wilson.

VI. Unknown.

VII. Constable, Philip E.

VIII. Unknown.
  Probably Claus Bruhn.

IX. Unknown both as to name and sex, burned.

X.   "   "   "   "   "

XI.   "   "   "   "   "

XII. Unknown.
  Described on coffin.

XIII. Unknown.
  Described on coffin.

NOTE:—The foregoing were copied from
"slips" in the possession of D. J. B. The
following were transcribed from the book kept
in the Morgue.   I. N. R.

14. Unknown.
  Supposed to be Mrs. Reese, wife of J.
  W. Reese.

15. Unknown.

16. Rosensteel, Mrs. J. M.

17. Bruhn, Claus.
  Buried.

18. Unknown.

19. Unknown.

20. Halstead, Rhea.

21. Unknown.

22. Unknown.
  Female. Sixteen years. White. Brown
  hair.   5 cts.

23. Kinney, Mrs.
  Age thirty-five. $103.   Two bunches
  of keys. Watch chain.

24. Unknown.
  Female. Fifteen years. Light brown
  hair.

25. Unknown.
  Male. Eleven years. Buried in Prospect.

26. Gallagher, Prof.
  Pocket book $1.31. Silver watch and
  chain. Two pocket combs. Pair cuff-
  buttons.   Bunch keys.   Collar-button.
  One handkerchief.   Sleeve-buttons.
  Charles Baines received the above.

27. Hoffman, Benjamin.

28. Brinker, Miss.
  Hair lip.

29. Hoffman, Minnie.

30. Hoffman, Helen.

31. Unknown.
  Very large. Alpaca dress. Two gold
  rings. Sent to Prospect.

32. Unknown.
  Male. Dark hair. Dark blue suit.
  Ring on finger with amethyst, with G.
  L. H. on stone. Pocket-book with 26
  cts. Cuff-buttons and collar-buttons.

33. Unknown.
  Male. Age eight. Light hair. Spring
  heel shoes. Red flannel undershirt.
  Calico waist. Canton flannel drawers.

34. Unknown.
    Female. Eleven years. Light hair. Red flannel dress. Blue waist. Barred shirt. Black stockings with red stripe on top.

35. Unknown.
    Female. Age thirty. 5 feet 6 inches height. Brown hair. Corsets. Red flannel shirt. Muslin drawers. Wart on left hand front finger. Two finger rings, one carved, the other ruby. Breast-pin.

36. Mangin, Mrs.
    Large. Taken by friends.

37. Unknown.
    Male. Cash in wallet, $312.51. Eighty. Taken by James Murphy, " K."

38. Unknown.
    Male. White. Heavy head of hair. Brown eyes. 135 pounds. Height 5 feet 6 inches.

39. Ebler, A.

40. Strayer, Mrs. James.
    Taken by friends.

41. Bricker, Henry.
    Open-faced watch with chain. Papers, keys, etc. Claimed.

42. Unknown.
    Male. Sent to Prospect.

43. Unknown.
    Female. Thirty-five years. Two small rings. Earrings.

44. Leslie, J. S.
    $46.25. Penknife. Bunch of keys and paper. Taken by " Deckart."

45. Unknown.
    Male. Thirteen years.

46. Strayer, Myth.
    Identified by family.

47. Unknown.
    Female. Thirty-five years. Black dress. Red flannel skirt. Black silk stockings. Small plain gold ring on left hand. Upper and lower false teeth. Small earrings.

48. Hughes, Emma.
    Claimed.

49. Ryan, John.
    Claimed.

50. Eshdale, James.
    A coupon book, Johnstown and Stony Creek R. R. 56 cts.

51. Jones, Thomas.
    $3.50.

52. Unknown.
    Male. Four years. Well dressed. Brown corkscrew coat. Blue waist. Black stockings.

53. Rowland, Louis.
    424 Bedford street. Bunch of keys. Large pocket-book with papers. Knife. 12 cts. Two old style door keys. Ring on left hand with " R " thereon. Gold watch and chain.

54. Unknown.
    Male. One old knife only. Supposed to be Mr. Evans, Machinist. " Kool" with W. H. Clater, 534 9th Ave.

55. Unknown.
    Female. Thirty-six years. Black and white woolen dress. Red woolen hose with black feet. Brown waist. Two gold rings, one plain and heavy, one light band ring with " L. S. H." on it. Garnet earrings.

56. Witt, Casper.
    Age sixty. Weight 225. 15 cts. One small key. One old knife. Taken by relatives.

57. Unknown.
    Female. Thirty-five years. Black cashmere dress. Jersey jacket. Black stockings. Button shoes. Dark brown hair. Scarlet underwear. Muslin skirt. Scapular. Green corded petticoat. Small gold ring. Height 5 feet 9 inches. Supposed to be Teny Rubert, married to Sabene.

58. Ripple, Jackson.
    Thirty-eight years. $47.16. Open-faced silver watch. Weight 185. Knife. Taken by Jack Watkins, Walnut Grove.

59. Unknown.
    Male. Age thirty-eight. Weight 165. One very small key. Black coat. Blue striped flannel shirt. " D. E. Beckley."

60. Unknown.
    Male. Age thirty-seven. Weight 160. Nothing but a rule.

61. Unknown.
    Male. Age thirty. Weight 150. Silver watch and chain. Two door keys. One comb. Penknife. Pocket-book. Small key. Leather belt. $32.36.

62. Brinkley, Dr. G. C.
    $49.85. Open-faced silver watch. Knife, books, papers, etc. Identified and taken by friends.

63. Roth, Mrs. Emil C.
    One scarf-pin. One stud. Taken by friends.

64. Unknown.
    Male. Thirty years. Weight 220. Open-faced silver watch. One knife. One rule. One tooth-brush. One lead-pencil. Book of rates E. L. A. S. 1000 mile pass book. Tape line. Pair cuff-buttons. Gave valuables to R. Duncaster in presence of Corporal F. W. Loesch.

65. Unknown.
    Male. 160 pounds. Age thirty-five. $2.50. Bunch of keys. Sent to Prospect. G. B.

66. Unknown.
    Male. Age thirty-nine. 165 pounds. Screw-driver. Electric wire keys. Plug of tobacco. Plyers. Knife. Wrench screw. Two passes for street cars. Papers marked W. E. Kegg found upon him. Mother lives in Harrisburg.

67. Unknown.
    Male. Age thirty-one. Weight 140. Dark clothes. No valuables or other articles.

68. Unknown.
    Female. Age twenty. Weight 110. Dark hair. No articles.

69. Benshoff, Arthur.
    Age thirty-five. Weight 150. Gold watch and chain. Two knives. Pocket-book with $1.25. Pair cuff-buttons. Two keys. Two collar-buttons.

70. Unknown.
    Male. Age thirteen. 10 cts. Small, round, black ball. Tin tobacco tabs. Small piece of lead-pencil. Scapulary. Sent to Prospect.

71. Unknown.
    Female. Age thirty-five. 150 pounds. Very few clothes on. Black skirt. Black stockings. Slippers. No money or valuables. Sent to Prospect.

72. Stattler, Frank E.
    Age twenty. Weight 148. Smooth face. Small gray barred coat. No vest. Flannel shirt ribbed in front, brass buttons in it. Plug of twisted tobacco. Bunch of keys. Button-hook. Name on key-ring was Frank E. Stattler, on reverse side was No. 121 Park Place. Key. Taken by his brother, in presence of D. J. Beale, D.D.

73. Supposed to be Davis, Miss Della.
    Age twenty-four. Weight 135. Blue calico dress with figure on it. Red hair. Small plain gold ring. Could not remove ring. Letter from her mother addressed Miss Della Davis, 142 Grant street, Johnstown.

74. Meyer, Mary F.
    Identified. Taken by her brother.

75. Meyer, Mrs. Elizabeth.
    Identified. Taken by her son, John Meyer. Valuables given to her son, John Meyer, Washington street barber.

76. Coad, Mrs. Mary.

77. Coad, Willie.

78. Coad, John.

79. Hollevan, Miss.

80. O'Connell, Captain.

81. Duvalt, Chas. B.

82. Unknown.
    Female. Age twenty-five. Black silk stockings. Calico waist, blue with white stars and white buttons, white and blue collar. Sent to Prospect.

83. Unknown.
    Boy baby. Age six months. Plaid skirt, red and black. Had shoes on. Found in front of Cambria Iron Co.'s office.

84. Unknown.

85. (No record.)
    Female. Age thirty. Weight 150. Blue gingham dress. One pin.

86. Unknown.
    Male. Age two years. Red and black barred blue woolen stockings. Supposed to be Hoffman.

87. Unknown.
    Male. Age seven to eight. Blue waist, crescent figure. Short knee pants, black and white.

88. Unknown.
    Male. Age nine or ten. Blue waist with white figures. Short knee pants.

89. Gaither, Harry.
    Western Union Telegraph despatch boy.

90. Unknown.
    Female. Age unknown. Weight 120. Blue calico dress with small crescent dots. White and blue apron. Black stockings, with red and gray stripes on the top.

91. Reese, Miss.
    Taken by her father. Age four. James Reese.

92. Ogler, Mary.
    Age eighteen or nineteen.

MORGUE "C"—MILLVILLE SCHOOL-HOUSE.

1. Prosser, Miss Bessie.
    Daughter of Charles Prosser, of Cresson. No valuables.

2. Unknown.
    Male. Age twenty-five or thirty years. Cameo ring with man's head. Initials R. A. W. Valuables. Supposed to be Manfield.

3. Byran, Elizabeth M.
    Age about seventeen. Of Germantown, Philadelphia. Brown dress. Bracelets, seven strands and locket with initials, "E. M. B." On Day Express.

4. Downey, Mrs. Mary.
    Sister of David Faloon. Thin silver ring on third finger of left hand. Can't take it off.

5. Unknown.
    Male. About fifteen years old. Supposed to be Paul Geddes. No valuables.

6. Unknown.
    Female. Age twenty to twenty-three. No valuables.

7. Overback, William H.
    No valuables.

8. Unknown.
    Female. Three band rings, one with initials "F. M." Earring in left ear. Right earring torn out.

9. Owens, Annie.
    Age one and one-half years. Body taken by her brother. Thomas J. Jones.

10. Lewis, Orie.
    Boy. Three years old.

11. Owens, Mary Ann.
    Wife of Moses Owens. Plain ring on third finger of left hand (can't take off). Breast-pin. Delivered to husband.

12. Jones, Annie.
    Daughter of James Jones. Conemaugh street, Johnstown.

13. Jones, Richard.
    Conemaugh Borough.

14. Unknown.
    Band ring on third finger of left hand. Ring with the words, "Gott, Schutz, Dick," engraved thereon.

15. Unknown.
    Male. Age thirty-five to forty. Possibly a Jew. No valuables.

16. Geddes, George.
    Jacob Nolen says that John Thomas (?) has a watch, book, and over $12 in money which was taken from body of George Geddes.

17. Rose, H. G.
    District Attorney of Cambria county, Pa.

18. Unknown.
    At first supposed to be George Helsel, but found to be a mistake.

19. Schelleimer.
    Male. Conemaugh Borough. Age thirty-five to forty. Red hair and moustache.

20. Williams, Mrs. D. J.
    Breast-pin given to her husband.

21. Prosser, Fanny.
    Daughter of Charles Prosser, of Cresson.
    Earrings. Silver ring on middle finger
    of left hand. Can't get it off.

22. Parsons, Mrs. Eva May.
    Breast-pin. Not taken off.

23. Myers, John.
    Son of Philip Myers, of Millville.

24. Jones, James.
    Point Johnstown.

25. Thoburn, Thomas.

26. Leech, Mrs. Allie.

27. Sharkey, Mary.
    Daughter of Neil Sharkey.

28. Unknown.
    Female. Age twenty to twenty-five.
    Brown hair. Black cloth coat. Gold
    watch and chain. Breast-pin. Plain
    gold ring, marked "H. B." to "M. S.
    McD." Supposed to have been a pas-
    senger east bound train.

29. Smith, Mrs. Hettie H.
    Wife of H. K. Smith, of Osborne, Green
    co., Ohio. Watch chain and two
    lockets. One locket lost in getting body
    out. Breast-pin. Pair of cuff-buttons.
    Pocket-book with $30. Valuables de-
    livered to her husband.

30. Unknown.
    Female. Mistaken for Mrs. Ogle.

31. Tross, Mrs. Margaret.
    Wife of J. W. Tross. Age about thirty-
    eight. Height 5 feet 4 inches. Brown
    hair, double plait. Upper teeth false.
    Old scar on left side of face. Light
    underwear. Button shoes. Black stock-
    ings. Checkered waist.

32. Burkhart, Mrs. Mollie.
    Plain gold ring on third finger of left
    hand. Could not be removed.

33. James, Mollie.
    Thirteen years old. Daughter of E. A.
    James, Jr., 117 Market street, Johnstown.

34. Davis, Frank.
    603 South 4th street, Johnstown.

35. Kenna, Mrs. Alice.
    nee Christy.

36. Boyer, Solomon.
    Franklin Borough.

37. Stophel, Mrs. Margaret.

38. Lucas, Mrs. Maria.
    Colored.

39. Unknown.
    Female. Burnt beyond recognition.

40. Unknown.
    Sex unknown. Burnt beyond recogni-
    tion.

41. Unknown.
    Female. About thirteen years. Black
    stockings with red tip. Burned beyond
    recognition.

42. Williams.
    Male. About fifteen years. Dark com-
    plexion. Weight about 100. Height 5
    feet. Brown suit. Blue shirt. 61 cts.
    Pass book. Glove on left hand. Money
    and pass book in express office.

43. Unknown.
    Male. Six years old. Light hair.
    Weight about 70. Height about 3 feet
    6 inches. Black and yellow pants. Coat
    red lining, brass buttons with eagles
    thereon.

44. Wilson, Dr. J. C.

45. Myers, Catherine.
    Wife of Philip Myers. Cinder street,
    Johnstown. Age thirty-one.

46. Unknown.
    Male. Badly burned. Supposed to be
    Patrick Fagan.

47. (1.) Unknown.
    Female. Age about thirteen. Badly
    burned. Supposed to be the daughter of
    Patrick Fagan.

47. (2.) Unknown.
    Female. Age about six months. Badly
    burned. Supposed to be the daughter of
    Patrick Fagan.

48. Unknown.
    Female. Badly burned. One heavy
    plain gold ring. One light plain gold
    ring. One old style carved ring. Can't
    remove them.

49. (1.) Unknown.

49. (2.) Unknown.
    Two bodies. Burned beyond recogni-
    tion. Female. With blue merino
    stockings. Male. Pair of red socks.
    Black pants. Ages cannot be estimated.

50. Unknown.
Burned beyond recognition. Head, arms, legs burnt off. Telegraph instruments and chair found with body. Handkerchief in coffin.

51. Murphy, John.
Iron street, Johnstown.

52. Beam, Charles.
Son of Dr. L. T. Beam, 142 Market street, Johnstown.

53. Unknown.
Female. Burned beyond recognition.

54. Unknown.
Male. Burnt beyond recognition.

55. Fitzharris, Mary.
Age nineteen. Franklin street, Johnstown.

56. (Same as 8.)

57. Tucker, Lilian G.
Age nineteen. Maple avenue, Woodvale. (Age eighteen to twenty ?). Dark hair. Hazel eyes. Weight almost 130. Height about 5 feet 6 inches. Two rings, one bearing initial "A." Figured wrapper. One tooth on right side filled with gold.

58. Unknown.
Female. Age about thirty-seven. Dark hair. Dark eyes. Weight about 110. Height about five feet 3 inches. Calico dress. Square-toed shoes. Colored shirt.

59. Unknown.
Female. Age about sixty. Fair complexion. Gray hair. Blue eyes. Weight about 110. Height about 5 feet 4 inches. Dark colored shoes.

60. Unknown.
Female. Age about twenty-two. Dark brown hair. Light blue eyes. Weight about 150. Height about 5 feet 4 inches. Buttoned shoes. Calico dress.

61. Hite, Samuel.
Male. Age thirty to thirty-five. Weight about 170. Height 5 feet 10 inches. Hair cut close. Hazel eyes. Dark pants. Working clothes. Laced shoes.

62. Unknown.
Male. Age three years. Height about 3 feet 5 inches. Light hair. Blue eyes. Barred woolen pantalettes with waist.

63. Blough, Emanuel.
Weight about 160. Height about 5 feet 8 inches. Light complexion. Black hair. Brown or hazel eyes. White undershirt. Black vest. Watch. Bunch of keys. Pocket-book. Looking-glass. 20 years in drug store. Buried on father's farm in Stony Creek.

64. Beam, Dr. L. T.

65. Murr, Charles.

66. Unknown.
Female. Child. Weight about 25 pounds. Height about 18 inches. Sandy hair. Blue eyes.

67. Buchanan, John S.

68. Levergood, Miss Lucy.

69. James, Mrs. John W.

70. Surany, David.

71. Seibert, Henry.

72. Potter, Joseph, Sr.

73. Vinton, Margaretta.

74. (No record.)

75. Howe, Mary E.
Washington street, Johnstown.

76. Owens, Thomas.
58 Conemaugh street, Johnstown.

77. Unknown.
Female. Age about forty-five. Weight about 115. Height about 5 feet 6 inches. Fair complexion. Black hair. Dark blue eyes. Red underwear. Black dress. Plain gold ring on second finger of right hand. Pocket-book containing buttons and 61 cts. Pocket-book containing $10 bill and one silver dollar.

78. Spitz, Walter L.

79. (No record.)

80. Morgan, Martha (Cinder street).
About twelve years old. Brown dress.

81. Rodgers, Mrs. Mary E.
Pocket-book $17.00. Comb. Nightcap.

82. Unknown.
Male. Weight about forty. Height about 3 feet 9 inches. Light hair. Coat, vest. Burnt beyond recognition.

83. Keedy, Mrs. Mary.

84. Zeller, Miss Rose.

85. (No record.)

86. Unknown.
    Male. Weight about 170. Height
    about 5 feet 9 inches. Head burned off.
    Dark lace shoes. Revolver and knife.

87. Gromley, Lillie.
    Mineral Point.   Weight about 125.
    Height about 5 feet 6 inches. Dark
    hair. Hazel eyes. Two plain gold
    rings on right forefinger. Body nude.

88. McDowell, Mrs. Agnes.
    183 Pearl street.

89. Peydon, Campbell.
    Son of John W. Peydon, 179 Clinton
    street.

90. Unknown.
    Portion of a body (burned).

91. Unknown.
    Portion of a body (burned).

92. (No record.)

93. Christie, Andrew Coulter.
    187 Maple avenue, Woodvale, Pa.

94. Bischop, Charles.
    $170 in paper and $75 in gold. Pair of
    new gum boots.

95. Ross, Joseph.
    Norreville.

96. Hurst, Nattie.
    Boy of sixteen or seventeen years
    (Johnstown).   Weight about 120.
    Height about 5 feet 3 inches. Sandy
    complexion. Small-pox marks on face.
    Light hair. Blue eyes. Dark clothes.
    White shirt.   One pair new gum boots.

97. Unknown.
    Female. Burnt beyond recognition.

98. McDowell, George.
    183 Pearl street, Johnstown.

99. Peydon, Georgianna.
    189 Clinton street.

100. Peydon, Julia.
     189 Clinton street, Johnstown.

101. Suiter, Homer.
     Age about eight. Weight about 50.
     Height 3 feet 9 inches. Light complex-
     ion. Sandy hair. Blue eyes. Blue
     waist. Dark pants. Barefooted. $1.00
     silver clasped in hand.

102. Hannekamp, Samuel E.
     Lincoln street, Johnstown.

103. Unknown.
     All burned.   Unrecognizable.

104. Unknown.
     Two bodies, all burned.

105. Unknown.
     One of the bodies in 104.

106. Unknown.
     Female. Badly burned. Unrecogniza-
     ble. Ring marked " K. T. B."

107. Fisher, Noah.
     Richland township. Weight about 135.
     Height about 5 feet 6 inches. Medium
     hair. Hazel eyes. Sack coat. Vest.
     Dark pants, striped.

108. Jones, Edgar.
     Age eleven to fourteen years. Weight
     about 75. Height 4 feet 3 inches. Dark
     hair. Gray eyes. Dark clothes. Blue
     dotted waist and new buttoned shoes.
     Pearl street, Johnstown.

109. Unknown.
     Female. Weight about 128. Height
     about 5 feet 6 inches. Blue eyes. Dark
     complexion. Handkerchief marked " E.
     Schotz."

110. Unknown.
     Female. Weight 130. Height about
     5 feet 3 inches. Dark hair. Hazel
     eyes. Thin ring on third finger of left
     hand.

111. Unknown.
     Child about two years old. Burnt and
     unrecognizable.

112. Unknown.
     Female. Weight about 160. Height 5
     feet 6 inches. Fair complexion.
     Brownish red hair. Gray eyes. Dark
     basque body. Light dress. Supposed
     to be Mrs. Christie.

113. Hause, Mollie.
     Weight about 135. Height about 5 feet
     9 inches. Dark hair. Hazel eyes.
     Satteen Polonaise. Black dress.

114. (No record.)

115. Owen, William Tumley.
     Age about twelve. Weight about sixty-
     five. Height about 4 feet 6 inches.
     Brown hair. Hazel eyes. Coat with
     belt. Dark high button shoes. Black
     stockings.

OUTSIDE VIEW OF A TEMPORARY MORGUE.

116. Unknown.
Female. Weight about 60. Height about 4 feet. Red hair. Black stockings and button shoes.

117. Unknown.
Female. Weight about 110. Height about 4 feet 6 inches. Blonde hair. Blue eyes. Some patches of quilt on body. One gold ring, wide, with two hearts on it.

118. Drew, Mrs. Mary.
Age about sixty. Weight about 140. Height about 5 feet 6 inches. Gray hair. Gray eyes. Blue striped calico dress. Gray striped flannel underwear. Plain gold ring on third finger of left hand. Identified by the husband, Mark Drew.

119. Hellriegel, Miss Elizabeth.

120. Unknown.
Male. Weight about 150. Height about 5 feet 9 inches. Brown hair. Light eyes. Dark complexion. Dark clothes. Blue flannel skirt. Barefooted.

121. Downs, Theresa.
Iron street, Johnstown.

122. Bradley, Viola.
Age eleven. Weight about 75 pounds. Height about 4 feet 6 inches. Light complexion. Hazel eyes. Calico apron. Red waist. Wore a truss. Of Maple avenue, Woodvale.

123. Peyton, John W.
198 Chestnut street, Conemaugh Borough.

124. Connors, Mrs. Mary.
Sister of Theresa Downs.

125. (No record.)

126. Downs, Mrs. Catherine.

127. Unknown.
Female. About sixteen years. Weight about 105. Height 5 feet. Light hair. Blue eyes. Light complexion. Blue stockings. Blue dress. Button shoes with rubbers on.

128. Unknown.
Female. 145 pounds. Height 5 feet 3 inches. Badly burned. Eyes burned out. Brown calico sack. Light dress. Low cut shoes. Ring on second finger of left hand. Small earrings.
13

129. Unknown.
Sex unknown. Too badly burned for recognition.

130. Unknown.
Male. Burnt beyond recognition.

131. Unknown.
Sex unknown. Burnt beyond recognition.

132. No record.

133. Nixon, Emma.
Age twenty. Weight 130. Height 5 feet 6 inches. Brown hair. Gray eyes. Black jersey. Blue dress. Set and plain ring on right finger. Small earrings.

134. Unknown.
Sex unknown. Burnt beyond recognition.

135. Unknown.
Female. Age eight. Height 3 feet 9 inches. Weight 65. Button shoes. Black ribbed stockings. Spotted calico dress.

136. Unknown.
Male. Age three. Height 2 feet 6 inches. Weight 40. Brown hair. Light eyes. Checkered dress.

137. Davis, Clara.
Age eight. Iron street, Johnstown.

138. No record.

139. Unknown.
Female. Age four. Height 3 feet. Weight 28. Black hair. Blue eyes. Mark on stomach looks like a burn.

140. McKee, John C. W.
Body removed by his brother, Harry W. McKee.

141. McHugh, John L.
East Conemaugh. Age fifteen.

142. Unknown.
Female. Age sixteen to eighteen. Weight 125. Height 5 feet 2 inches. White. Fair complexion. Auburn hair. Light eyes. Brown striped dress. Comb with glass beads.

143. Unknown.
Female. Age forty-five to fifty. Weight 160. Brown hair, blue eyes, old scar on neck. Button shoes.

144. Rodgers; Patrick.

145. Unknown.
Male. Age sixteen to eighteen. Weight 70. Height 4 feet 9 inches. Brown hair. Brown eyes. High button shoes.

146. No record.

147. Unknown.
Male. Weight 190. Height 5 feet 9 inches. Dark hair. Large seal ring on little finger of right hand; set gone. 10 cts.

148. Skillhammer, Lawrence.
Portage street, Conemaugh Borough. Male. Age eighteen. Weight 120. Height 5 feet. Brown hair. Gray eyes. Dark striped coat and pants.

149. Unknown.
Female. Weight 75. Height 4 feet 3 inches. Brown hair. Blue eyes. Eardrop with small balls attached. Pink bow in hair. Brown dress with red plaited front and cuffs.

150. Duncan, Mrs. J. C.
Woodvale. Weight 145. Height 5 feet 4 inches. Dark hair. Dark eyes. Red mother hubbard wrapper. Hair plaited. Red stockings. Gold breast-pin. Small ear-drop with set lost.

151. (No record.)

152. Unknown.
From club house. Female. White. Weight 115. Height 5 feet 2 inches. Brown eyes. Fair complexion. Long black hair. Barred gingham apron. Blue dress. Plain hoop ring, one set on left hand. Blood set.

153. Abler, George.
Portage street, Conemaugh Borough. Age eleven. Weight 85. Height 4 feet 2 inches. Light hair. Dark brown eyes. Red and white waist. Knee pants. Button shoes.

154. Abler, Louisa.
Portage street, Conemaugh Borough. Age twenty-five. Weight 125. Height 5 feet. Light complexion. Auburn hair, brown eyes, blue check dress, blue waist. Red undershirt. Red stockings. Bible. Earring-drop.

155. Unknown.
Male. Weight 150. Height 5 feet 7 inches. Light hair. Found in drift above Company's store. Slippers. Comb in pocket. Light barred pants. 70 cts. One bunch of keys. Two pocket pieces. Scapulars.

156. Willower, Mrs. Bertha.
Somerset street, Johnstown. Died in Prospect hospital.

157. Unknown.
Female. Age thirty. Height 5 feet. Dark brown hair. Blue eyes. Button shoes. Striped white and blue stockings. Earrings plain gold. Sacque with beads. Black quilted skirt. Three right teeth out. Eye-tooth taken off at gum.

158. Unknown.
Foot of female. High button shoe. Black merino stockings. W. K. Endsley's bank book.

159. Unknown.
Male. Boy. Weight 75. Height 4 feet 3 inches. Light complexion. Auburn hair. Knee pants. Blue waist. Little black waist. Red undershirt. Muslin drawers. Gaiters.

160. Unknown.
Male. Boy. Weight 75. Height 4 feet 2 inches. Found on Walnut street. Light complexion. Blue waist. Knee pants.

161. Unknown.
Male. Age thirty-five. Weight 160. Height 5 feet 9 inches. Light complexion. Blue eyes. Auburn hair. Blue shirt. White undershirt. Laced shoes. Red socks. Black pants. Black vest. "F. P. R." on arm and clasped hands under same.

162. Unknown.
Male. Age eleven. White. Weight 48. Height 4 feet. Fair complexion. Dark hair. Dark eyes. Red flannel shirt. Black and white striped coat.

163. Diller, Rev A. P.

164. Diller, Isaac.

165. Dinant, Lola.

166. Unknown.
     Female.   Age forty-seven to fifty.
     Weight 225.   Height 5 feet 6 inches.
     Auburn hair.   Red and blue striped
     petticoat.   Red flannel underwear.
     Pocket-book, $6.35 money.

167. Diller, Mrs. Maria.

168. Kilgore, Alexander.

169. Unknown.
     Male.   Age three to four years.   Height
     3 feet 6 inches.   Light complexion.
     Auburn hair.   Gray woolen sack.   Blue
     vest buttons.   Red and white striped
     calico dress.   Black woolen socks.
     Black and white flannel petticoat.
     Gauze undershirt.   Button shoes.

170. Unknown.
     Male.   Boy.   Age seven.   Auburn hair.
     Dark blue waist.   Blue woolen coat.
     Knee pants.

171. Unknown.
     Male.   Age fourteen.   Weight 110.   Height
     5 feet.   Auburn hair.   Gray woolen
     coat.   Knee pants.   Blue waist, brass
     buttons.   White undershirt.

172. Unknown.
     Male.   Age thirteen.   Weight 110.
     Height 5 feet 6 inches.   Auburn hair.
     Blue eyes.   Black pants.   Black jersey
     coat.   Blue shirt.

173. Unknown.
     Female.   Weight 90.   Height 5 feet 6
     inches.   Fair complexion.   Auburn hair.
     Hazel eyes.   Button shoes.   Black stock-
     ings.   White corsets.   Red striped body.
     White drawers.   Red skirt.   Plaid skirt.
     Black dress and bustle.   Plain gold ring
     on third finger of left hand.

174. Unknown.
     Female.   Age forty to forty-five.
     Weight 200 to 225.   Height 5 feet 6
     inches.   Brown hair.   Blue eyes.   Light
     complexion.   Plain heavy gold ring on
     third finger of left hand.   Button shoes.
     Black stockings.

175. Leslie, John T.

176. Thomas, E. M.
     All but hips and lower limbs burned
     away.   Bunch of keys with tag marked
     "E. M. Thomas."   Gun screw-driver.
     Pocket-book and buckeye.

177. Roberts.
     Gold watch, engraved Christmas 18—.
     A book, on front "M. H. R." Steel
     rim glasses. $65.95.   Gold pocket-rim
     spectacles.

178. Unknown.
     Male child, about ten years old.   White.
     Weight 60.   Height 3 feet.   Light com-
     plexion.   Auburn hair.   Gray eyes.
     Light muslin dress.   Black stockings.
     Button shoes.

179. Unknown.
     Male.   Age five years.   Weight 70.
     Height 3 feet 6 inches.   White.   Fair
     complexion.   Auburn hair.   Blue eyes.
     Black knee pants.   Red waist.   Blue
     undershirt.   Short stockings.

180. Unknown.
     Female.   Age sixty-five.   Weight 225.
     Gray hair.   Purse with $200 gold.
     Breast-pin.   Black waist.   Gingham
     apron. $30 in greenbacks.

181. Unknown.
     Female.   Age forty-five.   Height 5 feet
     6 inches.   Weight 100.   White.   Very
     long black hair, mixed with gray.
     White handkerchief with red border.
     Black striped waist.   Black dress.
     Plain gold ring on third finger of left
     hand.   Red flannel underwear.   Black
     stockings.   Five pennies in purse.
     Bunch keys.

182. Unknown.
     Female.   Age forty-five.   Weight 125.
     Height 5 feet 4 inches.   White.   Fair
     complexion.   Brown hair.   Gray eyes.
     Black set pin.   Calico dress.   Red
     underwear.   Black cloth laced shoes.

183. Unknown.
     Female.   Age fifty.   Weight 100.
     Height 5 feet 4 inches.   White.   Gray
     hair.   Gold necklace.

Here closes the P. R. R. depot morgue.   It
was moved to First Ward school-house, Mil-
ville, the 10th of June.

June 11th.

184. Unknown.
     Male.   Age forty-five.   Weight 180.
     Height 5 feet 10 inches.   Purse and
     small iron key on a ring.

185. Unknown.
Male. Age forty-five. Weight 180.
Height 5 feet 10 inches. White. Bunch
of keys. $1.13 loose. White bone
handle knife.

186. Unknown.
Female. Age seven. Right leg and
right arm only.

187. Unknown.
Male. Age forty. Weight 190. Dark
hair. Chin whiskers. Black and white
checkered shirt. All other clothing
gone.

188. Unknown.
Male. Aged. Beyond recognition.

189. Young, William.
Of Company C, 14th Regiment Penna.
National Guard. Age about thirty.
Weight 160. Height 5 feet 8 inches.
Hazel eyes. National Guard uniform.
Reported as having committed suicide.

190. Unknown.
Male. Age twelve. Weight 185.
Height 4 feet. Black hair. Found in
Charles Mesher's store above stone
bridge.

191. Unknown.
Supposed to be Dr. George Waggoner.
Age forty-five. Weight 170. Height 5
feet 8 inches. Fair complexion. Brown
hair. Full black suit of clothing. Purse
$1.57. Pocket-knife. Pencil. Several
letters. Large wallet. Tobacco box.

192. Unknown.
Female. Age thirty-five. Dark red
hair. Dark flowered calico waist. Blue
gingham striped apron. Blue woolen
dress. Low laced shoes. Plain gold
band ring on third finger of left hand.
Large door key; had been broken and
repaired.

193. Unknown.
Male. Age twelve. Light hair. Blue
striped waist and dress. Button shoes.

194. Unknown.
Male. White. Age forty. Black
pants. White shirt. Blue vest. Small
key. Engraved gold ring on third finger of left hand.

195. Creed, David.
White. Age fifty. Weight 160. Height
5 feet 8 inches. Silver watch, open-face.
Black pants. White shirt. Black coat
and vest. $108.65 in pocket-book.
Pocket-knife. Bunch of keys with tag
and name. Identified by his son.

196. Unknown.
Female. Age sixty. Weight 180.
Height 5 feet 8 inches. Black hair.
Gray eyes. Blue calico dress. Piece of
dress. Slate pencil and door key.

197. Hanish, Blanche.
White. Age twenty-six. Identified by
her father and shipped to Dayton, Ohio.

198. Unknown.
White. Age four years. Weight 50 or
60. Male. Dark hair. Brown eyes.
Plaid dress, no sleeves. Gray mixed
undershirt. Red flannel shirt. Supposed to be John C. Clark's son.

199. Unknown.
Male. Weight 90. Height 4 feet.
Dark gray pants with small black stripes.
Button shoes. Red shirt with white
stripes. Dark striped stockings.

200. Unknown.
Male. Aged. Height 6 feet. Black
hair. Blue check shirt. Red undershirt.
Jean pants. Working shoes. 11 cents
in pocket-book.

201. Unknown.
Female. White. Age twenty-six.
Weight 125. Height 5 feet 6 inches.
Black eardrops. Two black hair pins.
Gray skirt with red stripe. Blue stock-
ings. Button shoes. Medal and
"Agnus Dei" around neck.

202. Unknown.
White. Age two years. Weight 40.
Height 2 feet 6 inches. Black and
white flannel shirt. Supposed to be
John C. Clark's son.

203. Unknown.
Female. Weight 130. Height 5 feet
6 inches. Black hair. Blue and white
striped dress. Red undershirt. Two
plain gold rings on second finger of left
hand. Fur cape around neck. Supposed to be Mrs. John C. Clark.

204. Unknown.
Male. Age fifty. Weight 160. Height 5 feet 9 inches. Sandy hair. Plain ring on third finger of left hand (with initials inside "C. R. 1869.") Pair blood stone cuff-buttons. Black alpaca coat. Navy blue vest and pants. Congress gaiters. Red stockings. Pocketbook. Knife and pencil. $13.30 in change. Open-faced silver watch. Heavy plaited chain and locket. Inside of locket a star with S. H., words trademark alone a star. Chain trinket with Washington head. Reverse the Lord's prayer. Odd Fellow's badge on pin.

205. Unknown.
Male. White. Age fifty-five. Weight 185. Height 5 feet 8 inches. Key ring with Yale flat key and two door keys. Pocket-knife. Purse with street car ticket.

206. Unknown.
Female. White. Weight 150. Height 5 feet 6 inches. Auburn hair. Small earring, white setting. Plain gold ring on third finger of left hand. Calico dress. White corsets. Black and gray striped skirt.

207. Given, Jane.
White. Age twenty-nine. Weight 120. Height 5 feet 6 inches. Auburn hair. Breast-pin and gold setting. Brown and white dress. Barred gingham. Button shoes. Identified by D. M. Given.

208. Unknown.
Female. Head severed from body. Woolen dress. Flannel skirt and red woolen stockings.

June 12th.

209. Unknown.
Male. White. Age eighteen months. Weight 30. Height 3 feet. Light hair. White dress and skirt plaited.

210. Given, Benjamin.
Age about nineteen. Weight 130. Height 5 feet 10 inches. White. Sandy hair. Black striped vest. Flannel shirt. Black jean pants. Laced shoes. Pocket-knife.

211. Unknown.
Male. Age fifteen. Weight 100. Height 5 feet. Black hair. Dark blue vest. Blue and white striped shirt. Red flannel underclothing.

212. Unknown.
Female. Age six months. White dress with spots. White flannel skirt. Red woolen stockings.

213. Unknown.
Female. Age thirteen. Weight 75. Height 4 feet 3 inches. Auburn hair. Blue and brown striped skirt. White underclothing.

214. Roland, Rand.
White. Age twenty. Weight 150. Height 5 feet 9 inches. Sandy hair. Dark gray mixed woolen suit. Red flannel underwear. Identified by brother.

215. Roland, Emma.
Age eighteen. Weight 140. Height 5 feet 6 inches. Light hair. Long breast-pin with brilliants. White and black checkered body. Buttoned shoes. White and black striped stockings. Plain gold ring with coral setting. Steel spring gaiters.

216. Rabb, Elizabeth.
White. Age twenty-three. Weight 140. Brown hair. Red and green striped body. Brown striped skirt. White underclothing. Long gold breast-pin with stone setting. Plain gold ring with initials, "K. L. R." Plain gold ring and earrings with stone setting.

217. Unknown.
Female. Unrecognizable. Sandy hair. Red flannel dress.

218. Unknown.
Female. Age eleven. Weight 110. Height 4 feet. Brown hair. Blue and white barred handkerchief. Purple suit. Black and white striped flannel skirt.

219. Unknown.
Male. Age twelve. Weight 75. Height 4 feet 3 inches. Brown hair. Black overcoat. Short sack coat. Dark knee pants. Blue and white striped shirt. Button gaiters. Supposed to be Ernest Mayhew.

220. Unknown.
Female. Age sixty. Weight 160. Height 5 feet 6 inches. Fair complexion. Black hair mixed with gray. Black waist. Black and green striped skirt. Red flannel underwear. Canton flannel drawers. Heavy knit stockings.

221. Unknown.
Male. Age ten. Weight 60. Height 3 feet 4 inches. Auburn hair. Red calico waist. Dark knee pants.

222. Unknown.
Female. Age eighteen to twenty. Weight 100. Height 5 feet 6 inches. Auburn hair. Green and purple striped dress. White underwear. Two pair of stockings, one black and the other blue. High gum boots, similar to men's boots.

223. White, Mary P.
Age twenty. Weight 120. Height 5 feet 6 inches. Black hair. Black alpaca dress. Red basque. Black skirt. Red underwear. Black stockings. Button shoes. Plain gold ring.

224. Unknown.
Male. Age eight. Weight 80. Height 4 feet. Button shoes. Black stockings. Gray woolen coat. Blue calico waist. Red and black striped shirt.

225. Unknown.
Male. Age six. Weight 40. Height 3 feet 9 inches. Dark brown hair. White shirt. Light twilled cloth dress.

226. Unknown.
Female. Age thirty-five. Brown hair. Button shoes. White underwear. Gold ring, cameo setting with full figure of a woman.

227. Unknown.
Female. Weight 160. Height 5 feet 6 inches. Brown hair. Dark blue dress, blue and gray striped. White skirt. Woolen underwear. Wart on left shoulder. Pair of scissors. Piece of tape. Pocket-book $7.35. Lead pencil and pocket-knife.

228. Unknown.
Female. Age five or six. Weight 30. Height 4 feet. Purple coat with small black stripes. Red and black checkered skirt. Blue dress with small stars. Buttoned shoes. Brown stockings.

229. Unknown.
Female. Weight 140. Height 5 feet 7½ inches. Red underwear. Two pair stockings, one white cotton, the other black woolen. Plain gold ring on first finger of left hand. Gold band ring on third finger of left hand. Dress alternate black and red with black flowers. Ear-drops with black sets. Cloth gaiters and blue calico waist.

230. Unknown.
Female. Age twenty-five. Weight 160. Height 5 feet 9 inches. Black hair. Checkered apron. Red dress. Red striped stockings. Also blue mother hubbard wrapper with white spots. Red and black striped skirt. One thimble.

231. Unknown.
Female. Age fifty-five. Weight 140. Height 5 feet 2 inches. Blue calico waist. Light calico dress with dark diamond spots. Brown and white gingham apron. Gray skirt with white stripes.

232. Cope, Mrs. Margaret.
Age sixty-five. Weight 145. Height 5 feet 5 inches. Gray hair. Black dress. Red and black skirt. One pocket-book containing two five dollar gold pieces, and one piece of gold bullion and one ten dollar gold piece, one key and one cent. Also another pocket containing three pieces of old coin, two coppers and fifteen dollars in greenbacks. Body removed by her son, Warren W. Cope.

233. Unknown.
Female. Age sixteen. Height 4 feet 6 inches. Dark blue dress with light blue sleeve. Gum boots and black stockings. Had an "Agnus Dei" in her pocket.

234. Unknown.
Female. Age seventeen. Weight 130. Height 5 feet. Red hair. Green cloth dress. Blue checkered apron and white apron underneath. Gold ring with red set. Lace waist over top of dress.

235. Jones, Mrs. Alice.
Pocket containing papers and two cents.

236. Layton, William.

237. Unknown.
Female. Age forty. Weight 150.
Height 5 feet 10 inches. Brown eyes.
Striped dress. One plain gold ring.
Heavy black cloth jacket.

238. Ranney, Mrs. Rev. J. A. Kalamazoo,
Michigan.
Age sixty-five. Height 5 feet 4 inches.
Gray hair. Gray eyes. Dark dress.
Dark coat. Gold watch, open-faced,
with a short chain. Blank book. Iden-
tified 12th August by her sons, Matthew
and D. A. Matthews.

239. Unknown.
Female. Age thirty-five. Weight 160.
Height 5 feet 6 inches. Light brown
hair. Two gold rings on left hand, one
with amethyst setting and one plain,
marked " M. J. H."

240. McHugh, Mrs. B. A.
Residence, East Conemaugh.

241. Unknown.
Female. Age twenty. Weight 125.
Height 5 feet 4 inches. Dark brown
eyes. Pocket-book containing $43.35.
Small plain gold ring and one thimble.

242. Unknown.
Female. Weight 135. Height 5 feet 4
inches. Auburn hair. Light complexion. Dark dress. Blue underskirt.
Barred underdress. Blue and white
apron.

June 14th.

243. Unknown.
Female. Age six months. Weight 25.
Height 2 feet 6 inches. Black and white
skirt. White dress.

244. Unknown.
Female. Foot only. Black stocking.
High-buttoned shoe.

245. Unknown.
Female. Left foot of child. Black woolen
stocking. High buttoned shoe.

246. Unknown.
Female. Age forty-five. Weight 140.
Height 5 feet 2 inches. Gray hair.
One ear-drop, very strange pattern. Also
enciente.

247. Unknown.
Female. Age thirty-eight. Weight 145.
Height 5 feet 1 inch. Light complexion.
Dark hair. Dark eyes. Right hand
deformed. Striped calico dress.

248. Unknown.
Female. Age thirty-five. Weight 130.
Height 5 feet 1 inch. Dark hair. Low
shoes. Dark woolen stockings. Dress
of woolen goods, with small diamond
figures. Pocket-book with $6.10.

June 15th.

249. Unknown.
Male. Age eight. Weight 45 pounds.
Height 4 feet 2 inches. Light complex-
ion. Blue waist. Light barred knee
pants. Blue black ribbed stockings.
Buttoned shoes and patent heels.

250. Unknown.
Female. Age thirty. Weight 115.
Height 5 feet 4 inches. Blue calico
dress with star figures. Brown skirt with
two bands. Small coin purse, 20 cents.
One shoe buttoner. One plain band gold
ring.

251. Unknown.
Male. Age one year. Weight 20.
Height 2 feet 6 inches. Calico dress,
striped blue and white. Red flannel
skirt.

252. Unknown.
Female. Age fifteen. Weight 90.
Height 5 feet 3 inches. Brown dress.
Red flannel barred red and black. Black
and white barred underwear. Black
stockings, No. 5 shoes. Diamond ring
carved, one crescent pin, set with brilliants, with star in centre. One pair of
ear-drops.

June 16th.

253. Unknown.
Female. Age twenty-two. Weight 140.
Height 5 feet 7 inches. Light com-
plexion. Dark hair. Eyes unknown.
Black alpaca dress. White under-skirt.
Red waist, worked. Brown ribbed
stockings. No shoes.

254. Unknown.
Female. Age thirty-five. Weight 135.
Height 4 feet 10 inches. Dark garnet
dress. White stockings, No. 5 shoes.
No valuables.

255. Unknown.
Female. Age forty. Weight 140.
Height 5 feet. Hair dark and very long.
Black ribbed jersey. Black dress.
White and black striped skirt. Lady's
hunting-case gold watch and chain.

256. Unknown.
Female. Age ten. Weight 75. Height 3 feet 8 inches. Light hair. Eyes unknown. Shoes and one gum shoe. Ribbed stockings. Red flannel underskirt. Flannel drawers. Jacket with flannel skirt. Brown dress. One pair earrings.

257. Unknown.
Male. Age forty-five. Weight 150. Height 5 feet 9 inches. White. Light complexion. Dark shirt. Dark pants. Brown coat. White stockings. Pocketbook. Gold ring. Pocket-knife.

258. Unknown.
Female. Age four years. Weight 40. Height 3 feet. White. Light complexion. Eyes unknown. Barred dress. White lace collar. Black stockings. Cardinal jacket, with brass buttons. Barred underclothes. Child's gold breast-pin.

June 17th.

259. Bates, Mrs. Annie.
Racine, Wisconsin. Age sixty. Weight 120. Height 5 feet. Light complexion. Straw bonnet. Black gloves. One false tooth. White skirt. Black dress. White underwear. Valuables, receipt of deposit in First National Bank of Racine, Wisconsin, of $60.00, $74.20 in cash, three gold rings. Ladies' gold watch and chain, one trunk check marked C. 562. Breast-pin.

260. Phillips, Mrs. Robert.
Johnstown, Pa. Age thirty. Weight 125. Height 5 feet 6 inches. Light complexion. Dark hair. Dress, white and brown stripes, blue jersey. Valuables. Pocket-book containing $151.00. One small gold ring.

261. McConoughey, Mr. Wallace.
Johnstown, Pa. About three-fourths of body. No clothing. One large set ring.

262. Phillips, John.
Son of Robert Phillips, Johnstown, Pa. Age thirteen. Weight 70. Height 4 feet 10 inches. White and black striped waist. Checkered knee pants. Black stockings. Red belt around waist.

June 18th.

263. Unknown.
Female. Age forty-five. Weight 150. Height 5 feet 9 inches. White. Light complexion. Blue black dress. Figured waist and white underclothing.

264. Unknown.
Female. Age thirty. Weight 140. Height 5 feet. Blue calico dress with white spots. Woolen cloth waist barred gray and black. White muslin underclothing. Large ring.

265. Unknown.
Male. Burnt up almost. Small purse. Two watch keys. Door key and pocket handkerchief.

266. Unknown.
Female. Burned beyond recognition. Weight 115. Height 5 feet. Small gold ring.

267. Heckman, Mrs. Frances.
Age twenty-eight. Weight 160. Height 5 feet. Small rolled plate ear-drops. Received valuables of 267. John Burkhard, guardian of the above.

268. Knoor, Miss Emma.
Jackson street, Johnstown, Pa. Age 13.

269. Unknown.
Female. Age twenty-five. Weight 160. Height 5 feet 4 inches. Spotted cloth dress, gray and black. Flannel skirt, striped gray and black. Black cloth jersey, covered buttons. Valuables. Two gold rings.

270. Unknown.
Female. Age fifteen. Weight 100. Height 4 feet 6 inches. Fair hair. Light complexion. Blue and white barred calico dress.

271. Unknown.
Female. Age thirty. Weight 135. Height 5 feet. Dark hair. Plain cloth dress. Two gold rings, one pair ear-drops.

272. Trendle, John W.
Age twenty-five. Height 5 feet 9 inches. Striped brown and yellow overalls. Striped drawers. Large pocket-knife and five cents.

273. Unknown.
Male. Age forty. Height 5 feet 8 inches. Dark hair. Blue woolen shirt. $4.00 in cash.

SCENE IN THE PARK—OPERA HOUSE IN THE BACKGROUND.

274 Unknown.
    Female. Age twenty-three. Weight
    130. Height 5 feet 6 inches. Dark
    hair. Black woolen mitts. Black cloth
    jacket. Gold ring with torm of woman
    on set. Ear-drops, one broken.

June 19th.

275. Unknown.
    Female. Age six years. Height 4 feet.
    Hair long and brown. Plaid dress,
    belt with two buckles. High buttoned
    shoes.

276. Unknown.
    Female. Age twenty. Weight 130.
    Height 5 feet 6 inches. Red and black
    barred flannel skirt. Blue dress with
    white pearl buttons.

277. Williams, Carrie.
    Johnstown, Pa. Age twenty. Height
    5 feet 6 inches. Valuables. One ring
    with set. One chain with bracelet with
    small padlock attached. Two pins
    joined by chain. Received valuables of
    277. Harvey D. Williams.

278. Unknown.
    Female. Weight 150. Height 5 feet 4
    inches. Scapular around her neck.

279. Unknown.
    Male. Age twelve. Weight 60.
    Height 4 feet 6 inches. Brown hair.
    Striped waist, brown and white. Woolen
    knee pants, twilled blue cloth.

280. Unknown.
    Female. Weight 150. Height 5 feet
    6 inches. False teeth lower jaw.

281. Unknown.
    Male. Weight 150. Height 5 feet 9
    inches. Black and white barred
    flannel drawers. Door key. Tobacco
    pipe. Watch chain.

June 20th.

282. Unknown.
    Male. Weight 160. Height 5 feet 9
    inches. Red flannel drawers. Leather
    boots. Pipe. Pocket-knife.

283. Knorr, Miss Bertha.
    Jackson street, Johnstown, Pa. Age fif-
    teen. Weight 120. Height 5 feet 4
    inches.

284. Unknown.
    Female. Age seventeen. Weight 115.
    Height 5 feet 3 inches. White and
    black barred flannel skirt. Blue and
    white barred gingham apron. Black
    stockings.

285. Unknown.
    Female. Age thirteen. Weight 75.
    Height 4 feet 7 inches. Black stock-
    ings. Buttoned shoes.

286. Unknown.
    Female. Age ten years. Nothing but
    the bones.

287. Unknown.
    Female. Weight 140. Height 5 feet
    6 inches. Dark brown hair. Leather
    shoes with cloth top. Right foot and
    leg deformed.

288. Unknown.
    Sex unknown. Age about eighteen
    months. Blue and white striped dress.

289. Unknown.
    Sex unknown. Age about eighteen
    months.

290. Unknown.
    Female. Weight 150. Height 5 feet
    6 inches. Brown hair. Dark blue
    stockings with white soles. Buttoned
    shoes, with patent leather tips.

291. Reese, John.
    Son of James Reese, Conemaugh street,
    Johnstown, Pa. Age two years. Light
    hair. Black eyes.

292. Unknown.
    Female. Age twelve. Black and red
    barred flannel skirt. Green dress.

293. Unknown.
    Female. Weight 200. Black hair.
    Blue and white striped skirt. Striped
    calico dress.

294. Unknown.
    Female. Age nine. Weight 50.
    Height 3 feet 8 inches. Buttoned shoes.
    Red knit skirt. Maroon colored dress.

295. Unknown.
    Female. Weight 125. Height 5 feet 6
    inches. Black and white striped skirt.
    Brown dress with small steel stripes.
    Laced cloth gaiters.

June 21st.

296. Unknown.
Female. Age five years. Plaid dress, woolen goods, barred red, brown and green. Blue and white barred gingham bib. Small chased gold ring.

297. Unknown.
Female. Brown hair mixed with gray. Red skirt. Black jersey. Black dress. Canton flannel drawers. Buttoned shoes. Breast-pin.

2o8. Unknown.
Female. Dark blue woolen cloth dress. Buttoned shoes. Red skirt, with six inches of checkered cloth at top of band. $25.00 in paper. $1.68 in silver.

299. Benford, Miss Maria.
Hulbert house, Johnstown, Pa. Two plain gold rings, one marked "Sister" inside.

300. Unknown.
Female. Age nine. Black and white barred flannel skirt.

301. Unknown.
Female. Dark hair. Blue spotted calico dress. One small ear-drop.

302. Unknown.
Male. Weight 150. Height 5 feet 8 inches. Buttoned shoes. White handled knife. Cigar smoker, nickel. Small piece of steel chain.

303. Pritchard, Henry.
Market street, Johnstown, Pa. Open faced gold watch. Two pocket-knives. Three bunches of keys. Three door keys. Pocket-book, containing $1 in paper and $1.30 in silver.

304. Unknown.
Male. Age three. Weight 40. Height 3 feet 6 inches.

305. Unknown.
Female. Age twelve. Weight 80. Height 4 feet 2 inches.

306. Unknown.
Sex unknown. Only two feet.

307. Unknown.
Male. Age seven years. Weight 65. Blue waist, white stripes.

308. Benford, Miss Mary.
Hulbert house, Johnstown, Pa. One plain gold ring, one onyx set ring.

309. Unknown.
Sex unknown. Age seven months.

310. Unknown.
Female. Age four years.

311. Unknown.
Sex unknown. Burned beyond recognition.

312. Unknown.
Female. Burned beyond recognition.

313. Unknown.
Female. Burned beyond recognition.

314. Unknown.
Female. Buttoned shoes. Rubbers. $2.00 in bills. $5.00 in gold. 81 cents in change. Gold ring, garnet set.

315. Tacy, Peter L.
35 Maple avenue, Woodvale. Rubber coat and boots. Two feet rule. Pocket-book with $33.50.

316. Unknown.
Male. Silver open-faced watch and chain. Three keys. Pocket-knife. Bone tooth-pick. $6.31. Receipt from Charles S. Ruth to party named Schuner or Shuor.

317. Unknown.
Human foot. Laced shoe. Light stocking. Light drawers.

318. Unknown.
Female. Weight 140. Back comb and five cents.

319. Unknown.
Child. Sex unknown.

320. Unknown.
Male. Just one foot, No. 7 shoe.

321. Harris, Miss Winnie.
Daughter of John I. Harris, Chief of Police, Johnstown, Pa. Three rings. Ear-drops. Received by her brother.

322. Unknown.
Male. Weight 160. Height 5 feet 6 inches. One gold ring, cameo setting. Two pocket-knives. Bunch of keys. Door key. 38 cents in change.

June 22d.

323. Murrtha, Mr. James.

324. Murrtha, Florence.

325. Murrtha, infant of James Murrtha.

326. Murrtha, Frank.
   Son of James Murrtha.

327. Murrtha, James.

328. Hamilton, Jacob.
   Pocket-knife. Pair of shears. Eye-glasses. $37.00 in cash. Certificate of deposit for $1000.00 at John Dibert & Co.'s bank.

329. Ripple, Maggie B.

330. Unknown.
   Female. Only her feet.

331. Unknown.
   Male. Age eight. Weight 65. Height 4 feet 6 inches. Knee pants, black ribbed. Lace shoes. Blue waist. Black coat.

332. Unknown.
   Female. Breast-pin, collar-buttons, cloth dress, gray and white barred. No. on grave is 333.

333. Werty. Luther.
   Died at hospital. Check marked J. ? McK. No. 1698. Pocket-book. Pocket-knife. No money. No. on grave is 332.

334. Linton, Miss Minnie.
   Weight 140. Height 5 feet. Heavy jacket with heavy cord. Dress with large pearl buttons in front. Letter found on body addressed to Minnie Linton, Lincoln avenue, Johnstown, Pa. Signed, S. Clark Dougherty.

335. Unknown.
   Female. Weight 155. Height 5 feet 6 inches. Black hair. Woolen under-skirt, red, brown and white barred cotton underskirt, striped white and red. Black cashmere dress, with black glass buttons oval shape. Plain gold ring, with J. L. B. engraved on inner side.

336. Unknown.
   Female. Weight 115. Height 5 feet. Dark hair. Plaid dress, black, red and blue barred.

337. Beck, Mrs. William.
   Her child prematurely born was along with her. Weight about 140. Height 4 feet 5 inches. Brilliant ear-drops. Blue chintz dress, with yellow and white flowers.

338. Unknown.
   Adult. Only two charred feet.

339. Unknown.
   Adult. Only two charred feet.

340. Unknown.
   Adult. Only two charred feet. A bunch of keys found with the above three pairs of feet.

341. Lenhart, Annie.
   Short and stout build. Weight 110. Height 5 feet. Fine buttoned gaiters.

342. Unknown.
   Male. Age twelve. Height 4 feet. Knee pants. No means of identification.

343. Unknown.
   Male. Weight 190. Height 5 feet 11 inches. Clothes partly removed, and in stocking feet. No valuables.

June 23d.

344. Hiser, Mrs.
   Washington street, Johnstown, Pa. Weight 130. Height 5 feet 6 inches. Blue and white striped dress. Red handkerchief. Letter found on body signed S. F. Clarke.

345. Unknown.
   Female. Age about ten. Weight 75. Spring heel shoes. Blue and brown barred woolen waist. Black and red barred flannel skirt. High-buttoned shoes.

346. Unknown.
   Female. Weight 120. Height 5 feet 6 inches. Heavy plaid jacket with marble shaped buttons.

June 24th.

347. Unknown.
   Male. Age twelve to fourteen. Black corduroy coat, with two plaits down the back. Dark barred pants and blue calico waist with white flag figures.

348. Hammer, Daniel.
   329 Railroad street, Johnstown, Pa. Pair of overalls. Heavy leather boots. Pair of spectacles and tin case.

349. Conwey, Maude.
   Age about seven. Blue cloth dress. Hand-knit open-worked sacque. Identified by her mother.

350. Unknown.
Male. Height 5 feet 9 inches. Leather boots. Tin or nickel watch safe. Silver hunting-case watch and gold chain with charm representing surveyor's compass. Leather spectacle case. Gold spectacles. Door key. Upper false teeth.

351. Carroll, Rosie.
Railroad street, Johnstown, Pa. Gold ear-drops with pearl setting in centre. Gold breast-pin with brilliant setting. Small gold ring.

352. Unknown.
Female. Weight about 135. Height 5 feet 6 inches. Black jersey. Blue calico dress, with white spots. Red woolen stockings. Home knit red flannel skirt. White skirt. Gum garters.

June 25th.

353. Unknown.
Male.   Age twelve.   Weight 60. Height 4 feet 4 inches. Brown and gray striped knee pants. Blue coat.

354. Unknown.
Male. Age twelve to fourteen. Weight 100. Height 4 feet 6 inches. Brown cloth shirt, plaited in front, small plaits.

355. Keedy, Harry.
101 Centre street, Johnstown, Pa. Weight 150. Dark hair. Fine laced shoes. Badge of Junior Mechanics. 43 cents in change. Letters found on body. Valuables recovered by brother, T. P. Keedy.

356. Unknown.
Male. Weight 160. Height 5 feet 9 inches. Gold hunting-case watch and chain with charm attached. One wire sleeve supporter.

357. Unknown.
Female. Age about ten. Dark brown hair. Weight 65. Scapular around neck. Blue and white checkered bib. Calico dress, brown figure.

June 26th.

358. Hinckman, Henry C.
Age seven. Weight 45. Height 4 feet 4 inches. Gum boots. Blue waist with white stripes. Gray and black striped knee pants.

359. Unknown.
Female. Age six. Weight about 50. Height 4 feet 6 inches. Button shoes, spring heels. Red flannel skirt. Light calico dress. Small gold ring.

360. Unknown.
Female. Age eighteen months. Red flannel skirt. Red and white barred calico dress.

361. Unknown.
Male. Age fifty. Weight 170. Height 5 feet 6 inches. Leather boots. Red flannel drawers. Blue drill overalls. White woolen socks Gum coat. One week's growth of sandy beard, mixed with gray. Silver open faced watch, Elgin movement. Silver chain. Leather coin purse. Ten cents. Bunch of keys. Scapular around neck.

362. Ross, John A.
Crippled in both feet, and wore steel leg supporters. Name found on arm.

363. Unknown.
Female. Age six. Weight 40. Height 4 ft. Buttoned shoes. Black stockings. Blue and white barred cotton dress Brown hair, plaited with ribbon. Brown and white barred apron. Blue and yellow striped dress. Also red flannel dress. White underwear trimmed with embroidery.

364. Jacobs, Lewis.
Cambria borough, Broad street. One pocket-book. $1.95 in silver. Silver open faced watch. Black guard to it. Pocket-knife.

365. Hoffman, Harry.
Son of Godfrey Hoffman. Age six. Weight forty. Height 4 feet 4 inches. Buttoned shoes with spring heels. Home knit woolen stockings. Brown and white spotted necktie. Blue and white spotted calico dress. Red flannel skirt. Gray and black barred coat with black buttons.

366. Schmitz, Gustave.
Life insurance agent. $36.85 in cash. Gold watch, No. 16518. Gold ring marked M. S. to G. S., September 25, 1887. One band ring.

367. Unknown.
Male. Age about three years. Buttoned shoes. White muslin skirt. Dress with brown woolen waist. Brown, white and blue plaid skirt. Coat of brown cloth, same as dress waist, with large, white pearl buttons.

368. Hoffman, Godfried.
Washington street, Johnstown, Pa. Gold watch and chain. Bunch of keys. Pocket-knife. $4.65 in money.

369. Unknown.
Male. Age about eight. Knee pants. High buttoned spring heel shoes. Red woolen undershirt. Striped pants. Black stockings.

370. Unknown.
Male. Age about eight. Buttoned shoes. Red. white and blue waist, square, black pattern. Black corduroy coat. Black gray mixed pants.

371. Woolf, Mrs. Morris.
Locust street, Johnstown, Pa. Black jersey. Green and brown striped woolen dress. Blue and white striped skirt. $7.26 in change. One English penny.

372. Webber, E. Vincent.
Gold watch and chain. Pocket-knife. Door key. Bunch of keys. Small book and papers. Eighty-three cents in change.

373. Unknown.
Female. Age about six. Buttoned shoes, soles well worn. Red cloth dress. Red flannel skirt, with blue and white checkered waist attached.

374. Unknown.
Female. Buttoned shoes. Red shawl. Lower teeth false. Black and gray striped woolen skirt. Blue calico dress, white spots. White handkerchief. White and red striped skirt. Brown and white barred gingham apron.

July 1st.

375. Unknown.
Male. Weight 180. Height 6 feet. No clothing.

376. Daly, F. J.
Johnstown, Pa. Black cloth pants. Blue coat and vest. Purse with $8.00. Ring with set and name inside. Collar buttons. Bunch of keys.

377. Unknown.
Male. Age about ten. Weight 50. Black hair. Blue cloth knee pants. Blue and white striped waist. Identified afterwards as Francis Fores (Feris).

378. O'Connor, Rosanna.
Red and white striped skirt. Blue spotted calico dress. Plain gold ring, received by her mother, Ellen O'Connor.

379. Unknown.
Female. Age about ten. Buttoned shoes with spring heels. Red dress, trimmed with lace. Gray and white jacket trimmed with woolen lace. Black hair. Breast-pin.

380. Moore, Mrs. C. B.
Red and black striped skirt. Black cloth wrapper, buttoned in front to knees. Buttoned shoes. Black stockings. Heavy black coat.

381. Waggoner, Mrs. Mary.
Black dress with velvet collar. Buttoned shoes. Red skirt with ruffles. Blue and white ringed stockings. Long black tie or scarf. False teeth upper and lower. Plain gold ring. Small ear-drop. Leaf pattern.

382. Unknown.
Male. Age about ten. Buttoned shoes, spring heels. Black ribbed stockings. Black and gray mixed knee pants.

383. Unknown.
Sex unknown. No means of identification.

July 3d.

384. Unknown.
Female. Age ten. Red and black ringed woolen stockings, home knit. White dress trimmed with embroidery. Light calico dress with black figures. Red and white striped skirt. Buttoned shoes. Ear-drops, enameled black, with blue setting. Home knit lace collar. Scapular around her neck.

385. Oiler, John Esler.
Age about ten. Sandy hair. Black woolen stockings, home knit. Buttoned shoes. Blue cloth knee pants. Red waist with anchor figures.

386. Potts, Miss Jane.
    Dark dress. Black stockings. White underclothing. Gold watch and chain. Gold ring marked James Potts, died March, 1874. Pocket-book containing eighteen cents.

387. Unknown.
    Female. Age about twelve. Weight 65. Blue calico dress with white dots.

388. Unknown.
    Male. Age about three years. Buttoned shoes. Blue calico dress with small white vines. Red flannel skirt.

389. Unknown.
    Male. Age about six years. High-buttoned shoes with heel. Gray and black striped knee pants. Black stockings.

390. Young, Samuel.
    Male. Age about thirteen. Blue calico waist with white dots. White handled knife. Mixed woolen knee pants. One cloth slipper flowered. Receipt to Robert Bossett, from Geo. T. Swank, in payment of *Daily Tribune.* One month, dated May 1, 1889. Disinterred and removed to Braddock for burial by Frank L. Bridges.

July 4th.

391. Unknown.
    Female. Age about twelve. Buttoned shoes, spring heel. Red and black striped flannel skirt. Blue dress. Blue woolen stockings. Coat with fur collar. Blue and black barred flannel skirt. Blue and white barred gingham apron.

392. Unknown.
    Female. Height 4 feet 6 inches. Buttoned shoes, spring heels. Black ribbed stockings. Red and white striped skirt. Blue plaid dress. Plain gold ring.

393. Hoofman, Lizzie.
    Daughter of Godfred Hoofman, Washington street, Johnstown, Pa. Identified by her friends.

394. Unknown.
    Female. About fourteen. Light red hair. Part of a skirt of a petticoat, the band of which was made of ticking. The shoulder strap holding up the skirt was of same material. The body entirely nude, excepting two small pieces of skirt or petticoat. Found at Ten Acre in the river, July 3d. Buried in Decker's cemetery, Morrellville.

395. Unknown.
    Male. Age about 30. Height 5 feet 8 inches. Full suit of clothes of brown and red and black checkers. Red socks. Buttoned shoes. Rusty door key in one pocket. Nothing else about him to identify him, unless a ticket from Nineveh to Johnstown and return. Found in water at Ten Acre. Buried in Decker's cemetery, Morrellville, Pa.

July 5th.

396. Unknown.
    Female. Height 5 feet 6 inches. Weight 130. Buttoned shoes. Gum rubbers. Two gold rings chased. Gray woolen dress with red and white mixed stripes and brass buttons.

397. Downley, John.
    Residence unknown. Age about 55. Height 5 feet 6 inches. Weight 160. Sandy moustache. Bald in front, with large wart on right side of head. Hair mixed with gray inclining to curl. Middle finger of left hand stiff from some former injury. Injured July 4th, on P. R. R. and died from effects same day.

398. Unknown.
    Male. Height 5 feet 6 inches. Weight 150. Blue woolen shirt. Small heart on right arm.

399. Unknown.
    Female. Height 5 feet 4 inches. Weight 115. White muslin.

400. Unknown.
    Male. Height 5 feet 10 inches. Weight 170. Blue drill overalls. Blue, brown and white striped shirt. Gum coat. High gum boots. Bunch of keys. Pocket-knife, black handle. Small toothpick.

July 6th.

401. Unknown.
Female. Age about six. Red, blue, black and green plaid dress, woolen goods. Red flannel skirt. Brown and white gingham basque. Buttoned shoes, spring heel. Black stockings.

402. Unknown.
Male. Wore about No. 7 congress gaiters. Gray cotton socks. Green, black and brown barred pants. Gold hunting-case watch and chain. Mechanic's pin. Rubber finger ring in pocket. Supposed to be William F. Beck, husband of Mrs. Blanche Beck (337), years 29. Machinist, worked in Gautier. Two children, Alfred and Roy, drowned with them.

July 7th.

403. Lee, Dr. J. K.
Main street, Johnstown, Pa. Gold watch and chain with charm. $45.00 in cash. Bunch of keys with checks and name. Two pocket-knives. Valuables turned over to Mrs. Lee.

404. Alexander, Mrs. John G.
Height 5 feet. Weight 125. Brown hair. Buttoned shoes. White ribbed stockings. Leather heel protectors on foot. Wire bustle. Lady's brown cloth basque with plaid front. Lace collar. Rosette breast-pin, black, bound with gold and set with pearls.

July 9th.

405. Unknown.
Male. Age about ten. Black and brown striped pants. Black coat. Red and black barred necktie. High-buttoned shoes. Papers found on body.

July 11th.

406. O'Neal, John.
Height about 5 feet 10 inches. Weight 170. Dark brown hair. Barefooted. Jean pants. Gray woolen shirt. White cotton undershirt. Rosary and 25 cents in pocket.

July 12th.

407. Swineford, Mary A.
St. Louis, Mo. Lady's gold open-faced watch, stem-winder. Breast-pin. Pocketbook and papers. Harry Bischoff, St. Louis, Mo. Received valuables.

408. Unknown.
Female. Height 5 feet 4 inches. Weight about 140. Auburn hair. Buttoned shoes. One small ear-drop. Blue calico dress with small yellow stripes.

July 13th.

409. Unknown.
Female. Adult. Auburn hair. Buttoned shoes. Heavy quilted skirt. Flowered calico dress. $25.00 in gold and 38 cents in change.

July 14th.

410. Davis, Frederick.
Pittsburgh, Pa. Height 5 feet 8 inches. Age about thirty-six. Killed on P. R. R. July 14, 1889.

411. Unknown.
Female. Age about nine. Weight about fifty. Small earrings with ball attached. Gray jersey cloth vest and jacket, with large metal buttons, swan stamped upon them. Blue and black barred flannel skirt. High-buttoned shoes, spring heels. Black stockings.

412. Unknown.
Male. Adult. Body mangled. Heavy mill shoes. Black and brown vest.

413. Unknown.
Male. Age about thirteen. Buttoned shoes. Knee pants. Blue shirt. Black woolen stockings. Gum sling in pocket. Found near Walnut street. Height 4 feet 9 inches. Weight about 75.

414. Unknown.
Male. Black and gray striped pants. Red suspenders with drawers supporters. Black handle knife, two blades broken. 11 cents in change. Found in Conemaugh Borough.

415. Young, A. C.
Gum boots. Black pants. Silver tobacco box, with name and date, Jan., 1888. Silver open-faced watch and gold chain. Memorandum book of slaughter house, having a list of hides in it. Bunch of keys. Collar-button.

416. Unknown.
Female. Age about four years. Height 3 feet 3 inches. Blue and white checkered dress or apron. Garnet dress. Black stockings with supporters. Spring heel buttoned shoes. Gold ring with blue setting.

417. Cullin, Annie.
Cambria City. Found in residence of George Hamilton. Small gold ring, garnet set.

418. Female. Identified as Miss Girty Rees, daughter of James Rees, Johnstown, Pa.

419. Unknown.
Male. Age about fourteen years. Weight 90 pounds. Height 5 feet. Knee pants brown and black striped, good. Blue and white striped waist. Pearl button coat, gray, black and red mixed, wool. Blue silk tie with dots.

420. Unknown.
Male. Age fourteen years. Weight 90 lbs. Height 5 feet. Cotton pants. Dark coat. Blue calico waist, white spots. Found in Kernville.

421. Female. Identified as Miss Cora Wagoner.

422. Unknown.
Female. Height 5 feet 4 inches. Weight 125 pounds. Hair black. Small gold ear-rings. Button shoes. Brown and white ring hose. Blue and white flowered sateen basque. Blue and white barred skirt.

423. Unknown.
Female. Hair black. Weight 140. Height 5 feet 6 inches. Red knit skirt. White canton flannel drawers. Black and bronze barred wool basque. Black dress. Heavy black jersey cloth coat. Upper teeth false. Ladies' hunting-case gold watch. Chain with small bucket charm. Gold ring with set collar-button.

424. Unknown.
Male. Killed at Sheridan station, July 22d.

425. Identified as Mrs. Hart.

426. Unknown.
Child. Age about one year. Sex unknown. No clothing.

427. Unknown.
Female. Height 5 feet 6 inches. Weight 125 pounds. Striped skirt. Button shoes. Two rubbers. Black hose. Two teeth out right side upper jaw. One out left side. Front teeth good. Blue calico dress, white flowers. Pearl buttons. Wore scapulars.

428. Rand, Daniel.
Male. Died at Red Cross Hospital.

429. Unknown.
Female. Age about five years. Light hair plaited in back. White and blue stripe dress.

430. Female. Identified as Eliza Creed.

431. Male. Identified as John Lynch.

432. Female. Identified as Mollie Rabb.

433. Male. Shot on night of 5th of August. Identified as M. Nolan, of Philadelphia.

434. Female. Identified as Mrs. E. Vincent Webber.

435. Unknown.
Female. Height 4 feet 5 inches. Weight 75 pounds. Light hair, one plait in back, one on each side of head. Wore heavy brown cloak. Red dress trimmed with fringe around yoke. Pearl buttons. Woolen skirt. Blue belt around waist. Wore No. 11 shoe.

436. Female. Identified as the daughter of B. F. Hill.

August 8th, 1889.

437. Female. Height 4 feet 4 inches. Weight 80 pounds. Light hair, heavy, two large braids in back. Blue plush cloak. Blue stripe ticking skirt. Green plaid dress. Black hose. Ear-rings shape half moon, high button shoes No. 13. Ear-ring got by aunt, Mrs. Lou Pall. Name Katie Young.

August 9th, 1889.

438. Hamilton, Alex., Jr.
Identified by watch and bunch of keys with name on them.

August 10th, 1889.

439. Male. Identified as John Frank, Sr.

August 12th, 1889.

440. Unknown.
Female. Height 5 feet 3 inches. Weight 134 pounds. Brown hair plaited

SCENE AT MORGUE No. (FOURTH WARD ABOUT TO COFFIN A BODY.

and tied in knot in back. Gold filling upper jaw front teeth, gold filling in lower jaw, back teeth filled with silver, two front teeth lap over. Plaid dress. Blue cloth panel. Seersucker skirt. Black jersey, large buttons. Black hose. Button shoes. Lisle thread mitts. Large hair-pin.

441. Identified as Eben Hughes.

August 14th, 1889.

442. Unknown.
Female. Height 5 feet 4 inches. Weight 125. Dark hair. Red and black striped skirt, wine colored skirt. Black basque. Black silk dress. White collar. Large gold button, oval shape, engraved. Three pair hose, two pair black, one pair black and white stripe. Slippers tied with black bow. Heavy jersey. One rhinestone ear-ring. A round Harrison and Morton badge. Button shoes.

443. Bracken, Minnie.
Height 5 feet 2 inches. Weight 120. Very long dark hair, plait in back. Black cashmere dress. Black basque. Two rows of buttons, one on each side. Gingham apron. Black and gray barred underskirt. Low cut shoes, laced. Band ring, engraved.

444. Wiseman, Charles.
Boy. Two years old. Small button shoe spring heel. Blue calico dress with white stripes pleated in front, and pearl buttons. Black and white check underskirt.

445. Unknown.
Boy. Black pants with white thread run through. Spring heel button shoe.

August 17th, 1889.

446. Unknown.
Male. Height 5 feet 7 inches. Weight 155. Black pants. Blue and brown striped shirt pleated in front, pearl buttons. Gray woolen undershirt.

August 19th, 1889.

447. Unknown.
Female child. Black and blue plaid dress. Very small shoes. Black hose.

August 20th, 1889.

448. Unknown.
Male child. About ten years of age.
14

Sandy hair. Blue and red stripe waist. Gray pants, black thread run through. Canton flannel undershirt.

August 22d, 1889.

449. Unknown.
Male child. About five years of age. Red and white striped dress. Plaid underskirt. Home-knit stockings. Spring heel button shoes.

450. Fronheiser, Bessie.
Female. Age seven years.

451. Unknown.
Child. Sex unknown. Found near Sang Hollow.

August 31st, 1889.

452. Male. Height 5 feet 5 inches. Weight 130. Black hair. Full suit of black cork-screw cloth. Calico shirt, red and blue figures. Black tie, red stripe. Red flannel undershirt. Gray drawers. Home-knit hose. Button shoes. One dollar paper money. Key-ring. Two keys and button-hook. Collar-button. Cuff-buttons red set. Wore scapular. Supposed to be James Muller. Identified as James Muller.

September 1st, 1889.

453. Unknown.
Girl. Age about four years. Dark hair. Wine color dress. Gingham apron. White cotton undershirt. Small button shoes.

September 2d, 1889.

454. Murr, Maggie.
Female. Height 5 feet. Weight 100. Heavy brown hair, plat, and tied with black ribbon. Black and brown jacket. Plush collar. Steel buttons. Black dress. Skirt black and white. Plaid underskirt. Men's home-knit socks. Slippers. Rhinestone ear-rings ruby set, two sets lost out.

455. Hurley, William.

September 4th, 1889.

456. Unknown.
Male. Height 5 feet 6½ inches. Weight 140. White and black mixed frock coat and vest. Black cork-screw pants. White shirt. Gray woolen drawers. Home-knit socks. Red and

blue stripe handkerchief. Button shoes. Large buckeye in pocket.

457. Unknown.
Female. Weight 120. Height 5 feet 5 inches. Brown hair. Blue calico dress, figured half moon and stars. Pearl buttons. Wine color underskirt. Black dress skirt. Home-knit hose. Button shoes. One chased band ring. One plaited ring. Initials, I. P. or J. P.

458. Unknown.
Male. Height 5 feet 7 inches. Weight 145. Very dark brown hair. Black pants. No coat or vest. Gray woolen shirt. Purse $1.15 in money. Gum boots.

September 7th, 1889.

459. Unknown.
Male. Height 5 feet 11 inches. Weight 160. Brown hair. Plaid coat and vest. Black cork-screw pants. Red, white and blue stripe shirt. Cloth top button shoes. No socks. A Wood & Morrell store-book. Supposed to be J. Tyler.

460. Unknown.
Male. Height 5 feet 2 inches. Striped flannel shirt. Blue coat with four pleats. White cotton undershirt. Gray pants with black stripe. Black necktie with red stripe. Little jug charm in pocket.

September 11th, 1889.

461. Unknown.
Male. Height 5 feet. Black hair. Blue cheviot suit. Striped shirt. Heavy gray undershirt. Long black hose. Red bandana handkerchief. White handkerchief with blue polka dot border. Ladies' small open-face watch. Three watch chains. White handle pocket-knife. Mouth-organ. Key ring with keys. 4 foot pocket-rule and one Harmonie badge. Received the above valuables : Charles Brixner.

September 13th, 1889.

462. Unknown.
Female. Height 4 feet 9 inches. Heavy brown hair. Black dress buttoned in back. Brown and red stripe bosom, puffed at shoulders. Cord braid at waist. Elastic garter. Three white stripes black hose. Button shoes. One plain gold ear-ring. One ring, double heart.

463. Unknown.
Male. Height 5 feet 5 inches. Gray wool undershirt. Brown and black mixed pants. No coat or vest. White cotton drawers. Red bandana handkerchief. Blue and white cotton hose. Gaiter shoes. Key ring. 5 large keys. Gold charm.

464. Male. Height 5 feet 5 inches. Brown hair. Full suit of blue cheviot. Gray woolen shirt. Black ribbed hose. White handkerchief, red stripe border. Gaiter shoes. Instrument used for cutting washers or gaskets. Identified as Robert Buchanan.

September 14th, 1889.

465. Unknown.
Female. Height 4 feet 6 inches. Light brown hair. Plaid dress pleated in front. Two white underskirts, one wine color underskirt with blue waist and white dots. Black wool hose. No shoes. One necklace and locket chased with 5 rubies, the letters L. E. scratched on inside. One bar pin. Plain gold ring. Knife. Button-hook, and jacks.

466. Unknown.
Male. Height 5 feet 4 inches. Black cork-screw pants. Blue overalls. Cotton waist in pocket. Suit of gray woolen underwear. Dark wool shirt pleated in front. Brown socks. Gum boots. One round small tin plate with the Elgin Butter Co. eagle stamped on it in pocket.

September 20th, 1889.

467. Unknown.
Male child. Height 3 feet 8 inches. Black cheviot coat, knee pants, coat pleated in front. White waist figured with dog's head and red collar. Gum boots. Buckeye in pocket.

September 21st, 1889.

468. Unknown.
Male child. Age about one year. Blue polka dress. Gray underskirt. Black wool hose. Small button shoes.

September 23d, 1889.

469. Unknown.
Male child. Age about two years. Light hair. Gray wool dress pleated. Pearl buttons. White cotton underskirt

and red flannel skirt. Black hose.
Small button shoes.

September 24th, 1889.

470. Female. Height 5 feet 2 inches. Brown
hair with large hair-pin in shape of a
fan and four baskets. Long black and
white mixed cloak. Black silk dress.
Wine colored panel. Wine colored
basque, puffed sleeves. Black silk lapel
bosom. Black cuffs on sleeve. Ribbon
tied in bow around neck. Bar-pin attached. Two underskirts. Black hose.

September 26th, 1889.

471. Allison, Florence Edna.
Height 4 feet 6 inches. Dark brown
hair plaited and tied with ribbon. Black
and white stripe wool skirt. Black jersey. Long gingham apron, buttoned in
back, puffed at shoulders. White cotton
underskirts. White collar. Spring heel
button shoes. Black ribbed hose. One
plain ring set out. Received the above
described ring: Mrs. Allison.

472. Hoffman.
Killed at P. R. R.

473. McHugh, Gertrude.
Female. East Conemaugh. Dark
brown hair. Blue calico basque figured
with white squares. Blue wool skirt.
White underskirt. Orange color ribbon
tied in bow around neck. Black wool
hose. Button shoe. Found in Millville, in the cellar of H. W. Given's
store.

474. Identified as Mrs. Ed. Swineford of St.
Louis by her brother, Harry Bischoff,
passenger on day express.

475. Unknown.
Female. Quite aged. Height 5 feet.
Gray hair. No teeth. Black cloth cap
lined with red, and black wool cap with
black ribbon bow on top. White handkerchief around neck. Black cashmere
dress. Woolen underskirt. Brown
striped wool shawl. Lace shoes. Small
foot. Two purses containing $19.45, one
$2 bill, rest in silver, all halves and
quarters except $2 and four nickels.
Money returned to committee on valuables.

October 3d, 1889.

476. Kirkbride, Mahlon.
Identified by a stencil plate bearing name
and attached to a key-ring. Gold watch
and chain.

October 5th, 1889.

477. Unknown.
Male. Height 5 feet 7 inches. Brown
hair cut short. Smooth shaven face.
Two teeth out of upper jaw on right side,
one or two out on each side of lower
jaw. White cotton underwear. Black
pants. Black coat and vest with small
bar cloth covered buttons. Woolen
shirt, has evidently been blue. Pocket
on left side. Black overcoat with rubber buttons. Skull cap in pocket.

478. Meldom, Richard.

479. Unknown.
Female. Height 5 feet 5 inches. Brown
hair. Wool dress mixed goods, pleated
front on waist, belt of same goods as
dress. Wine color lining to collar and
black silk facing. Metal buttons, with
square figures in centre. Black ribbed
hose. Spiral garters. Cream color ribbon around neck. Button shoes, size
about 4½. Heavy jersey or coat badly
torn.

October 7th, 1889.

480. Unknown.
Male child. Light hair. Height 3 feet
3 inches. Plush dress. Blue skirt with
short stripes of black braid in front.
Green shirt laced front. Black wool
undershirt. Red undershirt. Black
ribbed hose. Black silk tie. High button shoes, spring heel.

481. Unknown.
Child. Sex unknown. Plaid wool
skirt. Barred gingham apron or dress.
Button shoes.

October 8th, 1889.

482. Schnurr, Robert.
Male. Brown hair. Height 5 feet 8
inches. Black diagonal coat and pants.
No vest. Cotton shirt, brown and white
stripe with small pleats in front. Coarse
gray woolen underwear. Heavy cotton
socks. Burlap apron. Gum boots. 2-

foot rule in pocket. Carpenter's lead-pencil. Nickel five cent piece. Identified by his wife.

483. Unknown.
Male. Height 4 feet 4 inches. Black hair. Black coat. Black knee pants supported by suspenders. Dark blue cotton shirt with white bar. Large upper front teeth.

484 Unknown.
Female. Light brown hair plaited. Plaid wool dress trimmed with wool crotchet lace. Black wool hose. Button shoes. Wore a scapular.

485. Unknown.
Male. Light brown hair. Black and gray mixed coat. Black and white striped pants. Black cotton hose. Button shoes. Large bar blue and white gingham waist.

October 9th, 1889.

486. Schauler, Miss Rose.
Height 5 feet 5 inches. Black hair plaited and put up in knot. Dress wine color with metal buttons. Black wool skirt with stripe. Brown wool hose, white feet. Button shoes. White linen collar with brilliant collar-button. Brilliant ear-drops. Jewelry received by her sister Mary.

October 10th, 1889.

487. Unknown.
Female. Brown black hair. Heavy woolen coat with rubber buttons. Large buckle with half moon on coat. Belt of same goods as coat. Barred cotton dress pleating in front, buttoned behind. Wine color skirt with ticking waist. Black hose. Spring heel button shoes with half soles. Bar pin with red settings. Chased band ring.

488. Unknown.
Male. Height 5 feet 8 inches. Light hair. Coat, pants and vest off. Collar and tie remained on neck. Blue collar with white dots. Separable collar-buttons. Blue and white polka dot tie. Dark wool pants. Coarse cotton socks. Derby hat and paint brush found with body. Lace shoes with half soles.

489. Unknown.
Male. Very large. Height 5 feet 7 inches. Brown hair. No coat nor vest. Heavy wool shirt. Collar attached. Black pants with white thread. Leather belt. Piece tar rope around waist. Piece white tape around body. No shoes nor stockings. White cotton underwear with pearl buttons. Stiff hat. Heavy band ring with letter Z and star inside on little finger of right hand.

October 11th, 1889.

490. Unknown.
Female. Black hair. Height 5 feet 5 inches. Basque and overskirt. Black and gray barred woolen goods. Black or gray wool skirt with two broad ruffles at bottom. White cotton hose, foot mixed with blue. Button shoes. Brown ribbon around neck. Scapular. Back tooth out right side lower jaw.

October 12th, 1889.

491. Unknown.
Female. Light hair, plaited, tied near middle. Cloak gray mixed wool goods. Large metal buttons. Apron with red bar. Plaid wool dress with metal buttons. White cotton vest. Black hose. Spring heel button, shoes, half soles, heels repaired.

October 25th, 1889.

492. Unknown.
Male. Apparently not old. Height 5 feet 6 inches. Brown hair. White shirt. Brown and mixed cotton socks. Gaiter shoes. Black corkscrew coat and vest. Black pants with white thread. Red bandana handkerchief. No collar or neckwear as near as could be told. Two collar-buttons, one a pearl, the other gold plated with set. One rubber sleeve holder with steel attachment. From pockets were taken a three-bladed knife, ring, shoe button, lead-pencil with pocket fastener, street car check and child's china ornament.

October 26th, 1889.

493. Unknown.
Female. Height 5 feet 4 inches. Brown calico dress, with large circular figure. Black lining with red polka dot. Two-skirts of gray and black barred wool. Apron of check shirting.

October 28th, 1889.

494. Lavelle, Michael.

November 1st, 1889.

495. Schrantz, John.

November 4th, 1889.

496. Unknown.
Female. Height five feet three inches. Brown calico wrapper with polka dots. Pearl buttons. White and black or blue striped collar. Dark striped velvet basque or overskirt, with ruffled fringe trimmings. Black lace tie. Red and black striped skirt, stripes one inch wide. Gray skirt. White muslin skirt. High heeled button shoes. Scalloped vamp. Gum rubbers, No. 5. Black stockings. Plated gold ear-ring with pendent amethyst set.

497. Unknown.
Boy. Probably ten or twelve years of age. Red and white striped jacket. Black knee breeches with white thread running through the material. Pleated underwaist.

498. Unknown.
Female. Height 5 feet 3 inches. False upper teeth. Perfectly natural lower teeth. Green cloth basque. Metal buttons. Brown and white gingham apron, with collar. Breast-pin, square shape.

499. Unknown.
Female child. About 3 feet high. Short flannel green and brown plaid with broad brown stripe. Black or gray flannel skirt. Canton flannel waist. White woolen chrocheted lace around skirt. Canton flannel drawers. Black home-knit woolen hose. White elastic supporters fastened to stockings by large black buttons. Brown and white gingham apron.

500. Jones, Tommy.

November 8th, 1889.

501. Unknown.
Child. Sex unknown. Found at Conemaugh furnace.

502. Unknown.
Found at Conemaugh furnace. Male child. No clothing whatever.

503. Unknown.
Boy. Ten or twelve years old. Dark cashmere Norfolk suit, plaited or corded down front and back. White waist. Concealed white buttons down front. One row small brass buttons each side of centre. Blue flannel shirt. Gray drawers buttoned to skirt by black buttons. Home-knit socks. Spring heel button shoes. Black handled pocket-knife with two blades. Medal in pocket with three horseheads thereon.

504. Unknown.
Found just below Lincoln bridge. Female. Light brown hair. Height 5 feet 2 inches. Canton flannel underwaist. No upper teeth. Three double teeth and one small tooth out on right side lower jaw, on left side first and fourth double tooth out.

505. Unknown.
Brought from Sheridan station. Boy. Knee breeches. Brown and black stripe gray flannel shirt with collar. Blue calico shirtwaist with light chain stripe.

506. Found in Stony creek near Bretheren Church. Little girl. Very light hair. Short gray flannel dress trimmed with three rows narrow braid, one and one-half inches from bottom, also three rows down front. Black hose. Spring heel button shoes. Identified as Irene Shumaker by her father, J. M. Shumaker.

November 23d, 1889.

507. Unknown.
Found foot of Main street in a cellar. Boy. Knee breeches black barred, coat of same. Supposed to be gray flannel shirt. Black ribbed hose, with elastic supporters. High top button shoes.

November 24th, 1889.

508. Unknown.
Found in Conemaugh river above Company store. Large man. Height near six feet. Sandy hair mixed with gray. Mustache and beard. Cork-screw vest. Black cloth pantaloons. White muslin or canton flannel underwear. White shirt and linen lay-down collar. Bone collar-button. Cuff-buttons in wristband of sleeve. White cotton socks. Lace shoes nearly new.

509. Unknown.
    Found near Sheridan station. Small child. Light hair. Child not more than ten years of age.
    November 29th, 1889.

510. Unknown.
    Bones of a human body brought from vicinity of Cambria works.

December 3d, 1889.

511. Unknown.
    Male. Found on river bank at Coopersdale.

MORGUE "D"—KERNVILLE.

1. Kolley, Mrs. R. H
2. Lonley, Sallie.
3. Marley.
    Child of John Marley.
4. Dixon, Mrs. R.
5. Dyer, Mrs.
6. Howard, James.
7. Craig, J. J.
8. Craig, Mrs. J. J.
9. Forkes, Rachel.
10. Fisher.
    Male child of Mr. Fisher.
11. Fisher, Margaret.
12. Fisher, George.
13. Fisher, Mrs. Margaret.
14. Fisher, John H.
15. Unknown.
    Servant girl of Mrs. Fisher.
16. Kinney, Mrs.
17. Roberts, Mrs. Milliard.
18. Palmer, Mrs.
19. Heffley, Ed.
20. Swank.
    Child of Neff Swank.
21. Swank.
    Child of Neff Swank.
22. Davis, Mrs. Walt.
23. Hocker, Mrs.
24. Ream, Mrs.
    Wife of Adolph.
25. Stuft, Wesley.
26. Swank, Jacob.
27. Swank.
    Baby of Neff Swank.
28. Bowman.
    Son of Luther Bowman.

29. Baker, Mrs. Nelson.
30. Hamilton, Jessie.
31. Delaney, Mrs. L. W.
32. Cooper, Otho.
    Colored.
33. Reese, Annie.
34. Reese, Winson.
35. White, Ella.
36. White, Maggie.
37. White, Menlo G.
38. Musser, Charles.
39. Brenner, Mrs. Edward.
40. Kunz (or Cunz).
41. Unknown.
    Female. Age about four months.
42. Quinn, Helen.
43. Howe, Gertrude.
44. Unknown.
    Female. Large woman.
45. Unknown.
    Female. Small-pox marked.
46. Evans, Mrs.
47. Bowman, Nellie.
48. Gageby, Mrs. Robert.
49. Holleran, May.
50. Findley, Elvira.
    Burnt below left ear. Ear-drops with glass set. Handkerchief. Lead-pencil.
51. Rhodes, Mrs. Link.
52. McClelland, George.
53. Spurline, John.
54. Potter, Mrs.
    Blue eyes. Brown hair. Black dress. Woodvale.

55. Unknown.
    Female. Oak-leaf breast-pin with three glass sets. Brown eyes. Black hair.
56. Hite, Mrs. Laura.
57. Kroger, Mr.
    Worked with H. Martin, Wire Mills. Gray eyes. Black hair. Black clothes.
58. Swank.
    Son of Neff Swank.
59. Luchenberg, Rev. John T.
    Black hair. Congress shoes.
60. Brady, John.
61. Arthur, Mrs. William.
    Black hair. Dark dress. Ear-rings. Breast-pin. Two plain band rings. One set of black stones.
62. Roebric, G.
    Johnstown Mileage book in pocket.
63. Unknown.
    Female. Age eight years. Gingham apron. Gray dress. Light hair. Ring on right forefinger.
64. Bantley, William.
    Black hair. Blue coat and vest.
65. Unknown.
    Female. Brown eyes. Calico dress. One ear-ring with red star set. Age thirty. Height 5 feet 6 inches.
66. Speer, Mrs. L. E.
    Gray silk dress. Gold watch. Breast-pin. One dollar gold ear-rings. Two dollar and a half gold breast-pin.
67. Unknown.
    Male. Boy. Short black pants. White plaited waist. Brown eyes. Short black hair. Twelve years old.
68. Shoemaker, J. M.
    Female.
69. Unknown.
    Female. Flat nose. Black hair. Black dress. Barred flannel drawers.
70. Unknown.
    Male. Eleven years old. Black hair. Short black pants.
71. (4) Unknown.
    Male. Nine years old. Black hair. Short pants with small bottle in pocket. Watch. Hatchet. Lead-pencil. Shoe buttoner.

72. (5) Unknown.
    Female. Five years old. Gingham dress. Red flannel drawers.
73. (6) Unknown.
    Female. Middle-aged. Long black hair. Blue calico dress with pearl buttons. Gingham apron. Brown canton skirt.
74. (7) Fox, Martin.
    Watchman at Wire Mill. Silver watch. Four bladed knife. Three bunches keys. Comb. 15 cents.
75. (8) Unknown.
    Female. Middle-aged. Breast-pin. Plain ring.
76. (9) Unknown.
    Female. Black hair. Barred calico dress. Black broadcloth coat. Ring, marked I. B. or J. B. B. I. or J. (?) Ear-drops set with white glass sets.
77. (10) English, John.
    Blue clothes. Silver watch. $3.90 in coin. Badge marked C. I. Co., employment.
78. (11) Unknown.
    Male. Ten years old. Brown hair. Black clothes, with patch on trouser knees. New shoes.
79. (12) Unknown.
    Female. Nine years old. Brown hair. Ear-rings with glass sets. Calico dress cut in two at waist.
80. (13) Will, Mrs. Elizabeth.
    Gray hair. Flannel skirt. Woodvale.
81. (14) Swank, Jacob.
82. (15) Unknown.
    Male. Twelve years. Brown hair. Black stockings. Black pants. Gingham waist. Jersey jacket. Fourth Ward Morgue.
83. (16) Livergood, Mrs. Jane.
84. (17) Alexander, J. G.
    $120.36 cash and valuables.
85. (18) Unknown.
    Female. Ten years. Short hair. Gold ear-rings with five blue sets. Gingham apron. Barred flannel skirt. Gum shoes.
86. (19) Unknown.
    Babe. Eighteen months old. Height 2 feet 6 inches. Gingham apron.

87. (20) Smith, Mrs. J. L.
88. (21) Unknown.
Female. Calico dress, red and brown. Black stockings. Pearl buttons on clothes. Plain gold ring.
89. (22) Unknown.
Female. Light gray hair. Black calico dress with white spots. Gold ring, octagon shape. Two pairs stockings.
90. (23) Zimmerman, Morgan.
Fourteen years old. Height 4 feet 9 inches.
91. (24) Unknown.
Female. Age three. Plaid dress. Red flannel waist. Worsted coat. $2.10.
92. (25) Humphrey, William.
93. (26) Unknown.
Male. Age twelve. Black pants and coat. Blue calico waist. Gum overshoes and shoes.
94. (27) Unknown.
Female. Age eighteen months.
95. (28) Unknown.
Male. Age seven years. Plaited waist. Knit stockings. Low shoes.
96. (29) Unknown.
Male. Age seven years.
97. (30) Voegeltz, Mrs.
Eighty cents in coin. $2.00 bill. Breastpin. Two small bags. Gold watch chain.
98. (31) Unknown.
Male. Large. Gray side whiskers. Dark clothes. Paper collar.
99. (32) Rhodes, L.
Large man. $1.10 coin. Papers, etc. One brass check No. 80.
100. (33) Unknown.
Male. Red moustache. Open faced silver watch. Congress gaiters. Bunch of keys.
101. (34) Unknown.
Male. Black hair. Heavy laced shoes. Overcoat.
102. (35) Unknown.
Male. Age twelve years. Light hair. Black pants. Toy pistol.

103. (36) Ream, Mrs. Adolph.
Two photographs. One gold ring. One paper needles. $1.00 bill. Two $5.00 gold pieces.
104. (37) Fetus, Mr.
105. (38) Owens, Mrs. Noah.
Gold head ring. Calico dress. Black hair.
106. (39) Unknown.
Female. One year old.
107. (40) Unknown.
Male. Two years old.
108. (41) Unknown.
Female. Eight years old.
109. (42) Unknown.
Female. Age twenty-four years. Short white hair. Gold ring enameled. Ruby glass ear-rings. Buff dress with yellow, brown and black spots.
110. (43) Akers, Alver.
111. (44) Bryan, William.
Moustache and goatee. Cork leg.
112. (45) Unknown.
Male. Age twenty-six.
113. (46) Park, Will.
Gold watch, paper, etc.
114. (47) Park, Miss.
115. (48) Park.
Female. Two years old.
116. (49) Park, Mrs.
117. (50) Unknown.
Female. Large. Black hair. Gold band ring. Slippers.
118. (51) Unknown.
Female. Age thirty years. Blue calico dress. Gold band ring. Gas key. Seventy-five cents in coin.
119. (52) Unknown.
Female. Black hair. Flannel skirt. Gold ear-rings.
120. (53) Unknown.
Female. Age twenty-four years. Scarred scarf pin No. 6.
121. (54) No record.
122. (55) Unknown.
Female. Supposed to be Annie Eager.
123. (56) Unknown.
Female. Large. Age twenty-four. Black hair. Ruby ear-rings. Brass hairpin.

CLEARING AWAY WRECKAGE—A BODY DISCOVERED.

NOTE:—The foregoing 123 names reported by W. G. Thompson, in charge of Kernville Morgue, June 14, 1889 (see list on file).

124. (57) Howe, Tom.

125. (58) Unknown.
Female. Age twenty-four. Black hair. Gold ring. R. O., 1886.

126. (59) Pike, W. W.

127. (60) Unknown.
Female skeleton.

128. (61) Pike, W. W., Jr.

129. (62) Pike, Stuart B.
Age nine years.

130. (63) Swank, Fred.
Age twelve. Knee pants. Music box.

131. (64) Unknown.
Female. Age twenty-four. Black hair. Black jersey jacket. Knit shirt.

132. (65) Unknown.
Female. Age thirty. Black hair. Blue calico dress. Two gold rings. Breakfast shawl.

133. (66) Lindell, Mary.
Calico dress. Breast-pin. Charm with different metals set in.

134. (67) Stuft, John W.
Woodvale.

135. (68) Unknown.
Female. Age twenty-two. Ear-rings with white set. Polka-dot necktie. Two rings, one engraved E.

136. (69) Unknown.
Male. Six years. Short pants. Dark blue suit. Gingham apron.

137 (70) Unknown.
Male. Large. Black hair. Black clothes.

138. (71) Unknown.
Female. Age forty. Calico dress. Gingham apron. Two rings with clover leaf pearl set. Breast-pin.

139. (72) Unknown.
Male. Age twelve years. Short black pants, old.

140. (73) Unknown.
Chinaman. White vest. Drilling clothes. Oroide watch. $5.15 coin. Thirty pennies.

141. (74) Unknown.
Male. Age fifty. Silver watch. Gold chain with charm, marked "God with us." Keys. Pocket-knife. Sacred heart. $2.56 money.

142. (75) Unknown.
Male. Age five years. Gingham apron. Red calico dress. Striped flannel shirt. Black stockings. Black hair. Stocking supporters.

143. (76) Unknown.
Baby. Age three months. Long white dress. Brown bib.

144. (77) Unknown.
Chinaman. Paper with Chinese letters. Keys. Necktie. Pin with square and compass. Lead dollar with hole in it.

145. (78) Unknown.
Male. Age seven years. Blue suit. Barred flannel skirt. Barred flannel waist with round pearl buttons. Spring heeled shoes.

146. (79) Unknown.
Female. Age fifty. Calico dress with red and white spots. Gingham apron. Crooked legs. All toes off left foot except small one.

147. (80) Unknown.
Female. Age about forty. Gingham apron. Canton flannel underclothes. Woolen stockings. Delaine dress with metal buttons. Ear-rings, with five point star set with glass.

148. (81) Unknown.
Female. Age thirty. Blue calico wrapper, brown and white stripes. Black stockings. Light brown hair.

149. (82) Unknown.
Female. Age twenty-five. Blue calico dress. Striped calico skirt. New buttoned shoes No. 2½. Black hair. Long coral breast-pin. Silk umbrella with two patches on it.

150. (83) Unknown.
Female. Age four years. Light hair. Red alpaca dress. Blue gingham with white buttons. Spring heeled shoes. Plaited underskirt with edging two inches wide.

MORGUE "E"—ST. COLUMBIA, IN CAMBRIA BOROUGH.

This Morgue was presided over by the Rev. Mr. Davin, the Roman Catholic pastor of that part of the city, and by his assistants. Priest Davin assured me that so great was the number of the dead brought to his church during the first days of June, and so complete was the confusion, that he was unable to give descriptions of most that passed through his Morgue; but that he merely counted them. He told me he was confident that the total number reached six hundred. Unfortunately Mr. Davin died before he had finished the report he was preparing for this history. Out of the records accessible I have been able to recover only the following names in connection with the St. Columbia Morgue.

Kratzer, Mrs. Mary.

Unknown.
Female. Dark eyes and hair.

Wise, Miss Annie.

Ault, George.

Unknown.
Boy. Dark hair and eyes. Scarlet underwear.

Cush, Joe.

Unknown.
Female. Dark hair. Brown eyes. Check apron.

Kane, John.

Boyle, Thomas.

Unknown.
Female child. About two months old.

Lambert, Mrs.

Child of John Wise.

Riley, Frank.

Unknown.
Female. Red dress. Blue calico overskirt.

Unknown.
Female. Supposed to be Mrs. George Ault.

Schuell, Mrs.

Unknown.
Boy. Fifteen years old. Dark hair. Gray eyes.

Cush, Daniel J.

Unknown.
Boy. About four years.

Unknown.
Girl. About eight years. Blue calico dress.

Unknown.
Female. Blue gingham apron. Blue dress, red braid bottom.

Scull, Mrs.

Unknown.
Female. Silver ring left hand. Heavy woolen stockings. No shoes. Blue calico dress.

Unknown.
Female child. Blue dress. Red flannel skirt.

Herman, E.

Frank, Katie.

Weiss, J., and boy.

Conthain, Mr.

Slick, Josephine.

Unknown.
Two small children.

Bishop, Julius.

Haas, Mrs.

Unknown.
Female. Supposed to be Mrs. Pearce.

Baby. Child of Justin O'Neill.

Unknown.
McHuaeney, Mr.

Unknown.
Three unknown females.

Riley, Mary.

Unknown.
Girl. Baby.

Unknown.
Girl. About seven years.

Nixon, Miss Emma.

McCann, John.

Lightner, James, and wife.

Howe, Gertie.

Child of Michael Hays.

Fogarty, Thomas.

Dunn, Miss Mary A.

Cush, Mrs. Patrick, Sr.

Cush, Mrs. Patrick, Jr.

Cooper, Mrs.
  Colored.
Unknown.
  A man with gray beard.
Howe, L. S
Kush, Jos.
Kane, John.
Kush, Emanuel.
Hester, Ann.
Harringan, Ella.
Child of John P. Hitch.
Brady, John.
Unknown.
  Woman.
Jockell, James.
Fisher, Amy.
New, Frank.
King, Mrs. S. F.
Shaefler, Jacob Sr.
Child of John Jones.
Bronson, Charles R.
Johnson, Mrs. John.
Johnson, John.
Pennell, Eldridge.
Ross, Jos.   .
Unknown.
  Two.
Unknown.
  Lady.
Fink, Mrs. Mary.
Smith, Mrs. John.
Sharpen, Jacob, Jr.
Holmes, Mrs. Eliza.
Unknown.
  Plain gold ring with S. T. How on.
  One ring with red set. Dark hair.
  Weight 135.
Garber.
Penninger, Mrs.
Frank, Miss.
Kurtz, Mrs. Mary.
Kurtz, Mrs. Catharine.
Lambert, Mrs. Ann.
Schnell, Mr.
Collohen, Mr. Frank.

Albetter, Mr.
Youst, Edward.
  A boy.
Wise, Mrs. Martin.
Cambiske, Mrs.
Cambiske, John.
Cambiske, Mrs.
Smith, Mrs.
Holtzman, Joseph.
Unknown.
  Lady.
Warren, Wm.
Morgan.
Unknown.
  Two.
Korass, Mrs. N.
Smith, Mr. Thomas.
Creg, Catharine.
Goleghter, Thos.
McConaghy, Jas. P.
Smith, Robt.
Smith, John.
Unknown.
  Three.
Shebaugh, Mrs.
Smith, William.
Ferdinan, M. W.
Unknown.
Berkshire, Ross.
Evans, Maggie.
Evans, Daisy.
Unknown.
  Five children.
Kerlin, Frank.
Kerlin, Edward.
Unknown.
Malcom, Cora.
Madam, John.
Barkly, George.
Skinner, John.
Worthington, Mrs. R., and child.
Stern, Bella.
Briscelle, Jessie.
Heaff. Mr.

Monteverde, Mr., and two children.
Osage, Christ.
Williams, P.
Overdorff, Isaac.
Knoble, Leonard.
Knoble, John.
Cole, John.
Pheby, Barney.
Sheiver, George.
Sheiver, Neil.
Plumer, Alvin.
Kelly, Charles.
Overdorff, J. R.
Wise, Mart.
Stinsman, Jos.
Yocum, Sam.
Oiler, George.
Overdorff, Jacob.

Unknown.
    Female. Light complexion. Dark hair.
    Two gold rings. One with set and the
    other with inscription, *Will to Mary*.
    Age twenty-one. Had ear-rings.

Hennings, Mary.

Maden, Mame.

Kerlin, Mrs. Mary, and husband.

Hennings, John.

Berkebile, Malin.

Edwards, Levi.

Mozo, Thos.

Bagley, Wm.

Rainbough, Henry.

Tomb, Chas.

Davis, Mr.

Thomas, Mr.

Crage, Annie.

MORGUE "F"—MORRELLVILLE.

As in the early management of the "E" or Cambria Morgue, so also, in that of the "F" or Morrellville Morgue, little system seemed to have been attained. Owing to the confusion, the piled-up débris and the swollen streams the superintendent of Morgues could not reach the place for several days. At Morrellville a saloon was appropriated for Morgue purposes, and different persons whose names could not be learned at first directed its affairs. The following, though, like Cambria, very imperfect, is all the superintendent was able to secure.

1. Keland, Frank.
2. Keland, Frank, Jr.
3. Dolan, Catherine.
4. Fisher, Emma.
5. Arms, Nicholas.
6. Caul, Mary.
7. Kinner, Lizzie.
8. Welsh, Thos.
9. Mirkey, August.
10. Thurn, Levi.
11. Purse, Mary Ann.
12. Shelden, H.

13. Strauss, Chas. (child).
14. Temple, Levy.
15. Nue, Elinore.
16. Heiner, August (Mrs.)
17. Newel, August.
18. Unknown.
    Man.
19. Unknown.
    Woman.
20. Boyle, Chas.
21. Jenkins, Thos.
22. Reese, Sarah.
23. Thomas, John.
24. Myres, Chas.
    Druker's Cemetery.
25 (1). Nadi, Frank.
    Perhaps Frank Wear.
25 (2). Unknown.
26. Unknown.
    Female. Aged about five years. Red flannel skirt. Weight about 45 pounds.

27. Unknown.
   Female. Height 3 feet 2 inches. Age five or six years. Weight about 45 lbs. Red flannel underwear. Black stockings. White skirt. Cotton undershirt. Heavy red wool coat.
28. Unknown.
   Male. Height 5 feet 6 inches. Brown hair. Age twenty-one years. Dark pants. No shirt. Laced shoes.
29. Unknown.
   Female. Age thirteen. Light cloth waist with oval brass buttons. One black stocking and one button shoe. Buried in *Morrellville*.
30. Unknown.
   Female. Aged about thirteen months. Weight about 15 pounds. Black and white striped dress with a black cross stripe.

The responsible persons at this Morgue report me that there were sixty-one additional unknown bodies of which, owing to the confusion and the necessity of immediate interment, no description could be given. Squire Ambrose held inquests over many of the bodies, and secured a depot for the valuables found on the persons of the drowned.

MORGUE "G"—NINEVEH AND OLD NINEVEH.

1. Fritz, Katie, Railroad street, Johnstown, Pa.
2. Fritz, Maggie, Railroad street, Johnstown, Pa.
3. Gold, Miss H., Railroad street, Johnstown, Pa.
4. Albetter, Miss, Cambria City.
5. Sheetz, Jacob, Conemaugh, Pa.
6. Oswald, Charles, Johnstown, Pa.
7. Viering, Mrs. H., Johnstown, Pa.
8. Clark, Thomas, Johnstown, Pa.
9. Fitzharris, Mrs., Johnstown, Pa.
10. Maclay, Mrs. Sarah, Market street, Johnstown, Pa.
11. Davis, Mrs. P., Johnstown, Pa.
12. Greenwood, Jennie, Cambria City, Pa.
13 (1). Mauser or Moses, Miss or Mrs., No. 59 Conemaugh street, Johnstown, Pa.
13 (2). Deformed foot, high heel on shoe.
14. Female aged forty, supposed to be Mrs. Gust M'Cue, Conemaugh, Pa.
15. Cornelison, Mrs. Maggie.
16. Saylor, Henry.
17. Gust, Edward.
18. Witch, Frank.
19. Dignan, Mrs.
20. Wolford, Frank.
21. Evans, Katie.
22. Hubburt, Bryan, Market street.
23. Garber, Mrs. John.
24. Anthony, Frank.
25. Unknown male, full grown.
26. Shonenviskie, Miss.
27. Hunkey, Miss.
28 (1). Sauerbrieskie, John.
28 (2). Mr. Haunerer.
28 (3). Samuel M'Claran. Buried at New Florence.
29. Unknown.
   Male. Age about forty. Light mustache.
30. Unknown.
   Female. Age forty-five. Black hair slightly gray.
31. Unknown.
   Male. Age about twenty. Dark hair.
32. Unknown.
   Female. Age forty. Gold filled teeth. Two rings.
33. Dobbins, J. R.
   Age four years. Light hair slightly gray.
34. Unknown.
   Male. Aged twenty-five. Large very light mustache.
35. Unknown.
   Female. Age eighteen. Light hair. Plain ear-rings. Plain ring on finger of right hand.

36. Unknown.
    Male. Age about twenty-one. Sandy hair. Very light mustache.
37. Unknown.
    Female. Age about forty-five years. Light hair slightly gray. Large mouth.
38. Unknown.
    Female. Age about forty-five. Large. Light hair turning gray. Plain earrings. Small plain ring on left hand.
39. Unknown.
    Male. Age fifteen. Light hair. Watch No. 1 on person.
40. Unknown.
    Female. Age about twenty. Very large. Light brown hair.
41. Unknown.
    Male. Age about fifty.
42. Unknown.
    Female. Age about twenty-two. Light brown hair. Left incisor tooth broken. Supposed to be Mrs. White.
43. Unknown.
    Female. Age about twenty-five. Tall and slender. Light hair. Breast-pin shape of star.
44. Ruberts.
    Male. Age sixty-five. Upper part of face shaven, also upper part of lower lip. Heavy gray beard on lower part of face. Long shaggy eyebrows.
45. Unknown.
    Female. Age about twenty. Brown hair. Fancy ear-rings with sets.
46. Unknown.
    Female. Age about fifty. Light hair partly gray. Silver ring and gold ring on second finger of left hand.
47. Unknown.
    Female. Age about four years.
48. Unknown.
    Female. Age about thirty. Tall. Brown hair.
49. Jones, Mrs. E. W.
    Vine street, Johnstown, Pa. Large. Age about forty-five. Black hair.
50. Unknown.
    Female. Age about sixteen months.
51. Unknown.
    Female. Age about sixty years. Large. Brown gray hair.

52. Unknown.
    Female. Age about twenty. Full face. Light hair.
53 (1). Unknown.
    Female. Age about fifty. Iron gray hair. Short full face.
53 (2). Frederick, Mrs.
    Age forty. Catholic. Large. Full face. Light brown hair. Plain gold ring on third finger of left hand. Taken back to Johnstown, Pa.
54 (1). M'Arreny, Mrs.
    Wife of Neal M'Arreny. Souvenir of Father Hollinger's scapular. Two plain hoop rings on third finger of left hand.
54 (2). Unknown.
    Female. Age fifty. Catholic. Light brown hair, slightly gray. Front teeth wide apart and protruding.
55. Unknown.
    Male. Age about thirty-five. Catholic. Height 5 feet 7 inches. Black hair and mustache. Supposed to be James Haltzman.
56. Unknown.
    Female. Age eighteen. Catholic. Light brown hair. Ear-rings with brilliants.
57. Unknown.
    Female. Age eighteen. Catholic. Light brown hair. Supposed to be Maggie Hipp.
58. Unknown.
    Female. Age about thirty. Tall and large. Light brown hair. Ring on third finger of left hand with set.
59. Unknown.
    Little boy. Age about four years. Medal with initials J. W. O.
60. Unknown.
    Little girl. Age about ten years.
61. Unknown.
    Girl. Age about eight years old. Supposed to be Sarah Wengle.
62. Unknown.
    Girl about ten years.
63. Unknown.
    Girl about six years.
64. Unknown.
    Girl about five years.

65. Unknown.
Boy about nine years.
66. Unknown.
Boy about six years.
67. Unknown.
Child about seven months.
68. Unknown.
Boy about two and a half years.
69. Unknown.
Boy about four years.
70. Unknown.
Child about two years.
71. Unknown.
Child about one year.
72. Unknown.
Male. Age about thirty-five. Black hair. Smooth face.
73. Unknown.
Male. Age about four years. Full face. Supposed to be Walter Jones. Disinterred and found not to be Walter Jones.
74. Unknown.
Male. Age about twenty. Light hair. Smooth face.
75. Unknown.
Female. Age about thirty-five.
76. Unknown.
Female. Age about nineteen. Black hair. Set band ring on third finger of left hand.
77. Unknown.
Male. Age about forty. Red hair and mustache.
78. Unknown.
Female. Age about thirty-five. Large gold ring on third finger of left hand.
79. Unknown.
Female. Age thirty-five. Black hair.
80. Unknown.
Male. Age about ten years.
81. Unknown.
Female. Age about twenty-five. Catholic. Stout. Brown hair. Band ring on third finger of right hand, hoop ring on left hand.
82. Unknown.
Female. Age about thirteen. Light sandy hair. Freckled.

83. Unknown.
Female. Age about thirty. Dark hair. Large plain band ring on third finger of right hand.
84. Unknown.
Male. Age about forty. Large. Heavy sandy hair. Red mustache.
85. Unknown.
Female. Age twenty-two. Catholic. Rather slender. Brown hair. Wore black belt with double clasp.
86. Unknown.
Girl. Age seven years. Light hair.
87. Unknown.
Boy. Age three years. Sandy hair.
88. Unknown.
Boy. Age nine years. Dark hair.
89. Unknown.
Boy. Age nine years. Light hair.
90. Unknown.
Child. Light hair.
91. Unknown.
Girl. Age four years.
92. Unknown.
Girl. Age four years. Dark hair.
93. Unknown.
Baby. Age two years. Red hair.
94. Unknown.
Child. Age two years.
95. Unknown.
Child. Age two years.
96. Unknown.
Boy two years. Supposed to be Mr. Bridge's child. Cambria City. Father a letter carrier.
97. Unknown.
Boy. Age four years.
98. Unknown.
Boy. Age four years.
99. Unknown.
Boy. Age five years.
100. Unknown.
Boy. Age seven years.
101. Unknown.
Child. Age five years.
102. Unknown.
Girl. Age two years. Golden hair.
103. Unknown.
Girl. An infant.

104. Unknown.
     Boy. Age five years.
105. Unknown.
     Boy. Age ten years.
106. Unknown.
     Boy. Age eight years.
107. Unknown.
     Boy. Age eight years.
108. Unknown.
     Boy. Age six years. Light hair.
109. Unknown.
     Boy. Age six years.
110. Unknown.
     Babe. Age eight months. Found with
     Mrs. Nitche.
111. Unknown.
     Boy baby. Age eight months.
112. Unknown.
     Child. Age one year.
113. Unknown.
     Male. Age about twenty-five. Black
     hair, smooth face.
114. Unknown.
     Female. Supposed to be the daughter
     of Daniel Convery, of Greensburg, Pa.
115. Gussie, Miss.
     Age twenty. Heavy set. Light hair.
116. Unknown.
     Child. Age eight months.
117. Unknown.
     Child. Age about twelve. Dark hair.
     Brown eyes. Supposed to be child of
     John Thomas.
118. Unknown.
     Baby. Age six months. Gold band
     ring on third finger of left hand.
119. Kidd, Joshua, Johnstown, Pa.
120. Unknown.
     Child. Age about three months.
121. Unknown.
     Child. Age about eight months.
122. Hammer, Mr.
     A mill man. Johnstown, Pa.
123. Unknown.
     Girl. Age four years. Light complex-
     ion.
124. Unknown.
     Boy. Age about three years. Supposed
     to be son of Andrew Baker, Johnstown,
     Pa

125. Unknown.
     Man. Age fifty. Bald head.
126. Unknown.
     Woman and child. Age of woman 45.
     Long gold breast-pin. Dark hair mixed
     with gray.
127. Unknown.
     Female. Age about eighteen. Dark
     hair. Small ring on third finger of left
     hand.
128. Unknown.
     Baby. Age about three years.
129. Unknown.
     Boy baby. Age about 6 months.
130. Unknown.
     Boy. Age about eleven years.
131. Unknown.
     Girl. Age about ten years.
132. Unknown.
     Girl. Age about ten years. Dark brown
     hair.
133. Unknown.
     Boy. Age about two years. Yellow
     hair.
134. Unknown.
     Girl. Age one year.
135. Unknown.
     Female. Age fifty-five. Catholic.
     Gray hair.
136. Unknown.
     Girl. Age four years. Dark hair.
137. Unknown.
     Girl. Age four years. Blonde hair.
138. Unknown.
     Female. Age twenty-two. Dark hair.
139. Wagoner, Henry.
     Cambria City.
140. Unknown.
     Girl. Age five years. Light hair.
141. Unknown.
     Age thirty. Brown hair.
142. Unknown.
     Baby. Age four months.
143. Unknown.
     Girl. Age eight years. Brown hair.
144. Unknown.
     Child. Age two months.

RESIDENCE OF DR. LOWMAN, NEAR THE PRESBYTERIAN CHURCH.

145. Unknown.
Male. Age about twenty-two. Brown mustache. Brown badge, O. O. S. of A. One band ring on finger of right hand.

146. Unknown.
Child. Age four years. Reddish hair.

147. Greenwood, Maggie.
Cambria City.

148. Unknown.
Child. Age two months.

149. Unknown.
Girl. Age two and a half years. Light hair.

150. Unknown.
Male. Age thirty-five. Brown hair. Supposed to be George B. Sutliff, Crawford county, Pa.

151. Unknown.
Male. Age fifty-five. Dark hair and stubby beard mixed with gray.

152 (1). Evans, Mrs.
Cambria City.

152 (2). Shiptman, Tony.
Cambria City.

153. Mashton, David.
Johnstown, Pa. Brought from Indiana Co., Pa.

154. Unknown.
Girl baby. Age two weeks.

155. Unknown.
Boy. Age twelve or thirteen years.

156. Workeestin.
Female. Age twenty. Full face.

157. Unknown.
Female. Age about sixty. Wore truss and had false teeth.

158. Unknown.
Child. Age about eighteen months.
This is the last of the six Indiana Co., Pa., bodies Nos. 153, 154, 155, 156, 157, 158.

159. Unknown.
Female. Age twenty. Medium build. Full face.

160. Unknown.
Female. Age about thirty-eight. Right wrist badly scarred and crippled at one time. Supposed to be enciente.

15

161. Stinson, Eliza.
Norristown, Pa.

162. Unknown.
Female. Age about fourteen. Black hair. Scar on side of face. Red and black flannel skirt. Wore a sacque. Blue stripe stockings.

163. Unknown.
Female. Age about fifty. Weight about 150. Hair half gray. Forehead slightly narrow. Teeth short and dark. Collar with scapular and cross crape around it. Wore blue calico dress. Large waist. Supposed to be Mrs. Griffin.

164. Unknown.
Female. Age about fifty-five. Gutta-percha comb holding heavy head of black hair. Six front teeth in lower jaw. One broken. Full face, large forehead. Large upper teeth, front second tooth on left side broken or removed. Large carved gold ring on third finger of left hand. Ring in possession of J. W. Young, clerk of County Commissioners, of Westmoreland county, Pa. Supposed to be Mrs. John Oswald.

165. Unknown.
Female. Age about sixteen years. Height 5 feet 1 inch. Light brown hair. Large front teeth not close together. One ring. Ring in possession of J. W. Young, clerk of County Commissioners of Westmoreland county, Pa.

166. Unknown.
Male. Age sixty or sixty-five. Full beard three-fourths gray. Top of head bald. No teeth above. Below stomach teeth and two side teeth. Supposed to be William Owens.

167. Schry, William.
Taken home to Johnstown, Pa.

168. Unknown.
Female. Age about nine years. Light brown hair. Handsome fine features. Supposed to be the daughter of Jacob Babb.

169. Unknown.
Male. Age sixty-nine. Light hair. Cow-lick on right forehead. Fair complexion. Heavy nose.

170. Unknown.
Female. Age about forty. Dark hair.
Medium build. Height 5 feet 4 inches.
Button gaiters. Common gingham
apron.

171. Unknown.
Female. Age about thirty-six. Black
hair. Very heavy build. Two strips of
muslin tied around the body.

172. Unknown.
Female. Age about thirty-five. Full
face. Heavy build. Black hair.

173. Unknown.
Male. Age about fifty. Large broad
face. Dark hair. Full face. German
look. Sandy mustache and goatee.

174. Unknown.
Male. Age twenty. Light brown hair,
cut very short.

175. Unknown.
Female. Age thirty. Very fair and
fine looking. Extremely heavy golden
hair.

176. Unknown.
Male. Age forty or forty-five. Weight
about 225. Red or sandy hair. Large
full face. Cut in upper lip. Small red
mustache.

177. Unknown.
Male. Age about four years. Red hair.
Two red skirts. Blue striped calico
dress. Black ribbed hose. Buttoned
shoes, tipped spring heels.

178. Unknown.
Male. Age fifty or fifty-five. Iron gray
whiskers and mustache. Supposed to
be Richard Worthington, a laborer, judg-
ing by receipts found on his person.
Receipts at Greensburg, Pa.

179. Unknown.
Age three years. In bad condition.

180. Unknown.
Female. Age twenty-five or thirty.
Ring on finger. Earring.

181. Unknown.
Female. Age thirty. Breast-pin.
Large waist, golden spotted.

182. Unknown.
Male. Age five years. Sandy hair.
Checkered waist. Ribbed knee pants.
Red underskirt. Black stockings darned
in both heels.

183. Unknown.
Male. Age three years. Sandy hair.

184. Unknown.
Female. Age ten years. Red underwear. Blue waist. Button shoes. Dark
hair. Full face.

185. Unknown.
Female. Age fourteen years. Two
gold rings on right hand. One with
two hearts, other with three sets. Mr.
Young, the clerk, has the rings.

186. Unknown.
Male. Age fifteen. Hair lip.

187. Unknown.
Female. Age forty-five to fifty. Large.
Weight 180 to 200. Light hair.

188. Unknown.
Female. Age twenty-five to thirty.
Earring. Black jersey. Blue and white
calico dress striped, sample retained.
Weight 165 to 175. Unusual heavy
head of hair.

189. Unknown.
Female. Age twenty-five. Height 5
feet 4 inches. Black hair. Rather small
face. Striped black and white skirt,
pleated front and pearl buttons. Two
gold band rings. Rings in possession
of R. B. Rodgers. Enciente.

190. Unknown.
Girl baby. Age about nine months.
Very bad condition. Found and coffined
at Tunnellton, Pa.

191. Unknown.
Female. Age eight or nine. Dark hair.
Red dress. Bright steel buttons. White
and black barred flannel skirt. Buttoned
shoes.

192. Grady, Mrs. John.
Identified by receipts found on her person. Body delivered to her husband
and taken to Morrellville, Pa.

193. Unknown.
Male. Age two years. Blue calico
dress, new, with white vine stripes.
Black and white plain skirts. Black
stockings. Buttoned shoes.

194. Unknown.
Female. Age ten years. Blue cam-
bric dress. Woolen skirt. Woolen
stockings. Buttoned shoes. Dark
hair.

This closes the records of the Nineveh Station Morgue. All of the above except two are buried at Hilhern Cemetery on a hill near town. These two are Nos. 161 and 192. The former is buried at Norristown, Pa., and the latter at Morrellville, Pa. The same number is given at the graves as in the records at Greensburg, Pa., now in the hands of the Westmoreland County Commissioners.

Mr. Hammer and Mr. Samuel M'Claren are the only exceptions to the above. They are put down as blank between Nos. 28 (2) and 28 (3). They were buried at New Florence.

The following were found at or near Old Nineveh, Indiana county, Pa., and are included in **MORGUE "H"** and numbered accordingly.

The first twenty-six were sent to Cambria City, Morrellville, Johnstown and elsewhere, for which see records. The other twenty-six were buried at Old Nineveh Graveyard or Riverside Cemetery, and are numbered from 1 to 26 inclusive. No. 1 commences at 221, and No. 26 closes at 246.

195. Eims, Mrs.
196. Lambreski, Mrs.
197. Stinely, Mrs., and her babe, two or three months old, sent to Cambria City.
198. Lentz, Mary.
    Sent to Cambria City, Pa.
199. Constable, Mrs.
    Sent to Cambria City.
200. King, Laura.
    Passenger on the day express. Given to R. B. Bates, Racine, Mich. Two breast-pins. One set diamond ear-drops. Two gold finger rings with sets. Gold watch and chain. $75 in money.
201. Unknown.
    Female. Age about thirty.
202. Hirsley, Harry.
    Age ten or eleven. Taken to Cambria City.
203. Hirsley, Edward.
    Age six or seven. Sent to Cambria City.
204. Stinely, Mrs.
    Buried at Johnstown.
205. Unknown.
    Female. Very large. Light complexion.

206. Martsen, Mrs. Joseph.
    Catholic medal. Sent to Cambria City.
207. Niche, Mary.
    Friends received valuables.
208. Louther, Mrs.
    Hungarian.
209. Unknown.
    Female. Weight about 200. Red hair.
210. Unknown.
    Boy. Age six or seven years. Fair complexion.
211. Atkinson, John.
    Age about sixty-five. Freight filler or car cooler. Buried in Union Cemetery, East Conemaugh.
212. Riley, Katie.
    Age eight or nine. Fair complexion. Long hair. Sent to New Florence.
213. Clark, Mrs. Owen.
    Sent to Cambria City.
214. Keelan, Mrs.
    Sent to Cambria City.
215. Griffin, Miss Mary.
    Sent to Morrellville.
216. James, Lena.
    Sent to Morrellville.
217. Shittenhelm, Tony.
    Age about ten years.
218. Kintz, Mrs. John.
    Sent to Cambria City.
219. Craig, Mrs. Catherine L.
    Sent to Cambria City.
220. Weir, Frank.
221. (1) Unknown.
    Female. Age about twenty. Weight 120. Light complexion and light hair.
222. (2) Unknown.
    Female. Age eight. Light hair.
223. (3) Unknown.
    Female. Age about sixty-five. Full face. Hair sprinkled with gray.
224. (4) Unknown.
    Male. Age thirty-five. Wore long stockings marked H. S. T.
225. (5) Unknown.
    Female. Age eight. Light hair. Blue eyes.

226. (6) Fitzpatrick, Emm: Buried in Morrellville.

227. (7) Unknown.
Female. Age about sixty-five. Dark hair. Weight about 140.

228. (8) Sweitzer, Mr.
Age seventy. Left leg off three inches below the knee. Grand Army Badge. Conemaugh Borough, Pa.

229. (9) Unknown.
Female. Age twenty. Black hair. Black eyes. Height 5 feet 6 inches. Heavy band ring lettered inside from H. W. S. to A. M. L., January 1, 1881.

230. (10) Unknown.
Female. Age thirty to forty. Height 5 feet 9 inches. Weight 250 to 300. Dark hair. Natural dent above right eye half an inch deep, like as if broken. Large lips. Short nose.

231. (11) Unknown.
Female. Age thirty-five to forty. Weight 175. Light brown hair. Gray eyes. Short nose. Round face. Rubber hair pins. Wort near ear. Gold ring, small.

232. (12) Unknown.
Female. Age sixteen. Height 5 feet. Weight 90 to 100. Light brown hair. Short nose. High forehead.

233. (13) Unknown.
Boy baby. Age two months. Brown hair. Blue eyes.

234. Hester, Mrs.
Cambria City.

235. (14) Unknown.
Female. Age twenty-one to twenty-five. Height 5 feet 6 inches. Long brown curly hair. Very heavy. Round face. Short nose. Chemise with red border. Ears were pierced. Shoes number 5 or 6. Blue calico dress.

236. (15) Unknown.
Female. Age sixteen to eighteen. Height 5 feet. Light brown hair with gray appearance. Blue calico dress. Red flannel underskirt. Slim waist. Number 4 shoes. High broad forehead. Short nose. Ear-drop in left ear round gold ball. Catholic.

237. (16) Unknown.
Female. Age forty to forty-five. Height 5 feet 10 inches. Weight 160. Black hair mixed with gray. Supposed to be nursing. Dark eye-brows. Turned up nose.

238. (17) Unknown.
Female. Age two to three years. Height 3 feet. Black hair. Very short nose. High and round forehead. Broad and full face. Banged hair.

239. (18) Unknown.
Male. Bunch of keys. On tab was " J. Kestler, 603 B. F. (Blast Furnace), Johnstown, Cambria county, Pa." Weight 160 to 175. Bald on top of head. Red hair, cut short.

240. (19) Unknown.
Female. Charred in Pershing's field in a burnt drift pile beyond recognition. Breast plate with name of Mrs. W. H. Wilson, Monongahela City. Plain white underskirt.

241. (20) A young woman; near her were found sixty-eight cents in silver. Small plated ring. Mr. Clark, of Armagh, Pa., an undertaker, has the ring.

242. (21) Unknown.
Female. Age fifty to fifty-five. Gray hair. A few gray hairs on chin. Bald on top of head. Height 5 feet 4 inches. Red flannel underskirt striped up and down. Left lower jaw deformed.

243. (22) Unknown.
Female. Age twenty-five to thirty. Hair brown and light. Height 5 feet 6 inches. Weight 160 to 175. Gingham apron. Body in advanced stage of decomposition.

244. (23) Unknown.
Female. Age about ten years. Black and swollen.

245. (24) Unknown.
Female. Age eighteen to twenty-five. Weight 100 to 120. Brown auburn hair. Height 5 feet 6 inches. Coat with large tin buttons. Corsets. White canton flannel drawers. Red short basque with red buttons on it. Black stockings. Full face. Buttoned cloth shoes, with patent leather tips.

246. (25) Unknown.
    Female. Age thirty to thirty-five. Height 5 feet 8 inches. Weight 150. Very black hair. Low round forehead.

247. (26) Unknown.
    Male. Age twenty-one to twenty-five. Height 5 feet. Weight 125. Black hair. Blue shirt with large bars on it. Mustache black. Round face. Brown overalls.

248. (27) Unknown.
    Female. Age eighteen to twenty. Height 5 feet 6 inches. Weight 115 to 120. Red barred flannel underskirt. Blue flannel underskirt. Blue calico apron with small round spot. Corsets. Leather belt with nickel buckle. No. $3\frac{1}{2}$ to 4 buttoned shoes. White cotton stockings. Low forehead. Gray eyes. Dark brown hair. Canton flannel drawers.

2.—IN THE CEMETERIES.

"But we have more dead in our hearts to-day
*Than the earth in all her graves."—*RICHARD HENRY STODDARD.

THE word CEMETERY is a Christian gift to sinning and dying humanity. It means a place of sleeping. It was not dreamed of in heathen philosophy. The grave was invested only with gloom, until the Son of Righteousness arose with healing in His beams. He said, "I am come a light into the world," and in His radiance His disciples saw that the tomb was the sleeping-place from which they who sleep in Jesus shall awake to life and light. Therefore they called their burial places cemeteries. Previous to the Christian era they were called "places of the dead;" they gave no intimation of a resurrection, a waking up in a better morn—a never-ending day. The inscription on the early Christian tombs, before the corruptions of Christianity began in the Western Church, was " requiescit in pace," he rests in peace ; not " requiescat," may he rest. Christianity has hallowed the grave while divesting it of the superstitions with which it was surrounded.

We sought resting places for our dead—not merely for sanitary reasons and for decency's sake, but out of our Christian consideration, both for the spirits of the departed and the living. Hundreds were unrecognized, and hence laid in graves unmarked save by a number. We could give them a Christian burial, though not knowing who they were. We trusted that many of them, at least, were resting in hope of awaking in that world on whose shores storms never arise and tempests never beat, and where the sunshine of the Lord makes perpetual calm amid the everlasting hills. Great numbers of bodies that had been hastily buried, were re-interred in the cemeteries. Many touching scenes occurred during this work. The recognition of the bodies by friends, parents, husbands, wives and children produced impressions that will never fade from the memory of those who were in charge of the work.

The following item from the daily press describes a scene as late as November 20th :

The people watching the exhuming of the dead, in expectation of finding missing friends, are used to the distressing sights which daily pass before them. But many were deeply touched last week when Mrs. Fenn identified her little daughter, Genevieve. The child's body had been buried at Nineveh just as found—with the little articles of clothing showing a mother's care, the tiny rings upon the fingers, and in the pocket a set of metal jack-stones with which she had been playing but a moment before the waters came and swept away father and seven children, leaving only the unhappy mother to pass her life in mourning. Mrs. Fenn's joy was great over finding the body, and all present rejoiced with her that the cruel flood had given up another of her dead.

On November 29th this report was published, which shows how large a number of unrecognized dead there were :

Mr. James M. Shumaker's force of men engaged in lifting and re-interring unknown dead finished their work yesterday. The figures are brief, but they speak volumes :

Grand View.—Raised, 135 ; known, 11 ; unknown, 122 ; identified, 2.

Prospect.—Raised, 362; known, 38; unknown, 308; identified, 16.

Morrellville.—Raised, 40; known, 3; unknown, 35; identified, 2.

German Cemetery, Morrellville.—Raised, 15; known, 3; unknown, 12.

Decker's.—Raised, 49; known, 5; unknown, 43; identified, 1.

Benshoff's.—Raised, 22; known, 5; unknown, 17.

Nineveh.—Raised, 182; known, 9; unknown, 162; identified, 11.

Old Nineveh.—Raised, 24; known, 1; unknown, 22; identified, 1.

Blairsville.—Raised, 11; known, 1; unknown, 9; identified, 1.

Sandyvale.—Raised, 4; unknown, 4.

The totals are: Raised, 844; known, 76; unknown, 734; identified, 34.

The work of raising the bodies at Nineveh of those who perished in the floods was completed Tuesday. The last car-load of those buried on the Nineveh side arrived here last night, and Wednesday they were hauled in wagons to Grand View.

The bodies buried on the Indiana side were lifted Tuesday. There were twenty-five of them. All but one were buried just across the river from Nineveh Station in a cemetery close to the bank of the stream. The one exception was a body that was interred in Hice's graveyard, about two miles below Nineveh. These bodies were all taken to Nineveh and placed in a box-car for shipment to Johnstown.

There was one identification. It was the body of Miss Maggie Dougherty, who was recognized by her sister Rosie, of Cambria.

Wednesday the bodies interred at Blairsville—thirteen in number—were begun to be raised. One of these, that of Mrs. Julia McLaughlin, is buried in the Catholic cemetery there and will not be disturbed. Another, that of Mrs. P. Carr, of Cambria, will be brought here for interment.

The removal of the bodies from Blairsville will complete the work under Mr. Shumaker and his force. The few remaining in other cemeteries will be exhumed by undertakers at those points and forwarded here for interment, in most instances.

IV.

THE WORLD'S SYMPATHY.

- - —

1.—SHOWN BY LETTERS, TELEGRAMS, CHECKS.

I felt the world weighed down with heavy care,
And heard sad cries in darkness everywhere ;
And heard them as I would be heard in prayer,
With large, sweet pity, taking instant share
Of the great burden of the laboring earth,
Holding one lifted heart of greater worth
Than scores of hopes and selfish birth.—ZADEL BARNES GUSTAFSON.

THE seamless robe of the Son of Man, woven throughout, typically signified the unity of humanity. As the Son of God, he had clothed Himself with humanity as a vesture. All the threads of the common life, which all men derived from God, and which had been unraveled and broken by sin, He gathered and wove together in Himself. On that night in which He finished His work of restoration, there were assembled men of different races ; and upon His cross, over His crucified and pierced body, they read the inscription in the three languages of the earth: "This is Jesus of Nazareth."

Amid that scene of tragic suffering, amid nature's portents, the brutal soldiers were seen casting lots for that seamless robe. It could not be parted without injury. True type of our humanity, He had worn it around His sacred body ; and it remains the sacred symbol of the oneness of mankind, which scenes of suffering and of death will ever display.

(278)

DR. BEALE'S TWO BOYS AND THEIR RESCUED DOG.

The human suffering at Johnstown touched the heart of humanity and demonstrated in noble strains that "the whole world is kin." From every civilized quarter of the globe the springs of sympathy were opened, and streams of supply and relief promptly flowed into our stricken valley. Telegrams and letters of sympathy and proffers of aid poured in from every direction. Hundreds and hundreds of telegraphic dispatches and thousands and thousands of letters were received within a few days, expressive of this sympathy. Postmaster Baumer, to whom, with Mr. Ogle, too much credit cannot be given for extemporizing a postoffice on the outskirts of the flooded districts, were hardly able with all their force to handle the immense mail matter which was daily received ; for sometimes my own letters averaged almost a hundred a day. It will be both interesting and instructive to put on permanent record abstracts from a few of them.

From North Adams, Mass., the Rev. Jno. S. Coyle writes me : "Your telegram reached me just as I was about to enter my pulpit. I made it the text for a plea for money, and I presume, as a consequence, several hundred dollars have already gone to John D. Roberts, whom you name as a proper person to receive it. I want to say that you are all in our hearts and prayers, as you are in the hearts and prayers of the whole world."

The Finance Committee were addressed thus from Salt Lake City : "The shock of your terrible calamity was felt in Salt Lake City, nearly 3,000 miles away, as though in sight. Reading the accounts of the appalling disaster, our eyes were suffused with tears. But mourning cannot raise up one life or heal one broken limb. We send money, therefore. A spectacle was witnessed a few evenings after your catastrophe, the like of which has never been seen since the city was built. Ten thousand people gathered in that wonderful building, the Tabernacle, to listen to a concert, the proceeds of which are to be sent to Johnstown."

The Rev. Dr. Hunter Corbett, of Chefoo, China, writes to me, under date of July 19th: " I cannot tell you how our hearts have been filled with sadness as we have read of the terrible calamities which have come upon your people. You all are constantly in our thoughts and prayers. Only God can comfort and sustain those who have lost those dearer than life. May God's richest blessings be upon every sad and bleeding heart! If we did not have full faith in the wisdom, the goodness and mercy of God, surely at such times we should be utterly cast down and be tempted to give up in despair. I am so glad to learn from the papers that your life has been spared. In a private letter it was reported that you were among the missing. I trust and pray that God still has many years of active service in store for you. You and your surviving people will be able to sympathize more deeply with poor China in the terrible calamities which fall so heavily and so often upon this people. Thousands, probably millions, were swept out of existence when the Yellow River left its source, and vast districts of fertile land, thickly inhabited, turned into lakes and desert land. Pray much for this people."

A distinguished American clergyman writes to me from Italy, under date of June 7th, as follows : " While traveling on the Continent I have read of the horrors at Johnstown. From a paper seen last evening I notice that God in his mercy has spared you. My heart bleeds for those who have perished, and for those who are left to mourn. I trust that your dear ones have escaped. I wish I was in a position to aid you. I have an American dollar here, which I inclose. Use it as you may see best; and may God in His goodness raise up friends for all you who are spared, and overrule this calamity for His glory !"

Among the letters received by me from other lands, no one is more highly prized than the following from a city in Queensland, Australia, which contained substantial aid to the amount of

£273 sterling: "On behalf of the citizens of Brisbane, we send you the inclosed draft as a small expression of our sympathy with the suffering survivors of the great flood which recently laid waste your fair valley. In the truest and deepest sense we feel the relationship which must ever exist between the people of the United States and British colonists in Australia, speaking as we do the same language, and united, as we are, in race fellowship. We would, therefore, send this small donation to the sufferers in the Conemaugh Valley, with assurance of a sympathy that cannot be expressed in a material way. We will be well pleased if this small gift is accepted as from brethren here to the suffering ones of the one great family in another land, and also as a token, in some small measure, of our anxiety to assist in bearing the burdens of suffering humanity. We request that you make such use of it as you may deem most expedient to make it reach the end intended—viz., the actual relief of some who have suffered through the great calamity. If you will, in due time, kindly send us a report of its distribution for publication here, we think it will do much to stimulate the spirit of generosity throughout our land, and be a means of bringing nearer the time we all hope for, when all the world will be united in the sympathetic Brotherhood of Humanity. We remain, Rev. and Dear Sir,

" Respectfully yours,

"W. M. GALLOWAY, *Mayor of Brisbane.*
"G. D. BUCHANAN, *Minister of Scots' Church, Brisbane.*
"JAS. CHAPMAN, *Hon. Treasurer.*
"R. LEE BRYCE, *Hon. Secretary."*

During the time I remained in charge of the morgues, I received over 3,000 letters and over 100 telegrams expressive of sympathy, and tendering help, a few of which are here given:

On June 2d a cablegram reached me regarding the person mentioned in the following letter and her husband, both of whom were drowned.   The letter that follows was written by Mrs. Bain, of Ayr, Scotland, June 5th, 1889 : "It is with a sore heart sympathizing with the unfortunate inhabitants that I write and ask if you can give me any information regarding my dear sister, Mrs. Craig, one of your church members.   I saw from yesterday's paper you were among the saved, and thought that with you might be my sister.   Words cannot describe how anxious my dear mother and all of us are about her safety."

Rev. B. F. Agnew, D.D., of Philadelphia, wrote the following on June 8th : "My heart aches for you all, and I want to be with you, but I have just recovered from a severe attack of bronchitis, and I have not felt able to camp out in the cold nights at Johnstown, or I would have been with you before this.   I have stayed at home and worked for you, and my church have given $1,600 in money, and on Sabbath we forwarded the first car load of blankets and clothing from our people; and the 32d Ward Committee have sent from the immediate neighborhood of my church over fifty large wagon loads of supplies to my dear old friends.

"Now, what else can I do for you all?   My ladies will ship a box of sheets, under-clothing, etc., to your address next Wednesday, and they want you to open it and take from it anything your own family may need.   Can you find time to write a few lines and tell me how the old church stands, and who are left of dear old friends ?   Can I be of any use if I go out there in a few days ?   The God of all comfort, who comforteth us in all our tribulation, comfort, sustain and strengthen you."

With a generous inclosure, the Rev. Dr. Jno. B. Grier, under date of June 7th, sent the following words of cheer: " My Dear Friend Beale :—We are thankful to God here that you and yours are safe, and that your church seems to be standing.   I put in an appeal for the people in this week's *Presbyterian*, and inclose you the first fruits.   It is committed to you with the idea that some of your flock may need special help, and to enable you to give aid to necessitous people, who may not otherwise receive relief. If you cannot use wisely among the Presbyterians, help all names and sects with it. We give you wide discretion in the use of anything we may transmit."

Rev. Wm. S. Lacy, of the Southern Presbyterian Church, addressed the following letter to Rev. Dr. Allison: "Our people have had their sympathies deeply enlisted in behalf of the Johnstown sufferers, and have given of their means generously, through the Citizens' Committee of Relief. The children of our Sabbath-school wished to add their mite, and wished it given to the needy of the Sunday-school of the Presbyterian Church in Johnstown. I have thus far failed to ascertain who is the pastor of the Presbyterian Church in Johnstown. But I see you are the Treasurer of the Board for Freedmen and the Committee on Temperance, and I know that Johnstown is a suburb in some sense of Pittsburgh. I, therefore, send to you and ask your kindness in appropriating it as desired."

Alfred Thomas, Esq., a prominent citizen of Columbus, Ohio, addressed me thus: "You have been much in my thoughts since learning of the dire calamity which has befallen your city. What scenes of suffering and desolation you must have witnessed! Our people at once commenced sending in donations of money, clothing, etc., through Mr. Deshler and our Board of Trade. Ohio, I am glad to know, was most prompt and efficient, through the good Governor and citizens, in sending aid to your surviving sufferers. Hold fast to God and His word. Let not your faith be shaken. 'When thou passeth through the waters, I will be with thee.'"

The Rev. S. M. Hamilton, of New York, has sent me the following communication, inclosing $25: "Last summer an Irish gentleman died in this city. Shortly before his death he had expressed a desire to send some money to the relief of Johnstown.

He was unable to carry out his wishes; but I have just received the inclosed money from his family, asking me to send it to you, that you may use it in any way that seems right to you. The gentleman, in whose memory it is sent, was a man of large heart, but not of large means."

Gifts ranging from twenty-five cents up to hundreds of dollars were received by myself and other individuals, and by the Finance Committee. One gift of twenty-five cents was inclosed in a letter to me written by a lady in Savannah, Georgia. Among letters received from children was the following from three little girls of Light St. Presbyterian Church, Baltimore: "Desiring to do something for the relief of yourself and other victims of the late terrible flood, we conceived the idea of giving an entertainment for that purpose. We immediately set to work to accomplish our object, and in one week made all necessary arrangements, and the entertainment was held on June 13th, in Triumph Hall, before an audience of over 300 people. Naturally, we felt a deeper interest in you, and decided that the money should be sent direct to you for your special benefit, but to be used in any way you might determine upon. The programme was carried out, with one or two exceptions, by little girls between the ages of 6 and 15 years. God has crowned our efforts with success far beyond what we expected, and we are glad to be able to send, through Mayor Latrobe, $93.41. Mr. T. L. McCully furnished twenty-three gallons of ice-cream, of which he donated ten gallons. The hall was donated by Mr. J. W. Parks, who is the agent, and a large number of cakes were given by many of your friends of South Baltimore. Hoping this money may do some good, we are,

"Yours truly,

"BESSIE McCULLY,

"FLORENCE HAYNARD,

"CORA OREM."

2.—SHOWN BY CHURCHES, SECRET SOCIETIES AND THE RED CROSS.

THE RED CROSS SOCIETY.

THE work of the Red Cross Society, under the personal direction of Miss Clara Barton, has been extensively published in the daily press and magazines, so that it is generally known and appreciated. Miss Barton, with a corps of assistants, appeared on the scene at Johnstown five days after the flood. As the founder and leader of the Red Cross Society, which had done noble and humane work in wars at home and abroad, and in calamities in other cities, she was gladly welcomed, and every facility was afforded her by the national and State authorities. She became prominent in the location and management of hospitals, through which the work of the Society was very largely done. Dr. Robert S. Wharton, the resident physician of the Philadelphia Branch of the Red Cross, was put in charge of the medical work. The efficiency of the work was greatly due to his experience and skill.

While some aspects of the operations of this Society have been quite freely criticised by the citizens of Johnstown, it did a great deal of good, which has been freely acknowledged by them in suitable testimonials.

Perhaps if the Society had confined its assistance to the sick, the wounded and crippled by the flood,—the classes for whom it was organized,—there would and could have been no occasion of complaint or criticism ; but, when it undertook the distribution of provisions and clothing, it at once assumed the risks with which such benevolence is always attended,—of being imposed upon, and of helping the lazy and shiftless to the neglect of the worthy and needy. This is precisely what happened. Complaints came to us from reliable sources that impostors, many of whom had arrived after the flood, were being furnished over and over again by this Society, while our own people, who were

penniless and homeless, and yet too noble to beg, received
nothing. Their cases—some of widows—were represented to the
Society, but, because they did not appear in person, they were
"neglected in the distribution." Whenever strangers, even with
benevolent purpose, attempt to do this work, they are liable to
make mistakes from their inability to distinguish between residents
and non-residents. Here was the great error in all departments
of the work of relief: they were, for the most part, committed to
non-residents, some of whom had never before been in Conemaugh Valley. The people of Johnstown and the other boroughs
were, therefore, put in the attitude of beneficiaries or beggars,
which the majority felt keenly. Out of this condition arose much
of the disaffection which was felt, though not loudly expressed,
towards the distributing work of the Red Cross Society. As late
as October 7th the regular correspondent of the *New York World*
thus writes from Johnstown : "They (the citizens) are beginning
to elbow out the outsiders who came here for revenue only, and to
demand that the city shall be allowed to rely upon its own resources. They frown upon the Red Cross Society, and declare
that it introduced pauperism by giving out provisions and clothing
to the more shiftless class, who will not do work of which they are
capable as long as they can eat the bread of charity."

That the services of Miss Barton, Dr. Wharton and the corps
of the Society were appreciated is evident from the receptions and
testimonials which were given them before their departure.

The Cambria County Medical Society passed the following
resolution :

Resolved, That the representatives of the Cambria County
Medical Society, residing in the Conemaugh Valley, hereby tender
to Miss Clara Barton, President of the American Red Cross, their
sincere and heartfelt thanks for the sweet spirit of charity and loving kindness which has prompted and controlled her actions with

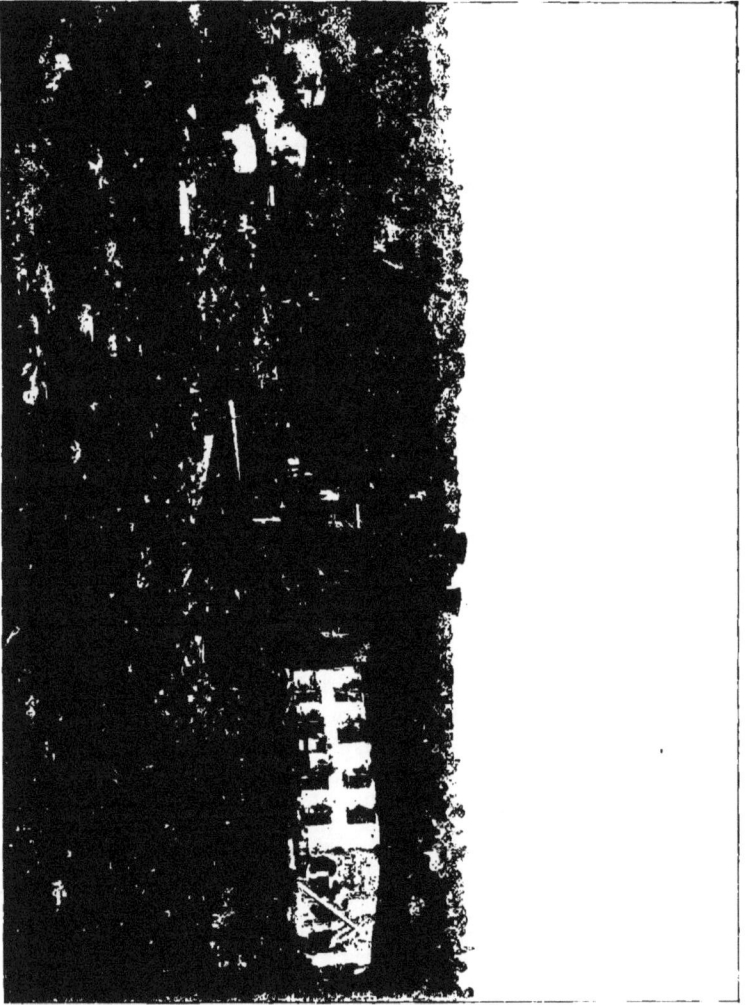

SCENE NEAR THE SITE OF THE HURLBUT HOUSE.

the stricken people of our community, and for the gracious manner in which she has aided us on many occasions.

The most valuable result of Miss Barton's work and mission is the UNION BENEVOLENT ASSOCIATION, with a Ladies' Branch. To this Miss Barton conveyed all the hospital property and requisites remaining in her possession. At a meeting of the two, the following preamble and resolutions were adopted by the Association:

WHEREAS, Miss Clara Barton has kindly tendered to the Union Benevolent Association the Infirmary on Locust Street, which she has fully and completely fitted up for the reception of patients and convalescents ; now, therefore,

Resolved, That the thanks of this Association be tendered to Miss Barton for this additional proof of her thoughtful and tender regard for the suffering people of Johnstown.

Resolved, That the President of the Association be authorized to consult with the President of the Ladies' Branch and arrange for the management by the Ladies' Branch of the Infirmary and property connected therewith.

And by the Ladies' Branch:

Resolved, That the President of the Ladies' Branch be authorized to consult with the President of the Association, and to appoint a committee of lady managers and members to take charge of the Infirmary which has been so kindly turned over to the Association by Miss Clara Barton.

Resolved, That the Ladies' Branch extend to Miss Clara Barton their thanks for the opportunity which she gives them of entering at once upon the work of caring for the sick and infirm, and that we will carry on the good work which Miss Barton has been performing for this community to the best of our ability.

16

THE UNION BENEVOLENT ASSOCIATION.

The Presidents of the Union Benevolent Association and the Ladies' Branch have given for publication a statement of the purpose of the Association and its workings. Copies of the constitution, which have just been printed, can be obtained from the officers. Mr. James King is Secretary, and Mr. W. C. Lewis, Treasurer. The constitution fixes the annual membership fee at $2 and a life membership at $10. The following statement is self-explaining:

JOHNSTOWN, PA., November 30, 1889.

To the Public :—The President of the Union Benevolent Association of the Conemaugh Valley and the President of the Ladies' Branch have been authorized to make the following statement for publication :

The Association is a charitable organization for the relief of the destitute. It is intended to be a permanent organization, and it is not in any way limited in its charities. It is not organized merely for the relief of flood sufferers, or to make good their losses by the flood. Such stores and funds as it can control will be used to prevent suffering among the destitute and worthy poor, and none others need apply for relief. The District Committees of the Ladies' Branch are charged with the duty of ascertaining the condition of the people within their districts and sections, so that if any persons are suffering for food, fire, clothing, or other of the necessaries of life, and are worthy of assistance, their distress may be relieved. In no case is it intended to give anything without personal investigation by the District Committee or District Visitor, and no attention whatever will be paid to any requisitions or recommendations where there have not been such personal investigation and such a report of the facts as will show that there is a necessity for relief. Any needy person, or any person having knowledge of a case of distress, should write the facts to the Union Benevolent Association of Johnstown, and the communication will receive attention by being referred to the proper committee for investigation and action. It is useless for the people to make personal application by besieging the members of the committees in their houses or going to the headquarters of the Association. Whenever any application for relief is granted, prompt notice will be given to the parties by the Secretary of the Association. The Association has but a small stock of supplies, and but a small amount of funds at its disposal, but it is now, and will be hereafter, able to relieve all cases of actual distress, and all such cases should be promptly made known to its officers. The visitors will also make known to the Committee in charge of the Infirmary any cases of infirm persons who cannot be made comfortable in their homes, and in such cases, when investigated and found to be of proper character, the Committee in charge of the Infirmary have authority to grant an order of admission. Persons able to make payment, or partial payment as inmates of the Infirmary, will be expected to do so.

We wish to say again, and say it emphatically, that the Association has the means of relieving any case of distress among our people. It is organized for this purpose, and it is unnecessary for any poor person in Johnstown to beg, and it is unnecessary for anybody elsewhere to beg for Johnstown. If there is anywhere, in the hands of committees, funds or stores contributed for Johnstown, and belonging to Johnstown, the Association would be pleased to receive them, and will endeavor to make good use of them.

HELEN MOXHAM.
CYRUS ELDER.

3.—SERVICES RENDERED BY THE PRESS.

It is difficult to express, in adequate terms, the value of the services rendered by the press. Among the first to come into our deluged and devastated city and valley were the ubiquitous reporters. They came primarily for news, and the immediate publication of the situation was necessary to our relief. But these gentlemen, who came to see and report, were moved by the scenes they beheld to sympathy and help. They freely bestowed money with which they had been supplied for personal expenses, and engaged in the work of rescue and repair, while they kept their pens busy in portraying the facts to the world.

The information they spread through the press—in the main truthful—awakened the sympathy of mankind, brought speedy relief from our own countrymen, and, soon afterward, from other countries.

They sent the pulsations of their own hearts back to the editorial office, and made the great heart of the cosmopolitan press swell with sympathy and leap to the work of mercy.

The thought and compassion of the civilized world were daily directed to and centered upon Conemaugh Valley and Johnstown. Proprietors, editors, reporters, printers and pressmen combined in the merciful work of relief. The newspaper offices in city and country were converted into subscription and collection agencies; and with the dispatch characteristic of the press, from these were received the speediest and most constant supplies of money and material. They came as if borne by the fabled Mercury, whose winged feet seemed scarce to touch the earth in his speed.

It would be gratifying and interesting to give all the items of aid rendered by the press, but I have only those that passed either through my hands or within my observation.

One of the most signal examples was that of the New York *Mail and Express*, of which Colonel Elliot F. Shepard is proprietor and editor. He was one of the first to communicate with me, not only with promises of large sums, as soon as they could be raised, but with immediate help in money, bedding, provisions and other things needed at once by the suffering survivors. These gifts and promises were accompanied with manifestations of sympathy and Christian concern for our people that gave to them additional value. The following letter, dated June 1st, the day after the flood, illustrates this:

Mail and Express,

NEW YORK, June 1st, 1889.

Rev. Dr. David J. Beale, Johnstown, Pa.

DEAR SIR:—Your heroic exertions in the calamities that have befallen your regions have been observed with keenest interest by many of your fellow-citizens. It is now both my duty and pleasure to forward you a contribution which has been made toward a fund for helping you to restore your church edifice by the Knox Presbyterian Church of this city, of which Rev. Dr. David G. Wylie is pastor.

We also inclose you a check for five hundred dollars, to be applied by you as you may think best, for the relief of the sufferers by the flood, or in the work of restoration or help in such form as you may elect.

We also beg to notify you that we have received a fund specially to aid and to be divided among the oldest male and female survivors of the calamity—a fund contributed by the Baptist Church of Mount Vernon, Westchester County, New York, and to ask you to select and name to us, five aged persons fulfilling this description, that we may remit to them the respective sums of one hundred dollars each.

We shall be pleased to hear from you in regard to any features of the great calamity and its mitigation.

May God bless our beloved country.

Yours most truly,

ELLIOT F. SHEPARD.

Colonel Shepard had telegraphed a contribution of ten thousand dollars immediately after the news of the disaster was received in New York. Mr. W. A. Deering ably represented the *Mail and Express,* and rendered us valuable service in many ways, besides writing truthful accounts of our calamity.

The reporters of the Pittsburgh papers were, of course, the first upon the ground, having been sent on Friday evening, May 31st, three hours after the flood, on a chartered train. They could not get farther that night than Bolivar. On the next morning they entered Johnstown and began at once their arduous work. They made use of the rudest accommodations and extemporized shelters among the ruins. They were soon afterward joined by their brethren from other cities, East and West. Not only were their services, as telegraphers and correspondents, valuable, as already intimated, but their presence was a comfort to us. We knew that they were a body of brave, intelligent men, upon whom we could rely in all emergencies, and for any assistance which we might be compelled to ask of them; besides this, their cheerfulness, good humor and encouraging words aided greatly in the recovery of our depressed spirits and mustering of our courage to carry on the work of reconstruction. Many of these gentlemen made themselves known to me, and offered their services in many ways that were consistent with their duty to their journals. It is not easy, indeed, it is not possible, to describe the influence upon our spirits of these intelligent, bright, cheerful men in the circumstances in which we were placed. But they often added to these words of encouragement, deeds of kindness and acts of self-sacrifice. I wish that all their names were known to me, that I might record them. I gladly name A. E. Watrous, H. S. Brown, F. J. Crute, of the Philadelphia *Press;* Wilson, of the *Times;* J. Hampton Moore, of the *Ledger;* Curley, of the *Record;* W. A. Deering, of the *Mail and Express;* and Herbert Smythe, of the Associated Press of Chicago.

Some of the journals established bureaus of relief in Johnstown where money and provisions were distributed. Mr. J. F. Graham, an editor of the New York *World*, established one where, up to July 1st, 1889, $9,688.00 were distributed to deserving sufferers

The most hazardous and difficult trip to Johnstown was that taken by Henry S. Brown, of the Philadelphia *Press*. He was sitting at his desk at 11 o'clock, Friday night, when he was ordered to the scene, and, without making any preparation for the journey, took the 11.20 train from the Broad Street Station. At Harrisburg all railroad communication with the West was interrupted. The Pennsylvania officials said it could not be restored for several days—in fact, it was not restored for two weeks. After studying the maps, the *Press* correspondent decided to drive to Johnstown, a proposition that was scouted by many people, who knew that all the country intervening had been ravaged by the flood. The Cumberland Valley Railroad took him to Chambersburg—a hundred miles from Johnstown as the crow flies, and much more than that by the country roads. Hiring a double team, he pushed across the Cumberland Valley and over the Tuscarora Mountains to McConnellsburg. Another team was in waiting, and he pushed onward. The roads were washed out, bridges were gone, and mountain streams were still swollen to roaring torrents. The horses had to be unhitched, and the wagon drawn across Licking Creek. On the side of Sidling Hill Mountain, the merest chance stopped the team on the brink of a yawning precipice. The wagon could only get within a few miles of Juniata Crossing, and the bed of the turnpike was, for a mile, a rushing stream, which the correspondent had to wade. On the other side of the Juniata he was met by another team that had been telegraphed for, and he drove through Everett and Bedford, and thence across the Alleghenies to Stoystown. Here another relay of horses was procured, and he got

into Johnstown on Monday, having made the terrible journey of
over one hundred miles in less than twenty-eight hours, by traveling day and night, without halting for food or rest. One of the
first faces he saw that he knew was that of F. Jennings Crute,
also of the *Press* staff. Mr. Crute had been told to get there by
rail, and he beat Mr. Brown by an hour. To accomplish this he
made a trip of nearly 800 miles, journeying by way of New York,
Buffalo and Pittsburgh. They were joined the next day by Mr.
A. E. Watrous, the city editor of the *Press*, and their reports attracted widespread attention. The other Philadelphia journalists
who took the same route as Mr. Brown, were John J. Curley, of
the *Record*, H. P. Wilson, of the *Times*, and Peter Bolger and
Arthur W. Morrow, of the *Ledger*. Mr. Curley had no sooner
entered the town than he narrowly escaped death by falling
through the trestle-work at the fatal bridge, and was seriously injured, but this did not prevent him from continuing his work. Mr.
Brown stuck to his post after all the other Philadelphians had been
recalled, and until he was stricken down with illness.

THE JOHNSTOWN PRESS.

In giving this willing and grateful testimony to the outside
press, we should not forget the local journals, *The Johnstown
Tribune, Democrat* and *Freie Presse*. Undaunted by the destruction and their losses, the proprietors and editors evinced a fortitude
and enterprise that could not be surpassed by the metropolitan
press. It was truly marvelous how speedily they mastered the
difficulties of the situation—how they secured the means and the
labor necessary to the collection of news and items and the daily
issue of their papers. They greatly facilitated the work of all who
had charge of the difficult task of recovery and reconstruction.
In their labors they were truly heroic, for those labors were herculean indeed.

JAMES B SCOTT CHAIRMAN PITTSBURGH COMMITTEE OF RELIEF.

4.—THE FUND DISTRIBUTION.

ERE the roar of the angry flood had subsided in Conemaugh Valley, the wires flashed the tale of horror to every city in Christendom. A dam that served no useful purpose had given way, and a city of thirty thousand people was inundated. Their business-houses and homes were destroyed, thousands perished, and the rest were left destitute and dismayed. The sympathy of the world was aroused, and quickly manifested itself in most substantial ways. Food and clothing came from near and afar to supply the immediate and most pressing wants of the suffering survivors. Trains were dispatched from Pittsburgh and Baltimore at once, and subsequently from other cities, with provisions and clothing, to which the people at way-stations contributed. Thus was the desire shown to administer without delay to the Conemaugh Valley sufferers.

For a few days after the flood there was no systematic distribution, consequently some avaricious persons obtained more than their proper portion. A number of farmers who lived miles away successfully demanded a share of the supply, on the plea that they had refugees in their homes. In some cases, they were charging board for these victims of the flood.

The sympathy of the world began to express itself in raising and sending money. Individuals, associations, societies, States, cities and towns, generously contributed. The civilized world with open hands poured out money, to what extent has never been, and perhaps can never be, accurately stated. Relief committees were appointed in cities and large towns. The Pittsburgh Chamber of Commerce acted as the financial agent, to whom a large portion of the contributions was sent. A local committee of finance was appointed in Johnstown by the provisional government formed immediately after the flood. The first relief the people had was from the fund in its possession. It was a *per-capita* distribution of ten dollars. The committee also paid all the expenses of government and the work of reconstruction during the existence of the local administration.

The committees in the various parts of the country and private contributors naturally communicated with or sent drafts to the Governor of the State. For a long time no definite information was received concerning the local authority, and the uncertainties of communication with it suggested this course. Governor Beaver then decided to appoint a commission, of which he was chief, to be called THE STATE FLOOD COMMISSION. This was to have the control and distribution of the funds, and the desire was officially expressed that all contributions of money should pass through its hands.

This arrangement was received favorably by the people and country at large, as it seemed to provide for a speedy as well as proper distribution. When, however, the Committee was announced, and not one of the residents of Johnstown or the Conemaugh Valley was upon it, surprise and disappointment and some indignation were expressed. The Governor, however, had offered a position on the Committee to four different residents, whose circumstances or other reasons prevented their acceptance— viz., John Fulton, James McMillen and John P. Linton. William Horace Rose also was appointed, but he had been severely injured by the flood, and, being absent from home, was not aware of his appointment. His son telegraphed the facts to the Governor.

Notwithstanding this, the citizens contended that there were many other men of like character and standing in Johnstown and vicinity, and that the Committee should not have been constituted without some of them upon it. They claimed this as their right of representation in matters affecting themselves in their calamity; that it was necessary to have those on the Committee who were bound to them by their domestic and civil ties, and had endured with them the perils and results of the flood. They also contended that a proper distribution of moneys depended largely upon personal knowledge of the people and community, by the Committee. The Commission was constituted with twelve members from different portions of the State—viz., James A. Beaver, Chairman; J. C. Bomberger, Treasurer; J. B. Kremer, Secretary; Edwin H. Fitler, Thomas Dolan, John Y. Huber, Robert C. Ogden, Francis B. Reeves, James B. Scott, Reuben Miller, S. S. Marvin and H. H. Cummin. This was the first occasion of the disaffection which subsequently became so outspoken. The next was when the Commission appropriated a quarter of a million of dollars to indemnify losses in lumber and other material property east of the Alleghenies, where there had been little or no loss of life or ruin of cities. The inhabitants of Conemaugh Valley said that the world's sympathy had been aroused not by the destruction of property, not by individual losses of lumber, rafts and mills; its great heart had been wrung by the cries of their drowning women and children, their fathers and husbands; by the destruction of their homes, and the wailings of the orphan. It poured out from its wealth and its poverty alike; it made the most willing sacrifices to send immediate help to the stricken, sorrowing, despairing victims of the Conemaugh flood. They declared that they would not have been the special subjects of the world's sympathy had it not been for this human aspect of the flood and the human sufferings from it. They had been previously subjected to inundation in which there were property losses similar to those east of the mountains, but they had not awakened any widespread sympathy or aid.

Delay in the distribution was another occasion of complaint. The suffering people, who were anxious to begin life again, could not understand why money which had been so quickly and generously given for this purpose should remain idle in the bank, and apparently be benefiting only clerical employees from other sections not affected by the disaster. The people clamored for the distribution, and the Local Finance Committee, whose standing the Governor and State Commission recognized, concurred with the people by an official request for it. In response, ten dollars *per capita* were paid to those who had passed through the flood with loss. This gave temporary relief, because in most instances it was paid to heads of families in aggregate sums. Dissatisfaction again arose from the requirement of an oath from the citizens on their "form of return" of their losses. The registration by the Board of Inquiry required every person to make a return upon a blank furnished of his or her loss in real or personal estate. The Board of Inquiry was composed of citizens of undoubted character and standing, well acquainted with the inhabitants of the district. For weeks they labored in going over the registration returns, and where they found the losses exaggerated they reduced them to what they believed was a just and true amount, calling in, from time to time, to aid them in ascertaining the facts, neighbors and acquaintances of the excessive claimants. Here the matter should have rested, but the Commission was not satisfied with the registration and the work of the Board of Inquiry, and one of their number devised a form of return to be sworn to as the basis upon which the distribution should be made. The return thus devised was regarded as inquisitorial and objectionable, and excited the condemnation of the conscientious portion of the community, who loudly protested not only at the delay in the distribution of the money, but at the inquisitorial shape of the questions addressed to the claimant by the Commission's form of return. An indignation meeting was called, and held in the Presbyterian Church, at which representative persons from all sections of the valley took part, and the action of the Commission

and the inquisitorial form of the return were denounced in resolutions. The indignation meeting brought its fruit. The representative of the Commission having charge of the returns took
occasion to explain that the blank did not mean what was stated
on its face, and some of the requirements were waived when many
of the returns were subsequently handed in. The meeting was
recognized as, in fact it really was, the first authoritative or representative meeting and declaration of the will and wants of the
leading people of the district, every ward, township, borough,
village or hamlet having had two or more of its best-known representative citizens participating in the meeting. The press of
the State recognized the fact and called the Commission to proceed
according to the wish of the stricken people, and hand over to
them the fund that had been so lavishly poured out for their relief.

The Board of Inquiry announced that they had ascertained
the losses ; that they were now delayed by the new form of the return required ; and that they found as the new returns came in the
amounts differed largely in many cases from the losses as they
had adjusted them. The query now arose, What should control—
the patient labor and inquiry of the Board, or the oath, in many
instances, of an unscrupulous claimant? To what extent persons
stretched their consciences in swelling the value of their goods
lost or destroyed will remain unknown ; suffice it to say the Board
of Inquiry found instances in which there was partial damage to
property where the amount claimed as damages exceeded all the
claimant was worth before the flood. In other cases, where the
party had been dodging creditors, claiming that his property was
so small that the three hundred dollar exemption would screen
him from his just debts, his sworn return showed that his losses
ranged from two to three thousand dollars. Cases like this the
Board of Inquiry could and would have reached ; the return required by the Commission prevented them from interfering,

because it was backed by the oath of the claimant. It is true that, in some few instances, the sworn return was for a less amount than the original schedule filed with the Board of Inquiry called for, but in the instances, for the most part, the difference was owing to the fact that portions of their goods had been found and restored between the dates of the two returns.

A scheme of division into classes was devised by which those made widows by the flood and having children were of the first class; and those made widows and having no children were of the second class: the aged, decrepit and injured were the third class; those who had lost all their property, and not of the first or second class, were of the fourth class ; those who had sustained considerable loss were of the fifth class ; and young persons able to take care of themselves, and persons who had much left, were of the sixth class. The Commission eliminated the sixth class from any share in the distribution, except what they had received of the *per capita* above referred to. A distribution of five hundred thousand dollars was ordered, giving to members of the first class six hundred dollars each; of the second class, four hundred dollars each; of the third class, two hundred dollars each; of the fourth class, one hundred and twenty-five dollars each; and of the fifth class, eighty dollars each. This distribution was hailed with delight, and did more to encourage the people and stimulate them to action than anything that had heretofore been done.

The Board of Inquiry was ready before the Commission for the final distribution. After having formulated their schedule, they were twice compelled to go over their entire work, by reason of the Commission having twice changed their scheme of distribution to the persons who had lost large amounts of property.

A period of six months elapsed before the final distribution was made. In it, members of the first and second class were paid, in accordance with their age and number of dependent children, from eighty to one thousand dollars. To the remaining classes, whose losses were in property, a percentage was allowed; those whose losses did not exceed five hundred dollars were allowed from fifty to eighty per cent. of their loss; those above five hundred dollars and under one thousand dollars, a sum according to the equity of their case, not to exceed six hundred dollars to any one person; those over one and under two thousand dollars were paid according to their circumstances, not to exceed eight hundred dollars to each individual. The fourth class was distributed to according to the equities of their cases, but no individual to receive more than six thousand dollars; to members of the fifth class a distribution was made according to the equities of the case, no one receiving more than two thousand five hundred dollars. The total amount of money disbursed in all the payments was in round numbers two million two hundred and thirty-six thousand dollars.

No statement has been furnished of the amount of money expended for commissary stores and other supplies, and until the Commission furnishes a detailed statement it will not be known what the sum last referred to is.

The local Finance Committee have never given to the public any statement of the amount that came into their hands, but it is believed that the sum aggregates one hundred and fifty thousand dollars; and that it will be honestly distributed or appropriated to some public purpose is not to be doubted.

While it may be asserted that mistakes were made and expenses incurred that might have been avoided, no imputation has been, or can be, cast upon the honor of the Governor or any member of the Commission.

The following are the resolutions adopted at the meeting of the citizens. They, with the foregoing, and the official statements of Mr. J. B. Kremer, Secretary of the State Flood Commission, are given as a part of the history, without comment by the author, in justice to all parties:

Resolved, That the citizens of Johnstown and vicinity respectfully yet earnestly request that the fund contributed for the relief of the sufferers by the disastrous flood which devastated the Conemaugh Valley be as speedily as possible distributed in money directly to the people for whose benefit it was donated, and that all purchases, contracts and expenses to be paid for out of this fund immediately cease.

Resolved, That any hoarding up of this fund to meet problematical future wants will materially diminish its usefulness and only result in delaying to a more distant time the restoration of homes, of business, of industry, and of confidence. It will do more good in the hands of the people *now* than at any time hereafter.

Resolved, That we repudiate as insulting to the manhood and intelligence of our citizens (now that the avenues of trade are opened up) the imputation that they cannot and will not wisely and economically disburse any funds placed in their hands, and, because of this imputation, the arrogant assumption that guardians must supervise our expenditures, control our disbursements, purchase our supplies, and make our contracts.

Resolved, That if the statement imputed to His Excellency, Governor Beaver, that "a million and a half dollars has already been expended in Johnstown and vicinity" has any foundation in fact, it is the strongest possible argument that expending relief funds in contracting for buildings, quartermaster, and commissary supplies is not a wise, judicious, or economical way of disbursing such funds when the ordinary sources of supply are opened up. Only by gross extravagance and carelessness could such a sum have been used here, and the people have received no adequate return for the expenditure of so large an amount.

Resolved, That the disbursement of the fund subscribed for relief directly to the sufferers by the flood will stimulate business,

DEBRIS ABOVE THE BRIDGE; CAMBRIA LOWER WORKS IN THE DISTANCE.

will provide work for our builders and trade for our merchants, will provide labor for our artisans, and will tend to restore confidence in the community, and will thus directly and indirectly help those for whom the fund was intended, while any other course, at this day, savors of jobs, redounds to the benefit of non-resident contractors and business men having no interest in this community, and unjustly discriminates against our own citizens.

Resolved, That it is unfair and unjust to exact an oath as to private income and relief before the bounteous charity of our countrymen can be distributed to its beneficiaries.

Resolved, That we hereby appeal to the custodians of funds at Philadelphia, New York, Pittsburgh and other localities to transmit the funds in their hands intended for Conemaugh Valley sufferers direct to our local Finance Committee to be distributed by that Committee immediately, in cash, upon requisitions of the Board of Inquiry upon such fair and equitable basis as may be adopted, and we invite the co-operation of such custodians in making such distribution.

Resolved, That our citizens have entire confidence in the good faith, skill and judgment of the Board of Inquiry appointed at a citizens' meeting and the local boards which they called to their assistance, and this meeting cannot look with favor on any attempt of strangers to supervise their work—perhaps reverse their findings, and, by exacting extra-judicial oaths and inquisitorial inquiries as to income and other relief, reflect on the proceedings of the Board, and, as we fear, delay for an indefinite period the distribution of that portion of the fund graciously allowed for present disbursement.

Resolved, That this meeting express its profound gratitude to the many thousands of people in our own and other lands who have so spontaneously and generously contributed to the relief of our people, and now only venture on this expression of opinion

17

because those here assembled believe they are in this way but expressing the sentiments of the generous donors of so bounteous a fund, as they are sure they express those of the intended beneficiaries.

Chal. L. Dick, Esq., thought the resolutions of the Committee were not strong enough; that the occasion demanded stronger language. Rev. Dr. Beale thought the resolutions should be adopted as read, with which view the meeting concurred, and the resolutions were adopted as read.

Official Statement as to the Johnstown Fund and the General Relief Work Performed.

OFFICE OF THE FLOOD RELIEF COMMISSION,

HARRISBURG, Pa., July 12th, 1889.

DEAR SIR :—At a regular meeting of the Flood Relief Commission, held on July 9th, a committee of three members was appointed to prepare for the information of contributors to the fund a statement of the general relief work performed. The committee makes report as follows :

In round figures the expenditures to date for relief in the Conemaugh Valley, Johnstown and vicinity, aggregate one million seven hundred thousand dollars. This includes the work of the Pittsburgh, Johnstown and Philadelphia committees and the Flood Commission ; also disbursements of the State in the abatement of nuisances and payment of the military detailed to staff and police duty.

Various committees in the West have been working through the Pittsburgh and Johnstown committees, and in the East through the Philadelphia Committee and the Governor of the State. The Flood Commission has been formed to create a unit of administration. In that Commission of which the Governor of Pennsylvania is the Chairman, the committees of Pittsburgh and Philadelphia and the State at large have representation. All the funds placed under the control of the Executive have been transferred to the Commission, and an implied understanding exists that the committees of Pittsburgh and Philadelphia will do the same. It is also desirable that all moneys now in the hands of other committees for this purpose be placed under the jurisdiction of the Governor and the Commission.

The Commission has held frequent meetings in various parts of the State. All its members, save one or two, prevented by uncontrollable causes, have made personal investigation of the several flooded districts of the State. Relief has been given in all needful directions with the greatest dispatch consistent with the best wisdom that could be brought to bear upon the case. Correspondence and conference have been freely invited for the information of the committees in the first instance, and the Governor and Commission subsequently.

The problem confronting the Commission in the Conemaugh Valley is of great magnitude, demanding the utmost celerity and the wisest and most delicate discrimination.

The number of persons to be fed have varied from a maximum of 31,950 to a present commissary roll of 7,000.

The number of distinct claims to be passed upon, many of them involving the interests of families or dependent relatives, aggregate nearly 4,000.

The Commission has sought to find the will of the donors of the great sums contributed for the relief of the sufferers, and believing that the following declaration of principles met the conditions, it was adopted and promulgated at a meeting held in Harrisburg on June 27th:

To the Public :—That the donors of the funds in the hands of the Flood Relief Commission may know how their generous gifts are to be disposed of, and that the expectant recipients of the same may not form erroneous views of and foster improper expectations for the same, it is now officially declared and announced that the following principles shall govern the distribution of relief:

1. That the said fund is in the nature of a charity to the needy, and not as a general indemnity for losses sustained.

2. That a distribution *per capita* would be manifestly unjust, as it would go alike to the rich and poor and alike to all sufferers, no matter what their needs or extent of their sufferings.

3. That a distribution by percentage on the amount of losses would be manifestly unjust, as it would result in giving the largest sum to the person having lost the most, without regard to the value of the remaining estate of such persons.

4. That this fund cannot be used for the benefit of any private or public corporation.

5. That the fund must go only to the most needy sufferers from the flood in accordance with the spirit of the trust imposed upon it by the donors.

At the unanimous request of the Commission, Hon. Hugh H. Cummin was requested to proceed to Johnstown and remain there as the resident representative and executive officer of this Commission in the Conemaugh Valley.

In accordance with the foregoing, Judge Cummin has fixed his office in Johnstown as the resident executive of the Commission, and is working energetically in harmony with the local Relief Committee and the leading citizens.

Supplies of food, shoes and clothing will continue to be given to the needy as required. It is hoped to shortly discontinue this form of relief. Four hundred portable houses and two hundred to be built on the spot are already contracted for. They will be made ready for use rapidly, as the local committee will indicate the places for them. The number will be increased, and the rate at which they will be supplied need only be limited by the ability to find ground upon which to put them. They will be fur- nished for occupancy as completed. Relief in other forms is also being given.

At Cresson, July 9th, the Commission held conferences with committees from Chicago, Williamsport and Johnstown.

In view of the magnitude of the relief required and the immense detail involved in a just apportionment of the funds in hand to the many curiously involved cases, the Commission, after hearing very fully and deliberately Messrs. McMillen, Elder, Moxham and Johnson, of the Johnstown Committee, resolved to appropriate five hundred thousand dollars, to be distributed among the verified claimants in the Conemaugh Valley, through its repre- sentative in Johnstown, Hon. H. H. Cummin, as soon as the checks for the payments can be prepared—the sums so paid to be considered as payments on account of a final adjustment to be made upon a carefully-devised system already approved by the Commission. The details are left to the judgment of Judge Cummin, but there is a tacit understanding that the distribution is to be upon the registration and classification of claims already made with much care by the Johnstown Committee. This cash will average considerably above $100 to each claimant, and is in addition to cash already distributed by the Johnstown Committee. This, it will be remembered, is beside the general relief work con- stantly going forward.

It will thus be observed that the total relief already afforded the Conemaugh Valley sufferers is in round figures two million two hundred thousand dollars.

The Commission increased the sum to be devoted to relief in the nineteen other counties besides Cambria to two hundred and fifty thousand dollars. The largest single sum will be required for the Williamsport district of Lycoming County—this in addition to various relief afforded by committees before the creation of the Flood Commission.

The sums required for the Johnstown district will cover all the moneys coming into the State from outside sources, with large amounts in addition. The appropriations for other localities are from general contributions made within the State of Pennsylvania.

It is the purpose of the Commission to gather and collate the accounts of all the work done everywhere for the relief of the flood sufferers, and place the same in a complete and permanent form for public use.   Very respectfully,

J. B. KREMER,
Secretary.

This official statement I received from Secretary Kremer, January 2d, 1890:

Received by the Flood Relief Commission to December 16, 1889:

Money sent direct to Governor Beaver,	.	$1,224,885
" received from the Pittsburgh Relief Com.,		560,000
" " " " Philadelphia " "		600,coo
" " " " New York " "		516,199

Total cash receipts, .	.	.	$2,901,084

Included in the "Governor's Fund" is $150,000 received from the Boston Relief Committee.

The Commission has distributed in *cash* in Johnstown, $2,060,000.

(Signed),   J. B. KREMER, Secretary.

The following amounts from foreign countries have been received by the Flood Relief Commission at Harrisburg: Ireland, $18,252.24; Mexico, $130.40; Canada, $4,464.65; England, $33,-158.36; Turkey, $876.57; Italy, $9.46; Austria, $481.70; Germany, $34,199.36; Prussia, $100; Wales, $68.60; Saxony, $2,-637.20; Persia, $50; France, $24,511.13. Total, $118,939.67.

On November 21st, Secretary Kremer spoke of the nature and difficulties of the distribution as follows:

The property losses of individuals and firms in the Conemaugh Valley are shown by the Commission records to be between $8,000,000 and $9,000,000. These do not include the Pennsylvania Railroad, the Cambria Iron Company, or the other large
corporations. Months of investigation have been devoted to making these records accurate. In the first place, each sufferer was
called upon to fill out a return of his losses. This was itemized
like a tax return. Opposite each item was put the value as estimated by the owner. Then local committees took hold of the returns, investigated each, and made an estimate of the value. After
that was done each claimant was required to make oath to the
value of what he had lost. The original figures underwent two
reductions. The committees cut down the original returns, and
the sworn returns were in many cases less than the reports of the
committees. Upon the final returns the Commission made the
awards. The work shows a list of fifty-eight hundred claimants.

In regard to relief for widows he said : One of the interesting
features of what may be called the flood census is the list of widows.
It contains one hundred and twenty-eight names. Widows
were placed in the first class of sufferers. They were provided
for before any payments were made in property losses. The Commission was in doubt how to deal with the widows. Various
propositions were made and discussed. The conclusion was that
the amount to be allowed the widows should be paid in cash rather
than in installments or in homes. The Johnstown widows have
received from $800 to $1,250 apiece. The claims of widowhood are now considered fully discharged. One of these widows
spent the first night after she was paid in the lockup. Several
have already parted with their money. But the cases where the
charity has seemed misapplied have been exceptional, the Secretary says. Nearly all the widows have expressed gratitude, and
have put the money to good uses.

V.

SHELTER AND REBUILDING.

The house of every one is to him as his castle and his fortress.—COKE.

I.—PRIVATE RESIDENCES AND PLACES OF BUSINESS.

OUR experience during the dreadful night of the flood and in the succeeding week made us realize vividly that the three great wants of man are food, vesture and shelter. The vast majority of us were without food; were inadequately clothed and without homes. The remorseless torrent had swept away everything we had, and, worse than all, many on whom the survivors had depended for the supply of these prime necessities to human life and comfort were buried beneath the wrecks in the valley, or were expiring under the injuries they had received.

The supply of food came as quickly from the sympathizing country as transportation was effected. For the first few days, before a complete system of distribution could be adopted, we managed to supply the hunger of the women and children by the self-sacrifice and fasting of many of us who were strong. Clothing of various sorts was sent from cities and towns, which was gladly received, to take the place of the soaked and dilapidated garments with which we emerged from the waters and were rescued from the debris. When, however, our anxiety concerning food and clothing was allayed, there loomed before us the awful fact that the vast majority of people were without homes, and for temporary shelter, even if that could be found, must depend on charity. But the few houses that remained in the city and the homes on the hill-

(318)

sides were not large. They were not constructed with a view to such a demand upon their hospitality and charity. Thus the problem of temporary shelter and future rebuilding became the most serious and difficult of solution.

There are times when men, and even women with their little ones, can do without comfortable homes or shelter. The pioneers of civilization, though possessing noble blood and having dwelt in lordly palaces, cheerfully endure the privations of the camp or bivouac and accept the dome of the sky as their only covering. The Pilgrims who left their homes in Old England and their hospitable shelter in the good old homes of Holland, and uncovered their heads to the bare heavens on the banks of the James River and on Plymouth's rocky shore, did not repine at the fact that there were no houses to enter, that the rude ones in which they were to dwell must be built by themselves; made of trees which must be felled and timber which must be hewed with their own hands. But they were providentially prepared for this. They were impelled to it by noble purposes and firm resolve to be free men under the open canopy of heaven rather than slaves under the gilded domes of royalty. Here were thousands who were the victims of a dreadful calamity. They had lived always in comfortable homes and knew nothing of the sufferings and privations of the homeless. They stood here gazing over the dire scene ; their homes gone, whose fragments were inextricably mingled with the wreck of forests and towns. They themselves but fragments of families, with torn garments and bruised limbs, had not where to lay their heads. They had not come out of a conflict with oppressors, with souls nerved to great sacrifices and enterprise. They were saved, and only saved, from the fury of the elements. The powers of nature had combined their strength in that narrow valley, and left its defenseless people crushed and homeless.

In this aspect of the disaster I felt the force of Bishop Tillotson's words: " Of some calamities we can have no relief but from God ; and what would men do in such a case if it were not for God ? "

The first temporary shelters were, of course, tents and hastily constructed shanties. In a few days the fields around the city presented the aspect of military camps. These tents were, however, inadequate and could not be the abode of women and children, as they were exposed to the hot sun and rains and the dreadful miasma and stench that pervaded the valley.

Now the great problem arose, when and how shall Johnstown be rebuilt with suitable residences and business houses ? In the retrospect we can see that the problem was made to seem more difficult than it really was. It was complicated by permitting hordes of strangers to come into the city, who either encumbered the situation by adding to the number to be fed and housed, or who engaged in labor that should have been exclusively given to the citizens. It would have been well to have permitted none to enter the precincts of the flood except those who came upon errands of mercy and were duly accredited with passes. The builders, masons, carpenters and laborers of the city should have been furnished with the material, means and implements to do the work of rebuilding ; only outsiders should have been employed when there was a deficiency of local laborers. This remark does not apply to those extensive and responsible contractors who only could furnish or speedily erect houses on a large scale. But it is a fact that thousands of outsiders came upon us, and both in labor and charity benefited from the moneys that were contributed solely for the sufferers, or were paid from public funds which should have been used in the employment of the impoverished citizens.

The first formal official action for the erection of business structures was a telegram of General Hastings to Hoover, Hughes & Co., of Phillipsburg, Pa. From their letter, herewith appended, it appears that nearly a month elapsed before the rebuilding commenced, and then for business purposes. The people were yet without homes, living in tents and shanties, or still depending on the hospitality of neighbors on the hills. A typical example of living, or rather existence, was given by the New York *World* correspondent four months after the flood: "Let us enter this house, for example. It is a frame house, once comfortable, but of little pretensions. The clapboards on front and sides have all been stripped off, laying bare the first and second floors. The roof was damaged, but has been repaired. There is no stairway, but a ladder leads to the upper floors. Up under the roof you will notice that a little glazed window has been put in, and behind it, in two garret rooms, so low that you would knock your head against the shingles if you tried to walk upright, lives, or rather camps, a family who never before knew the discomforts of roughing it. The wife lies on a bed of sickness—a sickness not improved, I imagine, by the knocking of the carpenters' hammers all about her. The husband gets a small income, enough to support him and a little better, but money is not so plenty with him that he can afford to push work on the house very much. If the share of the relief fund which is ultimately coming to him had been paid, as it ought, a month ago, his family would now be far better prepared to face the angry blasts of winter.

"This case is a fair sample of many. It is not an extreme one by any means—there are many better off, and many, alas! far worse."

Previous to this, a number of the Hoover, Hughes & Co.'s houses had been erected and were occupied. This correspondent remarks: "There were scattered over the plain many newly-constructed board-houses, wearing no other color than that of natural wood.

These were miserable little sieves, called Oklahomas, and the larger and better Hughes houses, which, though far from comfortable, must furnish shelter to thousands through the coming winter."

The disposal of the Hughes houses was by the House Distributing Committee to those who made application and who were approved by the committee. On July 19th, 1889, the names were published to whom one hundred and four two-story houses were allotted to be erected. This, of course, meant that it would be some time in August before they were ready for occupancy.

The outside world can never know the experience of the people of the Conemaugh Valley during the summer and fall. The patient endurance of the life that this gentle, refined American community was forced to live; their heroic self-control, in view of the fact that the means of relief, which their sympathizing countrymen had so quickly contributed, was so long withheld from them, cannot be fully appreciated. This community of intelligent and upright Americans was crowded together for months in all kinds of shelter and uncomfortable ways. They were, for the most part, brought up in Christian, comfortable homes, and accustomed to refined or gentle associations. They had sensitive natures, delicate instincts, which would hide their tortures of spirit rather than make them known. Many of these persons had lots where their vanished houses had stood, and four hundred dollars, within a few days after the flood, would have relieved their burdened hearts, and enabled them to provide a comfortable shelter for their families as soon as the removal of the debris and obstruction would permit.

A scheme for housing the people was adopted by which persons could obtain what was known as an "Oklahoma" at à certain price for a large or a small structure. At first there was great clamor for houses, and persons rushed to the committee to secure them. The wiser people abstained, and urged the committee, at least members of it, to abandon the system. A number of the houses arrived. After they were seen, the clamor for them ceased, and many who had obtained them regretted that the value of a flimsy building, unfitted for this climate, was to be deducted from the sum of their share of the fund for distribution. The demand ceased, and a few " Oklahomas " now stand as monuments of the folly of those who procured them.

JOHNSTOWN, PA., December 16th, 1889.

Rev. David J. Beale, Johnstown, Pa.

DEAR SIR:—As per your request we herewith submit a short history of our work done at Johnstown and in the Conemaugh Valley, brought about through the great destruction of property on the afternoon of May 31st. Prior to our coming to Johnstown for the commencement of our work very little had been done in the line of building, except the erection of commissaries and camps for flood sufferers and to quarter the large body of men engaged in clearing up the debris.

In answer to a telegram received from Gen. Hastings, our Mr. Hughes arrived at Johnstown on Wednesday morning at 3. A. M., and was obliged to pass the balance of the night at the Pennsylvania freight depot. Early next morning he presented himself to Gen. Hastings, who, as agent for the Flood Relief Commission, appointed him Master Carpenter for that Commission. He was informed that it had been decided to erect temporary store-rooms to enable the business men flooded out to resume business. These buildings it was decided to erect on the Public Park ground. Our Mr. Hughes at once submitted several plans, and on the afternoon of the same day, at request of Gen. Hastings, a special meeting of Council was held, granting the use of the Public Park grounds for the temporary store-room buildings for eighteen months, and also adopted one of the several plans submitted by Mr. Hughes. Governor James A. Beaver arrived from Cresson that same even-

ing and accepted our proposal to erect fifty 20x40 feet store-rooms
with offices above, to be completed in two weeks ; also arranged
with us to erect the three hundred and ten Chicago ready-made
houses as fast as they arrived.   On July 3d a contract was made
with the Flood Relief Commission for the erection of two hundred four-roomed houses constructed after a plan made and submitted by our Mr. Hughes. A further contract was made on August
3d for one hundred additional, with an option for one hundred
more if needed. The latter were ordered August 15th, making a
total of four hundred four-roomed houses known as the "Hughes"
house, which name they are liable to retain in the Conemaugh
Valley for years to come.

As soon as the contract for the temporary store-rooms was accepted, our Mr. Hughes telegraphed to our main office at Philips-
burg, Pa., for the material, and by Monday, June 24th, we had a
number of cars on hand, and on that same day the erection of the
temporary store-buildings was commenced. Between June 24th and
September 7th we erected all the Chicago houses and about three
hundred and seventy-five of the Hughes houses, out of the four
hundred ordered. We had sufficient force to complete the entire
contract by that time, but the Flood Commission desired to hold
back a number of houses to provide for cases which had been
overlooked.   During that time we employed an average of four
hundred and fifty men, and twenty-five double teams, and handled
over four hundred carloads of lumber and building material, which,
taking into consideration the many difficulties which had to be sur-
mounted, such as the almost impassable condition of the streets,
freight blockades, and the larger portion of the houses erected on
hillside and hilltops scattered east and west from Johnstown, from
South Fork to Morrellville, eleven miles apart, and north and
south, a distance of five miles apart, makes us feel rather proud
of our record.   By a special order of the P. R. R. Co., our cars

loaded with lumber at our mills were hurried through on fast freight time. At this point they were put at once into the Cambria Iron Company's yard, their engine promptly shifting them to our side-track, by which means we were enabled to get our material quickly, and put the work through with dispatch. Up to present date we have done the following:

The Flood Commission work, number of Chicago houses erected, three hundred and ten (one hundred and three section houses 16x24 and two hundred and seven 10x20 portable, known as Oklahoma); Hughes houses, four hundred; temporary store-rooms, fifty-five; Red Cross Hotel at Johnstown, headquarters for State Board of Health, and a large amount of special work ordered by the Commission. For private individuals and firms we have done the following: seven Hughes houses, a large brick addition to Cambria Iron Company's Club House, addition to Wood, Morrell & Co., Limited, store-room (now in the course of erection), several of the large buildings at Gautier's Works, one brick stable, three small frame stables, one large livery stable, two school buildings (one at Woodvale and the other in Cambria City), station for P. R. R. at East Conemaugh, double dwelling for P. R. R. at Johnstown, twelve dwellings and additions to same, repaired the brick residence of Mr. Trochneiser, and large amounts of small work too numerous to mention.

Very truly,

Hoover, Hughes & Co.

2.—THE CHILDREN AND THE SCHOOLS.

By the fireside still the light is shining,
The children's arms round the parents twining.—Muloch.

THE schools had closed on Friday afternoon for the week. The merry children had returned to their homes and put away their books, glad at their release from the school-room tasks.

They were anticipating and making arrangements for a happy holiday on the morrow. After dinner they were engaged in childish sports and games, making home bright with their cheerful faces, their sparkling eyes and ringing voices. Little girls with motherly instinct were absorbed with their dollies, arranging their wardrobes, and arraying them in their evening dresses, or telling them how dear they were to their own little mothers, and that they shall never, never let them go out of their sight. Little groups had gathered in some favorite home and were playing at jackstones or imaginary housekeeping. The boys were devising a game of baseball and other out-door sport, or tinkering about the house; perhaps they were teasing their sisters; at least they were doing what boys everywhere do to make a noise, a racket, through the house, and thereby make themselves more dear even to those whom they seem to annoy. Little babes were resting in their cradles and in their mothers' arms, or cooing at the pranks of the older nestlings. Some little ones were lying on beds of sickness on whom the anxieties and tender ministries of the home were centered.

The holiday never came; the sports were not to be enjoyed; but a long vacation came to those little ones, some of whom will never again enter the school-room. The dearly loved dollies were suddenly snatched from the little mothers. One little girl was found dead, with her dolly tightly clasped in her bosom. In the midst of all this childish life and glee came the avalanche of destruction. Amid the crashing and falling houses these little ones were thrown and dashed about, separated from parents and each other, some to perish, some to be rescued by strangers, many of them to be orphaned. This feature of the calamity goes closer to the heart of humanity than any other. The Rev. Mr. Diller was found near my church, with his babe in his arms and his wife by his side.

There is no home, however well defended, however exempt

DYNAMITE BLASTING ABOVE THE RAILROAD BRIDGE.

from the possibility of flood and tempest, in which our demolished homes do not awaken sympathy. The breaking up of their child-life, the scattered and buried bodies of their little ones, the sad lot of the rescued orphan—these are the saddest facts of the flood that touch humanity's heart.

The illustration of the happy little Fenn group, which providentially I have secured for this work, suggests to every sympathetic heart this whole chapter of the flood's history. The fathers and mothers of America need no pen to dilate on the scene ; to make them realize what are the unwritten and unutterable experiences of the parents of the once happy homes in Conemaugh Valley. Nor do they need to be reminded of those little ones whose fathers and mothers lie in our cemeteries or undiscovered beneath the mud of the streams and valley. Blessed are those whom the heavenly Father took into His own home to be there nurtured and developed into their immortal stature. *They* are *safe* as well as saved.

Great concern was expressed about the children, and we received special contributions for them and offers of adoption for many of those who were orphaned. But for some days there did not seem to be any children. We had nearly come to the conclusion that all had been drowned or killed. The day-schools and Sunday-schools could not be held, and the children who survived the flood were scattered over the country wherever shelter could be provided. There was no way, then, of ascertaining how many survived and who were dead or missing. Time alone could reveal this when the rolls would be called in the day and Sunday-schools.

There was a class of children to whom sympathy was not at first directed, who needed it more, for they had not enjoyed much of it in their sad and impoverished homes. It is the poor class. They, too, are the children of the great Father of us all. As their abodes were in the lower parts of the towns, many of them per-

18

ished. An example of child heroism is little Joe W. Dixon, a member of my church and Sunday-school. He is a newsboy of fifteen, whose father was employed in the Cambria Iron Works. He had made enough money to pay $150 for a news-stand just before the flood. As the wave swept over the city, a gentleman picked him up and carried him to a place of safety. From there Joe saw the flood carry away his stand with all his stock and capital. His father was drowned, his mother seriously injured. The family thus became dependent on him, and all his invested capital had been washed away. He went immediately to work selling papers, without complaint and with a brave heart, saying: "I've got to fix it somehow to do more business now than I used to: for my father is gone, and they will have to look to me." The ranks of commercial failure cannot show an example of greater fortitude and heroism.

The public and private schools, of course, were entirely broken up for the summer. The Sunday-schools, when they were resumed, showed many vacant places of teachers and scholars. It was by them that we first began to learn something about the fate and condition of the children. The Sunday-school, ever since it was inaugurated, has demonstrated in ten thousand ways its blessedness and its usefulness. It is in a time like that at Johnstown that its full value is known. If an atheist, an enemy of or an objector to the Sunday-school, could have been present in any of our schools when the teachers and children for the first time met after the awful days, his tongue would be henceforth silent. Heaven ever bless and preserve the Sunday-school. It is not only the nursery of the church on earth, but it is also the rallying place of the scattered family of God: it is the shadow of the home above where

"Around the throne of God
Thousands of children stand."

THE PUBLIC SCHOOLS.

The public schools of Johnstown were among the objects of its pride. There were few better anywhere. Their destruction was a great calamity, and their reconstruction became a serious and difficult undertaking. Contributions were made by teachers in other counties and districts for the help of our teachers.

The Board of Education has been equal to the exigencies, and is determined to see that the schools are maintained. It met on September 12th, and elected teachers for the ensuing term of eight months. Provision was made for opening twenty-four schools, to which the teachers elected were respectively assigned. The salaries authorized are, of course, inadequate, and will be until the taxpayers recuperate from their misfortune. A most noble and worthy act of philanthropy on the part of some wealthy person would be a gift of $2,400, to be equally divided among the twenty-four teachers, twenty-one of whom are ladies.

The State Superintendent of Schools and the Johnstown Superintendent gave notice that surviving teachers would be re-appointed without examination, and diplomas or certificates that were lost would be replaced on application.

The teachers who perished were: Mattie McDivitt, Emma K. Fisher, Laura Hamilton, Mary P. White, Jennie M. Wells, Minnie Linton, Maggie Jones, Rose Carroll, C. F. Gallagher, Mary Dowling, Kate McAneny, Miss Richards (classical), and Miss Diehl, of Shippensburg.

3.—THE CHURCHES.

On Friday afternoon, May 31st, the pastors of the churches were making final preparations for their Sunday sermons, doubtless giving them a cheerful tone, to be in harmony with beauties of the summer, which the Lord's day, June 2d, would usher in.

Those sermons were not preached, and doubtless will not be

for many months, if ever. There were no services on that day. The pastors who escaped, or were uninjured by the flood, were otherwise engaged. They had a Divine call to exercise the duties of their ministry in ways they never anticipated. Yet they learned by them more of the virtue and power of the religion of their Divine Master than they had ever known before.

The violent transformation from the beauty and bloom of spring merging into the calm and glory of summer, to a scene of tempest, flood, death, desolation and ruin, demonstrated, as sermons can never do, the reality and power of the Christian faith.

The churches were not in a condition to be occupied for that first Sunday. The dawn of Saturday revealed the sad fact that our stately and beautiful sanctuaries had suffered with the rest of the city. St. John's (R. C.), St. Mark's (Episcopal), the Welsh Baptist, Welsh Methodist, the Congregational, German Lutheran and German Reformed churches were destroyed. The rector of the Episcopal church, Rev. Alonzo P. Diller, the pastor of the German Lutheran church, Rev. John P. Lichtenberg, the Rev. E. W. Jones, D.D., of the Congregational church, and Rev. George Wagoner, M.D., of the United Brethren, perished.

The Baptist and Evangelical Association churches were very slightly damaged, and they were quickly ready for occupancy. The English Lutheran church was damaged only by water, and was soon repaired. The Presbyterian church, one of the largest in the city, was injured to a considerable extent, the floor having settled about a foot and a half. As the pastor had been appointed to take charge of identifying the recovered bodies, and as it was uncertain how long the church would be unfit for the use of the congregation, it was decided to utilize it, in its present condition, as a morgue under the immediate supervision of the pastor. Some persons objected to this on grounds of sentiment. The pastor and others deemed it a humane act and a religious duty. There were so many reasons for immediate identification of the bodies recovered—moral, legal and family. There were no large and protected rooms where the bodies, and the valuables which were found on them, would be secure from intrusion and robbery.

Regard for the dead and the living required us to suppress our sentiments, and yield, for a time, to what seemed to us a religious duty. We did what we had a right to suppose the Master of our faith would have done if He had been personally present. There were many occasions on which He offended the sentiments of His own disciples as well as the Scribes and Pharisees. Peter rebuked Him several times for doing what he imagined was unseemly for the Son of God. But He in turn rebuked Peter for knowing so little of the spirit and aim of His kingdom. He denounced the Pharisees unsparingly, whose false conception of holy things caused them to sink the consideration for human suffering and woe out of sight beneath their frigid literalism. They would hale Him before the authorities of the Church and turn Him out of the synagogue for healing the sick or raising the dead on the Sabbath day. They would not hesitate to take their own ox or ass from a pit on the Sabbath, which necessitated great labor, but condemned the Lord of the Sabbath for restoring the paralytic to health and giving him strength to walk and carry his bed. That Phariseeism is not yet extinct which will use holy things for its own financial or worldly advancement, and object to their use in behalf of stricken humanity when it offends its sentiment, or has not obtained its stiff-robed consent.

The first services after the flood were held on Sunday, June 9th, at my suggestion. I had personally called on Bishop Whitehead, of the Episcopal Church, Father Tahaney, of the Roman Catholic Church, and the pastors of the other churches, and arranged with them for services in different localities amid the ruins. Bishop Whitehead, of the Protestant Episcopal Church, conducted service in the Peelorville school-house; other services were held in the Pennsylvania Railroad station, and at the corner of Main and Adam Streets. Rev. Drs. George T. Purvis, of Pittsburgh; John Fox, of Allegheny City; J. Logan Sample, of the Black Hills, Dakota; Chaplain Maguire, of the Fourteenth Regiment; Rev. H. L. Chapman, of Cambria; Rev. James P. Tahaney, Rev. W. W. Moorhead, and Rev. D. J. Beale officiated at their respective appointments on this and succeeding Sabbaths.

Those services were indeed solemn and impressive. Divine worship had never been held and the Divine truth never preached under such circumstances. Around the assembled worshipers was a scene of destruction and desolation that was fearfully sad. The homes of those worshipers were scattered fragments, and their loved ones crushed or buried in the debris at their feet, and their plans and hopes in life destroyed.

Yet the storm and flood had not shaken their faith in God or in the promises of the Redeemer. They sang the songs of Zion, lifted up their hearts in prayer, and heard the assuring words of grace. They took heart from this worship to renew the struggle of life. They determined first of all to build again the " walls of Jerusalem ;" to " restore its waste places."

In this work the various denominations were assisted by their sister churches in other parts of the country. The Presbyterians sent in the aggregate about $16,000; $8,000 for the congregation, and nearly $8,000 for repairing the church and parsonage. The Baptists contributed $9,000. The Evangelical and Lutheran edifices suffered little damage and did not need much help. The Episcopal congregation has been enabled to erect a neat and comfortable chapel. Rev. W. H. Bates, pastor of the Reformed Church, says that he and the Committee of Classis have received for himself, for the rebuilding of his church, and for his people, over three thousand dollars. I could secure no reports from the other churches, except their grateful assurances that they received sympathy and aid from their sister churches.

"Where so much good work has been promptly performed it is difficult and might appear invidious to discriminate; but the service rendered by the various church organizations is worthy of being noted; and among such societies that were active in relieving the needy was that of the Presbyterian Church, under the wise direction of Rev. Dr. Beale, its pastor. Telegrams and letters poured unto him from all sections of the eastern part of this State, and from New Jersey and New York, asking for particulars as to the wants of the people, and boxes of food, clothing, and even bedding were sent to him 'as soon as railroad facilities permitted. A room was then secured at the corner of Main and Adam Streets, which was put in charge of Mrs. Dr. Beale, Mrs. Jones and Miss Duncan, of this place, Miss Graham, of Wilkinsburg, and Mrs. Dr. Marchand, of Irwin, who distributed edibles, wearing apparel, etc., to multitudes of every name, grade and profession who were left in destitute circumstances."—*Johnstown Democrat.*

VI.

MISCELLANEOUS.

I.—CONSOLIDATION.

THE most important feature of the reconstruction is the consolidation of the eight boroughs into the one city of Johnstown. An Act of Legislature was passed in the spring of 1889, providing for erection into cities of the third class towns or contiguous boroughs of not less than ten thousand inhabitants. Johnstown becomes the first city thus chartered under that Act.

This has been the aim of Mr. Arthur J. Moxham and others for a long time. They have urged it frequently, and the terrible disaster which was common to Johnstown proper and the boroughs determined them to renew efforts to effect the consolidation, and thus endow the new Johnstown with all the dignity, authority and advantage of a city. The considerations with which Mr. Moxham enforced this proposition are so forcible and applicable to other towns and boroughs in the State that a few of them are here presented, with a hope that they will follow the example:

"As a matter of common sense, if thirty thousand people want to do a thing, they can best do it by clubbing together and acting as a unit, and just now they have something to do. They have to get this place on its feet.

"A city with well-paved streets, cleanly sidewalks, and buildings which are pleasing to the eye; in which local transit is rapid and good, in which police protection and discipline are reliable, is just as sure to have a pleasanter, healthier and more pro-

(336)

gressive life, as a cleanly and well-regulated household is sure to enjoy life more than the household accustomed to slovenliness and dirt.   Let any public question arise, how much quicker the machinery of a city can be brought to bear in influencing results for its own good than that of seven or eight puny little boroughs.

"Would we have suffered the calamities of the flood if we had had a city organization here?   I answer emphatically, No.

"The facts which were known to all were these: A dangerous body of water existed in our neighborhood, and grave doubts were entertained on all sides as to the security of the structure which dammed it in.

"We then had the strange spectacle of the whole community, as a community, not even taking the trouble to investigate the possible danger.   The reason that nothing was done is very evident—simply this: That there has never been in these valleys a competent organization, representative of the community as a whole.   There have been a baker's dozen of organizations, each representing a homœopathic proportion of the community.   I will venture the assertion that if we had had a city organization, and consequently had become accustomed to acting as a unit, years ago would this question of the South Fork dam have been settled.

"Well, we have paid for our criminal carelessness—paid for it with the lives of those dear to us—paid for it with our homes, and with our savings.

"You cannot build even a house without tools to work with, still less can you control and influence public results without the proper machinery to do it with.   Take the history of affairs in Johnstown since the flood.   We have had many committees. Please point out to me among all these one committee, which, when it speaks on a general public question, can speak as representative of the whole community.   There is not one committee in existence that has not done its work nobly and well.   There is not one that has not earned the gratitude of the people ; but there is also not one, which, from the nature of the case, is to-day in a position to speak for the whole people.

" Many public questions have arisen and are arising from day to day, and they are put back to slumber, and no action taken upon them. Why? Because there is no machinery with which to reach the people excepting the cumbersome machinery of lots of little boroughs, and because life is too short and time is too quick for any sensible man to undertake the problem to try to get every little borough to think with the others on the same question.

" With a city organization our city would respond to every public need like a well-balanced piece of machinery ; with your borough organizations it takes dynamite to move you.

" With a city organization you would govern yourselves, and yourselves control the results which affect you. With your borough organization you are passive like a flock of sheep, and until a dog or wolf gets after you, or until something comes along with a bell on its collar to lead you, you do not move.

" I, for one, am looking forward to the election with great longing. I am hoping that it will be the beginning of a new life for us all, with the dead past so utterly put behind us that not even the name be left, and in the place of a lot of little mismanaged boroughs without a single collective name, but called Johnstown, by courtesy, I would like to see the birth of a new and vigorous city called Conemaugh Valley—a city that has witnessed the greatest sorrow of the times, and that has enjoyed the greatest tenderness. It cannot fail to have a grand future before it if it only profits by what it has learned—we have learned so much. "

That the consolidation has now been effected is due chiefly to the efforts and influence of W. Horace Rose, A. J. Moxham, John P. Linton, W. H. Story, Dr. J. C. Sheridan, Hon. John M. Rose and Rev. James P. Tahaney.

The population of the new Johnstown is as follows:

Cambria .	2,902
Conemaugh	3,971
Coopersdale	573
Grubbtown	497
Johnstown	10,253
Millville	2,680
Prospect .	819
Woodvale .	1,247
Total,	22,942

In addition to these boroughs, Moxham and the district lying above and along the Bedford Pike, and between the southern limit of Johnstown and the village of Walnut Grove, will become part and parcel of the city as soon as the proper proceedings can be had.

The population of Moxham is estimated at 1,000, and the other territory has fully 800. This would bring the total population of the new city up to 24,742.

If to this is added the population of that portion of Upper Yoder township lying immediately contiguous to Grubbtown, and whose citizens have joined with those of Moxham in asking the Court for annexation to Johnstown, then the population of the city will be over 25,000.

It is regretted that our friends at East Conemaugh and Franklin could not see their way clear to join us in the creation of the new Johnstown, but it is hoped they will eventually come into the family.

2.—ADDITIONAL ECHOES FROM THE FLOOD.

THESE papers of participants in the flood, and observers of its scenes and effects, were received too late to be inserted in the first part. They, however, give additional interest to the closing pages, and will be all the more appreciated for coming after the many details about the situation.

Mr. William F. Lewis, who has charge of the Cambria roll-shop, was on the Pennsylvania Railroad track opposite Rosensteel's tannery twenty-five minutes before the torrent came upon us. He then saw Mr. Haselbein and Miss Carrie Williams on a little knoll near the bridge that crosses the Conemaugh, with the spray of the swollen stream splashing around them. He waved his handkerchief at them, and Miss Carrie held up a piece of cheese and cracker in her hand, indicating that that was all the dinner they were having.

In about twenty-five minutes after, he (Mr. Lewis) was down at the Pennsylvania Railroad depot and saw the avalanche of water coming on the town. He saw the steeple of the German Lutheran church fall, then Mr. Kilgore's residence, and after that the Assistance engine-house. He noticed that the houses on Iron Street rose bodily and began to twist and grind one another to pieces; and after that everything changed as in a kaleidoscope, and he next found himself asking a man who stood by if it was really so that the town was swept away. The next morning the body of Miss Williams was found at the head of Main Street. He said that when the torrent came, men and women on Prospect Hill wrung their hands, tore their hair, and threw themselves upon the ground in agony.

Mr. Wener, wife and child were drowned. The child was found at the feet of its parents, and Mrs. Wener with her arm on her husband's shoulder.

On the day before the flood Mr. and Mrs. Webber, Mr. and Mrs. Curtis Williams, Mr. and Mrs. Longacre, Mr. William F.

Lewis, Miss Carrie Williams and Miss Menocher spent the day at the Viaduct and Mineral Point. They ate their lunch on the Old Portage Road, near the tunnel. When they reached Mineral Point they all joined in singing some patriotic and sacred pieces. The people gathered around them as they sang.

Mrs. S. W. Shields says : In the morning Charlie came home from town ; told me he could not get to the Johnstown office for high water, and then it was eight feet at Sandy Vale Cemetery. I was not surprised at all, knowing that was a most frequent occurrence. So we *waited* and *watched* the water until in the afternoon (Charlie staying at home). Then I proposed that the children and myself go up to Canan's to see what the water looked like. It was then coming into my yard. It was all the dry ground on that side of the street. The thought struck me that I had better make our-selves comfortable, for we might not get back ; yet at the same time I never dreamed that we would be washed out. But I paid attention to the monitor and made us all comfortable, and the clothes we put on we wore for weeks after. We were sitting on the porch, waiting and watching for what was to come. I looked over at the hill above the Conemaugh (after the whistle blew), saw the heavy black cloud and wondered what was in store for us, but did not speak. When Charlie asked what that noise was, I heard it and thought it was hail. Told all that were on the porch to come in *quick*, that we might be killed by what I thought was hail. We went in at once and up-stairs. Looked out ; saw one man wade across the street in water to his waist. I then looked up to the corner of Dibert and Morris Sts.; saw a man trying to catch a tree. The water was up to his neck, and with the same glance I saw two men and a woman trying to climb the electric-light pole. They were partly under water. Then I heard the call to come to the attic, which we all did with one accord. We had just reached it when I heard a terrible scream and breaking of glass. It was Miss Ida Hamilton, who screamed. She came to the attic, fell on her knees and thanked God for her escape, and also that her mother had been saved (in the house at the other side of theirs). She was a Catholic Christian. We had not been in the attic fifteen minutes when some one said: "There is Mrs. Tittle on a roof." Then began the work of breaking the windows. Some of the men got a plank across to Mr. Joseph's roof, their house having moved some twenty feet, but could not strike us, for the reason that we were on a terraced lot, four feet above the street. Who were the first brought in I cannot tell, but in a very short time the attic was full. Some cried, some prayed, and I waited, feeling that this was God's time now. We, I then thought, had had our time. Dick, Albert and Anna were standing with me. Dick asked: "Mother, will we die?" I answered: "I cannot tell; but one thing I *do* know, that God does all things well, and if He wants us to-night He will take us; if not, He will find a way for our escape. We will go and sit down, and see what the Lord will do," which we did, and Dick never asked another question. Mrs. Henry, from Market Street, and her family, made a very narrow escape. Just as their house, with the family on the roof, came past the market-house, it fell, throwing the bricks all over them, hitting Mrs. H. and her daughter, injuring them so that they were not over it for weeks. Mrs. McClay had left one of her servants, Mary Manealy, behind, which they lamented very much. Mrs. Henry insisted that, as their house came past Mrs. McClay's, they saw some one in the attic, on her knees; and about 4 o'clock, or just as soon as they could see, Mr. Murphy went across the roofs and found old Mary Manealy, safe and sound, wrapped up in Lizzie Tittle's fur-lined circular.

The little boy of B. F. Hills fretted all night for his papa and sister (she being drowned). He found his father next day on the hill. Mrs. Tittle brought in with her two little children, who had been taken in the afternoon to her house for safety; so when the big wave came she kept them. Their parents found them next day. Mr. and Mrs. Canan divided with every one that was brought in. When we came out the next morning, we walked out on planks laid on the sideboard, the upholstered chairs and extension tables through Mrs. Harshberger's house, over the roofs of some of the houses that were broken up. As I went I looked across to the hill that we were going to for refuge, and saw some men carrying some-one on a stretcher. They went to where I was going, and upon inquiry I found she was it wife of Mahlon Speck, who had been confined Thursday night; and on Friday, when the big wave came, she had to be taken to the attic. She lay there all night without a light, and no one with her but her husband. Saturday some men carried her out over the roofs of houses; and when I left her, on Monday morning, she was doing well. In Mr. Canan's attic there were sixty-nine persons. Of this number there were eighteen or twenty children. One of the men went out and got a loaf of dry bread, which was divided among the little ones; and it was from Friday morning until Saturday noon that no food crossed our lips.

Mr. Josiah T. Evans resided on Vine Street, and lived in good style, with his family. His children consisted of Maggie and her four brothers, all younger than she. Maggie was making preparations to visit Europe, expecting much enjoyment in the trip.

On Friday, the 31st of May, at the time of high water, Mr. E. finding the water in his house a foot high and rising, started with his wife, daughter and three youngest sons in a buggy, to go to the hillside. Fondly kissing them, they separated, with the understanding that, if possible, the buggy would be returned, to take the two elder boys to the same refuge.

But Mrs. Evans seems to have been frightened by the rising

waters, and entered the house of her friend, Mrs. Pritchard, who was alone with her four children. They all, the two mothers and their seven children, went to the attic, and there, looking out from under the mansard roof, they doubtless watched the ruin around them, until they themselves were swallowed up, when the three-story house was engulfed in the terrible flood, as it swept over that portion of the town, and they were all lost.

Mr. Evans and his two boys meantime remained in their own house, supposing that the mother and those with her were safe; and from the upper windows they beheld the surging waters rise and eventually fall, and they found themselves the next morning in their own house and safe. Had Mrs. E. and the rest of the children remained at home, they too would have been saved; but it was not ordered so of God!

Alexander N. Hart, says: "When the flood struck my house it began to tremble and move. I took my two little boys, aged respectively 2 and 8 years, by the hands and leaped with them from the second-story window upon a floating roof. My wife and sister followed us. After being whirled by the surging waters we were driven against Rev. Dr. Beale's house, where the family were huddled in his attic story. He helped us into the room, which our addition made more crowded. The fierceness of the flood and the sight of tumbling houses made us fear that our refuge would soon fall. We then determined, if possible, to escape over the floating and accumulating roofs and wreck to Alma Hall. Dr. Beale procured a rope, with which he let us down upon the roof of a floating house, which we secured to his residence. There were about twelve persons, women and children, besides Dr. Beale, Mr. Lloyd, and myself. Dr. Beale was the last to leave the attic, having secured our escape. With great labor we made our way over the roofs and debris. Strewed upon and

THE SITE OF WOODVALE—ONE MONTH AFTER THE FLOOD.

fastened in the wrecks were the dead and wounded and dying. It was a heartrending sight, and we did what we could on our way to help or comfort the sufferers. Among these I recognized Mrs. Young (since deceased), her daughter Rose and son-in-law, J. Fleming. We finally got into Alma Hall, where we spent the night amid scenes that are too sad to recall.

"Too much praise cannot be accorded to Dr. Edward W. Matthews, who, though suffering from broken ribs, devoted the night with Dr. Beale to helping others, dressing their wounds and setting broken limbs. One of the saddest things was the distressing cries of little children for water and food. The only water that could be obtained was the drippings from the roof of the adjoining bank, under which I held a pitcher.

"In the morning we got out of the second-floor windows, and, clambering for three squares over wrecks of houses, railroad cars, locomotives, trees and every other imaginable thing, with dead bodies all around us, we reached the ground, a sorrowful group indeed. Here I met with seventeen others, and we immediately proceeded to effect some sort of government for our protection and guidance. Mr. A. J. Moxham was chosen chairman, and I was appointed chief of police, with full powers to act. Without food for twenty-four hours, and with insufficient clothing, I organized a force of four hundred men and distributed them through the city, to protect property and the bodies of the dead from thieves, who had already begun to ply their nefarious vocation. I maintained this force until General Hastings arrived.

"I cannot end this account without paying tribute to Dr. David J. Beale, the pastor of the Presbyterian Church. During the whole time of the flood and afterward, he forgot himself in his care and ministering to us and our suffering people. Throughout that dreadful night in Alma Hall, he was incessant in his attentions, though his own wife and children were among the suffering multi-

19

tude. By his kind, consoling words, by his calmness and self-control, by his fervent prayers, directing us to our only help in this time of trouble, he made it possible for us to endure the horrors of that night. During the following weeks his work and services in the morgues and among the survivors have laid our citizens under obligations they can never fully discharge."

Mr. W. B. Tice, who had the handsome drug store at No. 31 Portage Street, has written thus his experience:

"My wife became alarmed at the rising of the water, so I removed her and my pet birds to the house of a friend, Nathan Oldham, in a more elevated portion of the city.

"About 9 A.M. I returned to my place of business. The water had begun to come into the store, so I went to work to save the most valuable articles on the top shelves, which being done I returned to my wife. She requested me to get her some clothing she had brought home and $160 in money which I had just got from the bank. While packing the clothes I heard a roar like thunder, one crash after another in quick succession, and on looking out of the window I beheld the most horrible sight I ever saw, and I hope I never may be called upon to witness such a scene again.

"The room I was in quickly filled with water, and in an instant I climbed on the roof by the aid of the spouting.

"The wall of water which came rushing toward me carrying everything before it seemed to be thirty feet in height, and in an instant, crash! and our building was raised aloft and whirled away by the mad, rushing, bounding and boiling waters of the Little Conemaugh. Eight men were on this roof, and all around us were screaming hundreds of men, women and children. Many of them were swept into eternity; some were praying, some weeping and wailing and some cursing.

"I was determined to keep my presence of mind and save myself and all others that I could. We sailed about three squares when the building struck the large brick store of Wood, Morrell & Co. I clung to the roof until it passed the store, when I leaped into the water and swam to a lumber pile, which floated into slack water up the Stony Creek, where I had a full view of the terrible disaster. The Wire Mills and Gautier Works fell, crushing all in their way. Whole families of my acquaintance were entirely wiped out of existence. All this time I was still floating around, and finally I was caught by the wild waters and whirled away and over the now famous stone bridge of the P. R. R. At this time the clock struck 4, and I then thought I would never hear the clock strike again. I was attracted by a voice, and, looking about, I saw a lady floating down at a rapid rate and singing:

> ' Jesus, lover of my soul,
> Let me to Thy bosom fly,
> While the raging billows roll,
> While the tempest still is high.'

This she sang as she sailed down the valley of death. I was again compelled to jump, and after being knocked about until almost exhausted, I reached another house-top, sailing at the rate of about fifteen miles an hour; but, getting close to shore, I again jumped, and a mill-man caught hold of my hand and assisted me to land; he was terribly excited and could not speak. I helped him to take two more men out. I went up on the embankment and looked across the bridge, which was filled full of debris, and on it were thousands of men, women and children, who were screaming and yelling for help, as at this time the debris was on fire, and after each crash there was a moment of solemn silence, and then those voices would be again heard crying in vain for the help that came not. At each crash hundreds were forced under and slain.

"I saw hundreds of them as the flames approached throw up their hands and fall backward into the fire, and those who had escaped drowning were reserved for the more horrible fate of being burned to death. At last I could endure it no longer, and had to leave, as I could see no more. I climbed the hillside where I could see the church on fire close to the house where I had left my wife, but I could not see the house, and did not know she was safe.

"A more terrible and lonesome night alone in the woods and rain I never spent, knowing that my friends mourned me as dead and I thought they were all lost.

"I remember one incident while I was on the house-top: a train of cars consisting of three or four coaches came puffing along the curve, and dashing into the water gave two puffs and was swept under the mad, rushing torrent.

"I could not cross the river to see my wife or let her know of my safety until the next day, and when I met her, there was once more a happy but penniless and homeless couple."

Colonel John P. Linton writes: "Before noon I was driven, with my family, into the second story of my house, which was situated on the lower end of Main Street, in Johnstown. By 3 o'clock the water was at least four feet high in the first story; and as my house stood on high ground, I would estimate it as nearly eight feet high in the street in front. Shortly before 4 o'clock we heard the loud and doleful whistling of the engines at the mill, which surely betokens a fire, and which we at the time supposed to be such an alarm. I have been informed since that this was intended to warn people that the South Fork dam had burst, and to prepare for the consequences. To us, even if we had understood the purpose of the alarm, it could have been of no avail, as an impassable flood of water already isolated our house, and we could not have fled to any place of refuge. Ah, what must it have been at about 4 o'clock (as I fix time from subsequent comparison of dates), for *then* I took 'no note of time;' an indescribable sound of rushing waters, crashing buildings and shrieking people was borne to our ears, and we rushed to the third story of the house. From the window in this story I saw the advancing torrent, many feet high, and bearing before it with terrific fury logs and broken buildings and crashing machinery, and preceded by what appeared to us as a cloud of smoke. The first wave seemed to follow the general course of the Conemaugh; the second, which followed in rapid succession, swept over Millville Borough, carrying everything before it, and the next, with scarcely a perceptible interval, swept along the Johnstown shore of the Conemaugh, tearing down and sweeping away all obstructions. Realizing at once the danger in which my family would be placed if our house was knocked down, and feeling that our most secure place was on the roof, I caused all the family to rush to a kind of observatory on the top of the house, and promptly followed them myself. By the time we reached the roof, the torrent had reached the stone bridge, had piled the debris high against the arches, and recoiling from this obstruction was setting back with but slightly diminished force, bearing up past my house many buildings. One of these buildings lodged for a time on the corner of the house, and a heavy volume of smoke issuing from it caused us to fear it was on fire, and added the dread of a conflagration to the other perils surrounding us. In a short time, however, the larger portion of our house fell, and the dreaded building floated away. Fortunately, when the larger portion of our house fell, that portion on which we stood remained projecting over the rushing waters, and thus seemingly suspended between death and life. Here we remained for nearly three hours, watching the waters carrying building after building to destruction, shivering in the cold, drenched with rain, and in the most fearful suspense. In the meantime we had noticed persons climbing over house-tops and debris to the High School building, about a block away from our house, and which still towered aloft apparently uninjured, the only edifice in our immediate neighborhood which stood on its foundation. All others had been swept away, leaving in their place a tangled mass of timber, broken planks, roofs and other debris. I dreaded remaining during the approaching night in our precarious situation, and before dark succeeded in getting my family out of a remaining attic window, and with much difficulty and peril succeeded in climbing over this debris, over water at least twenty-five feet deep, to the window of the school-house, into which we were helped. That night we spent with nearly two hundred others in the school-house, the scene of desolation around being lit up by the lurid light of the burning buildings at the stone bridge below and the Catholic church above. About 5 o'clock the next afternoon we were carried to the Kernville hill in boats.

"I purposely omit, as foreign to the purpose for which you asked this sketch, any effort to describe the tragic scene we witnessed from the top of our crumbling house. I also omit any attempt to analyze our sensations as we stood there and witnessed those scenes, and afterward journeyed with uncertain footsteps across constantly shifting and moving supports, over seething waters to the school-house. These, with all that occurred in our place of refuge during this night of calamities, are indelibly impressed on our memories; but who could describe them so as to convey even a faint idea of all we felt and saw and suffered!"

Charles R. Phipps writes: My first intimation that the rise of the water was unusually high was on my way to our office. I was informed that the machinery was stopped on that account. After going through the city, often wading across the streets, I obtained a horse and rode to Kernville to view the situation at the

upper end of the city. The lumber boom had broken and was rac-
ing down around the bend of the river. With everal other
horsemen I galloped down the street through two feet of water to
get across the bridge before the boom should strike it. As we
wheeled the corner to the bridge, the lumber, which had dragged
with it the Poplar Street bridge, struck the Kernville bridge, thus
stopping us until we discovered that it was not carried away. We
then crossed and rode into town. At noon we dined as usual without apprehending any further rise of the rivers or any disaster. After
dinner I wandered about the city for a half hour, and on my return
helped to raise a friend's piano above the floor, to be out of harm's
way. After entertaining myself in the house I found my dog in the
kitchen, and I made sport of his being afraid of the water in the
yard. This was about 4 P.M. In a few minutes the water began to
enter the room. We started to take up the carpets, but in less
than half a minute some one burst into the room, exclaiming
"The reservoir has broken; get up stairs, quick! quick!" We did
not get there too soon, for as we rushed up the stairs the house opposite crushed into ours, and behind it was a great wall of water
bearing on its surface, houses, trees, cars and almost every other
imaginable object. From the second floor we saw a three-story
brick-house fall to the ground. Our house moved off with the current, and, as it went, the two walls of the room we were in fell.
I jumped for the window of the house next door to ours, and from
there to the roof; but as it started off and seemed about to roll
over, I sprang into the waters to reach what was left of ours. As I
got on it the roof fell in, and we crawled to a pile of drift that was
whirling by. It lodged some hundred feet from the front street,
and we got to the floor of a brick-house which was poised at an
angle of about forty-five degrees. I helped the others up (three
ladies and two gentlemen). We then discovered that an old man had
been left behind. He was kneeling in water, on the second floor

of a part of the house, and with clasped hands as in silent prayer was looking toward the cross on the Catholic church. This was the venerable Judge Easly. We managed to get him safely to our frail refuge. When on the drift I saw the back of the Merchants' Hotel fall, and with it many persons who never rose above the water. We waited, expecting each minute to meet the same fate; for huge houses, barns, cars, etc., were crashing into the few places that were left as a refuge from the angry waters. On them were little children clinging to each other, mothers with babes in their arms, strong men and fathers, helpless but calmly awaiting their fate. The square above us was one raging torrent, which afterward calmed and glided noiselessly by where a few moments before were hundreds of happy homes. The silence of this river of death was interrupted by the occasional cry of a poor human being who was being carried on its bosom down to the flames a few squares below. About 8 o'clock the Catholic church, a square and a half away, between which and our little place of refuge this vast body of water glided, caught fire. This helped to warm us, but its fierce flames were driving out those who had taken refuge within its walls and on the surrounding houses. About 10 o'clock the great steeple, after supporting a vast flame that shot high in the air, fell, and the fine building was totally in ruins. This and the whole square that was burned, and the greater and more horrible fire at the stone bridge, added a horror to the night never to be forgotten— one that under other circumstances would have been called grand. We managed to get hold of some floating canvas and made a little tent, under which we (about fifteen in all) managed to get, and huddled close together to keep off some of the rain that continually poured down. My dog had followed us through it all, and as several of us had no shoes on, we made him lie on our feet to keep them warm. Several persons were pulled from the debris beneath our place of refuge, and were taken under our extemporized tent.

After sixteen long hours in this condition we managed to rig up a raft and poled ourselves to Jackson Street, where we once more touched dry land, and for the first time felt ourselves comparatively safe ; but we were only to witness the more horrible sight of seeing dead bodies by the hundred for the next month.

For fourteen years prior to the disaster of May 31st, Mr. Edward Mayhew and his family lived happily in Woodvale, their home being on Maple Avenue, a short distance above the tannery. At the time of the flood the household consisted of Mr. and Mrs. Mayhew and seven children. When the rush of water came all the members of the family gathered in an up-stairs room.

As soon as the flood came against the house, the structure began to go to pieces. Mr. and Mrs. Mayhew and one of the children—Edward, aged 14 years—climbed out of a window on the roof of the porch. Before Mr. Mayhew had time to get his other children out, the house had been smashed in and swept away with them in it, and he and his wife and his son were borne on the deluge down the valley.

At the Gautier Works the current turned them southward, and they were swept across Conemaugh Borough and out Jackson Street past St. John's Catholic church to the Stony Creek, where they succeeded in getting into a house through a window. Later they made their way across the debris to John Thomas' building, where they remained until 9 o'clock Saturday morning.

The children who were swept away in Mr. Mayhew's house were all lost. One of them—Joseph, aged 16 years—was found a week after the flood and taken to the Fourth Ward morgue. James, aged 22 months, was also found shortly after the flood.

The other four were all interred on Prospect, but it was only recently that Mr. Mayhew knew that their bodies had been recovered and where they were interred, these facts being learned by him upon a visit to the rooms of the Committee on Valuables. There he found two rings belonging to Jennie—his eldest daughter, aged 18—and a medal, some pictures, and an *Agnus Dei* belonging to Annie, his second eldest daughter, aged 12 years. After receiving the articles from the Committee on Valuables Mr. Mayhew had the graves on Prospect opened, and he fully identified the remains of his children.

Mr. John Brady was a stationer, his store being on the corner of Franklin and Locust Streets. His son Tom is bookkeeper for the *Daily Democrat*, from which we extract this account of the death of Mr. Brady and the thrilling escape of his family: "Tom, with his father, mother, three brothers and three sisters, was in the second story of the house—the dwelling and store were one building, built of brick—when the flood broke over the city. Three or four freight cars came along and struck the house, demolishing the entire Locust Street side. At the same time the wall separating the bed-room from the stairs and the wall running the entire length of the hall tumbled in, covering every one in the room with a mass of rubbish. Now comes the miraculous part. The floor, having nothing to retard it, commenced to float. It went slowly along with its load of living freight until it lodged against the debris at the Sixth Ward school-house, where Tom succeeded in getting his head above the timbers. Between the school-house and where the frail craft stopped was a solid mass of heavy timbers, frame-houses and wreckage of all kinds. Tom succeeded in getting his mother, brothers and sisters on the debris; but the father, who had been an invalid for some time, was drowned. Then the task of getting into the school-house commenced. Clambering on the roofs of houses that crushed against each other and went to pieces like so much paper, the brave party at last succeeded in reaching the haven of safety. The mother and daughters were pulled

into the building by means of a long pole held at each end by the
boys, then the others followed as best they could. They remained
in the school-house, in company with some forty-three others,
until Saturday noon, when the waters had abated sufficiently to allow
them to go out.

"Mrs. Brady, who sustained severe injuries, was removed to
Mercy Hospital, Pittsburgh, where she was taken with pneumonia,
and died on June 6th. Her remains were brought here and laid
to rest by the side of her husband, whose body was recovered two
days afterward, in Lower Yoder Cemetery."

Miss J. Louise Mueller writes: It is about thirty-eight years
since grandpa purchased the old home which we occupied. Never in
all that time, I am told, did the high waters come near it, until the
June flood of '87 rushed into our cellar, almost filling it. But on
that never-to-be-forgotten May day, 1889, when cellar and grounds
had been filled, and the waters, still rising, covered the piazzas, then,
about 11.30 A.M., came over the floors, it became evident that
the waters were really in our home. By 3 P.M. they had attained the height of the length of the piano-legs. From then until
about 3.45 they remained stationary. About 4 P.M. the warning
whistle was blown, and for a moment we were startled, wondering
what it could mean, when brother laughingly dismissed the subject
by conjecturing it was an alarm of fire in the midst of all that
water. Then, thinking it about time to look again after things on
the first floor, he descended, I following him down the dining-room
stairway within three steps of the bottom. Desiring to keep the
body of the piano dry, he made his way to the rear end of the
house to procure chairs on which it might be elevated. No sooner
had he disappeared through the hallway than I perceived the
water rapidly covering the top of the dining-table, on which the
contents of the book-case were piled; and, looking toward the

sideboard to prove—what I wished to make myself believe—that it was a defect of vision, I saw there also it was rising. Then, too, the door, through which brother had disappeared, closed. Fearing he might not soon perceive the rising of the water, I called loudly, but could not be heard. A great fear was beginning to steal over me; but, hoping still to convince myself that I did not see aright, or that a certain something was causing a rise in but that one room, I sped up the stairway, through the house, into the front hall, and down that stairway, to catch a glimpse of the piano and ascertain the height of the water on it. But oh! it was fast being covered. I could no longer doubt the floods were swelling.

Remembering where brother was, and that he could not escape up the kitchen stairway because it was packed with household goods, I reached the middle stairway again, like a flash, as I had come, and, calling frantically, was answered: "Yes, yes; I am coming. Do not get so excited." It required a big effort to get the door open, when an expression of much surprise broke from his lips; and, hastily handing me a few books, thinking to save some, he noticed the piano through the archway, and decided to save that if possible; while I, filled with wonder as to where so much water was coming from, rushed to the front upper windows facing north, and, as I neared them, I saw on opposite houses that the waters were fast covering the first-floor windows. Thrusting my head through an open window, and looking north-easterly, from which direction seemed to be coming an awful something, I saw what filled me with indescribable horror. A mountain of darkness from the very heavens down was pushing over on us, bringing houses and trees—a great mass of everything. The atmosphere was filled with spray, clouds of dust, flying particles of all kinds. My first impression was that the heavy clouds had broken down at that end of the heavens, and that the whole mass was gradually lowering. Then I wondered if it could be a cyclone, or of the nature of one, since there was such a strong breeze. Or, did it come directly from the Almighty's hand? "Anyway," I thought, "it is most evidently death-dealing, and this is Johnstown's last day." All this, from the blowing of the whistle up to that moment, had occupied but a few minutes.

Quickly returning, I found brother flying up one of the stairways, the waters following close. Calling to mamma, who had lain down to rest, to come and see the awful something that was coming upon us, I drew brother to the window and wanted to know if he had any idea what it was. He had none. We never for a moment thought of Conemaugh Lake; and, if we had, I presume we would not have decided that was it; for this dark, cloudlike mass, bearing down upon us with everything before it, had not yet dissolved itself into anything, so far as we could see. The fast rising of the waters I attributed to the fact that they were accumulating because of the pressure of this immense body of something.

For an instant we stood, then hurried out to the side upper piazza overlooking the lawn and orchard. Mamma then joined us, and for several seconds we stood looking upon the moving mass before us. A good part of our city, in wreck and ruin, was sweeping out Market Street toward the Stony Creek, almost immediately in front of us. Directly everything about us began to move but our own home. The building opposite crushed into our front piazza; the home across our yard, perhaps fifty feet away, turned on its side and moved off; our staunch old trees began to bend and sway like so many twigs. The crashing and creaking of the falling homes; the crunching of the moving particles driven by this black cloud; the dark waters about our feet; our own sensations as if all things, even old earth herself, moving off, getting away from us; the fact before us that this—we could not tell what—would probably overwhelm us at any moment—these horrors can never be forgotten. We wondered where all the people were, there were so few to be seen just then. We wondered, too, how long our strongly-built old home would withstand the power of that awful force.

Suddenly the floods seemed to receive a mighty impetus, and we found we must flee. It occurring to us that there might be safety upon the roof, away we sped to the attic, mamma having the presence of mind first to get the cage containing our lovely canary, "Little Fritz," and throw a covering over him. Into the attic we then went, and shortly found the skylight and got through it to the roof. By this time the dark mass of cloud had disappeared. A great body of water was rushing madly about, tearing westward on the north side of us, and rushing eastward on the south side, apparently a perfect whirlpool, and carrying wreckage with it to which the people were clinging; while we seemed to be stationary in the midst of those waters. Composing ourselves enough to find out where we were, we discovered that our home had faced about and floated diagonally across the square while we were getting up on the roof, and had quietly settled itself on the north side of the Market Street school-house, and that we were in a big jam, none of the surrounding wreckage, however, having struck us hard, and that little more than our roof was above water.

By this time people were springing up from everywhere out of the wreck, and many sought safety on our roof. Some were present from the extreme end of Johnstown proper. The rain began descending in torrents, the dark overhead seeming determined to wash us away too. And directly the easterly current which had swept *up* the Stony Creek came dashing down, taking with it portions of the wreckage in the jam, and it seemed to us we would surely be carried down to the stone bridge. But we were permitted to remain, and were thankful to God for His care of us. It was perfectly awful to see the people sweeping by or portions of their homes and fragments of all kinds, and with scarcely a hope of escape, entirely unable to steer their crafts to safety. We would look upon them, and scarcely ejaculate a sound, but just stare. All within our reach were aided, of course. Much aid was rendered rather mechanically. We did not have enough sense at times to greet our friends, but sat stupefied and stunned, staring at each other, each wondering how the other got there, but neither opening the mouth to question.

The rain poured down almost incessantly: all were suffering, though every contrivance to relieve the suffering was effected. After a time, the waters began to subside: many persons made their way into the attic of the school-house and rested, perhaps, on the joists all night. Brother returned to our attic at dusk, and, finding it dry, we descended, taking with us all who would go: so we spent the night there. The water had not touched it, so the three feather-beds in it were dry, and we proceeded to make ourselves as comfortable as circumstances would permit. The fear that our home might settle and go to pieces during the night was not verified. As we found later, it had not been in the way of any of the dreadful currents, so remained intact and was set upon the solid ground.

By morning the water-currents were confined to their channels again, though great pools were visible everywhere. Then, too, heads were seen protruding from openings of all sorts, and the ruin and desolation and death were viewed and numerous inquiries for everybody made; and much we wondered where our breakfasts were coming from, and when we would have homes again. The thought of receiving outside aid never came to us.

In the morning mamma, Henry, "Fritz" and I left the mud-soaked house, and, following a guide through that wilderness of wrecked homes, directly came upon the remains of two little children, side by side; and coming out on Main Street, just above our church, near Alma Hall, we started for the hills. We were so rejoiced to see the dear old church building there. Farther up the street, when making my way over the great piles of rubbish and buildings with much difficulty, "Fritz," which I was carrying in uncovered cage, suddenly took it into his pretty head to cheer us up, so burst into the sweetest melody he knows ; and for nearly four months since that day he continued almost incessantly his daily thanksgiving lays. But he seriously objects to being obliged to remain in-doors, so I presume his renditions will be discontinued until he is permitted to enjoy the out-door sunlight again. Still we are most glad to have this live flood-relic, and he certainly testified his gladness at having escaped the general fate of his kind by the sweet outburst on Main Street that morning after the flood.

We made our way to the hill, where a family took us in for a few days, when Mr. Wm. Thompson, of Morrellville, found us and took us to his home, he and his wife making us most welcome, and declaring that was our home until we should have another. We were there until the 1st of October, entirely rent-free, and shown every kindness.

Mrs. Mary Hamilton, of Lincoln and Cherry Streets, and five children, the eldest 12 years, were washed down to the stone bridge, the house resting on its end, the family clinging to the window-sills. Willie said: "Mamma, where is that God that Dr. Beale and Mr. Moore talk so much about, and said that He promised to save us?" A large planing-mill, belonging to Mr. Wesley Rose, had swept them down the stream, and now swept them back again to Napoleon Street, where they were rescued at Mr. Cunningham's, with forty-one other persons. In the journey she thinks she saw fifty or sixty persons sink underneath the waves. She saw some one throw an old coat to Mr. John Henderson, with

TRACK OF THE FLOOD.

Presbyterian Church at the left—Company's store and club house at the right.

which he covered his little boys, who were almost naked. Mr. Harry Hamilton (Mrs. Hamilton's husband) was in the private residence of Mr. Job Morgan, and was rescued while floating down to the stone bridge. He was badly injured, and separated from the family for three weeks, and is still under the physician's care. Mrs. Hamilton saw Henry Pritchard's house capsized, and the family crying for help as they went down to a watery grave.

Mr. and Mrs. Helsel and five children were swept over the stone bridge, and one boy (George), 17 years of age, was drowned in the passage.

Mrs. Jones, her four children, and Mrs. Phillips, a widow with five children, were rescued at Colonel Campbell's. These ladies are sisters.

Mr. Harry Campbell was on Conemaugh Street, and saw the Cambria Library washed away and many of the Woodvale people drown. He also beheld McConaughy's brick row and the two bridges washed away. In the morning, before the dam burst, he built a raft, and with another gentleman by the name of Lloyd succeeded in moving fifty or sixty from their own houses to higher places on the hills. These persons were afterward lost, as mentioned in a previous account.

Mrs. Ellen Hite, of Kernville, on the south side, was caught on the street and drowned while trying to climb an electric-light pole at the corner of Morris and Dibert Streets. Her screams were terrible.

Among the households on Vine Street none were more happy than that of Mr. John White, an aged man; the wife of his youth

20

and his children were still around him. They were all at home that day when the torrent came crushing their fine residence to pieces. Mr. White took his wife in his arms, but she was drowned despite all his efforts to save her. Besides the death of this estimable woman, the following members of the family perished : Maggie, Ella, Mina, Raymond, and Mrs. Jessie White Delaney. Lemuel Delaney, his son Jay, and sister-in-law, Miss Ida White, were carried to the stone bridge, while the father of fourscore years was drifted to the residence of Fred Krebs, in Kernville, whence, by the first Baltimore and Ohio train, he was conveyed to the town of Somerset.

Mrs. Hettie M. Ogle and Miss Minnie, her daughter, with four other young ladies, Master Willie Gaither and line repairer Jackson were imprisoned in the Western Union telegraph office by the deep water before the furious torrent struck them. Mrs. Ogle's son telephoned her until she was driven above stairs. The telegraph line had been destroyed before the torrent came. Mr. Charles Ogle is satisfied that his mother and those with her knew nothing of the supreme danger until they saw the approach of the avalanche. They were all lost in the flood. The ladies not mentioned above were Misses Mary Walters, Minnie Linton, Grace Garman and Jane Kush.

Rev. F. B. Cunz, a Lutheran clergyman and professor of German in our High School, was driven with his family, consisting of his wife and five children, to the upper story of his house on Napoleon Street. The house was dashed to pieces, and instantly Mrs. Cunz and four of the little children were drowned.

The part of the building to which Mr. Cunz and his son Herman still clung impinged against the residence of Rev. Horace Goodchild, the Baptist pastor, who, with his wife, was sitting on the parsonage roof. Here Mr. Cunz and his son were rescued.

Mr. Morrell Swank tells of the thrilling and terrible experience of himself and family on that ever-memorable Friday evening, as follows: "When the great flood struck my residence at No. 312 Main Street I was on the second floor with my wife and two children and servant girl. My house was crushed like an egg-shell right over our heads. My little son Roy was crushed to death in my arms. Just when I thought my last moment had come, the water raised the house and pushed us upward through the ceiling. In a few moments we were carried down a considerable distance below the Kernville bridge. My wife and I were only about four feet from each other, and she had the baby in her arms. I succeeded in getting loose, and took the baby from my wife and put it on a house-roof that was floating alongside of us. I then reached over to help my wife on the roof. Just then the water commenced to back up from the stone bridge, and I was whirled around out of reach of my wife, who drifted away, and she was drowned right before my eyes. Imagine my feelings when floating on the water about fifty feet deep, and houses crushing all around me loaded with human freight, the city all under water, the Catholic church burning, and the rain coming down in torrents. The baby and I were finally rescued about a quarter of a mile up the Stony Creek. My servant girl, wife, son, parents, one brother and a sister were drowned, and only three of their bodies have been recovered."

The following letter was written by Mr. George Barbour to a relative in Chambersburg, Pa.: "My mother, my wife and three children were all drowned. I have been almost crazy. I even did not think of writing to any of my friends. For a week I was kept busy trying to find their bodies. I had to climb the hills to get from one morgue to the other, and had no one to help me. Most of the time I had only one meal a day, and became so weak and sick that I had to stop. I found my dear wife and dear little girl. I had to carry the coffins over a mile to where the bodies were. As the bridges were all washed away I had to get a wagon and drive about four miles over the hills to the cemetery, and it was 8 o'clock in the evening when I got there.

"It was the hardest thing ever any man did, to put his own dear wife and child in a coffin and bury them himself; but it was the only thing I could do, and hundreds of others had to do the same.

"I could not find my poor dear mother and two little boys. One was about 7 years old and the other was our baby, about 3 months old. It was so nice, and everybody said it was the brightest and prettiest baby they had ever seen. Oh, if I had only stayed at home with them! I had taken them up to my sister-in-law's and told them to stay until I came back. I went to town and stayed longer than I intended to. It got clear and stopped raining, and they went back down town to our home, but could not get out any more.

"I was on my way home when the dam broke. I tried to reach the bridge, but when I was about a hundred yards from it, it gave way. I ran up the hill and saw my house and all the rest of the houses in our part of the town (Woodvale) move off. The roofs were filled with men, women and children, but they could do nothing. It didn't leave a house in Woodvale. I cannot describe it with a pen, but must try to tell you all. My cousin, Will Beck, was drowned, with his wife, two dear little boys, his mother-in-law and her niece. My mother-in-law, Mrs. Baker, was drowned, and also her 17-year-old daughter. James Baker, with his wife and child, and Edward Baker, his wife and two children, were all drowned. The Bakers were brothers to my wife. Edward Eldridge, my sister's husband, lost his mother and three brothers.

"I believe that completes the list of my relatives who were

drowned. I still have my two brothers, Thomas and James ; they and their families were saved. My cousin, Andy Beck, was also saved. They are all I have left. He was washed out and lost all he had. He has six children, and got them all out just in time. My brother Thomas hadn't time even to put on his coat."

C. C. Ramsey, who resided at 69 Main Street, says: "I arose at the usual hour, and found the waters rising very rapidly—so fast, in fact, that the water covered the first floor before we had time to remove carpets and furniture to the upper floors, at the same time forcing the entire family to the second floor. At the hour of 10 A.M. we were surrounded by at least ten feet of water, which closed all channels of escape from that hour, as the current which swept through the street was so strong that any ordinary boat could make no progress against it. However, a boat was a luxury that we did not possess.

"After 11 A.M. all was quiet even to the stillness of death; one could hear the swash of the waters, the voices of neighbors, or the bark of a dog. We were completely cut off from all communication, therefore, not knowing the South Fork reservoir had broken until it was upon us.

"The roar of the mighty wave fell upon our ears, and with one impulse we rushed to the third floor, which we gained just in time, as at that instant a string of flat cars, coupled together, struck the house, demolishing the two lower floors, leaving us the mansard, which floated toward the stone bridge. During this time we, with great difficulty, reached the roof, upon which we remained until we were wedged into the debris between the City Guard Armory and Lincoln Avenue, within a few hundred yards of the Morrell Institute. It is beyond description ; we can hardly remember, only we climbed over many houses, floating roofs, piles of debris, and finally the haven of safety was reached. During this time there continued a cold, driving rain which chilled one to the marrow. Fortunately the good people of the institute provided us with such protection as could be had in the shape of comfortables and blankets, which served a double purpose—protection from rain, and hiding from view the frightful scenes which were taking place about us.

"Darkness ensuing, the scene was made more appalling by the wreckage taking fire at the bridge. Roofs laden with human freight could be seen rushing into the seething flames to be roasted alive.

"Late in the evening we descended into the building, where we rested from the elements at least, and, on the following morning, with improvised rafts we reached terra firma, and were correspondingly happy, notwithstanding the fact we were without home or food."

Mary M. Butler resided before the flood at 112 Morris Street, Kernville. She says: "Brother John had been running all the morning between our house and his sister's, Mrs. Long, who resided on Vine Street in Johnstown.

"At dinner time brother John said to mother, 'You will have to get some warm clothes on and get ready to go up-stairs, as the water is rising and may come into the first floor.' Somewhere about 4 o'clock my sister happened to go to the window, and she heard a man passing, saying that the reservoir was broken. Then she said that we must take mother up-stairs. So we at once carried her up-stairs and put her on the bed, which was a roped bedstead. I had barely time to rush down-stairs to save something off the bed, which I succeeded in getting, that I could rescue from the rising water. Having secured those things, sister came down-stairs and hurried me, grabbing hold of my hands, when the rising waters pushed me up, and I had barely time to get on the bed, when, pushed by the waters, the bed arose, bearing us with it to within some eighteen inches of the ceiling.

"We all stayed in that condition all night; and although our house had been moved about a square from its foundation, we did not discover that fact until some time during the night. During the night the chimney, which had been for some time tottering and threatening to fall upon us, eventually took a sudden start and fell through the lower floor, crushing the bedstead on which my mother had lain ; and thus we also escaped that danger. During the night some neighbors called to us and asked if we were all there ; and then they asked us if we knew where we were; and not till that time did we know that our house had been moved from its foundations, and was now in the middle of the street. About 4 o'clock in the morning my brother Nathaniel found us, and after getting on the roof broke it in, and about 7 o'clock, with the aid of others, he succeeded in getting mother down through the large chimney-hole and bore her to a neighbor's house on Sherman Street. My sister and myself then succeeded in getting down through the same chimney-hole, and we then joined our mother.

"My brother John who had gone to town was never again heard of by us, nor has his body been recognized amongst the many that have been discovered and buried."

For several days after the flood Mr. Henry Viering, the well-known furniture dealer at the corner of Railroad and Jackson Streets, suffered great bodily pain from injuries received on the fatal Friday ; but his bodily pain was as nothing compared to his mental agony. He lost in the flood his whole family, consisting of his wife and three children. In an interview he said, substantially, as follows :

"I was at home with my wife and children when the alarm

came. We hurried from the house, leaving everything behind us.
As we reached the door, a friend of mine was running by. He
grasped the two smallest children, one under each arm, and then
hurried on ahead of us. I had my arm around my wife's waist
supporting her. Behind us we could hear the flood rushing.
In one hurried glance as I passed a corner I could see the fearful
flood crunching and crackling the houses in its fearful grasp, with
no possibility of escape, as we were too far away from the hillside. In a flash I saw my three dear children licked up by it and
disappear from sight, as I and my wife were thrown in the air by
the rushing ruins. We found ourselves in among a lot of drift,
driving along with the speed of a race-horse. In a moment or
two we were thrown with a crash against the side of a large frame
building, whose walls gave away as if they were made of paper,
and the timbers began to fall about us in all directions. Up to
this time I retained a firm hold on my wife; but I found myself
pinned between two heavy timbers, the agony causing my senses
to leave me momentarily: I recovered instantly, in time to see my
wife's head just disappearing under water.

"Like lightning I grasped her by the hair, and as best I could,
pinioned as I was above the water by the timber, I raised her above
it. The weight proved too much, and she sank again. Again I
pulled her to the surface, and again she sank. This I did again
and again without avail. She drowned in that grasp, and at last
dropped from my nerveless hands, to leave my sight forever!

"As if I had not suffered enough, a few moments later I saw
white objects whirling around in an eddy until, reaching again the
current, they floated past me. My God! would you believe me?
It was my children, all dead! Their dear little faces are before
me now—distorted in a look of agony—that, no matter what I do,
haunts me. Oh, if I could only have released myself at that time,
I would have willingly gone with them! I was rescued some time

after, and have been here ever since. I have since learned that
my friend, who so bravely endeavored to save two of the children,
was lost with them."

Rev. Dr. Davin, of Cambria City Roman Catholic Church,
saw the Conemaugh swell and overflow its banks, but this did not
cause him to leave his post. Finally, the water rose to the parlor
floor, and he began to think something unusual had happened.
Taking a man with him, he went to the Sisters' school, in water up
to his waist, and carried the Sisters, one after another, to his own
house. By the time this task was done, the great volume of water
had reached Johnstown and Cambria City. The rumbling and
crushing of houses and trees warned the inmates of the priest's
house to seek a place more secure, as the water was nearing the
second story of his handsome house.

To the third story the whole party went, and there spent the
night in frightful expectation that the worst would come every
minute. Several times the house shook ; and the shrieks of the
injured and dying, who were almost within arms' reach from the
windows, were something terrible. Father Davin then went to
his second-story window, and, at the risk of his own life, saved two
or three persons from drowning by pulling them through the
windows.

The horrors of that night preyed continually on Father
Davin's mind, and broke his constitution. The next night, when
the waters had subsided, Father Davin sent all in his house to the
hill for safety, but remained himself. His home and church were
partly destroyed, and two feet of mud left on the first floor. His
first work after he could get out was to look after the injured and
dead.

He turned the beautiful edifice into a morgue. As many as
one hundred and twenty-five bodies were in it at one time, and

there was not an hour of the day or night that Father Davin was not consoling the friends of the dead. In mud up to his knees he paced from altar to vestibule assisting in the removal of the dead.

During the afternoon of Sunday, June 1st, he walked down to the banks of the Conemaugh. Here he found three men robbing the body of a man. He ran and struck one of the villains on the head with his cane, stunning him. The miscreant soon recovered and dealt Father Davin a terrible kick on the side with a hobnail shoe, from the effects of which he never fully recovered.

The effects of the assault laid Father Davin up for some time, and until the time he died he complained of it. During the excitement in Johnstown, Doctor Davin's house was thrown open to every one, and here many a weary worker found a night's rest. He was earnestly advised after the flood by friends and doctors to take a vacation, but he steadily refused, giving as a reason that it looked to him like shirking duty when the wants of the people required his presence. A short time ago, however, he was prevailed upon to go to Denver, where he died. The last words he spoke on leaving were to his sister Stella:

"I am afraid I did not leave soon enough."

A coat was found in the wreckage, in a pocket of which was a Westminster Lesson Leaf with the following conclusions to the lesson: "What have I learned? 1. That we cannot escape from the power of God. 2. That we should promptly and willingly obey His commands. 3. That He sends the winds and storms to do His bidding. 4. That He is displeased with those who have the truth of God and fail to make it known."

One night in the morgue, after we had arranged the identified bodies at one side of the room and the unidentified at the other side, I assembled all the men at 1 o'clock and offered prayer.

Here, in the midst of eighty-four bodies, coffined, whose departed spirits were beyond the province of prayer, I felt that it
was a time to appeal to the living God for strength and comfort,
to impress our own spirits with the awfulness and suddenness of
death, to be prepared for it in whatever form it might come. I
felt also that the inexpressible sadness and gloom of our work
could only be relieved by Him who is the resurrection and life.

Among the curious revelations of disposition which the flood
made, this one perhaps exceeds all others. If there has ever been
an equal exhibition of meanness within recorded history it has escaped our observation. During the dreadful night a young
lady was rescued from the debris, where she would have died from
exposure, and was taken into the club-house. Her drenched and
ruined clothing was removed, and she had to attire herself in a
pair of pants belonging to one of the male guests. The party
who owned them hunted in every place for them and was informed
what disposition had been made of them. He demanded $8.00 in
payment, and it is understood that the young lady has since sent
him that amount. We hope that if he is ever married his wife will
" wear the pants."

While Rev. Drs. W. C. Cattell and Beale were walking
through the town about a month after the flood, they met Mrs. Fenn,
whose husband and seven children were lost in the flood on that
terrible afternoon, none of whose bodies had then been recovered.
She had been digging among the ruins of her home, this having been
her occupation every day for nearly four weeks. When Dr. Beale
and Dr. Cattell met her, she had just found a clock. It had been a pet
clock. She was sitting there hugging the clock to her breast as
if it were one of her babies. She is a member of Dr. Beale's
church, and was glad to see him. She told Dr. Cattell her story.

She related her experience on that dreadful day in a simple, straight-forward way and without a tear. She passed the clock over to Dr. Beale, and asked him to keep it for her. Dr. Cattell proposed that he should take it to Philadelphia and have it cleaned and placed in good condition again, promising to return it as soon as Mrs. Fenn was ready to receive it. He had hardly finished his proposition when the poor woman's face was bathed in tears: she had been able to tell the story of her dreadful sorrow with dry eyes, but one kind act from a stranger touched the well-spring of her heart, and made the tears course down her cheeks. Through the tender ministrations of Mrs. Beale and other ladies, this afflicted soul has been restored to the right use of her mind.

This clock was repaired and taken back on January 3d by Dr. Beale and presented to Mrs. Fenn.

The flood has brought out a "dark horse;" so we give him the prominence he deserves, and hand his name down to posterity.

The evening of the flood Mr. N. B. Hartzell's black horse was in the stable, which was near the gentleman's warehouse. The stable was washed away, and a neighbor of Mr. Hartzell told him he saw the building lifted up, and the horse floating off into the debris.

"I guess your horse is lost," the neighbor remarked, and Mr. Hartzell answered that he was afraid it was, and to that conclusion he came as Saturday passed and no trace of his animal was found. On Sunday some one said to him: "Hartzell, there's a horse up in the second story of your warehouse." At first he could scarcely credit the statement, but upon investigation he found that it was true, and that the horse was his own—the one he thought he had lost. When Mr. Hartzell entered the apartment where the horse was, it turned its head about and neighed and whinnied with evident pleasure at seeing its master. The horse had its halter on, with the hitching strap attached. The fastening had been pulled out of the trough. How the animal was transferred by the flood from the stable to where it was found is a mystery to Mr. Hartzell.

I insert this item from the *Johnstown Tribune*, of January 7th, 1890, as an interesting one in the personal history of the city:

SIR:—I see it stated in the obituary of Mrs. L. H. Roberts, who lost her life in the flood, that she was the first white child born in Johnstown, the date of her birth being given as October 20th, 1807. Now, Mrs. Catharine Burkhart, who also lost her life in the flood, going from Mineral Point, was born in Johnstown, April 9th, 1804, near where Col. Linton's house stood before the deluge came. When Mrs. Burkhart was yet a baby, her father, Abraham Hildebrand, built and moved up to where the Alma Hall now stands. Mr. Hildebrand then owned a considerable portion of the ground on which Johnstown is built. Mrs. Burkhart and Mrs. Roberts were playmates when children, were young girls together, and both could tell all about the great floods of long ago, little dreaming that both would live to see another and a greater flood, in which both should perish.   B.

Miss Nellie Secrist ran into Cover's livery stable for safety. She climbed into the hay-loft, immediately over the horses' heads. She says that the groans and shrieks of the poor animals in their death-struggles while drowning were fearful.

This is a pension which will receive the indorsement of the American people, from the President down through the rank and file: Sarah J. Mackin, a widow of Johnstown who lost all her earthly possessions in the flood, has been awarded a pension and back pay amounting to $5,966.

The entire money subscription to the *Mail and Express* for the Conemaugh sufferers amounted to $49,080.08. This does not include many of Colonel Shepard's personal gifts, and his other kind attentions to individuals and classes of sufferers. One of the most tender and beautiful of his benefactions was his sending to Asbury Park twenty-five ladies, and paying their expenses for a month at that delightful seaside resort. Nothing could have been more beneficial, as it afforded a resting place beside the sea, where, in the presence of its majesty, and with all the care and attention which Colonel Shepard's purse could command, they obtained relief which was inexpressible.

On Main Street is Thomas's general store. It is in the middle of the desolation. Three women were carefully climbing the piles of rubbish. One had a box under her arm. At this store workmen were wheeling out barrow loads of the dirt deposited over everything by the flood. The woman with the box stopped the workmen, found the man in charge, and said:

"I purchased these shoes before the flood. They are sevens. I want sixes. You made a mistake. I want them exchanged."

Mrs. Emma Robb, stepmother of Mrs. Overbeck, another of the survivors, lived at the corner of Morris and Willow Streets, south side. She is a widow, and with her only daughter she fled to the upper story of her house, taking some provisions with her. Both before and after the great tidal wave struck the house, mother and daughter worked heroically to save the terror-stricken and half-drowned unfortunates who floated past their windows. They succeeded in saving the lives of twenty-six persons, and early Saturday morning the whole party were carried on a raft to the upper part of Kernville. This was heroism compared to which Paul Revere's is tame.

Mrs. Joshua Carpenter, of Johnstown, was so affected by the fire in Seattle as to provide and prepare a box of clothing for those who had been burned out. The box was in her attic ready to be shipped on Saturday, June 1st. The flood came on Friday afternoon. Everything in Mrs. Carpenter's house was ruined except this box of clothing, which, being in the attic, was the only thing that escaped the waters. It was accordingly unpacked, and the clothing was judiciously distributed in her family and among her neighbors.

The dun mare of Mr. Frank Benford was standing in the alley between the Hulbert House and Hornick's Hotel when the great wave struck the town. Persons on the top of the Fritz House saw it go over her with the jam of buildings it had gathered in its wild roll. They thought of course she was killed. What surprise there was when on Saturday she was found perched up on one of the highest points of the wreckage, at a considerable distance from where she had stood—alive, but having become blind in the passage.

A farmer in Kansas shortly after the flood wrote to the Bureau of Information asking it to obtain a wife for him among those ladies who had survived it. He stated his age at 35, and wanted a wife of about 30. He owned a successful stock farm. The officers of the Bureau said that they had received many inquiries for relics, but this was the only one for a living relic, and she to become a wife. I think that the analysis of that young farmer's heart would show it to be healthy and full of blue blood. There was a nobility in this request. He was willing to take a woman who had no earthly possession ; he wanted to provide a home and life comfort for one who had been a victim of the disaster ; he was willing to trust total strangers to make the selection. He must be a man of unbounded benevolence and faith. Pity it is that more such men did not appear.

I wish the name of this New York lady was generally known. Her action displayed a woman's wisdom and sympathy. She selected from her and her husband's wardrobes all the suits they could possibly spare. Into the pockets of the men's suits she put a jack-knife, a hair-brush and a comb; into those of the women's gowns, a pair of stockings, a comb, a brush, a tooth-brush and a cake of soap. Several of the gowns she was saving for her summer's trip. She said, "I decided to let the Johnstown sufferers have them, and my husband will get me others."

Mrs. S. W. F., of Harrisburg, says: "My three children, Mary, Margaret and Samuel, have felt so sorry for the Johnstown people that on the 4th they had a pin and penny store for their benefit. On Sunday, when they heard the appeal for your church read, they decided to send the amount made, $1.68, to you. The pins the children gave for the little articles were sold for pennies."

A few days after the catastrophe a leading lady in Baltimore wrote: "Since the first news of the terrible disaster which has overwhelmed your little city, I have been watching the papers for tidings of you and yours. On Monday it was announced that you had been saved from the flood, but not until to-day have I noticed any positive assurance that your entire family had been spared. The pastors of the various churches here prayed most fervently and tenderly on Sabbath morning and night for the sufferers, and made earnest pleas for relief, which met with cheerful and liberal response."

Another Baltimore lady writes: "The inclosed sum, $1.85, is the

COMMISSARY DEPARTMENT AT THE P. R. R. DEPOT.

voluntary offering of twelve little girls (who have very little) to the Johnstown sufferers. They brought it to me, their teacher, for this purpose. I thought it best to send it to you, assured that through you it would go aright, small as it is. May I ask that you would, at your convenience, send me a postal card, just mentioning its receipt, so that I may read it to the girls, as I was the recipient?"

Dr. T. DeWitt Talmage writes: "Having seen your name in connection with the work of alleviation in your afflicted city, I write you expressing the absorbing sympathy felt by Brooklyn. The Committee of Relief close their labors to-day, and we report $95,905.28 raised and sent for the relief of Johnstown and adjoining suffering districts. But many of our citizens are in business in New York City, and therefore contributed through New York channels; so that, if those sums were added, we think from the hands and hearts of Brooklyn at least $150,000 must have been sent. As chairman of the Brooklyn Relief Committee, I thought it might be well in behalf of my fellow-citizens to write this letter, showing that our city has been greatly moved by your calamity. I will next week, on my way to Oregon, pass through your city. If I could be of any practical service I would stop off. What a fearful nervous strain you must all have been under, and how all the energies of the Christian ministers of your city must have been taxed in the effort to comfort the bereft!"

A lady from Rock Springs, Centre County, writes: "My heart goes out in deep sympathy for those who have lost dear ones. I met a Mr. McConaughey, a gentleman of seventy some years, last October. He told me his wife and daughters were members of your church. Now I notice among the dead a Miss McConaughey. Is she his daughter? Or are he and family safe? We here were

21

cut off from travel for so long or I would have gone to Johnstown willingly, if my service would have been needed, to wait on the suffering, but presume by this time you have all the help necessary. Now I trust God will bless you in your labors of love for Him; and you certainly are putting forth every effort to comfort the people, and trust they will look to our Heavenly Father, the Great Comforter."

The following communication reached me June 25th, accompanied by a kind note from the Governor:

"CHARLESTON, S. C.

Hon. Jas. A. Beaver, Harrisburg, Pa.

"DEAR SIR:—By direction of the session of Westminister Presbyterian Church of this city, I transmit you herewith my check for $64.22, same being amount of collection taken up in said church in aid of the sufferers in Johnstown who are connected with the Presbyterian Church there, and, as I have been informed that you are a ruling elder of the Presbyterian Church, deem it best to send the contribution to you, and would request you to forward the same to the pastor or session of the Presbyterian Church of Johnstown, and express to them our profound and heartfelt sympathy in the frightful calamity which has overwhelmed them, and which we of Charleston can take a measure of as no other city in the United States can, having ourselves experienced the horrors of cyclones and earthquakes, and remember with gratitude the munificent liberality and the generous sympathy of the people of the Keystone State. I have the honor to be

"Your obedient servant,

"J. A. ENSLOW,

" *Treasurer of Session, W. P. Church.*"

Captain W. R. Jones, of Braddock, received the following from Mr. Karl Wittgenstein, the iron king of Vienna, Austria:

"Dear Captain:—I ordered $1,000 to be sent to you on my account, and ask you to be kind enough and take the trouble to use this small sum as you think best to help the people who are suffering in Johnstown. It must be dreadful. I hope your family are all right.   Yours very truly,

"KARL WITTGENSTEIN."

3.—THE CALAMITIES OF JOHNSTOWN.

THERE have been so many frightful casualties at Johnstown that some people think it fated; others that it must be a very wicked place, and these are of the nature of judgments. These are hasty and unreasoning conclusions. We always make a mistake when we put such special interpretations on signal or single events. Johnstown is not more wicked than other towns of its size; indeed it compares favorably with other manufacturing districts, and can exhibit as large a proportion of God-fearing people and consistent Christians as any other. Yet it has been frequently the scene of sad calamities. On September 14th, 1866, occurred what was termed the Platform accident. A train from Pittsburgh carrying President Andrew Johnson and party stopped at the station. A large number of citizens had assembled on the platform to greet them. The President was introduced and made a short speech. Then calls were made for General Grant, Admiral Farragut and Hon. W. H. Seward. Suddenly with a crash the platform, which spanned the abandoned canal, went down and precipitated hundreds of people into its depths. There were shrieks and groans as the victims fell upon each other producing death and broken limbs. The train moved on, leaving a wailing mass of humanity and a death-shrouded town. Among those who were injured were Mrs. David Creed, Dr. George Wagoner, Lucy Levergood, Ahlum Cope, Mrs. Oliver Young, John H. Fischer and 'child, John S. Buchanan, Cyrus Tuttle, John Brady, Mrs. Wild, Jacob Hamilton and Daniel Unverzagt, who perished in the late flood. A large number of others received injuries, among whom was Rev. Dr. B. F. Agnew, of Philadelphia.

Before a month had expired after the broken dam disaster, while the country was yet mourning with us over its dire work, another frightful scene appears. Fire followed flood. As if that all-wasting flood had not done destruction enough, a disastrous conflagration seemed about to devastate what little was left of the stricken town. About 1 o'clock in the afternoon, the Market Street school-house was discovered to be on fire. This was located near the centre of the town, and was in good condition, having escaped the flood. The flames communicated with the other houses, and it seemed for a time that the rest of the town must go. Twenty-five tenements and three public school-houses were destroyed. General Wiley ordered out the troops at hand, and the section of the Philadelphia Fire Department which was stationed there responded to the alarm. By their speedy and efficient service the fire was soon under control and put out. Most of the buildings burned had been badly damaged by the flood.

After this scene we hoped to be exempt from horrors and peril. We felt that we had received our full complement of disaster, and that we might have rest after so much agitation and distress. On the night of December 10th, 1889, however, Johnstown was again startled by the cry of fire. Parke's Opera House was filled from floor to ceiling with a mass of people to witness the play of Uncle Tom's Cabin. That cry of fire outside was caught by some one in the gallery and repeated. A panic immediately seized the whole assembly. Everybody rushed for the exits. No one took time for second, sober thought. The rush was fearful.

Women shrieked and fainted ; men and boys yelled. In the mad rush, hundreds were trampled upon. Ten were killed and nineteen injured. It is a remarkable coincidence that this play was acted in the same building at its opening, February, 1869. This disaster was entirely causeless. There was no fire. Dr. A. N. Wakefield's hostler, before retiring, stirred up his fire. His quarters are in the rear of the doctor's residence. The smoke from the low chimney enveloped it. A passing observer, supposing that the residence was on fire, gave the alarm which was heard and repeated in the Opera House with fatal result. Every one of these calamities is traceable directly to the folly, ignorance and criminal carelessness or neglect of man. They therefore do not furnish any occasion for complaint of or repining at the Providence of God.

DR. T. DEWITT TALMAGE ON THE FLOOD.

The following letter of Dr. Talmage was written to the *New York World*, on July 20th, 1889, during his visit to Johnstown. The Doctor's ardent sympathy for us and his desire to ascertain our true condition inspired this visit. We received him as a "brother beloved," but we were in no condition to entertain him as we desired or as we had done. We had no homes to take him in, no tables to spread before him ; but our hearts were as wide and ready as ever to receive him whose voice is hailed with delight the world over, and whose presence is a benediction wherever he goes. Mr. A. J. Haws was host to Dr. Talmage.

I desired to strike out from this letter and other articles in the book all personal allusions to myself, but my friends and counselors in its preparation forbade it, on the ground that I was a part of the history for which the book is written—that I must subject my aversion to personal mention to the opinions and views of the contributors to the book and the history it contains.

Dr. Talmage wrote:

"When I first came here on Friday I was impressed with the courage and pluck of the survivors of the catastrophe. They will, with the help of outsiders, rebuild their city, and in five years it will be a more prosperous place than it ever was. They are an honest people, and can get any amount of commercial credit they ask for. Many of the citizens temporarily absent will return, and comfortable homes, large storehouses and great factories will stand where now are awful ruins. The stories circulated about the Johnstown people having lost their faith in God, and given up the Christian religion because of this calamity, I denounce as false and scoundrelly. The pastors tell me that there was not one such case. On the contrary, there are more prayer and Christian devotion than ever before. Even infidels pray. One of them, the afternoon of the disaster, in the upper room of a house which was rapidly filling with water, was overheard to pray: "O God! if you can give me any aid at this time, I will be very much obliged to you." All that story published through the land about the people of Johnstown in disgust burning their Bibles is a hemispheric falsehood.

"The work that has been done here by their own ministers and physicians and good men and women, and without compensation, should be spoken of everywhere. In applauding outside workers we have neglected to appreciate the Johnstown Howards and Florence Nightingales, who may be counted by the score, though they saved nothing from the wreck except the clothes on their persons. Let all the people North, South, East and West, and on both sides of the sea understand that in their gifts to the flooded districts they did not do too much or give too quickly. Not 5 per cent. of the anguish has been told.

"My heart is wrung with what I saw on Friday. Can it be possible that this is the beautiful and hospitable Johnstown that I saw in other days? Where once was a street suggesting Euclid Avenue, Cleveland, is a long ridge of sand, strewn with broken planks and twisted iron. At the moment when a great freshet which had been raging for hours had begun to assuage, a wave from twenty to forty feet high rolls over the already angry waters, and on that surmounting wave floated eight hundred houses, twenty-eight locomotives from the round houses and hundreds of people, many dead, many dying, a mass of helpless and appalled humanity. Two thousand dead discovered and two thousand missing make me believe that the story of how many thousand perished will never be told until the resurrection trumpet shall be sounded.

"To show how accustomed to scenes of death this district has become, on Friday, while a human body was being taken out of the ruins and I stood looking aghast at the spectacle and the laborers, no crowd gathered, and workmen a hundred feet away did not stop their work.

"Such an avalanche of wretchedness never slipped upon any American city. Horrors piled on horrors, woe augmenting woe; bankruptcy, orphanage, widowhood, childlessness, obliterated homesteads, gorged cemeteries and scenes so excruciating—it is a marvel that any one could look upon them and escape insanity. No fear that sympathy for Johnstown will be overdone! The two and a half million dollars contributed is a small amount compared with the thirty millions by this flood demolished.

"Was the work of devastation as great as I supposed? Far worse. Types cannot tell it. Only the eye can make revelation. But the worst part of it cannot be seen. The heart-wreck caused by the sudden departure of so many can be open only to one eye, and that the All-Seeing. Think of one family of fourteen all dead, except one, and that the wife and mother, and she the witness of their drowning! I saw the grave trench in which two hundred and sixty were buried, and the whole graveyard like a National cemetery, in which the unrecognized dead have a particular number placed above them and are recorded in the undertakers' rooms with a description of the body and clothes.   I can well understand how many of the survivors who had buried their kindred before this disaster occurred, thanked God that they were gone, saying: 'Oh, I am so glad that they escaped this.'

"Long after contributions of money have ceased, Johnstown will stand in need of the sympathy of all nations.   Let those who to-night have roofs over their heads and their families around them, or the bodies of their departed in garlanded sepulchres, give at least one prayerful thought to the shattered homesteads of Johnstown, and those who know not in what depth of river or what pile of debris the beloved form of father or mother or husband or wife or child may be slumbering.   Among the Johnstown people who have been heroic, assiduous and self-denying, I mention Rev. David J. Beale, D.D., who has presided over the morgues and been inspiration and hope and cheer to all people.   On the night of the disaster, having escaped with his family from the topmost window of his home and climbed across the roofs of floating houses, he entered the window of a tall building where there were, on the three floors, more than two hundred and fifty people, and he spent the night going from floor to floor praying with the distressed and frantic, and uttering words eloquent with good cheer.   But room would fail to write not of the five, but the five hundred acts of this tragedy of centuries.   T. DeWitt Talmage."

4.—PERSONAL SKETCHES.

ARTHUR J. MOXHAM.

There are unwritten histories of men whose heroic accomplishments in useful industry entitle them to greater fame than . the "hero of an hundred battles."   The man who, overcoming the

NEW BUSINESS HOUSES ON THE PARK, CORNER OF MAIN AND FRANKLIN STREETS.

disadvantages of a restricted life, without command of the ordinary resources of money and influence, rises by self-culture and persistent industry to prominence and success, is deserving of great honor. The men who "scorn delights and live laborious days" are educating themselves in a school from which they inevitably graduate with honor to themselves and with benefit to all who follow them. An example of this is one of Johnstown's most valued and valuable citizens, Mr. Arthur J. Moxham, President of the JOHNSON COMPANY, whose rolling-mills and iron-works are among the most extensive in the country.

Mr. Moxham comes from that sturdy, talented, heroic little country in the heart of England that has refused to be absorbed, and to this day holds the princedom which is succession to the throne of Great Britain—Wales. He was born in Glamorganshire, September 19th, 1854. At the age of 15, in 1869, he came to this country. He found his way to Louisville, Ky., and there engaged in iron manufacture until 1875. During this short period he made such rapid progress in the science of the iron industry as to become an expert as well as a practical workman. In 1878, he removed to Birmingham, Ala., where he organized the Birmingham Rolling-Mill Company, and built according to his own ideas and plans the Birmingham Rolling-Mills, which are the largest merchant mills in the Southern States. He retained the management of these for two years and then returned to Louisville. Shortly after this he was elected president of the Johnson Company at Johnstown, to which he moved in 1883. These works, comprising rolling-mills, the Miles foundry and a curve and switch work, have greatly prospered under his direction.

Mr. Moxham married Miss Helen Coleman, of an old and prominent Kentucky family. The public estimate was indicated in the choice of him, immediately after the flood, to be the chief of the provisional government.

GOVERNOR BEAVER.

General James A. Beaver was born in Millerstown, Pa., October 21st, 1837. His ancestors came from Alsace in 1740, and were
Huguenots seeking refuge and religious freedom in America. They
settled in Chester County, Pa., and became principal actors in the
affairs of the colony and the struggle for independence. In all the
wars of the country and in times of peace they have acted a leading part. James A. Beaver's father died in 1840, three years after
the birth of his son, and to his mother's care, training and influence
he owes his education and success. In 1846 she sent him to school
in Belleville, Mifflin County. In 1852 he was removed to Pine
Grove Academy, whence, in 1854, he entered the junior class in
Jefferson College. He graduated in 1856, and then read law
with H. N. McAllister at Bellefonte, Pa, and on arriving at age became his partner, and later, his son-in-law.

Here he joined the military company, " Bellefonte Fencibles,"
under command of Captain Andrew G. Curtin, afterward the
"War Governor of Pennsylvania." He was 2d Lieutenant of
this company at the secession of the Southern States, and on the
President's call for troops he offered himself. On the organization of the 45th Regiment of Pennsylvania Volunteers he was made
Lieutenant Colonel. On the new call for volunteers, in 1862, he
was commissioned Colonel of the 148th Regiment, having rendered
eminent service at Hilton Head, South Carolina, and other places.
His new regiment was first assigned to the Army of the Potomac,
in General Hancock's Corps, at Fredericksburg, and first engaged
in battle at Chancellorsville, May 2d and 3d, 1863, when it maintained the advanced position and suffered heavily, Colonel Beaver
being wounded at the head of the regiment. During the treatment of his wounds he was appointed, at his own request, recruit-
ing officer of Camp Curtin. He rejoined his regiment at Gettys-

burg, though his condition would not permit of his participating in the battle. He led it through the Wilderness campaign, 1864, and led the successful assault upon the Confederate works at Spottsylvania Court House. At the battle of Cold Harbor, June 3, 1864, Colonel Brooke having been wounded, he was put in command of the brigade, and held the advanced position under fire all day. On June 16th, 1864, he was again wounded in the first assault upon Petersburg. He returned to duty, although not in a condition to do so. He rode to the battlefield of Ream's Station in an ambulance, and just as he assumed command his right leg was shattered, necessitating amputation, rendering him incapable of active service. He was brevetted Brigadier General of Volunteers November 10th, 1864. He refused to be promoted, on the ground that it would remove him from the regiment with which he had enlisted and desired to remain until the end.

Governor Beaver has been successful in his profession of the law. His prominence has not been acquired by his self-seeking, personal efforts, for he has ever devoted himself closely to his own line of duty and life. He has been sought out by his fellow-citizens. He was elected a trustee of the Pennsylvania State University in 1873. He was elected Governor of the State in 1886, in which position he became the natural helper of desolated Johnstown.

Governor Beaver has been true to the religious teachings of his mother and the traditions of his Huguenot ancestors. He united with the Presbyterian Church and was elected to the ruling eldership. He holds this office to-day; and while his Christian views and sympathies are comprehensive, he is a consistent and earnest Presbyterian. This, perhaps, has something to do with one of his leading characteristics—that he is never loth to assume responsibility of duty and action when once he is satisfied that they attach to him.

GENERAL D. H. HASTINGS.

It is difficult to express in a few lines the value of General Hastings' services and the kindly regard the people of Conemaugh Valley entertain toward him. He arrived on June 1st, and during his stay discharged the difficult and delicate duties of his position in a manner entirely creditable to himself and satisfactory to the people. Colonel Spangler shows this in his report, in which he renders his testimony as an associate of General Hastings in the government and relief of our stricken valley.

General Daniel Hartman Hastings was born at Salona, Clinton County, Pennsylvania, February 26th, 1849. His father was a native of Ireland, and his mother of Scotland. Thus he combines in himself the blood of the two peoples who have made themselves notable in the history of the world in the struggle for civil and religious liberty.

His life until he was 14 was spent on a farm, alternately working and attending the district school. He so improved his opportunities as to be able at 14 to teach school ; and in 1867, when only 18, he was elected principal of the Bellefonte public schools, which position he held until 1875. During this time he pursued a course of higher studies, classical and English, and for part of the time was associate editor of the Bellefonte *Republican*. Here he read law with the firm of Bush & Yocum, of Bellefonte, was admitted to the bar in 1875, and entered into partnership with them, the firm becoming Bush, Yocum & Hastings. He subsequently associated with Wilbur F. Reeder, as Hastings & Reeder. In October, 1877, he married Miss Jane Armstrong Rankin, of Bellefonte.

General Hastings has always taken active interest in public affairs. In 1876 he was chief burgess of Bellefonte and is now a trustee of the Pennsylvania State University. Ever since he entered the National Guard of the State, it has improved. He has risen from the position of Captain to that of Adjutant General, to which he was appointed by Governor Beaver, January 18th, 1887.

REV. ALONZO POTTER DILLER.

Rev. Alonzo P. Diller, rector of St. Mark's Protestant Episcopal church, whose death is recorded in another part of the book, was greatly beloved by his own parishioners and highly esteemed by the whole community. He was a cultured gentleman, and efficient minister of the Gospel. He was a graduate of Franklin and Marshall College in Lancaster City, the residence of his father, who is a very influential citizen of that portion of the State. Mr. Diller was only about 30 years of age, and had attained a wide reputation in his denomination as a writer and preacher. He married one of Johnstown's most attractive and cultivated young ladies. Their death has made a vacancy in the Church and society which can scarce be filled. I have made m any efforts to obtain the particular incidents of his life and ministerial career, so as to publish a biographical sketch, but have not been successful.

REV. GEORGE WAGONER, M.D.

Rev. George Wagoner was born near Madison, Westmoreland County, Pa. His parents came from Germany. He was 64 years of age when he died. His father, Rev. George Wagoner, was a minister in the Allegheny Conference of the Church of United Brethren in Christ. Rev. Dr. Wagoner early became a sincere Christian, and a useful member of the same Conference. He spent many years in the active work of the ministry, and was an able expounder of the Word—very successful in winning souls to Christ and in building up the Church.

During the last years of his life, on account of ill-health, he was not able to preach and labor constantly.   He was located in Johnstown, and there organized a Sabbath-school and labored especially for the salvation of the young.   He was assigned to that charge by the Conference from year to year until his death. The charge was called Stony Creek Mission.   Up to the 31st of May, when the great flood came upon us, he conducted the Sabbath-school.   He had purchased ground on which he intended to build a chapel.

The terrible tempest and flood swept away Dr. Wagoner's house, which was a solid brick structure, drowning himself, his wife and his three unmarried daughters.

Mrs. Mary Wagoner, his wife, was 60 years of age; Miss Cora Wagoner was 23, Miss Lizzie 21, and Miss Frances 18 years.

Another daughter, Emma W., who was married to Mr. Frank Bowman, was also lost in the flood, with her two children, Jessie and Francis, 4 and 2 years of age.

The religious denomination of which this godly man and esteemed citizen was a minister, during a camp meeting at Cape May in the summer of 1889, held a memorial service to him.   His character, life and ministry were commended by his brethren in affectionate terms as worthy of all example.

REV. EDWARD W. JONES, D.D.

Rev. Dr. Edward W. Jones was the pastor of the Welsh Congregational church.   He was born in North Wales in 1832, and, after fifteen years in the ministry there, emigrated hither, and was for eighteen years pastor in Johnstown.   He ably and faithfully performed all the duties of the ministry, and had gathered a devoted flock around him.   He was a true shepherd, understanding and fulfilling his office of teacher and guide.   He possessed the sturdy and generous qualities of the Welsh people, their strength of intellect and religious principles. He and his entire household perished in the flood, with the little daughter of Mr. R. R. Thomas, who was at the time in his house. The body of Mrs. Jones is the only one of the family that has been recovered.

Of the 150 members of his church sixty were destroyed. All of these were worthy, industrious and useful people. Such a calamity as this alone would have spread a dark pall over the city. The church building as well as the parsonage was entirely swept away. Thus this congregation of most excellent people of God was most severely afflicted. Truly "out of the depths they cry unto the Lord." They now hold their services in the rooms formerly occupied by the State Flood Commission.

REV. J. PHILLIP LICHTENBERG.

Rev. J. Phillip Lichtenberg, the German Lutheran minister who was drowned, was born in Cassel, Germany. After graduating from the Gymnasium College at Hersfeldt, he entered the Marburg University, whence he went to Basle, Switzerland, to study the Arabic and Amharic languages, with a view to entering on missionary labor in Abyssinia.

In 1867 he was prevented from embarking on his mission there by the war against King Theodore. In this same year, he changed his plans, came to this country, and entered the Lutheran Theological Seminary in Philadelphia. After graduating in 1869, and being ordained priest, he received a call to Saugerties, Ulster County, N. Y. In 1878 he accepted a call to the Lutheran Zion Church of Utica, N. Y. After doing good work at this place, he came to Johnstown early in the month on the last day of which the great disaster befell us. On the 24th of May he wrote to Mr. Kessler a letter in which the following language occurs:

"Johnstown is beautifully situated, and has about thirty thousand inhabitants, many of whom are wealthy and cultured German Lutheran people. They were formerly divided among themselves, but have, through my unanimous selection, been happily united, and are now active and enthusiastic in church work. A new school-house will be built, and we have a fine teacher whose father and brother are preachers in Baltimore. I have formed a young men's society, and hope to make its membership over three hundred. I have also formed a young ladies' society. Every seat in the large church is rented, and never before did I see so many men in a congregation. I thank God for the change. He has done all things wonderfully well. My congregation is now engaged on a new constitution, and I can remain in the General Synod. The old constitution forbade this."

Before leaving Utica he sang " Jerusalem the Golden, I would I were in Thee." Sooner than he expected his wish has been granted.

JOHN FENN.

The circumstances attending the death of Mr. John Fenn are peculiarly sad and touching. He was one of the best and most enterprising of Johnstown's citizens—an honest man and sincere Christian. By honorable and persistent industry he had built up a successful stove and tinware business, and had in the home he was enabled to maintain a happy family group in his wife and seven lovely children. He was at the store when the waters arose to an unusual height, and, becoming alarmed for his loved ones, started for his home. He was overtaken by the fearful wave. He took refuge in the house of the editor of the *Johnstown Democrat*. Soon, however, that house was knocked to pieces, and he was thrown into the flood. Seeing that he must perish, he called to Mr. Henry Derritt to bid his wife and children farewell, and then was swept out of sight. His own house, at the same time, with

RED CROSS BUILDINGS ON SITE OF JUDGE POTTS'S FORMER RESIDENCE.

Mrs. Fenn and the children, was hurled away and demolished. The children all perished; Mrs. Fenn was saved in a wondrous way. She was unable for weeks by reason of sickness to obtain any clew to their remains. But finally the bodies of little Bismarck and Genieve were identified, and, later, the grave of her husband, in Prospect Cemetery, by a key-ring and pocket-book which had been preserved in the Presbyterian Morgue and numbered correspondingly with the grave. The picture of the Fenn group in another part of this book emphasizes the sad story of the destruction of Mr. Fenn's home, and of the lonely and childless widow.

JOHN DIBERT.

John Dibert was born in Somerset County, Pa., January, 1831. He came to Johnstown in 1846, where becoming a hardware merchant he accumulated property until he counted his wealth by hundreds of thousands. His magnificent residence on Main Street melted before the flood. He and his daughter, Mrs. Sue Weaver, and two grandchildren were drowned. Mrs. Dibert was severely injured by the falling of a part of the wall, but is recovering. Mr. Dibert became one of the very first influential citizens of Johnstown—a leader in all commercial and public enterprises. He was a valuable member of the Presbyterian Church, and was ever ready to advance its welfare and encourage the pastor. The loss to the Church can never be repaired.

James P. McConaughey, a nephew of the Rev. Dr. McConaughey, a former president of Washington College, Pa., was one of our most prominent citizens. His large residence on the corner of Walnut and Locust Streets was swept away as grass before a scythe. He, his wife and one son perished. He was one of the most even-tempered and upright men I ever knew. He was about 70 years of age.

22

Howard J. Roberts was cashier of First National Bank, about 60 years of age, and one of our most reliable citizens. He, his wife and youngest son, Otis, were drowned. He was recognized as one of the best bankers in Western Pennsylvania.

From the legal profession, Mr. Harry G. Rose, John N. Weakland and Theodore F. Zimmerman were lost. The bar of Johnstown in their death suffers a great bereavement.

The People's Building and Loan Association, of which Mr. Rose was solicitor, passed a series of resolutions, of which this one expresses the estimate in which he was held:

Resolved, That in his demise the bar of Cambria County has lost one of its shining lights, our Association a valuable officer, his wife a loving husband, society a leading member, and his companions a sincere friend.

Mr. Rose was also the District Attorney, and as such magnified his office, and discharged all its duties ably and to the praise of the courts. His death, just at the time when he had demonstrated his abilities and worth to the whole community, and as he had entered upon the strength of his manhood and powers, is beyond question one of the heaviest losses which Johnstown suffered by the flood.

The medical faculty lost Drs. L. T. Beam, W. C. Beam, J. K. Lee, J. P. Wilson, H. W. Marbourg and C. C. Brinkey, all of whom were skillful physicians, and had successfully established themselves in practice.

John G. Alexander, in 1882, removed with his family to Johnstown, where he took the same position in the Church and in society which he had occupied in his former homes. He was elected an elder in the Church, and superintendent of the Sabbath-school. These offices he filled with great faithfulness and acceptability.

Little is known of the immediate circumstances attending the loss of Mr. Alexander's life, and that of his wife, by the dreadful torrent that swept Johnstown and its people to destruction. He was spoken to by a friend shortly before, and returned to his house. The cold waters cover the rest of the story.

Out of 126 Hebrew citizens of Johnstown, thirty-two perished. Henry Goldenberg, A. J. Nathan and others who were drowned stood in the front rank as merchants.

The Roman Catholic churches, of which there are four in the borough, lost about a thousand of their people. Ex-Sheriff Ryan and J. J. Murphy were among the most prominent of this faith whom the flood swept away.

Mr. Jacob Swank was an honored Johnstowner. Born in Somerset County, he came to this city when about 30 years of age, and for three decades filled here an important place in society, in business, and in the Lutheran Church.

Among the rescuers at the stone bridge special praise is awarded Superintendent Hayes, Liveryman Young, Jacob Smith, Alexander Adair, and the son of Judge Potts.

5.—APOCRYPHAL STORIES.

THE PAUL REVERE OF JOHNSTOWN.

It may not be always desirable to disenchant the mind of illusions or to refute apocryphal stories of heroic achievement. When their purpose is to please the fancy, or incite to noble deeds, they may be allowed to stand. We do not even in this prosaic age moot the question whether the exploits of William Tell, or Arnold von Winkelried, or Joan of Arc, or Robin Hood and his merry men were historical, or only mythical, inspired by the spirit of resistance to tyranny and the desire to infuse the love of liberty into the breasts of men.

In times of war there are nearly always some who develop heroic traits and make the "circumstances of war" the occasion of some splendid deed.

In times of calamity there are those whose nature is so heroic as to forget their own peril in the desire to save others. Regardless of personal safety, they fly to the rescue. Some of these supreme ones have become immortalized in art and epic verse, but best of all in the hearts of mankind. Conemaugh Valley furnished many who will never be immortalized in song and story.

When a newspaper employs a correspondent, or the correspondent undertakes to manufacture a hero for a stipulated price, those who know of the fraud should expose it—especially if the conclusions, which will be inevitably drawn from it, reflect upon the common sense of the sufferers in the calamity.

A story was published in a leading daily and reprinted over the world of an alleged young hero who is said to have seized a horse and rode with speed through the valley and the streets of Johnstown, warning the people of the coming flood, crying, "To the hills: the dam has broken." It was said he did not leave the lowlands until he had completed the circuit of the city, and with the leaping, rolling flood fast upon his track sought to reach the hills, but was overwhelmed and drowned. I give my readers a part of this story from one of the books, as a specimen of imaginative heroism: "At last he completed the circuit of the city, and started in search of a place of safety for himself. To the hills he urged his noble steed   Tired out from its awful ride, the animal became slower and slower at every stride, while the water continued to come faster and faster in pursuit. Like an assassin upon the trail of its victim, it gained step by step upon the intrepid rider. But the hills are in sight. Yes, he will gain them in safety. No, he is doomed ; for at that moment a mighty wave, blacker and angrier than the rest, overtook horse and rider, and drew both back into the outstretched arms of death." This fate was very necessary to the story, as it rendered an interview of the hero by another impossible.

He was called the "Paul Revere of Johnstown." The name of the imaginary hero was Daniel Peyton. Everybody outside of Conemaugh Valley believed the story. Consequently, great surprise was expressed that the people did not heed the warning and escape to the hills—that they could be deaf to it thus publicly and heroically given. We were condemned for our supposed heedlessness or unbelief.

The answer which we make to this is, that there is not one word of truth in the story from beginning to end. There was not a single incident which could authorize or justify the tragic story. The great daily that published it was either imposed upon, or committed a gross fraud upon the world and perpetrated a cruel myth upon our people. Close investigation has not been able to locate a Daniel Peyton anywhere in Conemaugh Valley. The circumstances were all against the possibility of such an occurrence.

The South Fork dam and lake are nine miles in a straight line from Johnstown, and over fourteen miles by the turnpike. This road is the only way by which it is possible to ride from the lake to the city. The greatest speed of a horse for that distance would not accomplish the ride in less than an hour. Then the ride through the streets of Johnstown, provided man and horse were not exhausted, would occupy fifteen minutes more. Now, after the dam broke, the flood traveled as fast as the horse could run. The time of its passage was about twenty-five minutes, and the entire destruction occupied not more than half an hour. But the streets of Johnstown, besides the greater part of the Valley road, were under water. During the hours when this famous hero is said to have galloped through them, there were from three to ten feet of water in all our streets; and the housekeepers were engaged in removing carpets and furniture from their lower floors. The impossibility of a horse galloping through Johnstown between noon and 4 o'clock is at once apparent.

The fact is, that while there had been for years uneasiness in the public mind concerning the South Fork dam, when the flood came it was as sudden as an earthquake. The narratives of our most calm and intelligent citizens which this book contains show this. It was, as they all describe it, " One moment life, the next one death."

Rev. D. M. Miller, pastor of the Conemaugh Presbyterian Church, in a letter, says: " In regard to the warning having been given at Conemaugh Telegraph Station, the operators on duty that day affirm that they had received no intelligence in regard to the reservoir having given way; that the first intimation they had was the sight of the rolling mass coming down the narrow valley above them, apparently thirty or forty feet high; they dropped their instruments and fled from the signal-tower, barely in time to reach the elevated ground, wading knee deep in water much of the way."

Again, the Pennsylvania Railroad trains were lying at East Conemaugh, detained by water on the tracks. In them were leading officials of the company, and they had sent ahead to ascertain the condition of the road and the prospect of "going ahead." East Conemaugh is from one and a half to two miles nearer the dam than Johnstown. Nothing at this point was seen or heard of the furious and fateful rider.

Miss Ehrenfeldt, the telegraph operator at South Fork Station, gives this account: " Between 11 and 12 o'clock, A.M., that day, a man came into the station-tower and said I should telegraph to Johnstown that the dam would break. He seemed very much excited, and could not tell exactly what he wanted. Communication with Johnstown was cut off after the middle of the forenoon, and no message could go farther than Mineral Point. I tried repeatedly to get the office at Johnstown, but failed."

Thus writes Rev. G. W. Brown to me, inclosing the remarks of Miss Ehrenfeldt: "The people of Johnstown did not receive authoritative notice that the dam either would break or had broken, and did not deserve the condemnation passed upon them."

For the heroism of the event we must look at those brave men and women and children who, while being whirled and dashed about in the angry waters, and before the awful wreck that rushed down upon them, were bearing up and helping others to cling to means of rescue. God only knows how much of this heroism was enacted. We know of. some who saved others when it risked their own rescue ; we do know of some who died in the act of saving others. This was a greater, nobler heroism than that on horseback, real or imagined.

To clinch this refutation of the story, the following prominent citizens have given me authority herewith to attach their names as uniting with me in this endeavor to disabuse the public mind, and relieve our people from the imputation upon their good sense and common prudence :

JOHN HENDERSON,
F. D. JOLLY,
CHAS. ZIMMERMAN,
PROF. F. B. CUNZ,
A. W. LUCKHARDT,
SOL. REINEMAN,
G. W. MAPLEDORAM,
C. O. WILSON,
JOHN THOMAS,
L. M. WOOLF & SON,
WILL. B. DIBERT.

KRAMER BROS.,
C. SIMON,
J. EARL ODE,
IRWIN HORRELL, Burgess
of Johnstown,
J. E. SEDLMEYER,
F. H. ROBERTS,
JOHN D. ROBERTS CASTI,
CURT G. CAMPBELL,
ALEX. N. HART.

THE MIRACLE ABOUT THE VIRGIN'S STATUE.

One of the most preposterous of the stories that were perpetrated upon the wondering world was that of an alleged miracle in the Roman Catholic Church of St. Mary, Cambria City. The waters rushed into the church shortly after the congregation had retired from a service in worship of the Virgin Mary. The floor was submerged, the pews upset, and things pretty generally scattered and damaged. On the next morning the statue of the Virgin, which had been decorated with flowers, wreaths and lace, appeared uninjured. The report added that this was so, although the water had risen several feet above the height of the statue. This created such wide interest that I received inquiries from distant parts of the country about it. One theological student was greatly concerned, and wanted my explanation of the phenomenon.

The phenomenon explained itself. The statue and pedestal were made of wood. Consequently, they floated on the surface of the water. The pedestal, being the heavier portion, kept the statue in a perpendicular position above the waters, and when they subsided, it settled down, showing little effects of the flood. It would have been more of a miracle if it had been submerged and wet and bedraggled like the other objects ; for it is the nature of wood to float ; and if it had not floated, that would have been contrary to nature, and, therefore, a miracle.

Our intelligent Roman Catholic citizens were greatly chagrined that they were supposed to be so silly as to accept this most natural occurrence as a miracle. One of them said to me : "Do the people of this country think we are fools to believe such folly ?" Yet in a book on the Johnstown Flood there is this concluding sentence to the account: "Every one who has seen the statue and its surroundings is firmly convinced that the incident was a miraculous one, and even to the most skeptical the affair savors of the supernatural."

BIBLES BURNED AND FAITH ABANDONED.

This dispatch was telegraphed to the press on June 10th, eleven days after the flood:

"The people of Johnstown have lost all their faith in Providence. Many of them have thrown away their Bibles since the disaster, while others have openly burned them. They make no concealment of this.

"During the flood, one of the most upright and devout merchants of the town was rescued as by a miracle. It was with considerable difficulty that he was revived, but as he was lying on the bed a clergyman who was present dropped on his knees and earnestly began to pray.

"'Leave me,' cried the merchant. 'This is no time to pray or thank God. I never want to see your face again.'

"A lady who had lost her husband and four children was gathering together the relics of her home, when she came across the family Bible containing the record of her birth, marriage and births of her children. A stranger happened to pass, and, tearing the records out, she proffered the book to him. The man happened to be a clergyman.

"'Do you realize, madam, what you are doing?' asked the minister.

"'Perfectly,' was the reply. 'I have no further use for that book. I have always tried to be a consistent Christian woman. I brought up my four girls as strictly as I had been, but I cannot read that book any more.'"

As this went through the entire press of the country, the presumption was that it was an Associated Press dispatch. If so, its managers or agents are deserving of severest reprehension. If there were any individual cases like the above, or if the cases cited were genuine, this did not sanction this wholesale slander upon and insult to the common sense and Christian faith of the peo-

ple of Johnstown. Did the sender of that dispatch suppose that
people who had been trained in the Word of God in the home and
church, and who had proved its power and consolation in all the
experiences of life, would throw it away in the hour when most
they needed it? Had he so little conception of the nature and
strength of that conviction, wrought by the Spirit of God in the
heart of the Christian, to suppose that any calamity, any suffering, any death could eradicate it from that heart and convert
him to infidelity?

The fact is, infidelity inspired that dispatch. Those cases
never occurred.

The very terms of the dispatch, the particularity of the circumstances described, the animus that runs through its lines,
plainly indicate that it was the work of an enemy to the Bible and
the Christian ministry. It was the inspiration of the same being
who said to the Lord that if Job would lose all his wealth, his
children, his health, if he became involved in disaster, he would
give up his faith. This is the charge of Satan against the religion
of God:

"Doth Job fear God for naught? Hast thou not made an
hedge about him, and about his house, and about all that he hath
on every side? Thou hast blessed the work of his hands, and his
substance is increased in the land: But put forth thine hand now,
and touch all that he hath, and he will curse Thee to Thy face."
This was Satan's slander upon the faithfulness of God and the
strength of His righteousness to uphold His children. Satan meant
that religion is a matter of gain: God's righteousness a spider's
web that would snap at the first strain. Yet Job, when suffering
all the complicated calamities of life, when he let go everything
else, cried, "My righteousness I hold fast, and will not let it go."
And his experience has been verified by every man and woman
with a true faith in God. Witness those prayers in the darkness

of Friday night in Alma Hall, in the churches and other places of refuge. Witness that saintly woman who was being swept to her death in the waters, softly singing as she floated down :

> " Jesus, lover of my soul,
>   Let me to thy bosom fly ;
>   While the raging billows roll,
>   While the tempest still is high."

Witness the gathering again of the people in their sanctuaries, and renewing their vows to God and their Redeemer. This press dispatch was inspired by the same animosity with which Satan assailed the religion of Job.

The author wanted to make the world believe that the religion of the Bible is a sham. He used these poor stricken, flooded people of Johnstown, who gave him no occasion, to cast his aspersions upon the word and faith of God. The unbeliever takes up the charge of Satan and says, " Men are Christians for the sake of gain or power or influence. They do not serve God for naught. Take away the Christian's health or wealth, and you will take away his religion. Tear down his life, and he will tear down his altar. Touch his flesh and bone, and he will curse thee to thy face." This lie did not originate after the Johnstown flood. The devil had been going up and down in the earth tossing it to and fro. He who repeats it only echoes the charge of his master.

Part of that dispatch was designed to strike at the ministry. We are not ignorant of the device. The author overreached himself when he presented that alleged remark of the " most upright and devout merchant to the minister." He had no conception of real religion. If he had he would have known better than to have made such a remark come from an " upright and devout man ;" for the first characteristic of true religion is to be sanctified and strengthened by suffering. The religion of Christianity was born in suffering; and its Author was "made perfect—in His redeeming work—through suffering."

It so happened that the passing man to whom the enraged lady give the Bible after she had torn out the record of her birth was also a clergyman. How very minutely the scene was presented and the words recorded. That scene was born in the head of the author of the dispatch; and in front of that head it does not require close inspection to see the incipient horns of "the slanderer of God's children." No Christian woman could or would have spoken and acted as he alleges this one did. We have diligently inquired for the merchant, the minister and the lady, and have not been able to find or hear of them.

6.—THE FLOOD COMMISSION'S WORK.

On Thursday, January 16th, 1890, the Flood Commission held a meeting in Philadelphia. Governor Beaver presided. The other members present were J. S. Scott, S. S. Marvin, Reuben Miller, of Pittsburgh ; Francis B. Reeves, Robert C. Ogden and John Y. Huber, of Philadelphia. The Commission took up the question of caring for the orphans left by the flood. There are thirty-two children on the hands of the Commission who lost their parents in the great disaster.

Mr. Reeves said that he had made arrangements with a trust company which would insure the sum of $50 a year to each orphan under the care of the Commission. This arrangement contemplated the depositing with the company the sum of $98,900. The Commission approved of this plan, and appropriated that sum for the orphans' fund. There have already been paid to the guardians of the orphans $16,100 ; so the fund actually is $115,000. This fund, it is claimed, will just work itself out so that when the last child becomes 16 years of age the fund will have been exhausted.

Secretary Kremer's report showed that there had been left by the flood 116 widows, to whom have been paid $179,471, and to whom, for their children, will be paid $95,250 in annual payments ranging as the number and ages of their children.

The question of erecting and equipping a permanent hospital in Johnstown for the benefit of the Conemaugh Valley was discussed and agreed upon. There were appropriated for this purpose $40,000.

Francis B. Reeves gave out the cash statement of the Commission to January 15th, together with the appropriations made at the meeting as follows :

RECEIPTS.

Amount received by Governor directly	$1,225,872 83
Amount received from the Philadelphia Committee	600,000 00
Amount received from the Pittsburgh Committee . .	560,000 00
Amount received from the New York Committee	516,199 85
Total cash receipts by Commission	$2,902,072 68

EXPENDITURES.

Appropriations and expenditures, Johnstown	$2,430,393 69
Expenditures in other parts of the State	232,264 45
Distributed as specially directed by donors	2,271 85
Office expenses, Harrisburg	1,398 42
General expenses	1,318 70
First annuity to orphans	16,100 00
	2,683,747 11
Cash on deposit in Harrisburg	218,325 57
	$2,902,072 68

Above balance deposited, Harrisburg .	$218,325	57
Undistributed in Johnstown . .	36,384	03
Total money on deposit	$254,709	60
Less appropriated to other parts of State		
waiting payment	17,735	55
Net unapplied	$236,974	05
Appropriations made this day :		
Sundry claims ordered paid	$22,442	65
Appropriated for Williamsport Hospital .	5,000	00
Appropriated for Johnstown Hospital . .	40,000	00
Annuities to orphans . . . $115,000 00		
Less first payment . 16,100 00		
	$98,900	00
Balance at this date	70,631	40
	$236,974	05

J. B. Scott, in speaking of the money distributed, said : " The $2,430,000 distributed in Johnstown by the Commission does not include the money sent to the local finance committee, which is in the aggregate somewhere between $100,000 and $150,000. Nor does it include the money expended by the Pittsburgh Committee before the Flood Relief Commission was organized, which amounted to nearly $250,000. Then the money distributed by beneficial societies and private parties has not been taken into consideration. On the whole, therefore, there has been about $3,000,000 left in the Conemaugh Valley since the first of last June."

Secretary Kremer said : " The total number known to have been lost, as far as my information goes, is 2,228. The morgue records show about 2,000 bodies as passed through their care. During the last sixty days the Commission has had transferred from the various cemeteries, to its plot in Grand View Cemetery, 741 bodies. All but 87 of them were unknown, and there were about 40 identified by their clothing during the removal."

7.—THE LESSON OF THE FLOOD.

THE one great lesson which this disaster teaches and enjoins upon us is the wisdom, duty and necessity of constant watchfulness of ourselves and fidelity in the discharge of present duty. Watching, working and waiting ; at morn, at noon, at night, ever ready to labor on or to quit at the Lord's command. Death, wherever and whenever, and in whatever form it occurs, terminates our earthly career and fixes our eternal state. "But the end of all things is at hand ; be ye therefore sober, and watch unto prayer," said the Apostle Peter. The best preparation for the future life is the sober and watchful occupation of the present.

This has never been better expressed than in Whittier's poem on Abraham Davenport :

May Day, 1780, that there fell
Over the bloom and sweet life of the spring,
Over the fresh earth and the heaven of noon
A horror of great darkness like the night,
In day, of which the Norland sages tell—
The twilight of the gods.
Men prayed and women wept ; all ears grew
Sharp to hear the doom-blast of the trumpet shatter
The black sky.
*　　*　　*　　*　　*　　*　　*
Meanwhile in the old State House, dim as ghosts,
Sat the law-givers of Connecticut,
Trembling beneath their legislative robes.
"It is the Last Day! Let us adjourn,"
Some said ; and then as if with one accord
All eyes were turned to Abraham Davenport.
He rose, slow cleaving with his steady voice
The intolerable hush. "This well may be

The Day of Judgment which the world awaits;
Be it so or not, I only know
My present duty, and my Lord's command,
To occupy till He come. So at the post
Where He hath set me in His providence,
I chose for one to meet Him face to face—
No faithless servant frightened from my task,
But ready when the Lord of heaven calls,
And, therefore, with all reverence, I would say,
Let God do His work; we will see to ours:
Bring in the candles."

VII.

HISTORICAL SKETCH OF JOHNSTOWN.

BY W. HORACE ROSE.

[THE subjoined sketch was prepared by its author in the latter part of 1880, and, at the time, was published in a catalogue used at the "Methodist Loan Exhibition," which catalogue was only locally circulated. It is doubtful whether a half-dozen of the pamphlets are now extant. Being a brief and concise history of the rise and progress of Johnstown, it is here inserted, by permission of its author, as originally prepared, with the alteration of a few sentences made necessary to correspond with the change in the number of industries and increased population in the valley at the date of the great flood. It is a faithful sketch of the city, and illustrates the habits and characteristics of the industrious, prosperous and happy inhabitants of the Conemaugh Valley, which, in less than an hour, was made a place of mourning and a wilderness of waste !—D. J. B.]

WHETHER the "sugar-loaf" on the hill-top, south of the point of confluence of the Stony Creek and Little Conemaugh was the work of the "Mound-builders," or an altar, or a burial-heap of the first of the Indian tribes who peopled the regions of Laurel Hill, is a matter of conjecture, and the truth of the cause of the peculiar elevation will remain, to this generation at least, undetermined. But certain it is that, on the flat piece of ground lying between the waters of the two streams, at the base of a foot-hill of the Allegheny Mountains, was, long years ago, located an Indian town. When it was laid out, how many wigwams it contained, where the corn-patch was located; at what spot the flagstone, on which the hominy was pounded, lay; where the war-dance was performed, or the torture-stake planted, is now unknown. Local antiquaries, including the Chairman of the Committee on Local History of the Cambria Scientific Institute, are not agreed as to the name of the town. Some claim that it was called Kickapoo, others Kickneapawling; many maintain that Old Town was the correct name, while a few— and they seem to have the records, so far as the records exist, with them—that the true name was "Conemaugh Old Town."

The earliest record contained in the Land Office shows that on April 3d, 1769, one Charles Campbell entered, at Lancaster, an application for a tract of vacant land on the east side of Conemaugh Creek, between the Allegheny and Laurel Hill, in Bedford County, called "Conemaugh Old Town," which contained 249 acres and allowance of 6 per cent.; so that those who knew more of the town and its inhabitants, about the middle of the last century, than our local antiquaries, put on record their knowledge of names; and people who are not overly curious will settle down to the conclusion that Campbell gave to the Land Office the proper name of the tract, for the right to purchase which he presented his application.

Several conveyances of land were made, the patent for the same being issued April 26th, 1788, to James McLanahan, who, on September 30th, 1793, conveyed the tract to Joseph Johnson, *alias* Shantz, or Johns.

The exact reason Mr. Johns, as he was afterward known, gave for not knowing his own name has not been, as yet, settled. Eight years after his purchase he laid out on the lower end of his tract, at the confluence of the two streams, a town, calling it

Conemaugh. This town extended no farther eastward than Franklin Street, but contained eight streets, six alleys, a market square, a playground, a graveyard, a square for churches and schools, and a reservation of four lots for county buildings. The charter was recorded at Somerset, the land being at that date within Somerset County.

Johns was looking forward to the time, not when his little town was to be noted as a great manufacturing city, but a stately county seat for the new county then being called for by the residents of Northern Somerset. Conemaugh was at the head of water navigation westward. Blooms were hauled over the mountain by way of the Frankstown Road, and then shipped in flat-boats down the Conemaugh River. At an early day a forge was built on the Stony Creek, the dam being located opposite what is now Levergood Avenue. In 1828 the work on the main line of State improvements was begun, and Conemaugh was beginning to assume importance as the head of the western division of the canal and the terminus of the Allegheny Portage Railroad. In January, 1831, the town was duly incorporated into a borough by Act of the Legislature. On July 11th, 1842, the name was, by Act of Assembly, changed to Johnstown. Meanwhile Peter Levergood had become proprietor, and laid out the town above Franklin Street, and the lots which form what is now the borough of Conemaugh, erected by the Act of March 23d, 1849.

Back as far as 1832, prospecting for iron ore began, and resulted in the erection of furnace after furnace around Johnstown, until it became the center of numerous works conducted by George S. King, a resident of the town, in company with the famous iron master and pioneer furnace man, Dr. Shoenberger ; Cambria or "Calico" furnace, as it was called, owing to the mode of paying the employees, located three miles northwest of Johnstown, being the first erection near the town.

But the growth of Johnstown was slow, and, indeed, when the Central Railroad was built, and, in 1852, the business on the canal was practically abandoned, it looked gloomy enough for owners of lots, nothing but the trade of the furnaces being left to support the town. In 1853 Mr. George S. King succeeded in his great work of organizing the Cambria Iron Company, and the beginning of a new era dawned upon Johnstown. While there was some trouble in the management of the great iron works, and the industry seemed likely to fail, it was the foundation for the colossal establishment which, under its present efficient control and management, is now of world-wide renown.

The population of Johnstown proper is not a fair estimate of the place. Over 30,000 people are located in the irregular valleys of the Conemaugh and Stony Creek, but are divided into ten boroughs or municipalities, to wit: Johnstown, Conemaugh, Millville, Cambria, Coopersdale, Woodvale, Prospect, East Cone-maugh, Franklin and Grubtown; and three towns, Moxham, Morrellville and Walnut Grove, either of sufficient size to be incorporated, all of which boroughs and towns are collectively called Johnstown, as they are immediately contiguous or divided only by the streams in their meanderings through the mountains.

Located in the several boroughs are twenty-six churches, some of them stately edifices; twenty-two buildings, containing fifty-three rooms, are used for the purposes of the common schools, while for select and parochial schools three buildings and sixteen rooms are used.

A beautiful and expensive building, the free gift of the Cambria Iron Company, is dedicated to public use as a library, its shelves being filled with well-selected books.

A rolling-mill, two steel works, seven furnaces, with a host of shops of different kinds, the property of the Cambria Iron Company, a wire-drawing mill, a spring manufactory, two barbed-wire works, a tannery, two steam brick works, a steam fire-brick and cement works, a pottery, two woolen factories, two grist mills, five planing mills, two machine shops, two foundries, and the plant of the Street Railway Company, consisting of a rolling-mill, with divers machine shops, foundries and other divisions, with the Pennsylvania Railroad shops, are among the industries giving employment to thousands of sturdy men who dwell on the site of the old Indian village.

A street car line with a rapid transit road from Moxham to Johnstown connects the several towns together, affording easy and rapid communication. Nine iron bridges at different points span the two rivers, affording wagon communications between the towns, to say nothing of the bridges used by the Cambria Iron Company on their lines of railroad which gird the towns.

A gas plant and an electric light plant furnish the means of lighting the streets, dwellings and stores; while natural gas for manufacturing purposes and heating dwellings is carried a distance of forty miles, and distributed through the main portion of the valley.

The people are busy, industrious and prosperous. There is perhaps no town of its size in the Union where there are so few professional loafers—everybody seems not only willing to work, but has employment. It is essentially a town of homes, the majority of the married operatives at the several industries being the owners of their residences. For this reason the town is orderly, riots and disorderly conduct being the exception.

Located amidst the mountains, with two clear streams treading their way through the winding gorges, the scenery about Johnstown is of that kind where the eye is ever resting on changing views. The hill-sides, for the most part, are still covered with trees, and the carol of wild birds mingles with the music of a thousand automatic machines in the valley below !

The town is supplied with pure water by means of pipes laid from mountain streams. The climate is good; and health, prosperity and contentment are written on the countenances of the people.

But a span divides two great epochs in the history of the valley, guarded by the silent sentinel knob on the southern hill-top !

Where once the wild war-whoop broke the stillness, and was echoed back by the high hills, is now heard the steady hum of industry, while those echoing rocks are now broken to give entrance to the locomotive which brings from the bowels of the earth the "black diamonds" dug by a race more rugged than the fleet-footed braves, who, in the time past, chased the wild deer across the valley or slew the bear on the mountain-side !

Then the village was warned of the foe's approach by the swift-footed runner—now the thousands of workmen are directed by the telegraph and telephone ! Then the stealthy savage located the prowling wolf by the glare of its fierce eyes as it by night prowled about the outskirts of the village of wigwams— now on the same ground, under towering stacks and lofty iron roofs, amid the rattle of machinery, the rush of steam, and the scintillation of myriads of metallic stars, the engineer guides his locomotive by the effulgence of the electric light.